The Trinity, the Bible, and the Holy Spirit

Introductory Theology, Volume 1

By Grace Communion International

With articles by Joseph Tkach, Gary W. Deddo,
Michael D. Morrison, J. Michael Feazell, Paul Kroll, and others.

May 2015
Minor edits February 2019 and September 2020

ISBN-13: 978-1512336191
ISBN-10: 151233619X

CONTENTS

INTRODUCTION

This book is a compilation of numerous articles, most of them written independently of the others over the span of 20 years. There is some overlap, and perhaps even some contradictions, although all articles have been edited recently for this compilation. Some of the articles will be more relevant to your interests than others, so feel free to skip around according to which titles interest you. We hope that you find the collection useful.

In this volume, we discuss God, theology itself, how we use Scripture as the starting point for theology, details about the doctrine of the Trinity, and the Holy Spirit.[1] Due to the volume of material we have available, articles focused more on Jesus Christ are in a separate volume.

---

[1] Although speaking in tongues is not the most important thing to know about the Holy Spirit, we include a number of articles on that as well, since we have these articles available to address this contemporary controversy.

AN INTRODUCTION TO GOD

As Christians, our most basic religious belief is that God exists. By the capitalized word "God," we mean the God described in the Bible: a good and powerful spirit being who created all things, who cares about us, who cares about what we do, who is involved in our lives, and who offers us an eternity with his goodness.

Humans cannot understand God in totality, but we can have a solid beginning point for understanding who God is and what God is doing in our lives. Let's focus on the qualities of God that a new believer, for example, might find most helpful.

His existence

Many people, even long-time believers, want proof of God's existence. But there is no way to "prove" God's existence so that everyone is convinced. It is probably better to talk in terms of evidence, rather than proof. The evidence gives us confidence that God exists and is the sort of being the Bible describes. God "has not left himself without testimony," Paul told the pagans in Lystra (Acts 14:17). Well then, what is the evidence?

Creation. Psalm 19:1 tells us, "The heavens declare the glory of God." Romans 1:20 tells us, "Since the creation of the world God's invisible qualities—his eternal power and divine nature—have been clearly seen, being understood from what has been made." Creation itself tells us something about God.

It is reasonable for us to believe that something caused the earth, sun and stars to be the way they are. Scientists say the universe began with a big bang, and it is reasonable for us to believe that something caused the bang. That something, we believe, was God.

Design. Creation shows signs of order, of laws of physics. If various properties of matter were different, then earth would not exist, or humans could not exist. If the size or orbit of earth were different, then conditions on this planet would not permit human life. Some people believe that this is a cosmic accident; others believe that the more reasonable explanation is that the solar system was designed by an intelligent Creator.

Life. Life is based on incredibly complex chemicals and reactions. Some people believe that life had an intelligent cause; others believe that it happened by chance. Some have faith that scientists will eventually demonstrate a non-god origin for life. But for many people, the existence of life is evidence of a Creator God.[1]

Humans. Humans are self-conscious creatures who explore the universe, who ponder the meaning of life, who seek significance. Physical hunger suggests the existence of food; thirst suggests that there is something that can quench our thirst. Does our intellectual yearning for purpose suggest that there is in fact a meaning to be found? Many people claim to have found meaning in relationship with God.

Morality. Is right and wrong a matter of opinion, of majority rule, or is there some supra-human authority that defines good and evil? If there is no God, then humans have no basis for proclaiming anything evil, no reason to condemn racism, genocide, torture or any atrocity. The existence of evil is therefore evidence that God exists. If there is no God, then there is no basis for authority except power. It is reasonable to believe in God.

Greatness

What sort of being is God? Bigger than we can imagine! If he created the universe, then he is bigger than the universe—and not limited by time, space or energy, for he existed before time, space, matter and energy did. However, for further details, we must rely on revelation. We humans are not smart enough to figure out what God is like on our own—we must rely on him revealing himself to us.

2 Timothy 1:9 mentions something God did "before the beginning of time." Time had a beginning, and God existed before that. He has a timeless

existence that cannot be measured by years. He is eternal, of infinite age—and infinity plus several billion is still infinity. Mathematics is too limited to describe God's existence.

Since God created matter, he existed before matter, and he is not made of matter. He is spirit—but he is not "made of spirit." God is not made at all; he simply *is,* and he exists as spirit. He defines existence—he defines spirit and he defines matter.

God existed before matter did, and the dimensions and properties of matter do not apply to him. He cannot be measured in miles or kilowatts. Solomon acknowledged that even the highest heavens could not contain God (1 Kings 8:27). He fills heaven and earth (Jeremiah 23:23); he is everywhere, or omnipresent. There is no place in the universe where he does not exist.

How powerful is God? If God can cause a big bang, design solar systems, create the codes in DNA and manage all these levels of power, then he must be unlimited in power, or omnipotent. "With God all things are possible," Luke 1:37 tells us. God can do whatever he wants to do.

God's creativity demonstrates an intelligence greater than we can understand. He controls the universe, constantly causing its continued existence (Hebrews 1:3). That means he must know what is happening throughout the universe; he is unlimited in intelligence—he is omniscient. He knows whatever he wants to know.

God defines right and wrong, and is by definition right, and he has the power to always do right. "God cannot be tempted with evil" (James 1:13). He is consistently and perfectly righteous (Psalm 11:7). His standards are right, his decisions are right, and he judges the world in righteousness, for he is, in his very nature, good and right.

In all these ways, God is so different from us that we have special words that we use only for God. Only God is omniscient, omnipresent, omnipotent, eternal. We are matter; he is spirit. We are mortal; he is eternal. This great difference between us and God, this otherness, is called his *transcendence.* It means that he transcends us, is beyond us, is not like us.

Other ancient cultures believed in gods and goddesses who fought with one another, who acted selfishly, who could not be trusted. But the Bible reveals a God who is in complete control, who needs nothing from anyone, who therefore acts only to help others. He is perfectly consistent, his behavior is perfectly righteous and completely trustworthy. This is what the Bible means when it says that God is holy: morally perfect.

This makes life much simpler. People do not have to try to please 10 or

20 different gods; there is only one. The Creator of all is still the Ruler of all, and he will be the Judge of all. Our past, our present and our future are all determined by the one God, the All-knowing, All-powerful, Eternal One.

Goodness

If all we knew about God is that he had incredible power over us, we might obey him out of fear, with bent knee and resentful heart. But God has revealed to us another aspect of his nature: The incredibly great God is also incredibly gentle and good.

One of Jesus' disciples asked him, "Show us the Father" (John 14:8). He wanted to know what God was like. He knew the stories of the burning bush, the pillar of cloud and fire at Mt. Sinai, the science-fiction throne that Ezekiel saw, and the whisper that Elijah heard (Exodus 3:4; 13:21; 1 Kings 19:12; Ezekiel 1). God can appear in all these ways, but what is he really like? Where should we look?

Jesus said, "Anyone who has seen me has seen the Father" (John 14:9). If we want to know what God is like, we need to look at Jesus. We can learn a bit about God from nature; we can learn more from the way he revealed himself in the Old Testament, but we learn the most from the way that God has revealed himself in Jesus.

Jesus shows us what God is like. Jesus is called Immanuel, which means God with us (Matthew 1:23). He lived without sin, without selfishness. He is a person of compassion. He has feelings of love and joy, disappointment and anger. He cares about individuals. He calls for righteousness, and he forgives sin. He served others, even in his suffering and death.

God is like that. He described himself to Moses in this way: "The Lord, the compassionate and gracious God, slow to anger, abounding in love and faithfulness, maintaining love to thousands, and forgiving wickedness, rebellion and sin. Yet he does not leave the guilty unpunished" (Exodus 34:6-7).

The God who is above all creation is also free to work within creation. This is his *immanence,* his being with us. Although God is larger than the universe and everywhere within the universe, he is with believers in a way that he is not with unbelievers. The enormous God is always close to us. He is near and far at the same time (Jeremiah 23:23).

In Jesus, he entered human history, space and time. He worked in human flesh, showing us what life ought to be like in the flesh, and showing us that God wants more for our lives than merely flesh. We are offered eternal life, life beyond the physical limits we know now. We are offered spirit life, as the

Spirit of God himself comes into us to live in us and make us children of God (Romans 8:11; 1 John 3:2). God continues to be with us, working in space and time to help us.

The great and powerful God is also the gentle and gracious God; the perfectly righteous Judge is also the merciful and patient Savior. The God who is angry at sin also provides salvation from sin. He is mighty in mercy, great in gentleness. This is what we should expect from a Being who can create the codes in DNA, the colors in a rainbow and the delicate wisps on dandelion seeds. We would not exist at all, except for the fact that God is kind and gentle.

God describes his relationship to us in several ways. In one analogy, he is a father and we are his children. In another, he is the husband and all believers together are his wife. Or he is a king and we are his subjects. He is a shepherd and we are the sheep. In all these analogies, God puts himself in a situation of responsibility to protect and provide for the needs of his people.

God knows how tiny we are. He knows he could obliterate us in the snap of a finger, in the slightest miscalculation of cosmic forces. But in Jesus, God shows us how much he loves us, how much he cares for us. Jesus was humble, willing even to suffer, if it would help us. He knows the kind of pain we go through, because he has felt it. He knows the pain that evil causes, and he accepted it, showing us that we can trust God.

God has plans for us, for he has made us to be like himself (Genesis 1:27). He invites us to become more like himself—in goodness, not in power. In Jesus, God gives us an example to follow: an example of humility, selfless service, love and compassion, faith and hope.

"God is love," John wrote (1 John 4:8). God demonstrated his love by sending Jesus to die for our sins, so barriers between us and God might be removed, so we might live with him in eternal joy. God's love is not wishful thinking—it is action that helps us in our deepest need.

We learn more about God from the crucifixion of Jesus than from his resurrection. Jesus shows us that God is willing to suffer pain, even pain caused by the people who are being helped. His love invites us, encourages us. He does not force us to do his will.

God's love for us, shown most clearly in Jesus Christ, is our example: "This is love: not that we loved God, but that he loved us and sent his Son as an atoning sacrifice for our sins. Dear friends, since God so loved us, we also ought to love one another" (1 John 4:10-11). If we live in love, then eternal life will be a joy not only for us but also for those who live with us.

If we follow Jesus in life, we will also follow him in death, and then in resurrection. The same God who raised Jesus from the dead will also raise us and give us life eternal (Romans 8:11). But if we do not learn to love, then we will not enjoy everlasting life. So God is teaching us to love, at a pace we can follow, giving us a perfect example, changing our hearts by the Holy Spirit working in us. The Power who controls the nuclear furnaces of the sun is working gently in our hearts, wooing us, winning our affection, winning our allegiance.

God gives us meaning in life, direction for life, hope for life eternal. We can trust him, even when we suffer for doing good. God's goodness is backed up by his power; his love is guided by his wisdom. He has all the forces of the universe at his control, and he is using them for our benefit. "In all things God works for the good of those who love him" (Romans 8:28).

Response

How do we respond to a God so great and gentle, so terrible and tender? We respond with worship: awe at his glory, praise for his works, reverence for his holiness, respect for his power, repentance in the presence of his perfection, obedience in the authority found in his truth and wisdom.

To his mercy, we respond with thankfulness; to his grace, with our allegiance; to his goodness, with our love. We admire him, we adore him, we give ourselves to him even as we wish we had more to give. Just as he has shown his love for us, we let him change us so that we love the people around us. We use all that we have, all that we are, all that he gives us, to serve others, just as Jesus did.

This is the God we pray to, knowing that he hears every word, that he knows every thought, that he knows what we need, that he cares about our feelings, that he wants to live with us forever, that he has the power to fulfill every request, and that he has the wisdom not to.

God has proven himself faithful in Jesus Christ. God exists to serve, not to be selfish. His power is always used in love. Our God is supreme in power, and supreme in love. We can trust him in absolutely everything.

Summary: 5 facts to know about God

God is omnipotent—able to do whatever he wants. He is the Almighty.

God is immortal, constant in character, always reliable. He is the Eternal.

God is omnipresent—unlimited by space and time. He is always near.

God is omniscient—knowing all truth and all wisdom. Father knows best.

God is consistently good, never selfish. God is love.

For further reading

Now that you've had an introduction to God, wouldn't you like to know him better? We get to know God in several ways: through nature, through our experience with the Holy Spirit, through the Scriptures, through spiritual disciplines and through the words of other believers.

To learn more about God, read the Bible, especially the New Testament. Try a modern translation such as *The Message,* by Eugene Peterson, or *The New Living Translation,* published by Tyndale. For evidence of God's existence, we recommend the following (easiest listed first):

Paul Little, *Know Why You Believe*

C.S. Lewis, *Mere Christianity*

Lee Strobel, *The Case for a Creator*

Peter Kreeft and Ronald Tacelli, *Handbook of Christian Apologetics*

C. Stephen Evans, *Why Believe?*

James Sire, *Why Should Anyone Believe Anything at All?*

William Lane Craig, *Reasonable Faith*

C.S. Lewis, *Miracles*

Alister McGrath, *Intellectuals Don't Need God and Other Modern Myths*

For discussions of the attributes of God:

Max Anders, *God: Knowing Our Creator*

Paul Little, *Know What You Believe,* chapter 2

Gilbert Bilezekian, *Christianity 101,* chapter 2

J.I. Packer, *Knowing God*

Millard Erickson, *Introducing Christian Doctrine,* chapters 8-15

Donald G. Bloesch, *God the Almighty*

[1]Footnote on creation: The diversity of life is a separate question. Some people accept the theory of evolution; others reject it. Some people believe that the evolutionary theory describes the way that God produced biological diversity; others believe that God worked in some other way. The controversies about evolution are too complex to be resolved here; we simply

note that they do not affect the question of how life originated in the first place. We should also note that few people have studied evolution well enough to make their own conclusions about it; for the most part, they simply accept the word of "experts." That includes opponents as well as supporters of evolution. For further study, see *Three Views on Creation and Evolution,* edited by J.P. Moreland and John Mark Reynolds (Zondervan, 1999).

Things to think about

1. Do the evils in this world weaken our faith in God, or strengthen it?
2. If God is good, why did he make humans fallible, able to choose wrong?
3. What does God say about the way we use his creation?
4. How can God be distant to one person, but near to another?
5. Can we trust a God who has all power but isn't always good? Can we trust one who is always good but is limited in power?
6. In what way is God like Jesus, and in what way is he different?
7. Does God's mercy cause us to admire him, or to ignore him?

Michael Morrison

THE GOD REVEALED IN JESUS CHRIST

If we want the most accurate picture of God, we don't need to look any further than Jesus Christ. In Jesus we meet God as God really is. "Anyone who has seen me," Jesus said, "has seen the Father" (John 14:9).

Jesus Christ is the perfect revelation of the Father. "No one has ever seen God, but the one and only Son [Jesus]…has made him known" (John 1:18).

Through Jesus' words and actions, we hear and see what matters most to every human being—that God the Father loves us unconditionally. "God so loved the world that he gave his one and only Son, that whoever believes in him shall not perish but have eternal life" (John 3:16).

Even at our worst, God loves us. John continues, "For God did not send his Son into the world to condemn the world, but in order that the world might be saved through him" (verse 17). The Father sent Jesus out of his love and his commitment to save us.

Trinitarian-based

Jesus is God's self-revelation to the world. God has broken through to us by sending his eternal Son into our world. Jesus upheld the understanding that the one God is the object of our love and worship (Mark 12:29-31).

Jesus emphasized that God (Father, Son and Holy Spirit) was reconciling humanity to himself. That is why he instructed his followers to welcome people into right relationship with God by baptizing them in the name of the Father, and of the Son and of the Holy Spirit (Matthew 28:19).

The God we worship through Jesus Christ is the Triune God. The doctrine of the Trinity is central to how we understand the Bible and all points of theology that flow from it. That theology begins with an essential "who" question: "Who is the God made known in Jesus Christ, and who are we in relation to him?"

Trinitarian faith is based on a belief in the doctrine of the Trinity (the biblical teaching that there is one God, who is eternally Father, Son and Holy Spirit). Furthermore, it refers to a Christ-centered understanding of who God is.

Christ-centered

Christians recognize Jesus as the center of our faith and our devotion to God. Jesus reveals to us what God is like (John 6:37). "No one knows the Father except the Son and those to whom the Son chooses to reveal him" (Matthew 11:27). Trinitarian theology is first and foremost Christ-centered. Jesus is the unique Word of God to humanity and the unique Word of humanity to God (John 1:1-14). As the representative of all humanity, Jesus responded to God perfectly.

Jesus indicates that he is the key to understanding Scripture. He said to a group of Jewish religious leaders in John 5:39-40: "You diligently study the Scriptures because you think that by them you possess eternal life. These are the Scriptures that testify about me, yet you refuse to come to me to have life." Jesus, who is the focus of Scripture, is our source of salvation.

So we seek to understand the Bible through the lens of who Jesus is. He is the basis and logic of our faith—for he alone is the self-revelation of God.

Relationship-focused

Trinitarian faith is relational. Even before creation, there was a relationship of love between the Father and the Son (John 17:24). And in Jesus, that relationship of love is extended to all humanity. Jesus Christ, the only Son of God, has become one with us in our humanity to represent us as his brothers and sisters in the very presence of the Father (see John 1:14; Ephesians 1:9-10, 20-23; Hebrews 2:11, 14).

Human beings have turned away from God and broken the bonds of communion with God. But because of Jesus, God has reconciled us and renewed our relationship with him!

Not only that, as we respond to his call to us to share in that restored relationship, he comes to live in us by the Holy Spirit (Romans 8:9-11). In Jesus and through the Holy Spirit, we become God's treasured children, adopted by grace (Romans 8:15-16).

This means that Christian life and faith are primarily about four kinds of personal relationship:

- the relationship of perfect love shared by the Father, the Son and the Holy Spirit from all eternity,
- the relationship of the eternal Son with humanity, established when the Son became human in the person of Jesus,
- the relationship of humanity with the Father through the Son and by the Spirit, and,
- the relationship of humans with one another, in the Spirit, as children of the Father.

Who is Jesus?

"Who are you, Lord?" was Paul's anguished question on the Damascus Road, where he was confronted by the resurrected Jesus (Acts 9:5). He spent the rest of his life answering this question and then sharing the answer with all who would listen. The answer, revealed to us in his writings and elsewhere in Scripture, is the heart of the gospel and the focus of Trinitarian theology.

The Son of God, who is united from eternity to the Father and the Spirit, is now also joined to humanity because of his incarnation—his becoming a real flesh-and-blood human being (John 1:14). We summarize this by saying that Jesus is both fully God and fully human. That fact will never change, because he remains, in his divine nature and his human nature, the one mediator between God and humanity for all time (1 Timothy 2:5). His Incarnation did not end with his death or with his ascension. It continues forever. He was resurrected bodily and he ascended bodily. He will return bodily, the same as he departed. So when we say Jesus Christ, we are referring to God, and we are also referring to humanity.

As the One who is uniquely God (Creator and Sustainer of all) and also fully human, Jesus is the unique meeting place of God and humanity. Through the life, death, resurrection and ascension of Jesus, God and humanity were reconciled and human nature was regenerated—made new (2 Corinthians 5:17-18). In Jesus Christ all humans are reconciled to God. As the Lord and Savior of all humanity he has opened up the way for all to enter into an eternal union and communion with God.

Incarnation for salvation

The miracle of the Incarnation is not something that happened "once upon a time," now long past and simply affecting one person, Jesus. What he accomplished changed human nature itself, changed history, changed how the entire cosmos is "wired"—it is a new creation (2 Corinthians 5:17). The spiritual reality is, for now, hidden in Christ, and we still experience the effects of evil that still occur in this world. The Incarnation of the eternal Son of God, entering time and space and taking on our human nature to change everything forever, reaching back through all human history, and reaching forward to encompass all time. He has now become our Lord and Savior, not as an external agent, but from the inside, in his humanity.

As Paul teaches, God was, in Christ, reconciling the world to himself (2 Corinthians 5:19). Paul speaks of this transformation in Romans 7:4, where he says that even while we are alive, we are already dead to the law by the body of Christ. Jesus' death in human flesh for us, though a historical event, is a present reality that applies to all humanity (past, present and future). "You died," Paul says to the Colossians, "and your life is now hidden with Christ in God" (Colossians 3:3). Even before we die physically, we are given new life—made alive with Jesus in his resurrection.

Christ's incarnation and atoning work accomplished the renewal of our human nature. In him, God has reconciled to himself every human being, even those who lived before Jesus came.

In Ephesians 2:5-6 we read that those who trust in Christ share in his life, death, resurrection and ascension. Here Paul asserts that just as we are dead already in Jesus' substitutionary death, we have also already been "made alive together with him" and we are "raised up together with him" and "seated together with him in the heavenly realms." All this comes from God's grace and is experienced through faith—the faith of Jesus that he shares with us by the Spirit.

Jesus, the second Adam

In Romans 5, Paul addresses believers, but he also explains what Christ accomplished on behalf of all humanity even before anyone came to faith in God through Christ. Jesus Christ died for people who were still:

- "powerless" and "ungodly" (verse 6).
- "sinners" (verse 8).
- "God's enemies" (verse 10).

God accomplished his great work for us out of his "love for us" even while "we were still sinners" (verse 8). The result was that even "while we were God's enemies, we were reconciled to him through the death of his Son" (verse 10).

Paul goes on to explain that what Jesus Christ accomplished as the second Adam counteracts what the first Adam did. Through Christ, as the new head of all humanity, "God's grace and the gift that came by the grace of that one man Jesus Christ abounded for the many" (verse 15). Paul continues:

- The gift "brought justification" rather than condemnation (verse 16).
- "Those who receive God's abundant provision of grace and of the gift of righteousness reign in life through the one man, Jesus Christ" (verse 17).
- "One righteous act resulted in justification and life for all people" (verse 18).
- "Through the obedience of the one man the many will be made righteous" (verse 19).
- "Grace increased all the more" so that "grace might reign through righteousness to bring eternal life through Jesus Christ our Lord" (verses 20-21).

God did all this for us before we were even born. The benefit of what Jesus did so long ago extends to the past, to the present and into the future. Paul says, "how much more, having been reconciled, shall we be saved through his life!" (verse 10). This shows that salvation is not a one-time event, but an enduring relationship that God has with all humanity—a relationship formed within the person of Jesus Christ, who has brought God and humanity together in peace.

Jesus has not simply done something for us, he has done something *with* us by including us in his life, death, resurrection and ascension. Paul explains this in Ephesians 2:4-6:

- When Jesus died, we, in our sinful human nature, died with him.
- When Jesus rose, we, in our reconciled human nature, rose with him.
- When Jesus ascended, we, in our redeemed human nature, ascended and became seated with him at the Father's side.

Everything God has done in Christ shows us the mind, heart and character of the Father, the Son and the Holy Spirit. God is on the side of his people and all his creation. God is for us, even before we respond to him (verse 5). He has provided reconciliation and eternal life in communion with himself for every human being.

For all humanity

As Jesus made his way into Jerusalem for his final Passover with his disciples, the crowds shouted: "Hosanna! Blessed is he who comes in the name of the Lord! Blessed is the king of Israel!" (John 12:13).

Shortly thereafter, he proclaimed his impending death to those who went up to the Temple to worship. Jesus called to the Father: "Father, glorify your name!" A voice then thundered to the crowd: "I have glorified it, and will glorify it again" (verse 29).

Jesus told them the voice was for their benefit and that God's judgment on evil had come so that the prince of this world would be driven out (verses 30-31). He also said, "And I, when I am lifted up from the earth, will draw all people to myself" (verse 32). Jesus conquered evil in order to attract all people to himself. The apostles believed that Jesus died to redeem us all:

- 2 Corinthians 5:14: "Christ's love compels us, because we are convinced that one died for all, and therefore all died."
- Colossians 1:19-20: "God was pleased to have all his fullness dwell in him, and through him to reconcile to himself all things, whether things on earth or things in heaven, by making peace through his blood, shed on the cross."
- 1 Timothy 2:3-6: "This is good, and pleases God our Savior, who wants all people to be saved and to come to a knowledge of the truth. For there is one God and one mediator between God and mankind, the man Christ Jesus, who gave himself as a ransom for all people."
- 1 Timothy 4:9-10: "This is a trustworthy saying that deserves full acceptance… we have put our hope in the living God, who is the Savior of all people, and especially of those who believe."
- Hebrews 2:9: "We do see Jesus, who…suffered death, so that by the grace of God he might taste death for everyone."
- 1 John 2:2: "[Jesus is] the atoning sacrifice for our sins, and not only for ours but also for the sins of the whole world."

These passages show that Jesus died for all humanity, that is, in their place and on their behalf. Jesus did for us, as one of us, what we could never do for ourselves. This is what is meant by the vicarious humanity of Jesus (the word *vicarious* refers to a representative substitute).

In our place and on our behalf

Throughout the book of Hebrews, Jesus is depicted as our great High Priest, representing all humanity, providing on our behalf a perfect response to God. He is presented as the one who stands among us, in the midst of the congregation, and who leads us in worship (Hebrews 2:12-13). He represents us as our older brother. He has become one of us, sharing our very nature, learning obedience, being tempted as we are, but overcoming that temptation perfectly (Hebrews 2:14-18; 4:15).

Theologian Thomas Torrance explained it this way:

Jesus steps into the actual situation where we are summoned to have faith in God, to believe and trust in him, and he acts in our place and in our stead from within the depths of our unfaithfulness and provides us freely with a faithfulness in which we may share.... That is to say, if we think of belief, trust or faith as forms of human activity before God, then we must think of Jesus Christ as believing, trusting, or having faith in God the Father on our behalf and in our place. (*The Mediation of Christ*, p. 82)

Jesus is the one who, as we respond, perfects our faith and makes us holy (Hebrews 12:2; 2:11; 10:10, 14). He acted as one of us "in our place" or "on our behalf" (Hebrews 2:9; 5:1; 6:20; 7:25, 27; 9:7).

The response of faith

So how do we personally share in all that Christ has graciously done for us? How can we personally participate and be in communion with God who has, already, reconciled us to himself? We do so by trusting in him—by having faith that he, by grace, has accomplished for us all that is needed for our salvation. In short, we say we are saved by grace through faith (Ephesians 2:8).

Does this mean that we are saved by a faith that we work up? Does our salvation depend upon how great and sincere our repentance or our faith is? No, for salvation would then be dependent on something we do rather than dependent upon grace alone.

The good news is that our salvation does not depend on what we do—it does not depend on the strength of our faith or our repentance. It depends on the strength of our Savior, it depends on his faithfulness. He died for us. The gift has been given; our repentance and faith are simply responses to what God has given us. They are the way we accept and receive the free gift. Jesus has done everything necessary for our salvation from start to finish, so even our responses of repentance and faith are gifts of sharing in Jesus' perfect responses for us as our faithful mediator.

As Thomas Torrance explained, if we want to think of faith as a human activity, then we must think of Jesus as having done that for us as well. Just as he died for us, he lived righteously for us. As our representative, he presents to God a perfect response on behalf of all humanity. We are saved by his obedience (Romans 5:19)—and that includes his faith. Our salvation rests on Jesus—the perfect foundation.

As our High Priest, Jesus takes our responses, perfects them and gives them to the Father, all in the Spirit. As our mediator (1 Timothy 2:5), he ministers both from God to us and represents us in our relationship to God. So we join him in his response.

The role of human choice

What God has done in Christ to reconcile us to himself calls for a response. We are urged to accept him, to welcome and receive him. We do so by trusting in him and what he has accomplished for us. The Holy Spirit enables us to freely welcome the truth and walk in it. But God does not force us to accept the truth of his love for us. A love that forced a responding love would not be loving. God's love then calls for our decision to freely receive and freely love God in return.

Our choice is to either affirm or deny the reality that God loves us and has made every provision for us to be his children. Denial of this truth has consequences, but it will not change the reality of what God has done for us in Christ and thus who we are in Christ. Human beings choose to accept who Christ is or attempt to live in denial of who he is.

Real freedom is found in God, as theologian Karl Barth reminds us:

> The real freedom of man is decided by the fact that God is his God. In freedom he can only choose to be the man of God, i.e., to be thankful to God. With any other choice he would simply be groping in the void, betraying and destroying his true humanity. Instead of choosing freedom, he would be choosing enslavement. (*Church Dogmatics* IV.1, p. 43)

So what is our place in all of this? We choose to accept Jesus and all he has to offer or to reject him. Through the Spirit, God the Father is calling all people to place their trust in Jesus with a thankful and hopeful heart, and to share with other believers in the Body of Christ, which is the church. As we celebrate together in communities of faith and worship, our lives are transformed.

Personal response

Jesus called people to repent and believe (Mark 1:15). The early church continued this message, calling people to repent and be baptized (Acts 2:38) and to be changed (3:19).

Our response is important. The apostle Paul writes in Romans 5:17 that "those who *receive* God's abundant provision of grace and of the free gift of righteousness [will] reign in life." Abundant and freely given grace calls for us to *receive* it in faith. In Romans 5 Paul weaves together 1) elements of the reality accomplished by Christ on behalf of all humanity and 2) our response and participation in that relationship and reality. We must take care not to confuse what is true in Jesus for all humanity with each person's response to that truth.

God's gift is offered to all in order to be received by all. It is received by having faith in what God in Christ through the Holy Spirit has done for us. It is by faith in the grace of God that we begin participating in the relationship Jesus has restored, and start receiving the benefits included in that relationship.

We do not "decide for Christ" in the sense that our personal decision causes our salvation. Rather, we accept what is ours already in Christ, placing our trust in Jesus, who has already perfectly trusted for us in our place. When we accept the grace of Jesus Christ, we begin to participate in God's love for us. We begin to live according to who we really are, as the new creation that God, prior to our ever believing, made us to be in Christ.

Some people find it helpful to explain this using the terms *objective* and *subjective*. An objective truth is a reality, whereas our understanding of and response to that reality is subjective. There is a universal, or objective, truth about all humanity in Jesus, based on the fact that he has joined himself to our human nature and turned it around. But there is also the personal, or subjective, experience of this truth that comes as we surrender to the promptings of the Holy Spirit and join with Jesus Christ.

These categories of objective (universal) and subjective (personal) truth are found in Scripture. For one example, in 2 Corinthians, Paul starts with the objective nature of salvation: "All this is from God, who reconciled [past tense] us to himself through Christ and gave us the ministry of reconciliation: that God was reconciling the world to himself in Christ, not counting people's sins against them. And he has committed to us the message of reconciliation" (verses 18-19).

Here we find an objective truth that applies to all—God has already reconciled all to himself through Jesus, the incarnate Son of God. Paul then goes on in verses 20-21 to address the subjective truth: "We are therefore Christ's ambassadors, as though God were making his appeal through us. We implore you on Christ's behalf: Be reconciled to God."

How can all be "reconciled" already and yet some need to "be reconciled"? The answer is that both are true. All are already reconciled in Christ—this is the universal/objective truth—but yet not all embrace and therefore personally experience their reconciliation with God—that is the personal/subjective truth. God has a gracious attitude toward all people, but not everyone has responded to his grace. No one benefits even from a freely given gift if that gift is refused, especially the gift of coming under the grace of God in Jesus Christ in the power of the Spirit.

A second example of objective/subjective truth is found in the book of Hebrews where the author states in a straightforward manner, "For good news came to us just as to them, but the message they heard did not benefit them, because they were not united by faith with those who listened" (Hebrews 4:2) The benefits of a relational reality such as salvation can only be subjectively (personally) experienced when received by faith.

So while Christ is Lord and Savior of all, has died for all, and has reconciled all to God, not all will necessarily be saved. Not all will necessarily receive Christ who is their salvation. Not all will necessarily enter into their salvation, which is eternal union and communion with God as his beloved children. Some may somehow "deny the Savior who bought them" (2 Peter 2:1). While Scripture teaches the unlimited scope of Christ's atoning work, taking away the sins of the whole cosmos, it does not offer us a guarantee that all will necessarily receive the free gift of grace.

No explanation is given as to why or how this rejection of grace could happen. But rejection is presented as a real possibility, one that God has done everything needed to prevent. If there are those who reject Christ and their salvation, it will not be due to any lack or limit of God's grace. So we, sharing in the very heart of God, can also be those "not wanting any to perish, but all to come to repentance" (2 Peter 3:9).

What is our Christian mission?

Jesus' life and ministry provides the motivation for every aspect of our life, including our participation in mission and ministry with Jesus. The love of Christ compels us to take part in what Jesus is doing in the world through the Spirit. Out of love we declare the gospel and invite all people to receive and embrace it. In doing so, we hope what is true of them already in Christ will be experienced by them personally in faith. Like Jesus, we desire all to participate and receive all the benefits of Christ now. Then they, too, can join in Jesus' ongoing mission to draw others into a living relationship with their Lord and Savior. What greater joy and privilege could there be?

Our participation now in Jesus' love and life bears good fruit and personal joy that stretch into eternity. As we welcome the truth of the gospel, we can't help but worship our Lord and Savior!

Key Points of Trinitarian Theology

Following are some basic precepts of the theology presented in this book.

- The Triune God created all people through the Son of God, who also is known as the Word of God.

- We were created so that we could participate in the love relationship enjoyed by the Father, the Son and the Holy Spirit.

- We are enabled and qualified to participate in this relationship of love through Jesus Christ.

- The Son became human, the man Jesus Christ, taking on our human nature.

- He did this to reconcile all humanity to God through his birth, life, death, resurrection and ascension.

- The crucified, resurrected and glorified Jesus is the representative and the substitute for all humanity.

- As Savior and Lord of all humanity, Jesus now sits at the right hand of the Father, and he draws all people to himself by the power of the Holy Spirit.

- In Christ, humanity is loved and accepted by the Father.

- Jesus Christ paid for all our sins—past, present and future—and there is no longer any debt to pay.

- The Father has in Christ forgiven all our sins, and he eagerly desires that we receive his forgiveness.

- We can enjoy his love only as we believe/trust that he loves us. We can enjoy his forgiveness only when we believe/trust he has forgiven us.

- When we respond to the Spirit by turning to God, believing the good news and picking up our cross and following Jesus, the Spirit leads us into the transformed life of the kingdom of God.

Recommended Resources for Further Study

To study Trinitarian theology in greater depth, we recommend the following resources:

GCI articles

Grace Communion International has hundreds of helpful articles that address Christian belief and practice. See our website at www.gci.org.

GCI video programs

You're Included. This online program presents interviews with Trinitarian theologians and authors. View or download these interviews at www.youreincluded.org.

Books

- Michael Jinkins, *Invitation to Theology* (InterVarsity, 2001; 278 pages)
- Darrell Johnson, *Experiencing the Trinity* (Regent College, 2002; 112 pages)
- C. S. Lewis, *Mere Christianity* (HarperCollins, often reprinted; 225 pages)
- Fred Sanders, *The Deep Things of God: How the Trinity Changes Everything* (Crossway, 2010; 256 pages)
- James B. Torrance, *Worship, Community and the Triune God of Grace* (InterVarsity, 1996; 130 pages)
- Thomas F. Torrance, *The Mediation of Christ* (Helmers & Howard, 1992; 144 pages)

WHO IS GOD?

Charles Haddon Spurgeon was England's best-known preacher for most of the second half of the 19th century. In a sermon he gave when he was only 20, Spurgeon declared that the proper study for a Christian is the Godhead. Here is a quote from that sermon—it's one of my favorites:

> The highest science, the loftiest speculation, the mightiest philosophy, which can ever engage the attention of a child of God, is the name, the nature, the person, the work, the doings, and the existence of the great God whom he calls his Father. There is something exceedingly improving to the mind in a contemplation of the Divinity. It is a subject so vast, that all our thoughts are lost in its immensity; so deep, that our pride is drowned in its infinity. Other subjects we can compass and grapple with; in them we feel a kind of self-content, and go our way with the thought, "Behold I am wise." But when we come to this master-science, finding that our plumb-line cannot sound its depth, and that our eagle eye cannot see its height, we turn away with the thought, that vain man would be wise, but he is like a wild ass's colt; and with the solemn exclamation, "I am but of yesterday, and know nothing." No subject of contemplation will tend more to humble the mind, than thoughts of God.

As have many other preachers and teachers, Spurgeon reminds us that the great and central question of Christianity is this: "Who is God?"

God's own answer is not a proposition, but a person: the incarnate Son of God, Jesus Christ. As the self-revelation of God, Jesus is the focal point of our knowledge of God's nature. Jesus, who takes us to the Father and sends us the Spirit, teaches us to ask, "Who is God?," then bids us look to him for the definitive answer.

Throughout history, many great thinkers pondered the question, "Who is God?" Unfortunately, they often did not, or in certain cases (before the Incarnation) could not, make Jesus the living center of their investigations. Working from the central revelation of God in Jesus Christ, the doctrine of the Trinity was developed to answer the false reasoning and heretical ideas about God that had infiltrated the church in the first three centuries of its existence. Though the Trinity doctrine doesn't answer all questions about God's nature, it helps us focus on who God is without wandering away from sound doctrine.

The early Christians were not unique in developing errors of reasoning as they pondered the nature of God. Theologians and philosophers of every age got it wrong and our time is no exception. Old ideas have a way or repackaging themselves and worming their way into contemporary thinking. It is important that we are aware of two errors that are prevalent in our day. Both lead to wrong conclusions and a distorted picture of who God is.

The first error is a modern version of pantheism—the idea that God is a part of his creation instead of being distinct from it and Lord over it. Though Scripture tells us that creation tells us about God (Romans 1:20), there is an important difference between believing that God is *present to everything* and believing that *everything is God.*

Unfortunately, a belief in the divine spirituality of everything (often referred to as "the Universe") is common today. Hungry for spirituality and put off by traditional religion, many people are seeking "enlightenment" in obscure and fringe ideas. Go into any large bookstore and you'll find whole sections devoted to fantasy fiction and the occult. Video gamers are obsessed with ever more bizarre themes and fantastic creatures wielding supernatural powers. Technology is blurring the line between fantasy and reality, and the spiritual landscape is becoming cluttered with offbeat ideas.

The same thing happened in the early years of the church. People had an appetite for magic and mystery. As a result, many non-apostolic epistles and gospels were in circulation—offering a mix of truth and bizarre ideas about God, reflecting the popular culture of that day. Paul reminds us what happens when people lose their spiritual moorings:

> For although they knew God, they neither glorified him as God nor gave thanks to him, but their thinking became futile and their foolish hearts were darkened. Although they claimed to be wise, they became fools and exchanged the glory of the immortal God for images made to look like a mortal human being and birds and animals and reptiles (Romans 1:21-23).

A second prevalent error in our day concerning the nature of God is conceiving of God as a spirit force that dwells in everyone individually. From this perspective, God is viewed as a genie that we carry with us, making use of him as the need arises. It's as though God is a cosmic smartphone with all kinds of useful apps.

Following this line of faulty reasoning, we wrongly conclude that when we travel, we are taking God somewhere that he is not already present. God becomes dependent upon us and is limited by our limitations. As a result, God can't be more faithful than we are. Though this false idea may boost our sense of self-importance, it is a false sense of importance that negates the grace of God.

The truth of God's nature, revealed in Jesus, is the opposite of this error. As the authors of the New Testament remind us, God remains faithful even when we are faithless. Our true importance is related to our identify as children of the God who not only dwells within us by his Spirit, but far beyond us. Our calling is to join God in what he is doing. We do so with great anticipation knowing that he has been at work long before we arrive on the scene. We are greatly privileged to share in what the Holy Spirit is doing to turn people around and to draw them into a reconciled relationship with the Father and the Son.

The more clearly we understand who God is, the better will be our understanding of who we are and of our calling to live in communion with Christ by the Holy Spirit.

Joseph Tkach

KNOWING GOD

In Psalm 113:5-6, the psalmist asks: "Who is like the Lord our God, the One who sits enthroned on high, who stoops down to look on the heavens and the earth?"

We still are asking that question.

The self-help sections of bookstores and online catalogs offer seemingly countless books addressing ways to know God from Christian, quasi-Christian and other religious perspectives. Some of these books teach universalism; others teach pantheism or panentheism. Those with a New Age perspective inevitably promise keys to finding secret knowledge concerning God.

It seems that many people are seeking to know God or at least to connect with some sort of "higher power." That should not surprise us since God created humans in his image, giving us a "spiritual appetite." Theologian and philosopher Blaise Pascal is credited with saying that within each person there is a "God-shaped hole looking to be filled" [see footnote (1) for his actual words, translated into English]. That being so, one would hope that a person sincerely seeking to know God would receive clear direction from all Christian churches. Sadly, that is not always the case.

Given our limited minds, we humans are unable to fully comprehend all there is to know about God. Paul put it this way: "Oh, the depth of the riches of the wisdom and knowledge of God! How unsearchable his judgments, and his paths beyond tracing out!" (Romans 11:33). Though God lives in "unapproachable light" (1 Timothy 6:16), he has not left us completely in the dark. Note Jesus' remarkable statement in Matthew 11:27: "All things have been committed to me by my Father. No one knows the Son except the Father, and no one knows the Father except the Son and those to whom the Son chooses to reveal him." I love how the second-century Christian teacher Irenaeus explained this verse in *Against Heresies*:

> No one can know the Father apart from God's Word, that is, unless the Son reveals him, and no one can know the Son unless the Father so wills. Now the Son fulfills the Father's good pleasure: the Father sends, the Son is sent, and he comes. The Father is beyond our sight and comprehension; but he is known by his Word, who tells us of him who surpasses all telling. In turn, the Father alone has knowledge of his Word. And the Lord has revealed both truths. Therefore, the Son reveals the knowledge of the Father by his

revelation of himself. Knowledge of the Father consists in the self-revelation of the Son, for all is revealed through the Word.

This means that no one can know God unless and until God reveals himself. And he has chosen to reveal himself through Jesus. The word *reveal* comes from the Greek word *apokalupto* meaning to take off the cover—to disclose or reveal. It is the opposite of *kalupto*, which means to cover up; hide. The Old Testament speaks of the Shekinah glory of God, present within the innermost part of the Tabernacle behind the veil. No one was allowed beyond that veil except the high priest, and then only once a year. For most of the time, God remained hidden behind the veil. So when Jesus said he had come to reveal the Father, his followers were understandably intrigued.

When Philip asked Jesus to show the disciples the Father, Jesus replied: "Don't you know me, Philip, even after I have been among you such a long time? Anyone who has seen me has seen the Father" (John 14:9). God sent his Son to "pull back the covers" and reveal who he is through his Son. We must be careful not to let preconceptions of what God is like determine our thinking and behavior toward God. Only Jesus has perfect and complete knowledge of God. And he shares that knowledge with us.

Through the life and ministry of Jesus, we get the best look at what God is like this side of our resurrection in glory. Jesus alone is one with the Father and the Holy Spirit. He alone brings "insider knowledge" of the whole of God as the eternal Son of God. He alone is God's self-revelation in time and space, flesh and blood. In Jesus, God has come to us in person, meeting us face-to-face so that we may know him truly and personally.

Jesus shared himself and what he knew with his disciples, whom he called his friends. And he commissioned them, and those who follow them, to go into the world and make that knowledge known—not through books and programs offering esoteric, "hidden knowledge" or esoteric, private experiences. And certainly not through a complex web of philosophical arguments and counter-arguments. Jesus told his followers that they could come to know God through relationships, including relationships with each other and with those outside the Christian community. He said that the clearest sign that would point others to him would be the love that his followers have for each other—a love reflecting God's own love for all people.

(1) Here is what Pascal actually said (translated into English): "What else does this craving, and this helplessness, proclaim but that there was once in man a true happiness, of which all that now remains is the empty print and

trace? This he tries in vain to fill with everything around him, seeking in things that are not there the help he cannot find in those that are, though none can help, since this infinite abyss can be filled only with an infinite and immutable object; in other words by God himself" (148/428).

Joseph Tkach

WE WERE ALWAYS ON HIS MIND

The doctrine of the Trinity has been with us for more than 1,600 years. Most Christians consider it to be one of the "givens" of their faith, and don't give it much thought. Theologian J.I. Packer noted that the Trinity is usually considered a little-thought-about piece of "theological lumber" that no one pays much attention to.[1]

But whatever your level of understanding of the doctrine of the Trinity, one thing you can know for sure: The Triune God is unchangeably committed to including you in the wonderful fellowship of the life of the Father, the Son and Holy Spirit.

Communion

The doctrine of the Trinity teaches that there are not three Gods, only one, and that God, the only true God, the God of the Bible, is Father, Son and Holy Spirit. This has always been a concept that is difficult to put into words. But let's try. The Father, Son and Spirit, we might say, mutually indwell one another, that is, the life they share is perfectly interpenetrating. In other words, there is no such thing as the Father apart from the Son and the Spirit. There is no such thing as the Son apart from the Father and the Spirit. And there is no Holy Spirit apart from the Father and the Son.

That means that when you are in Christ, you are included in the fellowship and joy of the life of the Triune God. It means the Father receives you and has fellowship with you as he does with Jesus. It means that the love that God once and for all demonstrated in the Incarnation of Jesus Christ is no less than the love the Father has always had for you even before you were a believer and always will have for you.

It means that God has declared in Christ that you belong to him that you are included, that you matter. That's why the Christian life is all about love God's love for you and God's love in you.

God did not make us to be alone. To be created in God's image, as the Bible says humanity is (Genesis 1:27), is to be created for loving relationships, for communion with God and with one another. The late systematic theologian Colin Gunton put it this way: "God is already 'in advance' of creation, a communion of persons existing in loving relations."[2]

Mutual indwelling

This union/communion of Father, Son and Spirit was referred to as *perichoresis* by the early Greek fathers of the church. They used the word in the sense of *mutual indwelling*.[3]

Why does this matter? Because it is that very inner life of love in the Triune God that God shares with *us* in Jesus Christ.

Theologian Michael Jinkins describes it this way:

> Through the self-giving of Jesus Christ, through God's self-emptying assumption of our humanity, God shares God's own inner life and being in communion with us, uniting us to himself by the Word through the power of the Holy Spirit. Thus the God who is Love brings us into a real participation in the eternal life of God.[4]

Too "theological" sounding? Let's make it simpler. Just as Paul told the pagans at Athens, in God we all "live and move and have our being" (Acts 17:28). The God in whom we live and move and have our being is the Father, the Son and the Holy Spirit, each existing in the other in perfect communion and love. The Son became human so that we humans can join him in that perfect communion of love that he shares with the Father and the Spirit. All this we learn from God's own perfect revelation of himself in Jesus Christ attested in the Scriptures.

- "I am the way and the truth and the life. No one comes to the Father except through me. If you really knew me, you would know my Father as well" (John 14:6-7).
- "Don't you believe that I am in the Father, and that the Father is in me?... Believe me when I say that I am in the Father and the Father is in me" (John 14:10-11).
- "On that day you will realize that I am in my Father, and you are in me, and I am in you" (John 14:20).
- "I pray also for those who will believe in me through their message, that all of them may be one, Father, just as you are in me and I am in you" (John 17:20-21).
- "For God was pleased to have all his fullness dwell in him [Jesus Christ], and through him to reconcile to himself all things, whether things on earth or things in heaven, by making peace through his blood, shed on the cross" (Colossians 1:19-20).

Salvation flows from God's absolute love for and faithfulness to humanity, not from a desperate attempt to repair the damages of sin. God's gracious purpose for humanity existed *before* sin ever entered the picture (Ephesians 1:4). God has assured our future — he has, as Jesus said, "been pleased to give you the kingdom" (Luke 12:32). Jesus has taken us with him where he is Ephesians 2:6).

God has purposed to never be without us. *All* of us, for "God was pleased to have all his fullness dwell in him, and through him to reconcile to himself all things, whether things on earth or things in heaven, by making peace through his blood, shed on the cross" (Colossians 1:19-20). We often forget that. But God never does.

In his embrace

In Jesus Christ through the Holy Spirit by the will of the Father, we mortal, sinning human beings, in spite of ourselves, are graciously and lovingly held in the divine embrace of the triune God. That is exactly what the Father intended for us from the beginning. "In love he predestined us to be adopted as his sons through Jesus Christ, in accordance with his pleasure and will — to the praise of his glorious grace, which he has freely given us in the One he loves" (Ephesians 1:5-6).

Redemption starts with God's nature, his absolute and unquenchable love for humanity, not with human sin. Through the incarnation of the Son, his becoming one of us and making us one with him, God includes us humans in the all-embracing love of the Father for the Son and the Son for the Father. God made us for this very reason—so that in Christ we can be his beloved children.

This has been God's will for us from before creation. "For he chose us in him before the creation of the world to be holy and blameless in his sight. In love he predestined us to be adopted as his sons through Jesus Christ, in accordance with his pleasure and will — to the praise of his glorious grace, which he has freely given us in the One he loves.... And he made known to us the mystery of his will according to his good pleasure, which he purposed in Christ...to bring all things in heaven and earth together under one head, even Christ" (Ephesians 1:4-6, 9-10).

Through the atoning Incarnation of the Son, Jesus Christ, humans are already forgiven, reconciled and saved in him. Divine amnesty has been proclaimed for all humanity in Christ. The sin that entered the human experience through Adam cannot hold a candle to the overwhelming flood of God's grace through Jesus Christ. "Consequently," the apostle Paul wrote, "just as the result of one trespass was condemnation for all men, so also the result of one act of righteousness was justification that brings life for all men" (Romans 5:18).

Universal salvation?

So will everyone automatically—perhaps even against their will, enter into the joy of knowing and loving God? Such a thing is actually an oxymoron. That is, it is impossible for you to love someone against your will. God draws all humanity to himself (John 12:32), but he does not force anyone to come. God wants everyone to come to faith (1 Timothy 2:4), but he does not force anyone. God loves every person (John 3:16), but he doesn't force anyone to love him — love has to be voluntary, freely given, or it is not love.

Contrary to the idea of universal salvation, only those who trust Jesus are able to love him and experience the joy of his salvation. Those who don't trust him, who refuse his forgiveness or the salvation he has already won for them, whether because they don't want it or simply because they don't care, can't love him and enjoy fellowship with him. For those who consider God their enemy, God's constant love for them is a grossly aggravating intrusion. The more they are confronted with his love, the more they hate him. For those who hate God, life in God's world is hell.

As C.S. Lewis put it, "The damned are, in one sense, successful, rebels to the end; that the doors of hell are locked on the inside."[5] Or as Robert Capon explained: "There is no sin you can commit that God in Jesus hasn't forgiven already. The only way you can get yourself into permanent Dutch [trouble] is to refuse forgiveness. *That's* hell."[6]

Always on his mind

The doctrine of the Trinity is far more than just a creed to be recited or words printed on a statement of faith. The central biblical truth that God is Father, Son and Holy Spirit actually shapes our faith and our lives as Christians. The wonderful and beautiful fellowship shared by the Father, Son, and Spirit is the very fellowship of love into which our Savior Jesus places us through his life, death, resurrection and ascension as God in the flesh (John 16:27; 1 John 1:2-3).

From before all time the Triune God determined to bring humanity into the indescribable life and fellowship and joy that Father, Son and Holy Spirit share together as the one true God (Ephesians 1:4-10). In Jesus Christ, the Son of God incarnate, we have been made right with the Father, and in Jesus we are included in the fellowship and joy of the shared life of the Trinity (Ephesians 2:4-6). The church is made up of those who have already come to faith in Christ. But redemption applies to all (1 John 2:1-2). The gap has been bridged. The price has been paid. The way is open for the human race — like the prodigal son in the parable - to come home.

Jesus' life, death, resurrection and ascension are proof of the total and unwavering devotion of the Father to his loving purpose of including humanity in the joy and fellowship of the life of the Trinity. Jesus is the proof that the Father will never abandon us. In Jesus, the Father has adopted us and made us his beloved children, and he will never forsake his plans for us.

When we trust Jesus to be our all in all, it is not an empty trust. He *is* our all in all. In him, our sins are forgiven, our hearts are made new, and we are included in the life he shares with the Father and the Spirit.

Salvation is the direct result of the Father's ever-faithful love and power, proven incontrovertibly through Jesus Christ and ministered to us by the Holy Spirit. It's not our faith that saves us. It's God alone — Father, Son and Spirit — who saves us. And God gives us faith as a gift to open our eyes to the truth of who he is — and who we are, as his beloved children.

God's eternal and almighty word of love and inclusion for you will never be silenced (Romans 8:32, 38-39). You belong to him, and nothing in heaven or Earth can ever change that.

Endnotes

[1] James Packer, *God's Words* (Baker, 1998), 44.

[2] Colin Gunton, *The Triune Creator: A Historical and Systematic Study* (Eerdmans 1998), 9.

[3] Other theological terms that describe this inner communion of the Father, Son and Spirit are *coinherence,* each existing within the other) and *circumincessio* (the Latin equivalent of *perichoresis).*

[4] Michael Jinkins, *Invitation to Theology* (InterVarsity, 2001), 92.

[5] C.S. Lewis, *The Problem of Pain* (Collier, 1962), chapter 8, page 127).

[6] Robert Farrar Capon, *The Mystery of Christ* (Eerdmans, 1993), 10.

Joseph Tkach

WHO'S AFRAID
OF THE SCHIZOPHRENIC GOD?

Imagine a courtroom scene. It's you who are convicted, facing charges. Problem is, you know you are guilty. But as you walk in, you notice the judge gives you a reassuring nod of recognition, as if he had known you all your life.

He summons you to the bench. "Don't worry about a thing," he tells you with a warm fatherly smile. "I know all about this case. In fact, I'm going to be your defense attorney." The late theologian Shirley C. Guthrie would explain that this is the way we should picture what the Bible calls the Judgment. "Must we talk about the wrath of God?" Guthrie asked. "Yes," he answers. "But God's wrath is not like that of the gods. It is the wrath of the God who was in Christ reconciling the world to God's self" (*Christian Doctrine*, pages 261-262).

Theological strait-jackets

Unfortunately, instead of allowing Jesus' love, compassion and kindness to shape their understanding of God, many Christians gravitate toward what we might call a "forensic" model of salvation. The word "forensic" seems like a penal or legal term, which it is. This forensic model sees God the Father as stern and vengeful, a frightening God from whom we need Jesus to save us. It assumes that the starting place for understanding God is not Jesus Christ, but "the law," by which is meant the Old Testament legal system. This model sees the law as so important that even God is subject to it. Since God is concerned first about the penalty demands of his law and only secondly about the well-being of humans, he will punish them for lawbreaking in the same way that the State and human courts and legal systems do — through a straightforward proving of guilt followed by a guilty verdict.

Front and center in the forensic model is God's anger against sinning humanity. God is offended, and someone must pay. Jesus steps forward and takes the full force of God's wrath against human sin. That means we have had our penalty paid for us, but it does nothing for a restored relationship of love and trust. This "offended deity" picture forgets that first and foremost, God is love (1 John 4:16), that God is joyously working to bring "many sons to glory," and that our salvation was in his mind "before the foundation of the world" (Revelation 13:8, King James Version).

This forensic model also forgets something even more basic — that Jesus

Christ and the Father along with the Holy Spirit are the three Persons of the one God, and that the Son or Word made Incarnate in Jesus was the perfect revelation of the Father in human form. The Father is not some angry, vengeful deity that we need protection from; he is just like Jesus. Jesus, remember, is "the exact representation" of the being of God (Hebrews 1:3). The Father is full of compassion and mercy, a God who "desires mercy and not sacrifice," just like Jesus. Jesus is the starting place for understanding God; the law is not.

God is not schizophrenic. He does not have a split personality. There is not one "good God," Jesus, and one "bad God," the Father. There is one God — Father, Son and Spirit — who loves us unconditionally and has in Jesus made full provision not only for our sins to be forgiven and removed, but also for our full inclusion in the love relationship that the Son has shared with the Father from eternity.

Adoption

God is not in the business of training obedient valets, but in building a family. The apostle Paul used the word "adoption" in describing the kind of relationship that God has created for humanity in Jesus Christ (Ephesians 1:4-5). Through the Incarnation of the Son — by Jesus becoming one of us and taking up our cause as his own — God has drawn us into and made us part of the intimate relationship that Jesus has with the Father.

We see the power of this intimate love that God has for humanity in the parable of the Prodigal Son. The repentant son is welcomed home by the Father and restored to full rights of sonship (Luke 15:11-24). This depicts the God who was in Christ reconciling the world to himself (2 Corinthians 5:19). The death of Christ was not a vindictive act of divine child abuse, as some hostile critics of Christianity have charged. It was a divine rescue springing from God's love for us (John 3:16), an intervention designed to restore a purpose of which we were oblivious in our ignorance and darkness (verses 19-20).

Set against this majestic purpose, God's wrath can be seen for what it is — his anger — not at the humanity he sent Jesus to save, but at sin, that which destroys the relationship he has always intended for us in Christ. God is not some resentful, selfish parent in an emotional stew because we have not played by his rules. God is Father, Son and Spirit, loving, faithful and unconditionally committed to bringing humanity into the joy of knowing him for who he really is.

Mercy vs. judgment

God, however, will never be at peace with sin. The great human tragedy is that we have been totally unaware of the pardon and reconciliation the Father has brought about through Jesus Christ. We have loved darkness rather than light and have chosen to ignore what the Father offers us through the Son.

Through Christ, the disconnect between the world and God has been removed once and for all. The great majority of unbelievers are simply those who through weakness or ignorance are resisting the influence of the life-giving Holy Spirit of Christ, the Person of the Godhead who beckons to us to abandon our addiction to darkness and sin — who testifies in our hearts to God's saving, atoning and reconciling work in Jesus on our behalf (John 14:25-27; 15:26).

Jesus did not just *bring* good news, he *was* good news. The overwhelming emphasis of his teaching was mercy, not vengeance. His hallmark sayings reflect the God who is love, in whose mind mercy rejoices against judgment (James 2:13). Thus, what was hinted at in parts of the Old Testament becomes the major theme in the Gospels — "I will have mercy and not sacrifice." Jesus' word pictures show us a forgiving father, a Good Samaritan, seeking shepherds and splendidly generous employers, healings, exorcisms, a Great Physician who pleaded "Come to me, all you who are weary and burdened, and I will give you rest" (Matthew 11:28).

Neil Earle

GOD IS...

If you could ask God one question, what would it be? Maybe you would ask a big question: What is God's purpose for you? Or, what's going to happen to you after you die? Or perhaps, why does God let people suffer?

On the other hand, you might ask a question that seems minor but still perplexes you: Where did your puppy go after it ran away when you were 10? What would your life be like if you had married a lost sweetheart? Why did God make the sky blue?

But perhaps you might want to ask God about himself: Who are you? Or, what are you? Or, what do you want?

God's answer to such basic questions would go a long way toward answering other questions. Who and what God is, what God wants – these are aspects of God's nature. And the nature of God underlies everything else – why the universe is the way it is, who we are as humans, why our lives are the way they are, and what we should be doing with our time. Has anyone ever lived who didn't puzzle – at least a little – over such profound questions?

We humans can begin to grasp the answers. We can begin to understand the nature of God. Believe it or not, we can even come to share in that divine nature.

That is the subject of this series of articles – what we can know about God, at least a little bit. Thinkers throughout history have viewed God in different ways. But God reveals himself to us – through his creation, through his Word, and most especially through his Son, Jesus Christ. God shows us who and what he is, what he does, and even a lot about why he does what he does. He also tells us how we should relate to him now – and how we will relate to him in eternity.

Philosophers discuss the nature of God, but this series of articles is not based on philosophy. It is based on the Bible, which God uses to reveal himself to us. We accept the Scriptures as an authoritative source of information about who and what God is. This is written for people who want to know what the Bible says about God. Those who want a more philosophical approach, or those who are more skeptical of biblical authority, will need to turn elsewhere, although they may find these articles of interest, as well.

The book of Isaiah tells us that God reveals himself to people who are humble and repentant, to those who respect God's Word (Isaiah 66:2).

Jesus said, "If anyone loves me, he will obey my teaching. My Father will love him, and we will come to him and make our home with him" (John

14:23). God wants to make his home with us. When God does, our questions will begin to be more fully answered.

IN SEARCH OF THE ETERNAL

Humans have always wrestled with questions like "How did we get here?" and "What should we be doing?" and "Where are we going?" Their pursuit of answers often led them back to fundamental issues such as whether God exists and what God is like. They framed in different ways the ideas they came up with.

Twisted paths back to Eden

Throughout history, people built their religious concepts on their desires to understand human origins and the purpose of life. In their own ways, they wanted to make contact with and relate to the Source of human life – and, presumably, the Authority over human destiny. Unfortunately, the human inability to understand spiritual reality perfectly gave rise to disagreement and more questions:

- "Pantheism (Greek pan, 'all,' and theos, 'God') A term coined by John Toland (1670-1722), literally meaning 'everything God.' The view is that God is all and all is God. It differs from 'panentheism,' which views God as in all" (*Westminster Dictionary of Theological Terms,* 1996, p. 199). Pantheists saw God as being all that is, including all the forces and laws behind the universe. They depersonalized God and interpreted both good and evil as divine.

- Polytheists believed in many gods. Each of these gods could help or hurt, but none held absolute power. Polytheism was the basis of many Middle Eastern and Greco-Roman forms of worship, and of the spirit and ancestor worship found in many tribal cultures.

- "Theism (From Greek theos, 'God') Belief in a god. Also belief in one God (monotheism) in contrast to belief in many gods (polytheism)" (*Westminster Dictionary of Theological Terms,* p. 279).

- Monotheists embraced a personal deity as the source, sustainer and goal of everything. Three of the world's most influential religions are monotheistic – Judaism, Christianity and Islam. All three claim their descent from Abraham.

Does God exist?

Historically, every culture has had a sense that God exists. Atheism does not provide satisfactory answers to humanity's questions about who we are and why we exist. Atheism cannot explain purpose, or distinguish between good and evil. Atheism has no authority, no proof of its philosophical assumptions.

We see nature all around us, and science equips us to investigate the natural world. But science cannot explore the supernatural world. We cannot search for God with microscopes or deep space probes. If we are to know God, God must reveal himself to us. We want to know what the Creator is like, what his purpose is, and what must happen for us to come into harmony with him. So how does God reveal himself to us?

HOW GOD REVEALS HIMSELF

Imagine, for a moment, that you are God. You created all things – including human beings. You made humans in your own image (Genesis 1:26-27) and you want them to relate to you in a special way. Wouldn't you tell those humans about yourself? Wouldn't you tell them what you expect of them? Wouldn't you tell them how to come into the relationship you want to share with them?

People who believe that God is unknowable assume that God, for some reason, hides himself from his creation. But God does reveal himself, through his creation, in history, in the pages of the Bible, and through his Son, Jesus Christ. Let's look at what God shows us about himself.

Creation reveals God

Many people have looked at the cosmos and concluded from it that God exists, that God holds all power and that God works in order and harmony. Romans 1:20 tells us, "Since the creation of the world God's invisible qualities – his eternal power and divine nature – have been clearly seen, being understood from what has been made."

Looking at God's fabulous heavens made King David marvel that God even notices humans, who seem so insignificant next to God: "When I consider your heavens, the work of your fingers, the moon and the stars, which you have set in place, what is man that you are mindful of him, the son of man that you care for him?" (Psalm 8:3-4).

The patriarch Job questioned God. In reply, God described many of his marvels – and thus revealed his limitless authority and wisdom. Job was humbled by the exchange. You can read God's "speech" in chapters 38-41 of the book of Job. Job realized: "I know that you can do all things; no plan of yours can be thwarted.... Surely I spoke of things I did not understand, things too wonderful for me to know.... My ears had heard of you but now my eyes have seen you" (Job 42:2-3, 5).

God's purpose for humanity

What did God intend when he made all things and gave us life? Paul explained to the Athenians:

> From one man he made every nation of men, that they should inhabit the whole earth; and he determined the times set for them and the exact places where they should live. God did this so that men would seek him and perhaps reach out for him and find him, though

he is not far from each one of us. "For in him we live and move and have our being." As some of your own poets have said, "We are his offspring." (Acts 17:26-28)

Or, simply, as John wrote, "We love because he first loved us" (1 John 4:19).

History reveals God

Skeptics ask, "If God is real, why doesn't he show himself to the world?" This question assumes that God hasn't already shown himself to humanity. However, the Bible says that this assumption is not correct. From the time of the first family on, God has often communicated with human beings. But they, for the most part, have wanted nothing to do with God!

The story of Adam and Eve describes humanity's typical reaction. God created these people and spoke to them. But they disobeyed him, and then hid from him. "The man and his wife heard the sound of the Lord God as he was walking in the garden in the cool of the day, and they hid from the Lord God among the trees of the garden" (Genesis 3:8).

Disobedience separates us from God, makes us afraid of God, makes us want distance between us and God. The Bible is full of examples of how God reached out to sinning humans – but they rejected him. The book of Isaiah puts it this way: "Your iniquities have separated you from your God; your sins have hidden his face from you, so that he will not hear" (Isaiah 59:2). It is not that God is actually unable to hear, but that this is the person's perception.

Noah, "a preacher of righteousness" (2 Peter 2:5), warned his world about God's coming judgment. But they didn't listen – and they perished in the Flood. God destroyed sinful Sodom and Gomorrah in a fiery display (Genesis 19:28). But this supernatural rebuke did not convince anyone to change their ways.

Most of the Old Testament traces how God worked with the nation of Israel. But Israel often did not want to hear God. "Do not have God speak to us," they said (Exodus 20:19). God also intervened in the affairs of great powers such as Egypt, Nineveh, Babylon and Persia. But the effects were short-lived.

Many of God's servants met awful deaths at the hands of those to whom they brought God's message. People rejected the messengers of God because they did not like the message. They did not like what God was saying through his servants, because they did not like God.

Hebrews 1:1-2 tells us, "In the past God spoke to our forefathers through the prophets at many times and in various ways, but in these last days he has spoken to us by his Son." Jesus Christ came into the world to preach the gospel of salvation and the kingdom of God. The result? "He was in the world, and though the world was made through him, the world did not recognize him" (John 1:10). They killed him.

Jesus, as God in the flesh, was expressing God's loving concern for his people when he cried: "O Jerusalem, Jerusalem, you who kill the prophets and stone those sent to you, how often I have longed to gather your children together, as a hen gathers her chicks under her wings, but you were not willing" (Matthew 23:37).

God has revealed himself in many different ways, but most people have not wanted to see even the little part that they did.

The Bible record

The Bible reveals God in these ways:

- The Bible contains statements God makes about who and what he is.

- In Exodus 3:14, God revealed his name to Moses: "I am who I am." God's name reveals that God is self-existent, self-perpetuating life. The other names of God, found throughout the Bible, offer additional insight into who and what God is.

- "I am the Lord, and there is no other; apart from me there is no God.... There is no god apart from me, a righteous God and a Savior; there is none but me" (Isaiah 45:5, 21).

- In Isaiah 55:8, God tells us, "My thoughts are not your thoughts, neither are your ways my ways." God exists and acts on a higher plane than we humans do. We cannot understand all that he is, or all that he does.

- Jesus Christ described himself as the "I am" who lived before Abraham (verse 58). He was God in the flesh. He called himself "the light of the world" (John 8:12), "the gate" to eternal life (John 10:9), "the good shepherd" (verse 11), and "the way and the truth and the life" (John 14:6).

What a person does reveals much about what he or she is. In the same way, biblical statements about God's acts reveal him more fully to us.

"I am the Lord, who has made all things, who alone stretched out the heavens, who spread out the earth by myself," God says in Isaiah 44:24. God made all that is. And God rules what he made.

God also declares what he will do in the future: "I am God, and there is none like me. I make known the end from the beginning, from ancient times, what is still to come. I say: My purpose will stand, and I will do all that I please" (Isaiah 46:9-10).

God loves the world, and sent his Son for the salvation of the world. "God so loved the world that he gave his one and only Son, that whoever believes in him shall not perish but have eternal life" (John 3:16). Through Jesus, God is bringing children into his family. "He who overcomes will inherit all this, and I will be his God and he will be my son" (Revelation 21:7).

The Bible records the words of humans who describe what God is:

God has always interacted with people he chose to carry out his will. Many of those inspired servants left us, in the Bible, details about what God is like. "The Lord our God, the Lord is one," said Moses (Deuteronomy 6:4). God is one. The Bible proclaims monotheism, that there is only one God. (This concept will be taken up in more detail in chapter 3.)

Among the psalmist's many statements about God is this one: "For who is God besides the Lord? And who is the Rock except our God?" (Psalm 18:31). God alone deserves worship, and he strengthens those who worship him. The Psalms are full of insight about who and what God is.

Among the most comforting of Bible verses is 1 John 4:16, "God is love." A vital insight into God's love and his will for humanity is found in 2 Peter 3:9: "The Lord is...not wanting anyone to perish, but everyone to come to repentance." What is God's greatest desire for us, his creation, his children? That we be saved. And God's word does not return to him empty – it will accomplish what he sends it to do (Isaiah 55:11). Knowing that God intends to save us, and that he is perfectly able to do so, should give us great hope.

The Bible records the words of humans who describe what God has done and is doing:

God, as a loving Creator, formed humans in his own image and gave them dominion over the earth (Genesis 1:26).

Here's how God felt when he saw the earth corrupted by the evil that humans had chosen to do: "The Lord was grieved that he had made man on the earth, and his heart was filled with pain" (Genesis 6:6). God responded to the wickedness of the world by sending the Flood to start civilization over through Noah and his family (Genesis 7:23).

Centuries after the Flood, God called the patriarch Abraham and established with him a covenant through which "all peoples on earth will be blessed through you" (Genesis 12:1-3) – a reference to Jesus Christ, a descendant of Abraham.

When he formed the nation of Israel, God supernaturally brought them through the Red Sea and destroyed the Egyptian army: "The horse and its rider he has hurled into the sea" (Exodus 15:1).

The Israelites broke their agreement with God and gave themselves over to violence and injustice. Thus God allowed the nation to be attacked by foreign powers and, eventually, to be carried out of the Promised Land into slavery (Ezekiel 22:23-31; 36:15-21). Yet the merciful God promised to send into the world a Redeemer who would establish an everlasting covenant of righteousness with all those, Israelite or otherwise, who would turn to him in faith and repent of their sins (Isaiah 59:20-21).

In due time God sent into the world his Son, Jesus Christ. He proclaimed, "My Father's will is that everyone who looks to the Son and believes in him shall have eternal life, and I will raise him up at the last day" (John 6:40). God assured, "Everyone who calls on the name of the Lord will be saved" (Romans 10:13).

Today, God empowers his church to preach the gospel of the kingdom "in the whole world as a testimony to all nations" (Matthew 24:14). On the Day of Pentecost following the resurrection of Jesus Christ, God sent the Holy Spirit to unite the church as Christ's Body and to empower the preaching of the gospel, the good news of what God is doing (Acts 2:1-4).

The Bible is a book about God and humanity's relationship to him. Its rich message invites us to a lifetime of study to learn more about God, including what he is, what he has done, what he does, and what he plans to do.

But we know only in part. We are unable to know all there is of God, but we are able to understand what he has revealed to us. The Bible shows us that God is:

self-existing
not restricted by time
unbounded by place
unlimited in power
unlimited in knowledge
transcendent (having his existence beyond the physical universe)
immanent (involved with the universe).

What is God?

Suppose you are in a class in which a professor is trying to give the class a better understanding of God. She asks the students to close their eyes, relax and imagine God in their minds. "Think about what he must look like, what his throne would be like, how he would sound and what would be going on around him."

The students sit in their chairs, eyes shut, for a long time, each dreaming up a picture of God. "How are you doing?" the professor says. "Can you see God? Each of you by now must have some image. But do you know what?" – and then the professor shocks the class by exclaiming, "That's not God!"

"No!" the professor declares to the class. "That's not God! You cannot contain God in your mind! No human can have a full grasp of God, because God is God, and human beings are only physical, finite creatures! No image, no picture can do him justice."

Why is it hard to describe who and what God is? Because, as physical beings, our knowledge comes to us by way of our five senses – and human languages are designed in accordance with this knowledge. Our words, our grammar, our way of thinking, are all based on the physical world. But God is supernatural, eternal. He is infinite. He is invisible. We can still speak meaningfully about God, even though we are limited by our physical senses, but our words can never convey all that God is. We are limited in our languages.

What is "the image of God"?

Genesis 1:26 quotes God as saying, "Let us make man in our image, in our likeness, and let them rule over…all the creatures." Verse 27 tells us God followed through on his intent: "So God created man in his own image, in the image of God he created him; male and female he created them." Genesis 5:1 adds, "When God created man, he made him in the likeness of God."

How are we to understand what God means when he tells us we are made in his image and likeness? God's creation of humans in his image and likeness, recorded in Genesis 1:26-27, may be linked with the dominion God gave humans over the earth. In a sense, we act for God on earth when we exercise responsible lordship over the creation. "The context suggests that humanity is the image of God in the dominion it exercises over the rest of creation," notes *Harper's Bible Commentary* on Genesis 1:3-31 (Harper & Row, 1988, page 87).

The book *ABC's of the Bible* adds:

> Before undertaking his supreme creation, God announced his intention to make man in his image and likeness. The Hebrew word for "image" usually refers to a statue (often used in the Old Testament for pagan idols), while a different word for "likeness" suggests a physical resemblance. Later generations interpreted the terms more generally, however. They thought of themselves as resembling God

not in a physical sense, but in a spiritual sense by possessing...intelligence, and the capacity to make moral distinctions" (Reader's Digest Association, 1991, page 16).

Insight into the image of God can also be gained from a consideration of the distinction between the material body and the immaterial spirit within humanity's own constitution. The *Baker Encyclopedia of the Bible* states:

> Recent discussions have focused on the unity and integrity of man. Thus it is man as a physical-spiritual unity who is in the image of God as Spirit. This explains why the same words can be used both of God and man. God sees and hears as men do, but men do so in a way appropriate to their constitution as physical-spiritual creatures (with ears and mouth) and God in a way appropriate to his nature as spiritual and uncreated. (article "Image of God," Baker Book House, 1988, page 1018)

The image to which humans ultimately must conform is that of Jesus Christ. Romans 8:29 tells us God desires that we "be conformed to the likeness of his Son"—Jesus Christ. *ABC's of the Bible* states, "The New Testament added to the notion that man was created in the image of God by proposing that Jesus was the sole embodiment of divine perfection" (page 16).

We are unique among earth's creatures in that God endowed us with rationality, free choice and moral responsibility. By creating us in his own image, God has given us the incomparable capacity to have a personal relationship with him.

Spiritual realities, human language

God shows us facets of himself throughout creation. He has intervened many times in history. The Bible tells us much about him. He even manifested himself in various ways to various people in the Bible. Still, since God is spirit, his fullness cannot be seen or heard or touched or smelled. The Bible gives us truths about God by using words that physical beings in their physical realm can grasp. But those words are not capable of completely defining God.

The Bible describes God as a rock and a fortress (Psalm 18:2), as a stronghold and a shield (Psalm 144:2) and as a consuming fire (Hebrews 12:29). We realize that God is not any of these physical things in a literal sense. But these metaphors, based on what we as humans can observe and understand, reveal important truths about God.

The Bible even attributes human form to God, revealing aspects of his character and his relationship with humans. This is called anthropomorphism "(From Greek *anthropos,* 'human,' *morphe,* 'form') the attribution of a human quality to God, such as 'eyes,' 'hands,' or 'arms'" (*Westminster Dictionary of Theological Terms,* p. 13).

Biblical passages describe God with:

- a head and hair (Rev. 1:14),
- a face (Gen. 32:30; Ex. 33:23; Rev. 1:16),
- eyes and ears (Deut. 11:12; Ps. 34:15; Rev. 1:14),
- a nose and nostrils (Gen. 8:21; Ex. 15:8),
- a mouth (Matt. 4:4; Rev. 1:16),
- lips (Job 11:5),
- a voice (Ps. 68:33; Rev. 1:15),
- a tongue and breath (Isa. 30:27-28),
- arms, hands and fingers (Ps. 44:2-3; 89:13; Heb. 1:3; 2 Chron. 18:18; Ex. 31:18; Deut. 9:10; Ps. 8:3; Rev. 1:16),
- shoulders (Isa. 9:6),
- a chest (Rev. 1:13),
- a back (Ex. 33:23),
- a waist (Ezek. 1:27)
- and feet (Ps. 18:9; Rev. 1:15).

The Bible also describes how God wants us to relate to him, often using familial language. Jesus taught us to pray to "Our Father in heaven" (Matthew 6:9). God will comfort his people as a mother comforts her child (Isaiah 66:13). In Revelation 21:7, God promises, "He who overcomes will inherit all this, and I will be his God and he will be my son."

Yes, God calls Christians to a family relationship – to be his children. The Bible paints the picture in words humans can get their minds around. But the picture, to use a term from the world of art, is impressionistic. It does not give us a complete grasp of the ultimate, glorious, spiritual reality. The joy and glory of our ultimate relationship with God as his children is far greater than our finite words can express.

> To all who received [Jesus Christ], to those who believed in his name, he gave the right to become children of God – children born not of natural descent, nor of human decision or a husband's will, but born of God. (John 1:12-13)

In the resurrection, when the fullness of salvation and the kingdom of God have come, we will be able to know God fully at last. As Paul wrote:

"Now we see but a poor reflection as in a mirror; then we shall see face to face. Now I know in part; then I shall know fully, even as I am fully known" (1 Corinthians 13:12).

"Anyone who has seen me has seen the Father"

God's self-revelation, as we have seen, encompasses creation, history and the Bible. But God also revealed himself by becoming a human. He became like us and walked and served and taught among us. God's greatest act of self-revelation was in Jesus Christ. "The Word became flesh," John 1:14 tell us, and this divine Word we know as Jesus Christ. The Son of God set aside the privileges of being God and came to earth as a man – fully human, who died for our sins, was resurrected from the dead, and started his church.

Christ's coming disturbed the people of his day. Why? Because their picture of God wasn't big enough, as we shall see in the next two chapters. Yet Jesus told his disciples, "Anyone who has seen me has seen the Father" (John 14:9). In short, God had revealed himself in Jesus Christ.

THE LORD OUR GOD, THE LORD IS ONE

Judaism. Christianity. Islam. These three great faiths all look to Abraham as their father. Abraham differed from others of his day in one vital respect: He worshiped only one God – the true God. Abraham worshiped the one true God. Monotheism, the belief that only one God exists, marks the starting point of true religion.

Abraham was not born in a monotheistic society. Centuries later, God reminded ancient Israel: "Long ago your forefathers, including Terah the father of Abraham and Nahor, lived beyond the River and worshiped other gods. But I took your father Abraham from the land beyond the River and led him throughout Canaan and gave him many descendants" (Joshua 24:2-3).

Before God called him, Abraham lived in Ur, though his relatives may have lived in Haran. The people of both places worshiped many gods. Ur, for instance, was the site of a great temple tower dedicated to the Sumerian moon-god, Nanna. Other temples at Ur honored An, Enlil, Enki and Ningal. God called Abraham out of this polytheistic setting: "Leave your country, your people and your father's household and go to the land I will show you. I will make you into a great nation" (Genesis 12:1-2).

Abraham obeyed God and moved (verse 4). In a sense, God's relationship with Israel began when he revealed himself to Abraham, their ancestor. God made a covenant with Abraham. God renewed that agreement with Abraham's son Isaac and, later, with Isaac's son Jacob. Abraham, Isaac and Jacob worshiped the one true God. This set them apart even from their close relatives. Laban, a grandson of Abraham's brother Nahor, embraced numerous household gods or idols (Genesis 31:30-35).

God rescues Israel from Egyptian idolatry

Decades later, Jacob (whose name God changed to Israel) and his children settled in Egypt. The children of Israel remained in Egypt for nearly three centuries. The Egyptians also worshiped many gods. *The International Standard Bible Encyclopedia* points out: "The first observation of a person coming to the study of Egyptian religion is the large number of deities, many of them in animal form, or human form with animal heads.... It is possible to list at least thirty-nine gods and goddesses" (vol. 4, page 101).

The children of Israel grew in number in Egypt but became enslaved by their Egyptian hosts. God revealed himself as the one true God through a series of miracles that led to Israel's liberation from Egypt. God then made a covenant between himself and the nation of Israel. God's revelation of himself to humanity, as these events show, has always centered on monotheism.

He revealed himself to Moses as the God of Abraham, Isaac and Jacob. The name God called himself, "I am" (Exodus 3:14), implies that other gods do not exist in the same way God does. God is. They are not!

Because Pharaoh refused to release Israel, God humbled Egypt with 10 miraculous plagues. Many of these plagues showed that Egypt's gods had no power. For example, one of the Egyptian gods had a head in the shape of a frog. God's plague of frogs upon Egypt ridiculed the worship of that god.

Even after witnessing the devastating effects the plagues had on his nation, Pharaoh still tried to prevent the Israelites from leaving. God finally swept the Egyptians "into the sea" (Exodus 14:27). This action demonstrated the impotence of Egypt's sea god. The children of Israel sang triumphantly (Exodus 15:1-21), exalting the omnipotent God of Israel.

The true God found – and lost

God led the Israelites out of Egypt and to the foot of Mt. Sinai, where they ratified a covenant. God stressed in the first of his Ten Commandments that he alone was to be worshiped: "You shall have no other gods before me" (Exodus 20:3). The Second Commandment forbade the making or worshiping of idols (verses 4-5).

Time and again, Moses pleaded with the Israelites not to worship idols (Deuteronomy 4:23-26; 7:5; 12:2-3; 29:14-18). He knew Israel would be tempted to follow the Canaanite gods when they arrived in the Promised Land.

A saying known as the *Shema'* (after the Hebrew word for "hear," which begins the saying) captured Israel's duty to God. The *Shema'* starts: "Hear, O Israel: The Lord our God, the Lord is one. Love the Lord your God with all your heart and with all your soul and with all your strength" (Deuteronomy 6:4-5).

However, Israel again and again lapsed into worshiping the Canaanite gods, among them El (a standard term for deity that is also applied to the true God), Baal, Dagon and Ashtoreth (also known as Astarte or Ishtar).

Baal worship particularly troubled the Israelites. As they colonized the land of Canaan, they became dependent on crop production. Baal, the storm god, was worshiped in fertility rites. *The International Standard Bible Encyclopedia* states, "The fertility cult, by virtue of its focus on the fertility of land and beasts, must always have had an attraction in a society such as ancient Israel where economy was based primarily on agriculture" (vol. 4, page 101).

God's prophets warned the Israelites to turn from their waywardness. Elijah asked the people: "How long will you waver between two opinions? If the Lord is God, follow him; but if Baal is God, follow him" (1 Kings 18:21). God answered Elijah's prayer to prove that he alone was God. The people acknowledged: "The Lord – he is God! The Lord – he is God!" (verse 39).

God revealed himself not merely as the greatest of all gods, but as the only true God: "I am the Lord, and there is no other; apart from me there is no God" (Isaiah 45:5). And: "Before me no god was formed, nor will there be one after me. I, even I, am the Lord, and apart from me there is no savior" (Isaiah 43:10-11).

Judaism – strictly monotheistic

The Jewish religion of Jesus' day was not merely henotheistic (holding that God is the greatest of many gods) nor monolatrous (permitting the worship of God alone but acknowledging that other gods might exist). It was strictly monotheistic, meaning there is only one God.

According to the *Theological Dictionary of the New Testament,* on no other point were the Jews more united than on the confession "God is one" (vol. 3, page 98). Reciting the *Shema'* remains part of Jewish worship today. Rabbi Akiba, who was killed in Palestine during the second century A.D., is said to have been brought to his execution at the time of the reading of the *Shema'* and to have repeated Deuteronomy 6:4 throughout his tortures, breathing his last on the word *one.*

What Jesus said about monotheism

When a scribe asked Jesus which command was greatest, Jesus replied by quoting the *Shema':* "Hear, O Israel, the Lord our God, the Lord is one. Love the Lord your God with all your heart and with all your soul and with all your mind and with all your strength" (Mark 12:29-30). The scribe agreed: "Well said, teacher.... You are right in saying that God is one and there is no other but him" (verse 32).

In the next chapter, we will look at how Jesus' coming gave the New Testament church a deeper and broadened concept of God. (Jesus claimed to be the Son of God and to be one with the Father.)

Jesus reaffirmed monotheism. As the writers of the *Theological Dictionary of the New Testament* point out: "Early Christian monotheism is confirmed rather than shattered by the Christology of the [New Testament].... According to the Gospels Jesus himself sharpens the monotheistic confession" (vol. 3, page 102).

Mark 10:17-18 records one of Jesus' clearest affirmations of monotheism.

When a man addressed him as "Good Teacher," Jesus answered: "Why do you call Me good? No one is good but One, that is, God" (New King James Version).

What the early church preached

Jesus commissioned his church to preach the gospel and to make disciples of all nations (Matthew 28:18-20). This soon involved preaching to Gentiles who were still immersed in polytheism.

When Paul and Barnabas preached and performed miracles at Lystra, the reaction of the people showed how steeped they were in polytheism: "When the crowd saw what Paul had done, they shouted in the Lycaonian language, 'The gods have come down to us in human form!' Barnabas they called Zeus, and Paul they called Hermes because he was the chief speaker" (Acts 14:11-12). Hermes and Zeus were two gods in the Greek pantheon. The Greek and Roman pantheons were well known in the New Testament world, and worship of the Greek and Roman gods was widespread.

Paul and Barnabas responded vigorously with the message of monotheism: "We too are only men, human like you. We are bringing you good news, telling you to turn from these worthless things to the living God, who made heaven and earth and sea and everything in them" (verse 15). Even then, Paul and Barnabas could scarcely restrain the people from sacrificing to them.

In Athens, Paul found many altars set up to honor different gods – even one with the inscription: "TO AN UNKNOWN GOD" (Acts 17:23). He used that altar as a starting point from which to explain monotheism to the Athenians.

At Ephesus, brisk sales of idols accompanied the worship of the Greek goddess Artemis. After Paul preached about the one true God, the idol trade slackened. The silversmith Demetrius was adversely affected economically. He told his fellow artisans, "Paul has convinced and led astray large numbers of people.... He says that man-made gods are no gods at all" (Acts 19:26).

Here is another case of one of God's servants preaching that gods made by hand are not gods at all. Just as the Old Testament does, the New Testament proclaims but one true God. The other gods aren't.

No other God

To the Christians at Corinth, Paul stated explicitly, "We know that an idol is nothing at all in the world and that there is no God but one" (1 Corinthians 8:4).

Monotheism underpins both the Old and New Testaments. God called

Abraham, the father of the faithful, out from a polytheistic society. God revealed himself to Moses and Israel, and founded the old covenant on the worship of himself alone. God sent prophets to reiterate the message of monotheism. Finally, Jesus Christ himself reaffirmed monotheism. The New Testament church that Jesus founded fought against worship that fell short of true monotheism.

The church, from the days of the New Testament forward, has consistently preached what God long ago had revealed: "The Lord our God, the Lord is one."

JESUS REVEALS GOD

The Bible teaches that God is one. There are not two Gods, or three, or a thousand. Christianity is a monotheistic religion. That is why the coming of Jesus Christ aroused such strong controversy in the communities of his day.

"A stumbling block to Jews..."

God revealed himself to humanity through his Son, Jesus Christ, who is "the radiance of God's glory and the exact representation of his being" (Hebrews 1:3). Jesus called God his Father (Matthew 10:32-33; Luke 23:34; John 10:15) and said, "Anyone who has seen me has seen the Father" (John 14:9). He boldly claimed, "I and the Father are one" (John 10:30). After Jesus' resurrection, Thomas addressed him as "My Lord and my God!" (John 20:28). Jesus Christ was God.

Judaism could not accept this. "The Lord our God, the Lord is one," said the *Shema'* (Deuteronomy 6:4), which had long undergirded the Jewish faith. Yet here was a man with profound scriptural insight and miracle-working power who claimed to be the unique Son of God. Some Jewish leaders acknowledged that Jesus was a teacher come from God (John 3:2). But God's Son? How could God be one, and yet Jesus Christ also be God?

"For this reason the Jews tried all the harder to kill him," says John 5:18. "Not only was he breaking the Sabbath, but he was even calling God his own Father."

The Jews eventually condemned Christ to death because they thought he had, by his claims, blasphemed:

> The high priest asked him, "Are you the Christ, the Son of the Blessed One?" "I am," said Jesus. "And you will see the Son of Man sitting at the right hand of the Mighty One and coming on the clouds of heaven." The high priest tore his clothes. "Why do we need any more witnesses?" he asked. "You have heard the blasphemy. What do you think?" They all condemned him as worthy of death. (Mark 14:61-64)

"...Foolishness to Gentiles"

On the other hand, the Gentiles could not accept Jesus for who he said he was, either. The Greek philosophers thought that nothing could cross the gap from what was eternal and unchanging to what was temporal and material.

So the Greeks scoffed at John's statement: "In the beginning was the

Word, and the Word was with God, and the Word was God.... The Word became flesh and made his dwelling among us. We have seen his glory, the glory of the One and Only, who came from the Father, full of grace and truth" (John 1:1, 14).

For the unbelievers, this unbelievable story didn't end there. Not only did God become a human being and die, but he was raised from the dead and returned to his former glory (John 17:5). Paul wrote to the Ephesians that God had raised Christ "from the dead and seated him at his right hand in the heavenly realms" (Ephesians 1:20).

Elsewhere, Paul addressed the consternation with which the Jews and Greeks greeted the astounding story of Jesus Christ:

> Since in the wisdom of God the world through its wisdom did not know him, God was pleased through the foolishness of what was preached to save those who believe. Jews demand miraculous signs and Greeks look for wisdom, but we preach Christ crucified: a stumbling block to Jews and foolishness to Gentiles. (1 Corinthians 1:21-23)

Not everyone could understand and rejoice at the wonderful news of the gospel. Paul went on: "But to those whom God has called, both Jews and Greeks, Christ [is] the power of God and the wisdom of God. For the foolishness of God is wiser than man's wisdom, and the weakness of God is stronger than man's strength" (verses 24-25). And in Romans 1:16 Paul exclaimed, "I am not ashamed of the gospel, because it is the power of God for the salvation of everyone who believes: first for the Jew, then for the Gentile."

"I am the gate"

During his life on earth, Jesus, God in the flesh, smashed a lot of long-held and cherished – but false – beliefs about what God is, how God lives and what God wants. He illuminated truths that were only hints in Old Testament. He said that no one could be saved except through him: "I am the gate; whoever enters through me will be saved" (John 10:9).

"I am the way and the truth and the life," Jesus announced. "No one comes to the Father except through me" (John 14:6). And: "I am the vine; you are the branches. If a man remains in me and I in him, he will bear much fruit; apart from me you can do nothing. If anyone does not remain in me, he is like a branch that is thrown away and withers; such branches are picked up, thrown into the fire and burned" (John 15:5-6).

Jesus is God

Jesus did not do away with the monotheistic command in Deuteronomy 6:4. Rather, Jesus expanded beyond what anyone had imagined what it means for God to be one. The Gospel of John says that, while God is one and only one, the eternal Word existed with God and was God (John 1:1-2).

When the Word came in the flesh, though he was fully divine, he voluntarily set aside the prerogatives of divinity.

> [Jesus], being in very nature God, did not consider equality with God something to be grasped, but made himself nothing, taking the very nature of a servant, being made in human likeness. And being found in appearance as a man, he humbled himself and became obedient to death – even death on a cross! (Philippians 2:6-8)

Jesus was fully human and fully divine. He held all the power and authority of God, but he voluntarily, for our sakes, subjected himself to the limitations of human existence. During this period of incarnation, he, the Son, remained one with his Father in heaven.

"Anyone who has seen me has seen the Father," said Jesus (John 14:9). "By myself I can do nothing; I judge only as I hear, and my judgment is just, for I seek not to please myself but him who sent me," he said (John 5:30). And, "I do nothing on my own but speak just what the Father has taught me" (John 8:28).

Just before his crucifixion, Jesus told his disciples: "I came from the Father and entered the world; now I am leaving the world and going back to the Father" (John 16:28). Jesus came to earth to die for our sins. He came to found his church. He came to start the preaching of the gospel in all the world. Jesus also came to reveal God to humanity. In particular, he opened human understanding to the Father-Son relationship that exists within the Godhead.

The Gospel of John, for example, largely devotes itself to recording Jesus' work of revealing God the Father to humanity. Jesus' Passover discourse (John 13-17) is of special interest in this regard. What a startling truth about the nature of God! Even more startling is Jesus' further revelation about how God intends for humans to relate to him.

Humans share in the divine nature!

Jesus told his apostles: "Whoever has my commands and obeys them, he is the one who loves me. He who loves me will be loved by my Father, and I too will love him and show myself to him" (John 14:21). God wants to unite humans to him in a profound relationship of love – the love that the Father and Son share. God is revealed to those in whom that love works.

Jesus went on to explain: "If anyone loves me, he will obey my teaching. My Father will love him, and we will come to him and make our home with him. He who does not love me will not obey my teaching. These words you hear are not my own; they belong to the Father who sent me" (verses 23-24).

God lives in those who come to him through faith in Jesus Christ, committing themselves to live in allegiance to him. Peter preached: "Repent and be baptized, every one of you, in the name of Jesus Christ for the forgiveness of your sins. And you will receive the gift of the Holy Spirit" (Acts 2:38). The Holy Spirit also is God, as we shall see in the next chapter. The Holy Spirit lives in the believers.

Paul knew that God lived in him: "I have been crucified with Christ and I no longer live, but Christ lives in me. The life I live in the body, I live by faith in the Son of God, who loved me and gave himself for me" (Galatians 2:20). Because Christ lives in us and the Holy Spirit lives in us, God lives in us. But there is only one God.

God revealed himself fully in Jesus Christ. "For in Christ all the fullness of the Deity lives in bodily form" (Colossians 2:9). What can this revelation mean to us? By partaking of Christ, through faith in him, we can be partakers of God's own divine nature! Peter summed it up by saying,

> Divine power has given us everything we need for life and godliness through our knowledge of him who called us by his own glory and goodness. Through these he has given us his very great and precious promises, so that through them you may *participate in the divine nature* and escape the corruption in the world caused by evil desires. (2 Peter 1:3-4)

Christ – the perfect revelation of God

How did Jesus Christ reveal God?

- Jesus revealed God's character in all he did and taught.
- Jesus died and was raised from death so that humans may be saved and reconciled to God, and that they may receive eternal life. Romans 5:10-11 says: "If, when we were God's enemies, we were reconciled to him through the death of his Son, how much more, having been reconciled, shall we be saved through his life! Not only is this so, but we also rejoice in God through our Lord Jesus Christ, through whom we have now received reconciliation."
- Jesus revealed God's plan to form a new spiritual community — the church — transcending racial and national barriers (Ephesians 2:14-22).

- Jesus revealed God as the Father of all who are reborn in Christ.
- Jesus revealed the glorious destiny God has promised to his people. The indwelling presence of the Spirit of God gives us a foretaste of that future glory here and now. The Spirit is "a deposit guaranteeing our inheritance" (Ephesians 1:14).
- Jesus also witnessed to the existence of the Father and the Son as one God. Our understanding of God's unity must allow for Father and Son, must allow for more than one Person within the Godhead. New Testament writers frequently applied the Old Testament names for God to Christ. By doing so, they showed not only what Christ is like, but what God is like, for Jesus is the revelation of the Father, and he and the Father are one. We learn about God as we study what Jesus Christ is like.

ONE IN THREE
AND THREE IN ONE

The Bible never compromises the fact that God is one. Yet, Jesus' incarnation and work give us a greater depth of understanding of the way in which God is one. The New Testament testifies that Jesus Christ is God and that the Father is God. There is *more than one* Person in the *one* God.

The New Testament, as we shall see, also presents the Holy Spirit as divine and eternal. Whenever we say that the Holy Spirit does something, we mean that God does it. The Holy Spirit is God. That means the Bible reveals one God who exists eternally as Father, Son, and Holy Spirit. It is for this reason that Christians are to be baptized "in the name of the Father and of the Son and of the Holy Spirit" (Matthew 28:19).

Throughout the centuries, many ideas have been developed that might seem, at first glance, to make these biblical facts easier to understand. But we must be careful not to accept any idea that contradicts what the Bible says. Some ideas might make things seem simple, in the sense of making God easier to comprehend and easier to picture in our minds. But what is important is whether an idea is consistent with the Bible, not whether it is simple or easy.

The Bible tells us there is one and only one God, and then presents us with more than one Person called God. The Father is called God, the Son is called God, and the Holy Spirit is called God. All three are eternal, and all three do things that only God can do. So there is one God, and three in the One.

"One in three" – or "three in one" – is a concept that, at first glance, appears illogical. But neither is it logical for us to assume that God could not be more than what we would expect if we simply sat down, with no revelation, to figure it out for ourselves.

God reveals many things about himself, and we believe them, even though we cannot explain them all. For example, we cannot completely explain how God can be without beginning. This is beyond our ability to understand. We cannot explain what eternal existence is like, yet we know that God is without beginning. Likewise, the Bible reveals that God is one and only one, yet is also Father, Son, and Holy Spirit. We believe it even though it is not simple or easy to explain. We believe it because the Bible reveals it.

The Holy Spirit is God

Acts 5:3-4 calls the Holy Spirit God:

> Peter said, "Ananias, how is it that Satan has so filled your heart that you have lied to the Holy Spirit and have kept for yourself some of the money you received for the land? Didn't it belong to you before it was sold? And after it was sold, wasn't the money at your disposal? What made you think of doing such a thing? You have not lied to men but to God."

When Ananias lied to the Holy Spirit, Peter says he was lying to God. He was not trying to deceive an impersonal force or an intermediate agency — he was trying to deceive God.

The New Testament ascribes to the Holy Spirit attributes that belong only to God. For instance, the Holy Spirit is omniscient, or unlimited in knowledge. "God has revealed it to us by his Spirit. The Spirit searches all things, even the deep things of God.... No one knows the thoughts of God except the Spirit of God" (1 Corinthians 2:10-11).

The Holy Spirit is omnipresent, or unlimited in place. "Do you not know that your body is a temple of the Holy Spirit, who is in you, whom you have received from God?" (1 Corinthians 6:19). The Holy Spirit is in believers everywhere, not limited to any one place (see also Psalm 139:7-8).

The Holy Spirit regenerates Christians, giving them new life. "No one can enter the kingdom of God unless he is born of water and the Spirit. Flesh gives birth to flesh, but the Spirit gives birth to spirit" (John 3:5-6).

The Holy Spirit speaks and foretells the future. "The Spirit clearly says that in later times some will abandon the faith and follow deceiving spirits and things taught by demons" (1 Timothy 4:1).

The Holy Spirit is equated with the Father and the Son in the baptismal ceremony. Christian converts are baptized "in the name of the Father and of the Son and of the Holy Spirit" (Matthew 28:19). There is one name, but three are included in the One.

The Spirit creates out of nothing (Psalm 104:30). Only God can create like that.

Hebrews 9:14 says the Holy Spirit is eternal. Only God is eternal.

Jesus told the apostles: "I will ask the Father, and he will give you another Counselor to be with you forever – the Spirit of truth. The world cannot accept him, because it neither sees him nor knows him. But you know him, for he lives with you and will be in you" (John 14:16-17).

Jesus identified the Counselor as the Holy Spirit: "The Counselor, the

Holy Spirit, whom the Father will send in my name, will teach you all things and will remind you of everything I have said to you" (verse 26). The Counselor convicts the world of sin, an accomplishment that can rightly be ascribed only to God. He guides into all truth, something only God is capable of doing. As Paul affirmed, "We speak, not in words taught us by human wisdom but in words taught by the Spirit, expressing spiritual truths in spiritual words" (1 Corinthians 2:13).

Father, Son, and Holy Spirit: one God

When we understand that God is one, and that the Holy Spirit is God, just as the Father is God and the Son is God, we have no problem understanding a passage like Acts 13:2: "While they were worshiping the Lord and fasting, the Holy Spirit said, 'Set apart for me Barnabas and Saul for the work to which I have called them.'" Here Luke presents the Holy Spirit as speaking. The Holy Spirit is God at work in the church, speaking and calling people to do God's will.

The biblical revelation of the nature of God is beautiful. When the Holy Spirit speaks, or sends, or inspires, or leads, or sanctifies, or empowers, or gives gifts, it is God speaking, sending, inspiring, leading, sanctifying, empowering or giving gifts. But since God is one, and not three separate beings, the Holy Spirit is not a separate God.

God has one will, the will of the Father, which is also the will of the Son and of the Holy Spirit. It is not a matter of two or three separate God Beings deciding to be in perfect agreement with each other. This would contradict scriptures such as Isaiah 44:6-8. It is a matter of one God, one will. The Son is the very expression of the will of the Father. Similarly, the Holy Spirit constitutes the will of the Father at work in the world.

Paul says that "the Lord is the Spirit," and he speaks of "the Lord, who is the Spirit" (2 Corinthians 3:17-18). He says "the Spirit gives life" (verse 6), which is something only God can do. We know the Father, only because the Spirit enables us to believe that Jesus is the Son of God. Jesus dwells in us and the Father dwells in us, but that is only because the Spirit dwells in us (John 14:16-17, 23; Romans 8:9-11). Since God is one, if the Spirit is in us, then the Father and the Son are in us. The three can be distinguished, but not separated.

Paul equates the Spirit, the Lord, and God in 1 Corinthians 12:4-11. He says it is "the same God who inspires" in verse 6, and he says "these are the work of one and the same Spirit," and goes on to declare that the Spirit does all this as the Spirit wills (verse 11). How can the Spirit will? The Spirit wills because the Spirit is a person, and the Spirit is God, and God is one, and the will of the Father is the will of the Son and of the Holy Spirit.

To worship God is to worship the Father, the Son, and the Holy Spirit, the one and only one God. That does not mean we are to single out the Holy Spirit and worship the Holy Spirit as though the Holy Spirit is a separate Being. We do not direct our worship to the Holy Spirit specifically, but to God, who is Father, Son, and Holy Spirit. It is God in us (the Holy Spirit) who causes us to worship God. The Comforter (like the Son) will not speak on his own (John 16:13), but what the Father gives him he will speak. He does not direct us to himself, but to the Father through the Son. Likewise, we don't normally pray specifically to the Spirit – it is the Spirit in us who helps us in our prayers, and intercedes for us (Romans 8:26).

Unless God himself is in us, we would not be turned toward God at all. Unless God himself is in us, we would not know God, and we would not know his Son. That is why all the credit for our salvation goes to God and not to us. The fruit we bear is the fruit of the Spirit – that is, God's fruit, not ours. But God gives us the privilege, if we will accept it, of participating with him in his work.

The Father is the Creator and Source of all things. The Son is the Redeemer and Savior, and the one by whom God created all things. The Holy Spirit is the Comforter and Advocate. The Holy Spirit is God in us, the one who leads us to the Father through the Son. Through the Son, we are cleansed and saved so that we can have fellowship with him and the Father. The Spirit stirs our hearts and minds and inclines us toward belief in Jesus Christ, who is the way and the gate. The Spirit gives us gifts, the gifts of God, including faith, hope and love.

All this is the work of the one God, who reveals himself to us as Father, Son, and Holy Spirit. He is not a different God from the God of the Old Testament, but in the New Testament something more is revealed about him: He sent his Son as a human being to die for our sins and to be raised to glory, and he sent us his Spirit – the Comforter – to dwell in us, to lead us into all truth, to give us gifts, and to conform us to the image of Christ.

When we pray, reaching God is the goal of the prayer, yet it is also God who leads us toward that goal, and it is also God who is the Way along which we are led toward the goal. In other words, it is to God (the Father) we pray; it is God in us (the Holy Spirit) motivating us to pray; and God is also the Way (the Son) along which we are being led toward that goal.

The Father initiates the plan of salvation. The Son embodies and executes the atoning, redemptive plan for the salvation of humanity. The Holy Spirit applies the benefits, or gifts, of redemption to empower the actual salvation of the faithful believers. All this is the work of the one God, the God of the Bible.

Paul ended 2 Corinthians with the blessing: "May the grace of the Lord Jesus Christ, and the love of God, and the fellowship of the Holy Spirit be with you all" (2 Corinthians 13:14). In this verse, Paul highlights the love of God, which is shown to us through the grace he gives us in Jesus Christ and the unified fellowship with himself and one another he gives us through the Holy Spirit.

How many "Persons" is God?

Many people have only a hazy idea of what the Bible teaches about the oneness of God. Most do not really think about it. Some imagine three separate Beings. Some picture one Being with three heads. Others think of one Being who changes from Father to Son to Holy Spirit whenever he wills. It is easy to make such mistakes.

Many people use the word Trinity as a definition of the biblical teaching about God. However, if asked, most would not be able to explain what the Bible actually teaches about how God is one. In other words, what many people envision when they speak of the Trinity is not biblical. Some of the confusion lies in the use of the word Persons.

The word Persons, which is normally included in English-language definitions of the Trinity, causes people to think of three Beings. "One God who is three Persons – Father, Son, and Holy Spirit," is a common way the Trinity is explained. But the ordinary meaning of the word "person" is misleading when it is applied to God. It gives the impression that God has limits, and that his threeness lies in being three separate individuals – which is not the case.

The English word "person" is derived from the Latin word *persona*. The word *persona* was used by theologians to describe the Father, the Son, and the Holy Spirit in the Latin language, but it did not convey the same meaning as the English word "person" conveys today. It was a word originally used for a role that an actor portrayed in a play. It was also the word for "mask," because actors wore different masks for each character they portrayed.

Even this concept, though it does not allow the error of three Beings, is still weak and misleading when referring to God. It is misleading because the Father, the Son, and the Holy Spirit are not mere roles being played by God. An actor can play only one role at a time, quite unlike God, who is Father, Son, and Holy Spirit all the time.

Even though a Latin theologian may have understood what was meant by the word *persona,* the average person today would not. The English word "person" is easily misunderstood by the average individual when referring to God, unless it is accompanied by an explanation that "Persons" in the Godhead should not be thought of in the same way as "persons" like humans.

When most English-speaking people think of one God who is three Persons, they cannot help but think in some way of three separate Beings. In other words, the terms *persons* and *beings* are usually thought of, in English, as meaning the same thing. But that is not how God is revealed in the Bible. There is only one God, not three. The Bible reveals that Father, Son, and Holy Spirit are the way the one true God of the Bible is, the way God exists always.

One God: three Hypostases

When we express the biblical truth that God is one and at the same time three, it is helpful to use words that do not imply three Gods. God's oneness cannot be compromised. The problem is, all words that refer to created things tend to mislead by their very context in ordinary language. Most words, including the word Persons, tend to confuse God's nature with the created order. On the other hand, all our words in one way or another refer to the created order. So it is important to know what we mean, and what we do not mean, when we use any word in reference to God.

A helpful word, and one that was used by Greek-speaking Christians in expressing the oneness and threeness of God, is found in Hebrews 1:3. This passage is helpful in several ways. It states: "The Son is the radiance of God's glory and the exact representation of his being, sustaining all things by his powerful word."

From the description of the Son as "the radiance of God's glory," we learn a number of things. The Son is not a separate Being. The Son is not less divine than the Father. The Son is eternal, just as the Father is. In other words, the Son is to the Father as radiance or brightness is to glory. One cannot have radiance without the source of radiance, or a source of radiance without the radiance itself. Yet we distinguish between God's glory and the radiance of that glory. They are distinct, without being separate.

Likewise, there is much to learn from the words "the exact representation of his being." The Son is the full and complete expression of the Father. What God is in his being, the Son also is.

Now, let's look at the Greek word translated "being" in this passage. Some versions translate it "person." The word from which "being" and "person" in this passage are translated is *hypostasis*. It comes from Greek words meaning "standing under." It refers to that which "stands under," or that which makes something what it is. Hypostasis could be defined like this: "That without which something cannot be." It could be called "the ground of being."

God is personal

Hypostasis (in plural form, hypostases) is a good word to use of the Father, the Son, and the Holy Spirit. It is a biblical term, and it does not so easily confuse God's nature with the created order.

The word Person may also be used, as long as one understands that Person must not be confused with the way humans are persons. One reason the word Person is helpful, if it is understood correctly, is that God interacts with us in a personal way. It is wrong to say that God is impersonal. We do not worship a rock or plant, or an impersonal "power that is behind the universe." Rather, we worship a "living Person."

God is personal, but he is not a person in the way humans are persons. He says, "I am God, and not man – the Holy One among you" (Hosea 11:9). God is Creator; he is not just another part of his creation. Humans have a beginning, grow up, have a body, are separate from one another, grow old, increase or decrease in size, strength, etc., and die. God has none of those characteristics, but is nonetheless personal in his relationship to humans.

God is infinitely more than any human word can convey, yet he is personal and loves us dearly. God has revealed much about himself, but he has not revealed everything about himself – some things we are simply incapable of knowing. As finite beings, we cannot totally grasp the infinite. We can know God as he reveals himself to us, but we cannot know him exhaustively, because we are finite, and he is infinite. What God has revealed to us about himself is true. It is relevant. It is intimate. It is marvelous, and it is thorough. But we must never think we know everything about God. God has revealed all we *need* to know, and what he has revealed is wonderful!

God calls on us to continue to "grow in the grace and knowledge of our Lord and Savior Jesus Christ" (2 Peter 3:18). Jesus proclaimed, "This is eternal life: that they may know you, the only true God, and Jesus Christ, whom you have sent" (John 17:3). The more we know God, the more we realize how small we are and how great he is.

HUMANITY'S RELATIONSHIP WITH GOD

In an earlier chapter, we tried to frame a question that would capture what it is that humans want to know about God. What one question would we want to ask God, if we had the chance?

To our fumbling question "Who are you?", the awesome God who made and rules the cosmos replies, "I AM WHO I AM" (Exodus 3:14). God declares himself to us in creation (Psalm 19:1). He has interacted with the human family ever since he made us. Sometimes he speaks through thunder, quaking or fire, and sometimes he speaks in a gentle whisper (Exodus 20:18; 1 Kings 19:11-12).

In the biblical record, God reveals information about himself and inspired reports of how people responded to him. God also reveals himself through Jesus Christ and the Holy Spirit.

But we want to know more than who God is, don't we? We want to know why he made us. We want to know his will for us. We want to know what he has in store for us. We want to know not just *about* him — we want to know *him*.

What is our relationship with God now? What should it be? And what will our relationship be in the future? God made us in his image (Genesis 1:26-27). The Bible reveals a far more profound future than we can now imagine.

Where we find ourselves now

Hebrews 2:6-11 tells us that we are made "a little lower than the angels." Yet God has crowned us with "glory and honor" and put everything under our rule. His future intent for humanity is to leave "nothing that is not subject to him. Yet at present we do not see everything subject to him."

God has prepared an infinitely glorious and joyous future for us. But something stands in the way. We find ourselves in a state of sin, alienated from God by our transgressions (Isaiah 59:1-2). But the breach has been healed. Jesus tasted death for us so that he might bring "many children to glory" (Hebrews 2:9-10).

Revelation 21:7 says that God desires to unite us with him in a family relationship. Because of God's love for us and what he has done for us, and what he is doing for us now as the Author of our salvation, Jesus is "not ashamed to call [us] brothers and sisters" (Hebrews 2:10-11).

So what should we be doing now?

Acts 2:38 instructs us to repent of our sins and to be baptized – to figuratively bury the old self. Those who believe that Jesus Christ is their Savior, Lord and King are led by the Spirit (Galatians 3:2-5). As he opens our minds to understand the gospel, we repent – turning to God from the selfish, worldly, sinful ways we followed in the past. In faith, we enter into a new relationship with him. We are reborn (John 3:3), given a new life in Christ through the Holy Spirit, regenerated by the Spirit through God's grace and mercy and the redemptive work of Jesus Christ.

What happens then? We "grow in the grace and knowledge of our Lord and Savior Jesus Christ" (2 Peter 3:18) for the remainder of our lives, destined to take part in the first resurrection, after which we will "be with the Lord forever" (1 Thessalonians 4:13-17).

Awesome inheritance

God "has given us new birth into a living hope through the resurrection of Jesus Christ from the dead, and into an inheritance that can never perish, spoil or fade – kept in heaven for you, who through faith are shielded by God's power until the coming of the salvation that is ready to be revealed in the last time" (1 Peter 1:3-5).

In the resurrection, we will be given immortality (1 Corinthians 15:54) and a "spiritual body" (verse 44). "As we have borne the likeness of the earthly man [Adam]," says verse 49, "so shall we bear the likeness of the man from heaven [Jesus]." As "children of the resurrection," we will no longer be subject to death (Luke 20:36).

Could anything be more wonderful than what the Bible says about God and our future relationship with him, a relationship that can begin right now? We will "be like him [Jesus], for we shall see him as he is" (1 John 3:2). Revelation 21:3 says that, in the time of the new heaven and new earth, "the dwelling of God is with humans, and he will live with them. They will be his people, and God himself will be with them and be their God."

We will be one with God in holiness, love, perfection, righteousness and spirit. As his immortal children, we will be the family of God in its fullest sense, sharing complete fellowship with him in perfect and everlasting joy. What a marvelous and inspiring message of hope and eternal salvation God has for all those who are prepared to believe!

The Name of God — YHWH

When God called to Moses out of the burning bush, telling him to free the Israelites from bondage in Egypt, Moses asked: "Suppose I go to the Israelites and say to them, 'The God of your fathers has sent me to you,' and they ask me, 'What is his name?' Then what shall I tell them?" (Exodus 3:13).

God answered Moses, "I AM WHO I AM" (verse 14). The Hebrew word for "I AM" is *ehyeh,* which comes from the verb "to be." It can also be translated as "I SHALL BE."

God further told Moses: "Say to the Israelites, 'The Lord, the God of your fathers...has sent me to you'" (verse 15). Although the Hebrew word for "Lord" is *adon*, the word translated "Lord" in verse 15 is different. It is spelled with the four Hebrew consonants YHWH – "the tetragrammaton" (Greek for "four letters"). The word is related to *ehyeh* and also comes from the verb "to be." Both words have the sense of "being actively present."

Although most scholars pronounce the tetragrammaton as Yahweh, the correct pronunciation is not known for certain. The Hebrews avoided saying the tetragrammaton because they believed that doing so might take God's name in vain. When reading a passage of the Hebrew Bible that contained it, they referred to God by another one of his names – *adonai* or "my Lord."

The oldest known manuscript fragments of the Septuagint leave the tetragrammaton untranslated. Later manuscripts, probably reflecting Christian editing, render the tetragrammaton as *kyrios,* Greek for "Lord." Later, English versions rendered the personal name YHWH as the impersonal "the LORD." They used all capital letters for "Lord" to indicate they were translating YHWH, rather than *adon* or *adonai.*

The text of the Hebrew Bible originally had only consonants. When vowels were added in the 10th century A.D., the vowels of *adonai* were also used for the tetragrammaton, reminding the readers to pronounce the word as adonai. In the 16th century, Latin translators combined the vowel points of *adonai* with the consonants of the tetragrammaton to produce the artificial form *Iehoua.* In 1530, Tyndale rendered the tetragrammaton as *Iehouah* in his translation of Exodus 6:3. Subsequently, the I became J, and the u became v, and Jehovah became the standard spelling. The King James Version uses this spelling (Psalm 83:18 is one example), but the KJV usually translates YHWH as "the Lord" and *adonai* as "the Lord."

GOD'S NAMES AND TITLES

The names of God and the words used for God found in the Old Testament reflect a Semitic world's commitment to the relationship between the nature of anything and the name of that thing. The name could not be divorced from the nature of the actual being of the thing. The revelation of God belongs to the divine freedom of the Self-Naming God. The various names of God in his acts with his people in the world cannot be divorced from his actual nature and being. All the names of God must refer to who he truly is with Israel and the world.

The most common name of God found in the Old Testament – YHWH (used 6823 times) – refers to the great I-AM of God, established in his divine freedom to be present with Israel in the Exodus tradition. The fundamental assertion of the five books of Moses or the Pentateuch is that YHWH is none other than the Elohim (used 2550 times) of the world.

It is the nature and being of this one that would establish both the redemption of his people and the creation of the world. Deuteronomy 32:3, in the Song of Moses, the poet declares that he will proclaim the name of YHWH, he will praise the greatness of "our" Elohim. There is a strong polemic inherent in the use of these names that demythologizes the world of the ancient deities. With the use of these names, Israel confessed the unique power of the oneness of the "Lord our God" (Deuteronomy 6:4).

The names YHWH and Elohim are usually translated by the English words LORD and GOD. We should understand these names as referring at once both to the Deliverer of Israel and the Creator of the universe – the heavens and the earth.

In a few places, the King James Version translated the consonants YHWH with the vowels from the word *Adonai;* the resulting hybrid was "Jehovah." The four consonants of the name that the Jews would not pronounce in the synagogues of Judaism were read aloud as "Adonai," and the scribes recorded the practice in a conflation of the consonants from YHWH and the vowels of Adonai. Transliterated in the King James Bible, the word Jehovah was produced.

Modern scholars believe that in some sense YHWH is to be associated with the verb "to be" in Hebrew, and may have been pronounced something like "Yahweh." That is the way the name is sounded among most scholars today. Many Jews cling to their reverence for the name and in their congregations, when they see the Tetragrammaton (YHWH) in the texts, they say, "Ha Shem," meaning "the Name."

The important thing to understand is that "Lord God" refers us to the actual nature and being of the actual existence of his deity with us in the world. Because of his actions in delivering Israel from Egypt, YHWH is the name confessed by the people of God, and Elohim, the name associated with his creation in the beginning of the world, is affirmed as being none other than YHWH. We do not exhaust the ways the Lord God in his divine freedom chose to interact in covenant with his people. There are many other names of God in the Old Testament.

Associated directly with the Lord God (*YHWH Elohim*) is the name *Elohim* in construct form with the fathers of Israel. He is the God of Abraham, Isaac, and Jacob/Israel (Exodus 3:13-15). Other forms of *YHWH* may be observed: *YHWH Yireh* (Genesis 22:14, "He sees"), *YHWH Rophekah* (Exodus 15:26, "He heals"), *YHWH Nissiy* (Exodus 17:15, "My Banner"), *YHWH Meqaddishkem* (Exodus 31:13, "He makes you holy"), *YHWH Shalom* (Judges 6:24, "Lord of peace"), *YHWH Tseba'oth* (1 Samuel 1:3, "Lord of hosts"), *YHWH Tsidqenuh* (Jeremiah 23:6, "Lord, our righteousness"), *YHWH Shammah* (Ezekiel 48:35, "He is there"), *YHWH Elyon* (Psalm 7:17, "He is most high"), *YHWH Ro'iy* (Psalm 23:1, "He is my shepherd"), and others.

The book of Ezekiel may be understood as a prophecy that shows that God does not name himself in vain: "I am YHWH" is announced over and over again throughout the book. The rhetoric is clearly that, when the prophecy is fulfilled, the whole world will know him for who he truly is.

Combinations of terms with *El* or *Elohim* are also frequent in the Old Testament. Genesis 14:18-22 possesses a play on the names for the Lord God, and it claims the *El Elyon* (God Most High) as the begetter (*Qoneh*) of the heavens and the earth is the one who is Abram's Shield or Protector. *El Shadday* (God of Provision, Genesis 17:1) was known among the ancestors of Israel (Exodus 6:3), long before the great I-AM had given Moses the name YHWH, with which Moses could confront Pharaoh.

El in certain combinations can refer to angels, mighty heroes or humans, as well as the supreme God. *El Olam* (God of Forever, Genesis 21:33) bears the interaction of God's eternity with created time. *El Rachum* (God of Compassion, Exodus 34:6) signifies the way God is in the conception of Israel, even in spite of Israel's opposition to who he truly is. *El Emunah* (God of Faithfulness, Deuteronomy 32:4) refers to the God whom Israel can trust with her future.

The confession in Exodus 34:6-7 shapes a "credo" that forms much of Israel's understanding of the Lord God in covenant with her and the development of her history in the world. Here *YHWH* is the *El* of that compassion, favor, patience, and great grace and truth that is inherent in the way the great I-AM has chosen in his divine freedom to be present with Israel's past, present and future.

Besides these combinations of names with *YHWH* and *El* or *Elohim,* the term *Adonay* can be employed in the superlative to refer to the Lord of Lords (Deuteronomy 10:17). In Genesis 15:1, the Word of YHWH calls himself for Abram a *Megen* (Shield). In Exodus 31:13, YHWH calls himself the one who makes Israel holy (*Meqadish*), a name especially important in the Levitical law (Leviticus 20:8; 21:8; 22:32). In his interaction with his people, he is of a dynamic nature and being.

YH and a shortened form *YHu* can be found throughout the ancient Near East to signify a deity in the pantheons of some city-states as well as the God of the Old Testament (Exodus 15:2 and with many names of places and people). *El* and *Elohim* are commonly found among the mythologies and cosmogonies of the ancient civilizations. These names for the gods of the temples and palaces in the city-states of the ancient civilizations are also reflected in the pantheons of the Greek gods. The Canaanite *Baal,* Mesopotamia's *Marduk,* and the Greek *Zeus* may all be understood as storm-gods bound up with the fertility myths of these peoples.

These gods are the background for the names of the Lord God that we find in use in ancient Israel. But Israel employs what was common in this background with unique significance. The names of the Lord God in the biblical usage could never be understood free from the actual being and nature of the one true Creator and Redeemer of the world in opposition to the other gods. He is to be known in Israel as the great I-AM, the one who makes Israel the people of God (cf. Hosea 1:9). She is to know this one for who he truly is in the world (cf. the "I am YHWH" of the book of Ezekiel). This is the prophetic power of the self-revelation of the self-naming God that lies behind the use of the divine names and titles in the Old Testament.

Thus, the use of the words Greek *Kyrios* and *Theos* in the New Testament resounds in the Greco-Roman world the names of *YHWH* and *Elohim* in the Old Testament.

John McKenna

A GOD OF CHAOS?

Do you ever feel you're in a chaotic mess? I'm spending much of my time either trying to avoid chaos or get out of it. Earlier this year—you know, New Year's resolutions—I had the bright idea to reorganize my home office. I know what, I'll (meaning my husband) build some shelves in the office closet to hold the printers and other equipment taking up my space.

Well, one thing led to another. Electrical and computer cables had to be redirected. Files had to be moved out of the closet to make space for the shelves. Everything was piling up in my office, so we could hardly get in and out.

Moving that equipment into the closet allowed us to get rid of some furniture, which meant moving around the other furniture. It was chaotic for days and it wasn't long before I was apologizing to Ed and sorrowfully regretting my bright idea.

But then, all was put back in order. I had more space. The office looked much better, and Ed didn't hurt his back. I promised him it would be years before I would change that office around again.

God likes order. It says in Genesis 1 that God created raw material out of nothing. And he took that chaotic mass of raw material and made a universe out of it. One planet he focused on in particular was our earth.

Genesis 1:1-3 (New Revised Standard Version): "In the beginning when God created the heavens and the earth, the earth was a formless void and darkness covered the face of the deep, while a wind from God swept over the face of the waters. Then God said, 'Let there be light'; and there was light." We know the rest of the story.

With the subject of this article firmly in mind, I looked at several translations. The earth was "without form and void"; "formless and empty"; "void and vacant"; "unformed and void"; and finally in the Living Bible, "a shapeless, chaotic mass."

Yes, I finally found the words I was looking for: *chaotic mass.*

God makes order out of chaos. But then, as he made everything, didn't God also make the chaos? He had to make that shapeless, chaotic mass to begin with. Who is this God we worship? What's he really like?

I know God is creative—wonderfully creative. No two snowflakes alike, no two fingerprints the same. When I watch in wonder at cloud formations swirling around changing patterns or at the ever-changing colors in a sunset, I'm looking at a moving canvas of art never to be repeated in quite the same way.

Before you scoff at abstract paintings, look at the most beautiful abstracts ever by viewing Hubble telescope's photos of the stars, nebulas and the constellations. Or look at organic structures under a microscope. No one can create abstracts as beautiful as God creates.

And what about us humans? We start out tiny as the head of a pin, then through ingesting animal and vegetable products we grow into adults. How can wheat, rice, milk, beef, green beans, or here where I live in Texas, chicken-fried steak and biscuits and gravy grow a human being? Yet here we are, made out of a mess of seeds, grasses, fish and animals.

A meteorologist studying weather patterns in the 1960s came to the conclusion that because of the endless variations in the weather, we could never accurately predict the weather. It was too chaotic. The study was famous for saying even the flutter of a butterfly's wings could change the weather—the butterfly effect. This eventually led to what is called Chaos Theory.

I won't attempt to explain that theory, but in later studies what scientists considered chaotic: how weather changes, how tree branches grow, how blood veins branch out, all individually different and unpredictable, some brainiac came up with a formula that worked across these so-called chaotic patterns. To scientists' astonishment, they found order even in chaos. There's so much we have yet to learn about the mind of God.

Our God is the greatest artist, greatest architect, scientist, biologist, zoologist, physicist—greatest everything because he created everything. I wonder how much Christ knew in his physical form about what he created. The Bible writers are more concerned with what Christ did and taught, so few are the clues to what Christ understood about the world he lived in.

He changed water into wine. Did he understand the molecular structures he was working with? Did he need to? He healed people. Again, did he know exactly how the healing took place? Not sure if it mattered to him. His purpose was not to reveal the secrets of the universe but to redeem, reconcile and save us.

We live in a chaotic world full of people living chaotic lives. Before surrendering my will to God, I could describe my life as "without form and void." Many are out there living in desperation, yearning for some kind of escape from the mess they've made of their lives. That's where Christ comes in like the conquering hero he is.

Who is this God who calls himself the Creator? Jesus came to show us. He came to reveal the sovereign God. Some say we can learn about God through looking at his creation. That may be true to a point. As 17-century

English poet John Milton wrote:

> "The planets in their stations list'ning stood,
> While the bright pomp ascended jubilant.
> Open, ye everlasting gates, they sung,
> Open, ye heavens, your living doors; let in
> The great Creator from his work return'd
> Magnificent, his six days' work, a world"
> (*Paradise Lost*).

Yes, a magnificent work indeed. But God cannot be examined through microscopes or telescopes. He is spiritual. Jesus came to let us know who God really is. Even scientific minds marvel at his creation, but only Jesus could let us know how much God loves us.

Sheila Graham

WHY BOTHER WITH THEOLOGY?

Many people find theology to be complicated, confusing and even irrelevant. They wonder why they should bother with it at all. "Surely," they exclaim, "the Bible isn't that difficult! Why read the works of head-in-the-clouds theologians with their long sentences and fancy terms?"

Sadly, it is common to ridicule what we don't understand. But doing so is a formula for continuing in ignorance and possibly falling prey to heresy.

I acknowledge that some academic theologians are hard to understand. In fact, it is unusual to find a genuine scholar who is also a gifted communicator. People in academic circles often deal in lofty ideas, and speak and write mainly with their peer group in mind. They leave it to others to bring those ideas down to earth. The situation is not unlike the difference between the practices of science and technology. The experimental scientist in his laboratory discovers a new process or material, and leaves it mostly to others to harness the idea into something practical for the ordinary person.

Theology has been called "faith seeking understanding," and we should not despise it. As Christians we trust God, but God has made us to want to understand the one we trust and why we trust him. Our God apparently wants us to grow in our knowledge and trust in him, having our minds more and more transformed. But knowledge about God is not something that we humans can just come up with on our own by thinking it out. The only way we can know anything true about God is to listen to what he tells us about himself.

God has chosen to preserve the revelation of himself to us in the Bible, a collection of inspired writings compiled over many centuries under the supervision of the Holy Spirit. However, even the most diligent study of the Bible does not automatically convey to us a right or full understanding of who God is. Most heresies come from wrong understandings of who God is, often promoted by one or a few individuals who fail to grasp how God has revealed himself in the Bible and ultimately in Jesus Christ, and who have given little or no attention to the biblically based teaching of the church down through the ages.

What then do we need? First, we need the Holy Spirit to enable our minds to understand what God reveals in the Bible about himself and give us the humility to receive it. The Bible and the work of the Spirit together are sufficient to bring the humble reader (or hearer) with a mustard seed's worth of faith to an initial trust that repents of unbelief and acknowledges that Jesus is Lord and that he alone brings us God's gracious salvation. Second, growth in our knowledge of who God is calls for a comprehensive grasp of the whole of Scripture with Jesus Christ standing at the center of it all. No one can do that for themselves in even a lifetime. We need the wisdom of others. Third, we may misunderstand some or much of what we read in the Bible due to assumptions we bring with us into our study of the Bible. We need help to remove these obstacles to spiritual growth. Fourth, we will not instantly know how best to communicate our understanding to those around us. Some are specifically called to help sort all these things out. And this is where theology comes in.

The word *theology* comes from a combination of two Greek words, *theos*, meaning God, and *logia*, meaning knowledge or study—*study of God*. Theologians are those members of the body of Christ who are called to synthesize and sum up the biblical witness to the nature, character, mind, purposes and will of God. In doing this they survey the results of others in the history of the church who attempted to do the same. They also analyze our contemporary context to discern the best words, concepts, stories, analogies or illustrations that most faithfully convey the truth and reality of who God is. The result is theology. While not all theologies are equally faithful, the church is wise to make use of those results that do help it keep its proclamation of the Gospel resting on the firm foundation of God's own revelation of himself in Jesus Christ according to Scripture.

The church as a whole has an ongoing responsibility to examine its beliefs and practices critically, in the light of God's revelation. Theology, therefore, represents the Christian community's continuous quest for faithful doctrine as it humbly seeks God's wisdom and follows the Holy Spirit's lead into all truth. The church ought to make use of those members of the Body who are specially called to help it do just that. Until Christ returns in glory, the church cannot assume that it has reached its goal. That is why theology should be a never-ending process of critical self-examination. Theology can thus serve the church by combating heresies, or false teachings, and helping us find the most faithful ways we can speak the truth in love today in our current context.

My point is that theology — good theology based in a profound respect for the biblical revelation and a sound understanding of its intent, background, context and comprehensive meaning for today — is a vital ingredient to a growing Christian faith. The 21st century is posing unprecedented challenges that are not addressed directly in the inspired Scriptures. Times change, but "Jesus Christ is the same yesterday and today and forever" (Hebrews 13:8). At the Last Supper, Jesus told his disciples, "I have much more to say to you, more than you can now bear. But when he, the Spirit of truth, comes, he will guide you into all the truth. He will not speak on his own; he will speak only what he hears, and he will tell you what is yet to come. He will glorify me because it is from me that he will receive what he will make known to you. All that belongs to the Father is mine. That is why I said the Spirit will receive from me what he will make known to you" (John 16:12-15).

So let's not despise the understanding that comes from good theology, even though it sometimes comes wrapped in difficult language. As the "resident theologian" to the people you serve, strive to understand it and then serve it up to your people in a way they can also understand.

Joseph Tkach

THEOLOGY IN PERSPECTIVE

Sound theology is important, for unsound theology distorts our understanding of God and our relationship with him. However, it's important to note that we are not saved by theology. And so we need to keep it in perspective.

Christianity has never been theologically or doctrinally perfect. We often hear preachers urging people to "get back to the faith once delivered." By this, they usually mean the early apostolic church, which they assume had a complete and uncorrupted understanding of the faith. However, those apostolic churches were not perfect. They too had to grow in their understanding of what was "sound doctrine."

In fact, much of the New Testament is polemic — meaning that it was written to correct various wrong ideas. In Corinth, for example, some Christians were tolerating incest, suing one another in court, offending each other by their understanding of what they were permitted to eat and becoming drunk at the Lord's Supper. Some thought they should be celibate even if married and others thought they should divorce their non-Christian spouses. Paul had to correct these ideas, and history tells us that he had only limited success. But the people were Christian despite their lack of complete doctrinal understanding.

There are many examples of the disciples failing to understand Jesus, even when he was with them. For example, after Jesus miraculously fed thousands of people, he and the disciples got into a boat and Jesus warned them, "Watch out for the yeast of the Pharisees and that of Herod" (Mark 8:14). The disciples concluded that Jesus meant that, since they hadn't brought any bread they would have to buy some on the other shore; moreover, they shouldn't buy any bread from a Pharisee or Herodian because something was incorrect about the yeast they used.

Why didn't they just ask Jesus what he meant? Perhaps because they were afraid of looking foolish (that happens today, too!). Jesus chided them for not understanding something that they should have been able to grasp. The disciples didn't need to worry about bread or yeast. Jesus had just shown that he could make bread miraculously. They could remember facts (verses 19-20), but they didn't always draw right conclusions from those facts. The miracle of the loaves was not just a way to save money — it also had a much deeper meaning that the disciples had failed to understand (Mark 6:52). It figuratively symbolized the fact that Jesus is our source of life.

I am encouraged to know that Jesus' own disciples frequently didn't fully comprehend what he was doing. Nevertheless, Jesus still co-ministered with them, as he does with us. It demonstrates that any "success" we have is the result of God's guidance, not our human ability to figure things out exactly.

Those first disciples were thrown into confusion by Jesus' death even though he explained it to them more than once. But, like us, they could only absorb so much at a time. If you follow the flow of the conversation at the Last Supper, you can see by their questions and frequent attempts to change the subject that the disciples did not understand what was going on. So Jesus told them, "I have much more to say to you, more than you can now bear. But when he, the Spirit of truth, comes, he will guide you into all the truth" (John 16:12-13).

After his resurrection, Jesus appeared to his disciples and instructed them for 40 days, after which he ascended to heaven. While with them, he said, "Do not leave Jerusalem, but wait for the gift my Father promised, which you have heard me speak about. For John baptized with water, but in a few days you will be baptized with the Holy Spirit" (Acts 1:4-5).

Jesus' words were fulfilled on the day of Pentecost. And as we read in Acts 2:4, the disciples were filled with the Holy Spirit and through his guidance, what had been isolated facts and an unsound theology came together in a new and exciting way. The apostle Peter preached his first public sermon, urging his audience to repent, to believe in Jesus Christ as their Messiah and to receive the gift of the Holy Spirit (verse 38). On that day, some 3,000 people were baptized and became the people of God (verse 41). The church had been born.

From that day on, the Holy Spirit has continued to guide the church into "all the truth," helping her to "prove the world to be in the wrong about sin and righteousness and judgment" (John 16:9). The New Testament writers, led by the Holy Spirit, showed those first Christians how to live godly lives in the turbulent environment of the first century. He is doing the same with us today, as we struggle to "get it right" while facing the complex and controversial challenges of our time.

We need to remember then, that the ultimate object of our faith and the only object of our worship is our Triune God, not our theological statements. We want to tune our theological understandings as best we can to do nothing less and nothing more than serve our faith in and worship of the Father, Son and Spirit. By the Spirit and the Word our theological understandings can be continually sanctified. This coming week on Pentecost Sunday we celebrate the descent of the Spirit that gave birth to the church. While not yet perfect, the children of God have been given the good and perfect gift of the Spirit, who will in the end enable all of us to share in Jesus' own perfection!

Joseph Tkach

THEOLOGY:
WHAT DIFFERENCE DOES IT MAKE?

"Don't talk to me about theology. Just teach me the Bible."

To the average Christian, theology might sound like something hopelessly complicated, frustratingly confusing and thoroughly irrelevant. Anybody can read the Bible. So why do we need head-in-the-clouds theologians with their long sentences and fancy terms?

Faith seeking understanding

Theology has been called "faith seeking understanding." In other words, as Christians we trust God, but God has made us to want to understand who we are trusting and why we trust him. That's where theology comes in. The word *theology* comes from a combination of two Greek words, *theos,* meaning God, and *logia,* meaning knowledge or study—study of God.

When properly used, theology can serve the church by combating heresies, or false teachings. That is because most heresies come from wrong understandings of who God is, understandings that don't square with the way God has revealed himself in the Bible. The church's proclamation of the gospel needs to rest on the firm foundation of God's own revelation of himself.

Revelation

Knowledge about God is not something that we humans can just come up with on our own by thinking it out. The only way we can know anything true about God is to listen to what God tells us about himself. The main way God has chosen to reveal himself to us is through the Bible, a collection of inspired writings compiled over many centuries under the supervision of the Holy Spirit. But even diligent study of the Bible, in itself, cannot convey to us right understanding of who God is.

We need more than mere study—we need the Holy Spirit to enable our minds to understand what God reveals in the Bible about himself. The bottom line is that true knowledge of God comes only from God, not merely by human study, reasoning or experience.

The church has an ongoing responsibility to critically examine its beliefs and practices in the light of God's revelation. Theology is the Christian community's continuous quest for truth as it humbly seeks God's wisdom and follows the Holy Spirit's lead into all truth. Until Christ returns in glory, the church cannot assume that it has reached its goal.

That is why theology should never become a mere restatement of the church's creeds and doctrines, but should rather be a never-ending process of critical self-examination. It is only as we stand in the divine Light of God's mystery that we find true knowledge of God.

Paul called that divine mystery "Christ in you, the hope of glory" (Colossians 1:27), the mystery that through Christ it pleased God "to reconcile to himself all things, whether things on earth or things in heaven, by making peace through his blood, shed on the cross" (verse 20).

The Christian church's proclamation and practice are always in need of examination and fine-tuning, sometimes even major reform, as it continues to grow in the grace and knowledge of the Lord Jesus Christ.

Dynamic theology

The word *dynamic* is a good word to describe this constant effort of the Christian church to look at itself and the world in the light of God's self-revelation and then to let the Holy Spirit conform it accordingly to be a people who reflect and proclaim God as God truly is. We see this *dynamic* quality in theology throughout church history. The apostles reinterpreted the Scriptures when they proclaimed Jesus as the Messiah.

God's new act of self-revelation in Jesus Christ brought new light to the Bible, light that the Holy Spirit opened the eyes of the apostles to see. In the fourth century, Athanasius, bishop of Alexandria, used descriptive words in the creeds that were not in the Bible in order to help Gentiles understand the meaning of the biblical revelation of God. In the 16th century, John Calvin and Martin Luther contended for the renewal of the church in light of the demand of the biblical truth that salvation comes only by grace through faith in Jesus Christ.

In the 1800s, John McLeod Campbell attempted to broaden the Church of Scotland's narrow view on the nature of Jesus' atonement for humanity, and was thrown out for his efforts.

In modern times, no one has been more effective in calling the church to a dynamic theology rooted in active faith than Karl Barth, who "gave the Bible back to Europe" after liberal Protestant theology had nearly swallowed up the church by embracing Enlightenment humanism and the "natural theology" of the German church, and ended up supporting Hitler.

Listening to God

Whenever the church fails to hear the voice of God and instead gives in to its own assumptions and presuppositions, it becomes weak and ineffective.

It loses relevance in the eyes of those it is trying to reach with the gospel message. The same is true of any part of the Body of Christ when it wraps itself up in its own preconceived ideas and traditions. It becomes bogged down, stuck or *static,* the opposite of *dynamic,* and loses its effectiveness in spreading the gospel.

When that happens, the church begins to fragment or break up, Christians become alienated from one another, and Jesus' command that we love one another fades into the background. Then, gospel proclamation becomes merely a set of words, a proposition that people unthinkingly agree with. The power behind it to offer healing to sinful minds loses its force. Relationships become external, only surface contacts that miss the deep union and communion with Jesus and one another where genuine healing, peace and joy become real possibilities. Static religion is a barrier that can prevent believers from becoming the real people God intends them to be in Jesus Christ.

'Double predestination'

The doctrine of election or double predestination has long been a distinctive, or identifying doctrine, in the Reformed theological tradition (the tradition that stands in the shadow of John Calvin). This doctrine has frequently been misunderstood, distorted and the cause of endless controversy and distress. Calvin himself struggled with this issue, and his teaching on it has been interpreted by many as saying, "From eternity God has decreed some to salvation and others to damnation."

This latter interpretation of the doctrine of election is usually described as hyper-Calvinistic. It fosters a fatalistic view of God as an arbitrary tyrant and an enemy of human freedom. Such an approach to the doctrine makes it anything but good news as proclaimed in God's self-revelation in Jesus Christ. The biblical witness describes the electing grace of God as astonishing, but not dreadful! God, who loves in freedom, offers his grace freely to all who will receive it.

Karl Barth

In correcting this hyper-Calvinism, the preeminent Reformed theologian of the modern church, Karl Barth, recast the Reformed doctrine of election by centering rejection and election in Jesus Christ. He carefully laid out the full biblical doctrine of election in Volume II of his *Church Dogmatics* in a way that is consistent with the whole of God's revelation.

Barth forcefully demonstrated that within a Trinitarian context, the doctrine of election has one central purpose: it declares that God's works in creation, reconciliation and redemption are fully realized in the free grace of God made known in Jesus Christ.

It affirms that the triune God who lives eternally in loving communion graciously wills to include others in that communion. The Creator Redeemer deeply desires a relationship with his creation. And relationships by nature are dynamic, not static. Relationships penetrate the abyss of our existence and turn it into real life.

In the *Dogmatics*, where Barth rethought the doctrine of election in a Trinitarian, Creator Redeemer context, he called it "the sum of the gospel." In Christ God elected *all* of humanity in covenant partnership to share in his life of communion by freely and graciously choosing to be God for humanity.

Jesus Christ is both the Elected and the Rejected for our sakes, and individual election and rejection can be understood as real only in him. In other words, the Son of God is the Elect on our behalf. As the universal elected man, his vicarious, or substitutionary, election is at the same time both to the condemnation of death (the cross) in our place and to eternal life (the resurrection) in our place. This atoning and reconciling work of Jesus Christ in the incarnation was complete in the redeeming of fallen humanity.

We must therefore say yes to God's yes for us in Christ Jesus and embrace and begin to live in the joy and light of what he has already secured for us— union, communion and participation with him in a new creation.

New creation

In his important contribution to the doctrine of election, Barth writes: "For in God's union with this one man, Jesus Christ, he has shown his love to all and his solidarity with all. In this One he has taken upon himself the sin and guilt of all, and therefore rescued them all by higher right from the judgment which they had rightly incurred, so that he is really the true consolation of all." Everything changed at the cross. The entire creation, whether it knows it or not, has been, is being and will be redeemed, transformed and made new in Jesus Christ. We are becoming a new creation in him.

Thomas F. Torrance, premier student and interpreter of Karl Barth, served as editor when Barth's *Church Dogmatics* was translated into English. Torrance believed that Volume II was some of the finest theology ever written. He agreed with Barth that all of humanity has been redeemed and elected in Christ. Professor Torrance, in his book *The Mediation of Christ*, lays out the biblical revelation that Jesus is not only our atoning reconciler through his vicarious life, death and resurrection, but serves as our perfect response to God's grace.

Jesus took our fallenness and judgment on himself, assuming sin, death and evil in order to redeem the creation at all levels and transform everything that stood against us into a new creation. We have been freed from our depraved and rebellious natures for an internal relationship with the One who both justifies and sanctifies us.

Torrance goes on to explain that "the unassumed is the unhealed." What Christ has not taken upon himself has not been saved. Jesus took our alienated mind on himself, becoming what we are in order to reconcile us to God. He thereby cleansed, healed and sanctified sinful humanity in the depths of its being in his vicarious loving act of incarnation for us.

Instead of sinning like all other human beings, he condemned sin in our flesh by living a life of perfect holiness within our flesh, and through his obedient Sonship he transformed our hostile and disobedient humanity into a true, loving relationship with the Father.

In the Son, the triune God took up our human nature into his Being, and he thereby transformed our nature. He redeemed us and reconciled us. By making our sinful nature his own and healing it, Jesus Christ became the Mediator between God and a fallen humanity.

Our election in the one man Jesus Christ fulfills God's purpose for the creation and defines God as the God who loves in freedom. Torrance explains that "all of grace" does not mean "nothing of humanity," but *all of grace means all of humanity*. That is, we cannot hold onto even one percent of ourselves.

By grace through faith, we participate in God's love for the creation in a relational way that was not possible before. That means that we love others as God loves us because by grace Jesus Christ is in us and we are in him. This can happen only within the miracle of a new creation. God's revelation to humanity comes from the Father through the Son in the Spirit, and a redeemed humanity now responds by faith in the Spirit through the Son to the Father.

We have been called to holiness in Christ. We enjoy freedom in him from the sin, death, evil, misery and judgment that stood against us. We reciprocate, or return, God's love for us through thanksgiving, worship and service in the community of faith. In all his healing and saving relations with us, Jesus Christ is engaged in personalizing and humanizing us—that is, in making us real people in him. In all our relations with him, he makes us more truly and fully human in our personal response of faith. This takes place in us through the creative power of the Holy Spirit as he unites us to the perfect humanity of the Lord Jesus Christ.

All of grace really does mean all of humanity. The grace of Jesus Christ who was crucified and resurrected for us does not depreciate the humanity he came to save. God's unconditional grace brings into the light all that we are and do. *Even in our repenting and believing we cannot rely on our own response, but in faith we rely only on the response that Christ has offered to the Father in our place and on our behalf!* In his humanity, Jesus, the new Adam, became our vicarious response to God in all things, including faith, conversion, worship, celebration of the sacraments and evangelism.

Ignored

Unfortunately, Karl Barth has generally been ignored or misinterpreted by American evangelicalism, and Thomas Torrance is often presented as too hard to understand. But to fail to appreciate the dynamic nature of theology displayed in Barth's reworking of the doctrine of election causes many evangelicals and Reformed Christians alike to remain caught in the behavioralism trap, struggling to understand where God draws the line between human behavior and salvation.

The great Reformation principle of ongoing reformation should free us from old worldviews and behavior-based theologies that inhibit growth, promote stagnation and prevent ecumenical cooperation within the Body of Christ. Yet today doesn't the church often find itself robbed of the joy of grace as it shadowboxes with all its various forms of legalism? For this reason the church is not uncommonly characterized as a bastion of judgmentalism and exclusivism rather than as a testament to grace.

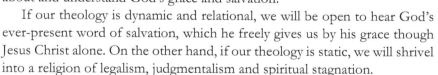

We all have a theology—a way that we think about and understand God—whether we know it or not. And our theology affects how we think about and understand God's grace and salvation.

If our theology is dynamic and relational, we will be open to hear God's ever-present word of salvation, which he freely gives us by his grace though Jesus Christ alone. On the other hand, if our theology is static, we will shrivel into a religion of legalism, judgmentalism and spiritual stagnation.

Instead of knowing Jesus as he is in a way that seasons all our relationships with mercy, patience, kindness and peace, we will know judgment, exclusivity and condemnation of those who fail to meet our carefully defined standards of godliness.

New creation in freedom

Theology does make a difference. How we understand God affects the way we understand salvation and how we live the Christian life. God is not the prisoner of some static, humanly reasoned idea about what he must and should be.

Humans are not capable of reasoning out who God is and what he must be like. God tells us who he is and what he is like, and he is free to be exactly how he chooses to be, and he has revealed himself in Jesus Christ as being the God who loves us, is for us and who chooses to make humanity's cause—including your cause and my cause—his own.

In Jesus Christ, we are freed from our sinful minds, from our boasting and despair, and graciously renewed to experience God's *shalom* peace in his loving faith community.

Recommended reading

- Michael Jinkins, Invitation to Theology
- Thomas Torrance, The Mediation of Christ
- Karl Barth, Dogmatics in Outline
- James Torrance, Worship, Community and the Triune God of Grace
- Thomas Torrance, The Christian Doctrine of God, One Being Three Persons
- Thomas Torrance, The Trinitarian Faith
- Ray Anderson, Theology, Death and Dying
- C. Baxter Kruger, *The Great Dance*
- Robert Farrar Capon, *Parables of Judgment*
- Donald Bloesch, The Christian Foundations series (seven books)

Terry Akers and J. Michael Feazell

THEOLOGY AFFECTS THE WAY WE LIVE

Ideas have consequences. The way we think about God affects the way we respond to him. In other words, our *theology* affects the way we live. Some people think theology is dull and irrelevant, but perhaps that is because they think God is dull and irrelevant; they would rather get on with their life without dragging God into the discussion.

Everyone has a theology, whether they know it or not. They have some concepts of what God is like. They may think he is distant and unconcerned, or harsh and angry, or even that he doesn't exist. All these ideas affect the way we live. If we believe God is distant and unconcerned, we may be angry because we are suffering from the sins of other people, and God doesn't seem to care. We may need help, but God doesn't seem to answer our cries for help. Or we may indulge our baser desires or take advantage of others, thinking God doesn't care one way or the other.

Living by faith

My point is that the way we *think* about God affects the way we live. This is implied throughout the Bible, which repeatedly connects doctrine and behavior.

God cares about us, Jesus said, so we should not worry. Worry comes from a lack of faith that God is good, powerful, merciful and will not cease to love us and do what is good and right for us. If we don't trust God, we may think that he doesn't care, or that he doesn't have the power to take care of us, or that he is harsh, unforgiving or unpredictable toward us.

But when we trust in God, we do not worry even when bad things happen to us. We are confident that God is faithful to us, suffering with us, holding us, and that he will use even our pain to make us stronger and bless us. He works all things, even bad things, for good. He brings light out of our darkness. Our belief about God's power and love affects the way we react to the situations we face.

Paul uses a similar kind of logic in his letters. He explains that we are saved by grace through the work of Jesus our Savior, and then he writes, Therefore we should be living sacrifices, set apart to do God's will, putting off the old self and putting on the new, acting like the new people that God has declared us to be. In other words, our theology should affect the way we live.

The book of Hebrews uses similar logic at several points. After explaining a concept, the author says, Therefore let us hold fast to our confession, therefore let us approach the throne with confidence, therefore let us encourage one another. He sees a close connection between ideas and consequences, between doctrine and practice.

Need for an accurate view

Since the way we think about God affects the way we live, we want to have the best understanding of God we can. If we think of God as a powerful physical being, then we will tend to focus on physical life, on external behavior, on a future based on physical things. We will tend to neglect spiritual qualities such as grace and love, and give little attention to concepts such as the heavenly and the eternal.

On the other hand, when we think of God as eternal and triune, then we see a God for whom relationships are essential to his very being, for whom love is essential, a God who gives himself when he gives his Son, a God who lives within us when his Spirit is in us.

The triune God is a God who has fellowship with us directly, not through intermediaries. In contrast, a God who is only Father, but not Father, Son and Holy Spirit, unity in trinity, is more likely to be seen as aloof, distant, legalistic, stressing law rather than mercy. This is how many people view God. If such a God sent his Son to die on the cross, he would be sending another being to appease his angry judgment, rather than (as actually happened) taking humanity into his own being and redeeming it through union with his own sinless Son, with whom he, with the Spirit, is One God.

It is not my intention here to discuss the nature of God in detail. We have already published quite a bit of material on that, and most of it is included in this volume. We have an article summarizing it and listing a number of books for further study (see above). It highlights two qualities of God — his greatness and his goodness. God always uses his enormous power to further his covenant of love and grace toward his people. He is gentle, loving, slow to anger and full of mercy.

Trust

Here, I want to focus on the "so what" question. How is this relevant to us? What difference does it make in our lives? How do we respond to a God who is simultaneously powerful and gentle? When we realize that God has all power to do anything he wants, and that he always uses it for the good of humanity, then we can have absolute confidence that we are in good hands.

He has both the ability and the covenanted purpose to work all things, including all our rebellion, hatred and betrayal against him and one another, toward our redemption and glorification in Jesus Christ. He is completely trustworthy — worthy of our trust.

When we are in the midst of trials, sickness, suffering and even dying, we can be confident that God is still with us, that he cares for us, that he has everything under control. It may not look like it, and we certainly do not feel in control, but we can be confident that God isn't caught off guard. He can and does redeem any situation, any misfortune, for our good.

We need never doubt God's love for us. "God demonstrates his own love for us in this: While we were still sinners, Christ died for us" (Romans 5:8). "This is how we know what love is: Jesus Christ laid down his life for us" (1 John 3:16). The God who did not spare his own Son can be counted on to give us through his Son everything we need for eternal happiness.

God did not send somebody else: The Son of God, essential to the Godhead, became human so that he could die for us and rise again for us (Hebrews 2:14). We were redeemed not by the blood of animals, not by the blood of a very good man, but by the blood of the God who became human.

We can be confident that he loves us. Every time we take communion, we are reminded of the extent of his love for us — both of his death wherein we are forgiven, and his resurrection wherein we are given union with him and presented holy and blameless to God. He has earned our trust.

"God is faithful," Paul tells us. "He will not let you be tempted beyond what you can bear" (1 Corinthians 10:13). "The Lord is faithful, and he will strengthen and protect you from the evil one" (2 Thessalonians 3:3). Even "if we are faithless, he will remain faithful" (2 Timothy 2:13). He is not going to change his mind about wanting us, about calling us, about being merciful to us. "Let us hold unswervingly to the hope we profess, for he who promised is faithful" (Hebrews 10:23).

He has made a commitment to us, a covenant with us, to redeem us, to give us eternal life, to love us forever. He will not be without us. He is trustworthy, but how do we respond to him? Do we worry? Do we struggle to be worthy of his love? Or do we trust him?

We need never doubt God's power, either. This is shown in the resurrection of Jesus from death. This is the God who has power over death itself, power over all the beings he created, power over all other powers (Colossians 2:15). He triumphed over all things through the cross, and this is demonstrated through his resurrection. Death could not hold him, for he is the author of life (Acts 3:15).

The same power that raised Jesus from death will also give immortal life to us (Romans 8:11). We can trust that he has the power, and the desire, to fulfill all his promises toward us. We can trust him with everything — and that's a good thing, since it is foolish to trust in anything else.

Of ourselves, we will fail. Left to itself, even the sun will fail. Our only hope is in a God who has power greater than the sun, greater than the universe, more faithful than time and space, full of love and faithfulness toward us. We have that sure hope in Jesus our Savior.

Joseph Tkach

THEOLOGY AS A FRAMEWORK
FOR LIFE AND MINISTRY

Theology is important to us because it offers a framework for our belief in God. But there is a lot of theology out there, even within the Christian faith. One of the things that is foundational for GCI as a denomination is our commitment to what's known as "Trinitarian theology." Although the doctrine of the Trinity has been widely embraced in the Church down through the ages, some have called it the "forgotten doctrine," because it is often overlooked.

However, at GCI, we believe that the reality of the Trinity changes everything. The Bible teaches that our salvation depends upon the Trinity. It shows us how each person of the Godhead plays a vital role in our lives as believers. God the Father has adopted us (Ephesians 1:5) as his "dearly loved children" (Ephesians 5:1). This is because God the Son, Jesus Christ, has completed his work, and he is enough for our salvation (Ephesians 1:3-7). We can be confident in our salvation because God the Holy Spirit dwells in us, as a seal of our inheritance (Ephesians 1:13-14). Each member of the Trinity plays a unique role in welcoming us into God's family.

Even though we worship God in three divine persons, the doctrine of the Trinity can sometimes feel like it's difficult to live out in a practical way. But when our understanding and practice conforms to this central doctrine, it has the potential to transform our daily lives. I see it like this: The doctrine of the Trinity reminds us that we cannot do anything to earn our place at the table – God has already invited us and accomplished the work necessary to get us there. Thanks to salvation through Jesus and the indwelling of the Holy Spirit, we can come before the Father, caught up in the love of the Triune God. This love is available to all who believe because of the eternal, unchanging relationship of the Trinity – at no cost to us.

However, this doesn't mean that we don't have a chance to participate. Living in Christ means that God's love enables us to care for those around us. The love of the Trinity overflows to include us, and through us, it reaches others. God doesn't *need* us to complete his work, but he does *invite* us, as his family, to join with him. We are empowered to love because of his Spirit inside of us. When I recall that his Spirit dwells in me, I feel my own spirit grow lighter. The Trinitarian, relational God wants to free us to have richer relationships with him and with others.

Let me give you an example from my own life. As a minister, I can get caught up in "what I do" for God. Just the other day, I was meeting with a group of people. I was focusing so much on my own agenda that I forgot to pay attention to who else was in the room with me. When I realized my worry about accomplishing things on God's behalf, I took a moment to laugh at myself – and to celebrate that God was there with us, guiding us. We don't have to be afraid of making mistakes when we know that God oversees it all. We can serve him joyfully. It transforms our daily interactions when we recall that there is nothing God can't redeem. Our Christian calling is not a heavy burden, but a wonderful gift. Because the Spirit of God indwells us, we are liberated to participate in his work without worry.

You may know that one of GCI's mottos is "You're included." But do you know what that means to me? It means that we seek to love one another the way the Trinity loves – to care for one another in a way that celebrates our created difference while still coming together. The Trinity is a perfect model of love. Father, Son, and Holy Spirit enjoy perfect unity, while remaining distinct divine persons. As Athanasius put it, "Unity in Trinity, Trinity in Unity." The love expressed within the Trinity teaches us the significance of loving relationships within God's kingdom.

Trinitarian theology defines the life of our denomination. Here at GCI, it motivates how we care for one another. We want to love those around us, not because we need to achieve something, but because our God is a God of community and love. God's Spirit of love guides us to love others, even when it isn't easy. We know that his Spirit is not only in us, but in the lives of our brothers and sisters as well. This is why we don't just meet together to worship every week – it's why we also eat meals together, why we eagerly anticipate what God might do in each other's lives. It's the reason we offer help to those in need in our own neighborhoods and around the world, why we pray for the sick and those who are struggling. It's because of our belief in the Trinity.

When we grieve or celebrate together, we seek to love each other as the Triune God loves. When we live out Trinitarian theology in everyday life, we embrace our call to be "the fullness of him who fills everything" (Ephesians 1:22-23). We are showered with the Father's love through the salvation of his Son and the presence of his Spirit – and through the care of his body. From a meal made for a sick friend, to rejoicing with a family member's accomplishment, to a donation that supports the work of the church, we are able to live out the good news of the gospel.

Joseph Tkach

AN INTRODUCTION
TO TRINITARIAN THEOLOGY

I. Introduction: why we need to learn this

A. Stating the topic

We say that we have a "Trinitarian theology." However, lots of churches accept the doctrine of the Trinity, and their theology is at least somewhat Trinitarian, but we emphasize the Trinity more than most churches do. Sometimes we say that we have a Trinitarian Incarnational theology, or a Trinitarian Christ-centered theology. None of these are completely distinctive terms, but they do mention some of the emphases that we have.

We call our theology Trinitarian because the doctrine of the Trinity is not a side point, or just one of many other doctrines. We are trying to be more consistent with it, to let it be the organizing principle for other doctrines. Whether we are talking about sin or salvation or the church, we want to ask, how does the doctrine of the Trinity help us understand this particular doctrine? How is it all connected with the nature of God, and of who God is in his innermost being?

We are trying to understand a little better some points about God's relationship with humanity: his purpose in creating humanity, the way in which he saves us, and how we should respond to him. We believe that our theology is true to the Bible, and that it helps make sense of what we are doing on the earth and in the church. It helps tie different doctrines together.

B. Not trying to criticize others

In the process of explaining our theology, we find that our beliefs are sometimes a little different from other theological traditions, and in some points of doctrine, we conclude that those other Christians are mistaken. This does not mean that we think they are non-Christian, or that those people won't be saved. We all make mistakes, and we have no doubt made a few of our own.

We all believe that we are saved through the life, death and resurrection of Jesus – and it is good for us to have that in common with many other Christians around the world.

Thankfully, we are saved not by having absolutely perfect theology, but we are saved by Christ, by grace, by trusting in Jesus to do for us what we cannot do for ourselves. Other Christians are doing the best they can, and we are doing the best that we can, to understand the Bible, and to understand the meaning of life and how it all fits together. Our purpose here is not to criticize other people and other theologies, but simply to do the best that we can in explaining what we believe, and how we think it is true to the Bible, and how we think it helps us understand what our life is all about.

C. A desire to understand as much as we can

This is what the early church called "faith seeking understanding." We already understand some things about God, and we believe them, but we are convinced that this is something we'd like to know more about, and so we try to know as much as we can. We have fallen in love with Jesus, and we'd like to learn more about who he is, and the relationship he has with us, and what he has in mind for our future.

We could also describe our goal as an act of worship: we want to praise God for who he is and what he has done and what he has promised to do in the future – and in order to praise God for these things, we need to understand what they are. The goal is to explain things as best as we can, based on the Bible and the way that God has revealed himself to us ultimately and personally in Jesus Christ.

D. Practical significance

We will not try to cover all the biblical or historical evidence for the doctrine of the Trinity. We have published other articles about that. What we would like to focus on here is the practical significance of the doctrine.

At first, it seems like the doctrine of the Trinity is just information about God: God is three persons in one being. But what does that have to do with us? Does it make any difference to us here on earth?

Well, yes.

That is because persons have relationships with one another, and relationships are important for all of us. God created us to have relationships similar to the relationships that exist for all eternity within the Triune God. The Divine Persons in the Godhead have relationships, and persons here on earth have relationships, too, and there is supposed to be some similarity in the kind of relationships we have.

The Bible tells us that "God is love" (1 John 4:8). Not that he has love, but that he IS love. That is descriptive of who he is and how he lives in eternity, how he interacts with other persons. Even before God created the universe, even before God created angelic beings, he was love. When God was the only thing there is, God was love—love among the triune Persons.

So, before God created anything, what would God be like? If there is only one person in God, there would be no one to love, because love means caring for and caring about someone else. But if God were somehow loving but alone, that would mean that God would be unable to fully be or express some of his internal nature. God would be deficient. The statement that "God is love" would be meaningless, if God were only one Person, because the love could not be expressed.

The doctrine of the Trinity tells us that even before God created anything, he could be love, because the Father loved the Son, and the Son loved the Holy Spirit, and the Spirit loves the Father, and so forth. There was love within the Triune God, even before anything had been created. The three Persons were distinguishable from one another, but united to one another in love. This is important for who God is, and it's important for who we are, as well.

II. Trinitarian theology is centered on Jesus Christ

As mentioned in the introduction, we sometimes say that we have a Trinitarian, *Christ*-centered theology. And some people wonder, if all three Persons in the Godhead are fully divine, and *equal* in being divine, then why should we center our theology on *one* of them in particular?

A. Jesus is fully divine

We are simply acknowledging that God is revealed to us *most clearly* in the Person of Jesus Christ. Jesus is where God has chosen to make himself *visible* to us. Jesus is the <u>Word</u> made flesh—God the Son become human. He has revealed himself in a way that we could see him, touch him, hear him and see how he lives. Jesus is the way that God has chosen to reveal himself to us.

In John 14:8, Philip asked Jesus: "Lord, show us the Father and that will be enough for us." Jesus responded in verse 9: "Don't you know me, Philip, even after I have been among you such a long time? Anyone who has seen me has seen the Father" (New International Version).

Jesus is not saying that God the Father is 5 foot 8 inches tall, with brown hair and a Jewish nose. But he is saying that in his most important respects, his character, purposes, heart, and mind, *God the Father is like Jesus Christ* – and that is in terms of the way he interacts with others. The compassion that Jesus had shows us exactly what God is like. The zeal for righteousness, that's what God is like. The willingness to sacrifice for others, God is like that, too. Jesus helps us see what God the Father is like – and the Holy Spirit is like that, too.

When Jesus became incarnated as a flesh-and-blood human being, he was showing us in a tangible and visible way what the Triune God is like. The apostle Paul says, "The Son is the image of the *invisible* God" (Colossians 1:15). Even though we cannot see God directly, Jesus shows us what he's like, in a way that we *can* see and hear.

Colossians 2:9 says, "In Christ all the fullness of the Deity lives in bodily form." Jesus is the summary we are given of what we need to know about

God. We can never know God completely – he is simply much bigger than our minds are capable of comprehending – but we are able to have an accurate understanding of at least *some* things about God, because Jesus embodies all that any human being can know of God, and he came to reveal God to us.

John 1:18 says, "No one has ever seen God, but the one and only Son, who is himself God and is in closest relationship with the Father, *has made him known.*"

B. Jesus is fully human

All orthodox Christian theology includes the teaching that Jesus is fully human. That might seem obvious to many people – he was born as a baby, grew as a boy, and he died. As the Bible says, in John 1:14, "The Word *became flesh* and made his dwelling among us." He didn't just put on a costume that made him *look* human – no, he was a real human being. He ate ordinary food, breathed air like an ordinary person, his fingernails grew and he got thirsty and tired. When he scraped his knee, he bled real blood, and when they crucified him, he died just like other people would have.

He was fully God and fully human – both at the same time. We've never seen that combination before, but with God, all things are possible, and so if that's what he did, then we have to make room in our theology for it. God can do one-of-a-kind things that aren't comparable to anything else. The Incarnation of the Son of God is that unique kind of thing.

There are a number of reasons as to why a divine Person would become a human being. He came to communicate to us on a level we could understand; he came to die for us; he came to experience life as a human so that we could know for sure that he understood what it's like for us to be human.

But one thing I want to point out now is that just as Jesus shows us what God is really like, he also shows us what *humanity* is really like. Jesus simultaneously shows us divinity and humanity – and that implies that there is an important similarity between God and humans, and I'll explain more about that in a minute.

C. Connecting human beings to God

Jesus has a unique role. He has been part of the circle of God's triune life, and he's been part of the human circle of life, and because of that, he provides a unique connection between humanity and God. In a sense, he is a bridge between the two, a bridge we use to participate in the God circle. Not that we are part of the Trinity, of course, but in and through his humanity, we do share in God's life.

2 Peter 1:4 says, "He has given us his very great and precious promises, so that through them you may *participate* in the divine nature." So in some way we participate in what God is. We are in the family of God, or the kingdom of God. We are in fellowship with God, in a *relationship* with God – and this is all made possible by Jesus.

1 Timothy 2:5 says, "There is one God and one mediator between God and mankind, the man Christ Jesus." A mediator is a person in the middle, in this case, a person serving to connect humanity with God. Of course, God initiated this; he is the one who sent Jesus to earth to become a human being, and to be resurrected back into heaven to make this connection work. Jesus is the key link or connector between humanity and God.

And the doctrine of the Trinity is important for this understanding. For our connection with God, for our future with God, it is essential that our mediator be fully God in his own right. No human being is good enough to *earn* a connection with God, who is infinitely far above us in power and glory and wisdom and righteousness. No created human being could rise up to God's level as Creator, but God is able to put himself at *our* level.

Jesus is perfect in righteousness and holiness, and yet one of us. He is the pathway by which other human beings are brought *into* the presence of the holy and perfect God.

The doctrine of the Trinity says that Jesus is fully God, and the doctrine of the Incarnation says that Jesus became fully human, and he continues to be both divine and human, and with that combination, now we are ready to talk about a relationship between God and humanity.

III. Humanity in the image of God
A. Created in his image

Jesus shows us what God is like, and he also shows us what humanity is supposed to be like, and this implies that there is some important *similarity* between God and humans. And this is not because humans are good enough to rise up to the level of God. No, it all comes from God as a gift given to us. He is the one who created us this way in the first place.

We find it stated in the very first chapter of the Bible, in Genesis 1, verses 26-27:

God said, "Let us make mankind in our image, in our likeness, so that they may rule over the fish in the sea and the birds in the sky, over the livestock and all the wild animals, and over all the creatures that move along the ground." [27] So God created mankind in his own image, in the image of God he created them; male and female he created them.

And that is what God did, and God said it was good.

So humanity was created "in the image of God," to somehow look like God and to represent God here on earth. Now again, we are not supposed to think of skin color or hair color or the number of fingers on our hands. All those things are incidentals that only apply to creatures. What is really important is that humanity should be like God in a *spiritual* sense, and we see just that emphasis in Galatians 5:22, where the apostle Paul describes the results of the working of the Holy Spirit in us: "love, joy, peace, forbearance, kindness, goodness, faithfulness, gentleness and self-control." Humans are supposed to be like God in *these* ways.

Now we can ask the Trinitarian question: In what way does the doctrine of the Trinity help us understand what humanity is? And the answer is, that just as the Persons in the Trinity interact with one another in love, so also we as persons ought to interact with all other human persons *in love.* That's the first fruit of the Spirit, and the way that we were made to be like God. Love should be the basis for our lives and our societies.

Just as the Triune God is essentially relational, with the Persons defined in reference to one another, so humans are also essentially *relational,* and our identity as persons depends on our relationships with other people. "Who we are" depends on the relationships we have with others. No one is a solitary individual; the meaning of life is not in *self*-existence, but it is to be found in our relationships with each other, in the way we live and think about other people. We were created to be in right relationship with the Triune God and also to be in right relationship with other in a way that mirrors Jesus' own relationship with the Father and the Spirit.

B. Sin defaces the image

Well, you know the story. Humans didn't want life on the terms that God had given them. They wanted to have life follow their own definition, doing their own thing, instead of having to do God's things. So instead of love, joy and peace, they choose selfishness, and they got strife and unhappiness.

So, what does the doctrine of the Trinity reveal to us about the nature of *sin?* How does it help us better understand what sin is?

Well, if good is defined as humanity being the image of God, then it helps us to see that sin is doing things that are <u>unlike</u> God. If God is a relational being, and humans were created to be in relationships of love, then sin is a disruption in our relationships – problems in our relationships with God, and problems in our relationships with one another.

As a practical matter, we have rules that describe what a good relationship is. In a good relationship, we don't lie to each other, we don't steal from one another, we don't dishonor or disrespect the other, and so forth. Avoiding these problems doesn't necessarily *create* a good relationship, but breaking these rules *hurts* our relationships. Laws do not exist for their own sake, but in order to serve something more important, and that is relationships based on love.

When humanity rejected God, we also rejected him as the source of the *love* that we need. We were created to be like God in that respect, but we went in a wrong direction.

C. God restores the image -- in himself

The Old Testament doesn't say much more about the image of God. But the New Testament picks up the phrase "image of God" and applies it to Jesus Christ. We have already looked at Colossians 1:15: "He is *the image of the invisible God.*" He is the image that Adam failed to be. He tells us and shows us in a *visible* way what God is like in the invisible, spiritual world.

Hebrews 1:3 tells us something similar: "The Son is the radiance of God's glory and *the exact representation of his being.*" When we see Jesus, we see what the Father is like in relationship to Jesus. So, we expect God to be like Jesus, in his compassion and mercy and love.

D. We are in the image of Christ

This concept becomes directly relevant to us when we see that the Bible talks about us being formed in the image *of Christ.*

We can see this in 2 Corinthians 3:18: "We, who with unveiled faces all reflect the Lord's glory, are being transformed *into his likeness* with ever-increasing glory, which comes from the Lord, who is the Spirit." That is, we look more and more like him – and again, that's not talking about his physical shape, size and color – it's talking about the way he is spiritually, that is, in relationship to the Father and the Spirit from all eternity.

- Galatians 4:19 talks about how "Christ is formed in you."
- Ephesians 4:13 talks about how "we all reach unity in the faith and in the knowledge of the Son of God and become mature, attaining to the whole *measure of the fullness of Christ.*"
- Colossians 3:10 says we "have put on the new self, which is being renewed in knowledge *in the image of its Creator*" – and that is Jesus Christ.

And since Christ is the image of God, when we become more like Christ, we are being brought back toward the image of God that we were created to be, that we are supposed to be. Right now, it is a spiritual transformation, a *mental* and ethical or relational transformation, and eventually, it will be a physical transformation as well, all based on God's original plan.

This concept is seen in a different way in Romans 5. In that chapter, Paul is comparing the first man, Adam, with Jesus Christ. Verse 14 says that Adam was a type, or a model, "a pattern of the one to come." Paul goes on to show that just as the first Adam brought in sin and death, the second Adam brought in righteousness and life. Just as we shared in the results of the first Adam, so also we share in the benefits of the second Adam. Paul summarizes it in verses 18-19:

> Just as one trespass [i.e., Adam's sin] resulted in condemnation for all people, so also one righteous act [that of Jesus] resulted in justification and life *for all people*. For just as through the disobedience of the one man [Adam] the many were made sinners, so also through the obedience of the one man [Jesus] the many will be made righteous.

All humanity was included in the results of the first Adam, and all humanity is included in the results of the second Adam, Jesus. It's not just a few people that God chose ahead of time, and it's not just one particular nation, or one particular social class – God's plan is for everyone he has created – and that means everyone. Jesus really is Lord of all.

Adam messed it up, but Jesus did it right—and in Christ, all humanity has a fresh start on being "the image of God." Jesus is the key to our transformation – not only is he the model that we copy, but he is also the engine that drives the whole process. He supplies the power and the direction.

IV. The covenant relationship
A. The covenant formula

Even though the Old Testament does not use the phrase "image of God" very often, it does talk about the relationship we have with God, and the term it uses for that most of the time is *covenant*. We can see the basic idea in Exodus 6:7: "I will take you as my own people, and I will be your God." And we see it in

- Leviticus 26:12: "I will walk among you and be your God, and you will be my people."
- Jeremiah 7:23: "I will be your God and you will be my people."

- Ezekiel 36:28: "You will be my people, and I will be your God."

Old Testament scholars call this the "covenant formula." It's found more than 20 times in the Bible. It is an adaptation of words that people in the ancient Middle East used for marriages, and adoptions, and for political treaties.

In a marriage, it would go something like this: "I will be your husband, and you will be my wife." In an adoption, it would be "I will be your father, and you will be my son." And in a political treaty, it would be adapted: "I will be your king and you will be my people." It is declaring a relationship that the people intend to be permanent, a relationship that now defines who they are in relation to the other.

In the Law and in the Prophets, God repeatedly talks about covenants between God and humanity. He makes covenants with Abraham, Isaac, Jacob, Aaron and David. In the covenant, he says, I have made with you a covenant relationship, and as you live according to it, then our relationship will be a good one. *The goal* is to have an ongoing relationship.

B. A new covenant promised

But as you know, the people of Israel didn't do it very well. They broke the covenant time and time again. And eventually through the prophets God promised that there would be a *new* covenant, made in the hearts of the people, that God's Spirit would be in them. This is not something that the people could achieve for themselves – it would be something that God would have to do *for* them. He would *give* them a new heart, a new Spirit.

- Jeremiah 31:33: "This is the covenant I will make with the people of Israel after that time," declares the Lord. "I will put my law in their minds and write it on their hearts. I will be their God, and they will be my people."

- Ezekiel 36:26-27: "I will give you a new heart and put a new spirit in you; I will remove from you your heart of stone and give you a heart of flesh. 27 And I will put my Spirit in you and move you to follow my decrees and be careful to keep my laws."

In Isaiah 42:6, God promises to make his servant "to be a covenant for the people and a light for the Gentiles." The covenant relationship between God and humanity would be focused and embodied in one person – the one we now know as Jesus Christ. The covenant that we have with God is found in him; he is the covenant for all the people; our connection to God depends 100 percent on him.

C. Other relationship terms in the New Testament

The New Testament says that we have this new covenant in Christ. The

Lord's Supper reminds us that we have a new covenant in the blood of Christ. But this is not the only relationship term in the New Testament. It uses several descriptions. For example, it calls us children of God; we are *adopted* into the family of God.

- Romans 8:15 says, "The Spirit you received does not make you slaves, so that you live in fear again; rather, the Spirit you received brought about your adoption to sonship."
- Ephesians 1:5 says, "He predestined us for adoption to sonship through Jesus Christ."

This means we become part of God's family, with rights and privileges that are part of being in the royal family. We are dramatically moved into a new social class.

Paul uses a different relationship term in 2 Corinthians 11:2: "I promised you to one husband, to Christ, so that I might present you as a pure virgin to him." This marriage concept is used in the book of Revelation, too, Revelation 19:7: "Let us rejoice and be glad and give him glory! For the wedding of the Lamb has come, and his bride has made herself ready." And in Revelation 21, verses 2-3:

> I saw the Holy City, the new Jerusalem, coming down out of heaven from God, prepared *as a bride* beautifully dressed for her husband. And I heard a loud voice from the throne saying, "Look! God's dwelling place is now among the people, and he will dwell with them. *They will be his people,* and God himself will be with them *and be their God."*

There is the covenant formula again, this time used in the context of a wedding. God will live with us, and we will live with him. We will be his children, adopted as brothers and sisters of Jesus Christ, part of the royal family forever. Through Jesus, we are brought into fellowship with the Triune God, sharing in his sonship.

Another way to describe this is "the kingdom of God." That biblical phrase just means being part of the universe in which life is lived in the way that God lives. We become part of the ruling family, with the privileges and responsibilities of that.

It means that eternal life is *not just living for a really long time* – it means that we live *with each other, and with God,* forever and ever. It is social, not solitary, because that is *the way that God made us to be.* We were made in his image, and he is social, and not solitary. The doctrine of the Trinity helps us understand who we are, what life is all about, and how God is bringing it about for us.

The Triune God who began a good work in us is sure to finish the job, creating humanity to be a reflection of what God himself is: Persons in perfect community and harmony.

V. Salvation is more than a verdict

Understanding where we started, and where we will end up, can help us understand a little more about what *salvation* is. Some people think that salvation is just a matter of going to heaven when you die. But when it comes to salvation, there's a lot more to it than just a change in location.

And some people think that salvation is just a matter of getting a favorable verdict on the day of judgment. There's going to be a day of judgment, they warn, and everybody is guilty of sin and deserves to be thrown into hell. But if you believe in Jesus, that guilty verdict will be changed to "innocent."

Well, it is *true* that there will be a day of judgment, and that everyone is guilty of sin, and that Jesus allows us to escape the verdict we deserve, and he allows us to enter a heavenly paradise.

But that is all in the future, isn't it?

But doesn't salvation have anything to do with life right now? Yes, it does. There's more to salvation than just a change in our future verdict.

A. Restoring us to God's image

Salvation means that we are rescued from *sin,* and from the results of sin. It means that God's original plan gets back on track – and the original plan is that we were made in the image of God and we were to live in that covenant relationship. It is a *spiritual* likeness that God wants us to have, and that can be summed up in the word *love.* We are to love God with everything we have, and we are love other people in the way that we love ourselves.

Now I think it should be clear that just changing our location isn't going to restore us to being like God. Just changing the final verdict isn't going to make us the people we were meant to be. The goal in salvation is to change *us* – so that we are spiritually like God, really be his children in a way that mirrors Jesus' own sonship. That's the original plan, and God hasn't given up on it. He sent Jesus to show us the way and to <u>be</u> the way, for all humanity to be brought back into fellowship with the Triune God. The Father initiated the plan, the Son of God carried out key steps in the plan, and the Holy Spirit also has *an ongoing role* in the transformation, the change that we all need. Let's briefly look at each of those.

B. The role of the Father

Some people describe the gospel as the Father setting the rules, and getting angry at us because we have broken the rules. He says that we deserve to die, but then the Son has compassion on us and volunteers to pay the penalty for us. So the Father pours out his anger on his own Son, and then he says, "Well, justice has been done. Those sinners can come into my kingdom, because the penalty has been paid." So we have an angry Father and a compassionate Son who is able to get his Father to change his mind.

Maybe that's the way it works in some human families, but that's not the way it works in the Triune God. It's not true to the Bible, and not true in any system of theology, whether it's Trinitarian or Calvinist or Catholic or Eastern Orthodox.

Trinitarian theology reminds us that Jesus is fully God. He is just like God the Father. He is just as angry as the Father is, and just as *loving* as the Father is. He didn't change the Father's mind about anything. Rather, he *reveals* the Father's mind – the Father wants us to be saved just as much as Jesus does. Let's look at a couple of scriptures that show that.

John 3:16 says it well: "*God* so loved the world that he gave his one and only Son, that whoever believes in him shall not perish but have eternal life." God the Father loves humanity and he wants us to be saved, not to be condemned or punished.

Romans 5:8: "God demonstrates *his own love* for us in this: While we were still sinners, Christ died for us." God did not demonstrate his love for us by sending *somebody else* to die. It is only because Christ is God, that *his* death could demonstrate the love of God. They have equal love for us, equal compassion for us. The Triune God is in *full agreement* on our salvation. Father, Son and Spirit created us for a purpose, and they are working together to bring us to completion.

C. The role of the Son

Even though the Father initiated the plan, we often forget that, and usually think of Jesus as the Savior, the one who carried it out. He has the more visible role.

And how did Christ save us? Christians usually think that we were saved by Jesus' death on the cross. That is an important part of the picture, but it is only *part* of the picture.

1. The first step in our salvation was the Incarnation, when Jesus was made a flesh-and-blood human being. He took our nature as his own. That is when he became the second Adam, the new *leader* of all humanity. Just as we were all guilty because of the sin of Adam, so also we are made righteous in the righteousness of Jesus, because Jesus came to give all humanity a new beginning (Romans 5). This doesn't work in terms of DNA and genetics – it is a *spiritual* reality,

that the Incarnation includes all of us in the salvation that Jesus brings. Jesus reconnects all humanity in himself.

2. The next step in our salvation is that Jesus had to *live*. He had to live a righteous life, without any sin – because if he sinned, then he would simply be like one of us, needing to be saved. He would not even be able to save himself, and certainly not anyone else. But since he is our Creator and he lived without sin (he had a perfect relationship with the Father and the Spirit and, as much as could be done from his side, with all humans), we are allowed to share in his righteousness.

3. Third, Jesus had to *die* for us. The wages of sin is death, the Bible says, and death is the result we would *expect,* if we try to live independent from the creator and sustainer of the universe. Jesus, as a mortal human being, experienced death, the result of our sins. He took our sins upon himself, so that we might share in his righteousness. Since the Creator of all humanity became a human, he had an essential unity with all of us. As our Creator, he was able to accept responsibility and the consequences for all of our sins, and to die for the sins of all humanity.

4. Fourth, Jesus had to be resurrected. In 1 Corinthians 15:17, Paul said, "If Christ has not been raised, your faith is futile; you are still in your sins." Romans 5:10 says that we are "saved by his life." Jesus is able to save us from death because he himself has overcome death. He has been there, done that, and now he can do it for us, too.

5. Last, Jesus had to ascend into heaven as one of us, fully human, and be restored to complete fellowship with the Father and Spirit. The Bible says he ascended bodily into heaven, as a glorified human being, and he is now at the Father's right hand, which is a figure of speech meaning the most honored position. His is eternally, even now, our mediator, our intercessor, praying for us, and *transforming* us to become more like he is. By the Spirit he is sharing with us his regenerated and perfected humanity.

Our salvation is not complete with just the forgiveness of sins. We definitely *need* that, but if that's all we got, we'd still have a big problem, because we all have a tendency to sin again, and we want to be *freed* from that tendency. Paul calls it a slavery to sin, and we want to be liberated from that slavery. And so, by sending us his Spirit, all that Jesus had done for us on earth and completed for us in heaven, is now being worked out in us. Jesus by his Spirit is continuing to work for our transformation.

We can rightly say that we are saved by the death of Jesus, but that is only part of the picture. A more complete statement is that we are saved by the incarnation, life, death, resurrection and ascension of Jesus. If that's too much to say at one time, then just say that we are saved *by Jesus*. We are saved by who he is, and what he has done.

How did Jesus save us?

Let's focus on the death of Jesus for a few minutes, because it is a very important part of the picture, and perhaps the most distinctive part of Christian theology. How is that the death of Jesus can do anything for our salvation?

One common explanation is that our sin requires a penalty, and Jesus serves as a substitute to pay the penalty on our behalf. This is called the penal substitutionary theory of the atonement, and it is so common that some people think that it's the only legitimate explanation. But there is a danger in this theory, and the Bible gives us other ways to explain it, as well.

1) The danger: a focus on punishment

First, the danger. A problem can arise if we focus on the "penalty" part of the theory, by suggesting that God had to *punish* Jesus for all the sins that we committed. This suggests that one Person in the Godhead is inflicting pain on another Person in the Godhead; this suggests separation rather than unity in the Triune God. And this does not seem like a very righteous thing for God to do; we do not allow substitutions in our penal codes and systems of justice.

This theory acts as if the primary problem with sin is the punishment, as if the primary problem with crime is that our prisons are getting full. But this is focusing on the results, and not the real problem. It focuses on the verdict, and it still leaves people with a problem: we all have a tendency to sin, and the death of Jesus does not address that problem. The problem is not just in the things that we do, but in the kind of people that we are.

What has happened here is that people have let a legal metaphor, a figure of speech, become the controlling description of what God is doing. Remember, all our words are based on human experiences, and the meaning of our words depends on how they are used in human affairs. And when God sometimes uses courtroom terminology to describe sin and salvation, we should not let *our* concepts of legal procedure to be the final description of what God is doing. When we say that the penalty of sin is death, we should not think that "penalty" is an exact description of what is going on, as if God is obligated to inflict punishment for every transgression of his law.

No, it seems that "consequence" would be a more appropriate term. The result of sin is death, even without God having to step in to inflict it. And when Jesus died for us all, he experienced the consequence of our sin, the result of the way of life human beings chose, but God did not have to step in to perform additional pain and suffering so that Jesus could pay the penalty we deserved. No, he suffered and died without any need for extra punishments coming from God.

Now, God does pronounce a judgment on sin. He says, If you sin, you're going to die. He does not say, If you sin, I'm going to kill you. No, death is a *natural* result of us turning our backs on the one who gave us life. God doesn't have to do anything extra to us, in order for us to suffer from the results of sin, and to die from the results of sin. We experience the judgment, the result he warned us about, without him having to do anything extra to punish us. And he didn't have to do anything extra to Jesus for Jesus to die for our sins. When God did intervene, he gave Jesus life instead of death.

That's what he does for us, too. God is angry about sin, but as Ezekiel says, he takes no pleasure in the death of the wicked (18:23, 32). Death does not serve his purpose. His goal is salvation, not punishment. The reason that he sent Jesus to us is so that we could *escape* the consequences of sin. He wants to *rescue* us, not punish us. We should not force God into our legal metaphor.

Trinitarian theologians accept the idea that Jesus' death was substitutionary, that Jesus died as a substitute for us. But we generally avoid the word "penal," because that word suggests that God the Father punished his one and only Son, and did something to increase his pain. It puts legal requirements and demands as putting requirements on what God has to do, as if law and punishment is the most important description of what good relationships ought to be. When we bring the doctrine of the Trinity into the picture, it helps us see that *punishment* is not the right way to think about it.

2) Biblical descriptions of salvation

If the Bible does not describe the death of Jesus as a punishment required by some law that God had to obey, how does it describe it? In a number of ways. Time does not allow me to say much about them, although we could easily spend a lot of time for each.

1. Jesus said that he would die as a ransom: "The Son of Man did not come to be served, but to serve, and to give his life as a ransom for many" (Mark 10:45). The word "ransom" suggests a payment that we might give to a kidnapper. Some people in the early church made

elaborate theories of how Jesus paid a price to Satan, as if Satan had some legitimate claims over us. But I think they were making the mistake of letting a figure of speech turn into an exact description of what was going on.

2. We see a similar figure of speech in the word "redemption." That was the word people used to get friends and relatives out of slavery. They bought them back; that is the literal meaning of the word "redeem." Jesus bought us with a price, Paul says, but we should not think that anyone actually *received* that payment. It is a figure of speech. The Old Testament says that God redeemed the Israelites out of slavery in Egypt, but he certainly did not pay anyone in order to do it. We should not let the figure of speech dictate to us what actually happened in spiritual reality.

3. The Bible describes Jesus as a sacrificial lamb. John the Baptist called him the "the Lamb of God, who takes away the sin of the world!" (John 1:29). The apostle Paul says that "Christ our Passover has been sacrificed" (1 Corinthians 5:7). But here again, the picture is not exact. Passover lambs were not designed as payments for sin – but they were associated with escaping slavery and death.

4. Jesus is called "an offering and a sacrifice to God" (Ephesians 5:2). In the Old Testament, there were a wide variety of sacrifices – some for sin, some for purity rituals, some for thanksgiving, and so forth, and Jesus fulfilled the symbolism of all of them.

5. Jesus is our place of atonement. Romans 3:25 says, "God presented Christ as a sacrifice of atonement." Some translations say *propitiation,* and some say *expiation,* and scholars have argued about that for a long time. The Greek word meant one thing in a pagan context, and another thing in a Jewish context, but the Greek word is also the word used for the mercy seat on top of the ark of the covenant, the place where the high priest sprinkled blood on the day of atonement. So the NIV quoted above calls it the "sacrifice of atonement." But the sacrifice was never actually done at the mercy seat; a better translation would be "the place of atonement," without trying to be more precise than the word actually is. Jesus is the place, or the way that our sins are atoned, so there is nothing between us and God, so that we are restored to fellowship with God.

6. Reconciliation is a similar term; it refers to people who were once enemies or alienated, but are now on good terms with each other.

Romans 5:10 says, "While we were enemies we were reconciled to God by the death of his Son."

7. Justification is another important term. Some theologians say it is the most important term of all, the one that makes sense out of all the others. Romans 5:9 says that we are "justified by his blood," or by his death on the cross. Justification means to make something right. The word could be used for making a relationship right, or it could be used for making something legally right. In a trial, a person could either be found guilty – condemned – or found righteous (cf. 2 Corinthians 3:9). When the judge declared a person to be in the right, this was justification. This can be a helpful way of looking at salvation, but it misses out on the fact that God wants more from us than to be declared legally innocent – he also wants us to be in fellowship with him forever. Yes, we are guilty of a crime, but the solution is not just to let us out of jail, but it is to transform who we are, so that we are more like Christ.

8. In Colossians, Paul gives us another interesting way to look at the death of Jesus: "Having disarmed the powers and authorities, he made a public spectacle of them, triumphing over them by the cross" (2:15). By his death on the cross, Jesus won a victory! He defeated spiritual powers that were fighting against us. Paul does not explain the logic in how that works, but he says that it does.

The Bible uses a few additional figures of speech, but the point is already clear, that there are several ways to look at it, and we should use all of these ways together. Trinitarian theology says that the meaning of human life is to be found in relationships, and relationships cannot be put into precise formulas. But we can state some basic facts about it.

First, Jesus became a human, a real human, and he was mortal. Even if the Jews and the Romans didn't kill him, he had a mortal body that would eventually get old and he would die. He was part of the Godhead, but he became part of humanity, and he accepted all of the negative consequences of that. Why did he do it? Out of love. God loved us so much that he sent his only Son to die for us, and the Son loved us so much that he did it.

So Jesus has connected the world of heaven and earth, divine and human. And in his death, Jesus demonstrated that he was indeed a real human, completely in union with humanity. He completed his identification with us, sharing in everything that it means to be human. And by doing that, he reversed the curse that was against us (Genesis 3:19; Galatians 3:13). He was able, on behalf of all humanity, to suffer the consequences of sin, and yet

dust
return

curse
pt
the law

since he was personally without any sin, death did not have a legitimate claim on him. He had to be resurrected, and as the new Adam, the new head of humanity, he sets the pattern for what will happen to all of us, and that's resurrection – not just a life that lasts forever, but a life that is in fellowship with the Triune God.

D. The role of the Spirit in our salvation

OK, the Father sent the Son to save us, and the Son did his work. Does that mean that there's nothing left to do until the Last Judgment? No, certainly not! Trinitarian theology reminds us that we should expect the Spirit to have an important role in our salvation.

Shortly before Jesus died, he told his disciples:

> It is for your good that I am going away. Unless I go away, the Advocate will not come to you; but if I go, I will send him to you…. When he, the Spirit of truth, comes, he will guide you into all the truth…. He will tell you what is yet to come. (John 16:7, 13-14)

So, even though Jesus completed *his* earthly job, part of the work must be completed after Jesus goes away – and that work is done by the Holy Spirit, the Advocate, the Comforter, who is sent by Jesus.

What does the Holy Spirit do in our salvation? Lots of things. We don't need to present a complete theology of the Spirit here, but let's mention a few points:

1. First, the Spirit gives us new birth. In John 3, Jesus told Nicodemus, "No one can enter the kingdom of God unless they are born of water *and the Spirit*…. You must be born again" (vv. 5, 7). We need a *new start in life,* and in one sense, Jesus gave all humanity that when he became "the second Adam." But for individuals, this is done by the Holy Spirit.

2. The Spirit also enables us to understand the gospel message. In 1 Corinthians 2:14, Paul writes, "The person without the Spirit does not accept the things that come from the Spirit of God but considers them foolishness, and cannot understand them because they are discerned only through the Spirit." Unbelievers might understand what the words of Scripture mean, but people don't accept those words as *true,* without the Spirit leading them. The Spirit helps us see the truth about God, the truth about ourselves, and helps us continue growing in the truth. As John 16 says, the Spirit teaches us and guides into the truth. No one has all the truth *yet,* so this is still a work in progress.

3. Third, the Spirit helps us realize that we *are* born again, that we are children of God. Romans 8:15 says, "The Spirit you received brought about your adoption to sonship. And by him we cry, 'Abba, Father.'"

4. The Holy Spirit *sanctifies* us, or sets us apart for God's use. 2 Thessalonians 2:13 supports this: "God chose you as firstfruits to be *saved* through the sanctifying work of the Spirit and through belief in the truth."

5. The Spirit gives us power over sin. "If you live according to the flesh, you will die; but *if by the Spirit* you put to death the misdeeds of the body, you will live" (Romans 8:13). As the Spirit leads us, helps us understand, and gives us strength, we are to stop doing bad things and start doing more good things. This does not mean that we stop all sin, but that our basic orientation in life is now toward the good. Christian life and good behavior are part of the process of sanctification. The Spirit sets us apart for God's use, and God wants to use us for good.

6. As already mentioned, the Spirit produces results in our lives, of love, joy, peace, and other good qualities. These are the good results God wants to see in us. This is a transformation in our attitudes as well as our actions – we are being changed from the inside out.

More could be said on each of these points – and we could add some more points. Our main purpose right now is just to make the larger point that the Spirit has a vital role in our salvation – we cannot be saved without the work of the Spirit in our lives. Salvation is a Trinitarian work, involving the Father, Son, and Spirit working in harmony to bring us back to the kind of persons we are supposed to be.

VI. What next? How do we respond?

We have already seen some of the ways that God is working in our lives: He is restoring in us the divine image, so that we are living representatives of who he is and what he is like. It is a *spiritual* image, started when God said, "Let *us* make mankind in our image, in our likeness." So we were made to be like God, and since Jesus is the perfect image of God, we are being conformed into *his* image, changed so that we are more like he is. And the Spirit is doing that work in us, producing in us the fruit of the Spirit: love, joy, peace, and other attitudes and actions that help us have better relationships. This is part of the ongoing work of salvation that God is doing within us.

But a time is coming when we will be transformed into God's image in additional ways, too. Romans 6:5 says, "If we have been united with him in a death like his, we will certainly also be united with him in a *resurrection* like his." Our physical nature will be changed, and we will share in the glory of Jesus Christ.

In 1 Corinthians 15, Paul describes the resurrection, and he says in verse 49, "just as we have borne the likeness of the earthly man [that's Adam], so shall we bear the *likeness* of the man from heaven [that's Jesus]." We will have the image of Christ in a more glorious way.

1 John 3:1-2 gives us a similar picture:

> How great is the love the Father has lavished on us, that we should be called children of God! And that is what we are! The reason the world does not know us is that it did not know him.²Dear friends, now we *are* children of God, and what we *will be* has not yet been made known. But we know that when he appears, *we shall be like him,* for we shall see him as he is.

We will be like he is; we will be even more fully made in his image.

All humanity has been created in the image of God, made for this very purpose. We are already his children, already "in his image" in one sense, but there is more to come. As we are transformed into his image in this life in the way we live and think, we will be transformed *more completely* into his image when we are resurrected into glory and given immortality and incorruptibility. This is the wonderful future God has prepared for us.

And what conclusion does John draw from this wonderful promise? He says it in the very next verse: 1 John 3, verse 3: "Everyone who has this hope in him purifies himself, just as he is pure." When we want to be like God is, then we want to be *like him in our thoughts and actions*. It's the same picture, the glory that God has designed for us, that we should be like he is.

As noted earlier, there's a lot more to eternal life than just living forever. A never-ending life of suffering would *not* be good, and that is not what God wants us to have. Rather, he wants us to have a never-ending life of love and joy, of good relationships – relationships with millions and billions of other people who *help* one another and *love* one another.

And the good news of the gospel, the good news of the Bible, the good news of salvation, is that not only do we live forever, but that we will live *with God*. That's the best part of all: God wants us to live with him. We can see this in the last book of the Bible, Revelation 21:1-4:

> Then I saw "a new heaven and a new earth," for the first heaven and the first earth had passed away…. ³I heard a loud voice from the

throne saying, "Look! God's dwelling place is now among the people, and he will dwell with them. They will be his people, and God himself will be with them and be their God. 4 He will wipe every tear from their eyes. There will be no more death or mourning or crying or pain, for the old order of things has passed away."

God will live with us, and we will live with him. We will be his children, adopted as brothers and sisters of Jesus Christ, part of the royal family forever. And the Bible tells us that we are *already* his children. We already have a relationship with the Father, Son and Spirit.

But how can our vision of *future* life affect the way we live now? Here's another thought that many Christians struggle with: If salvation is by grace, why does the New Testament have so many commands about what we are supposed to do? Is it grace for how we get in, but works *after* we get in? No, not at all.

It is because God is not just giving us existence that lasts forever – he is giving us life of a certain *quality,* life that is based on love rather than selfishness and competition. That's the kind of life we will enjoy in eternity, and that's the kind of life that is *good,* not just in the future but also right now. When the New Testament gives us commands, it is *describing* for us the kind of life that God is giving us, the life of the age to come. Grace says: I am giving you a never-ending life of joy. The commands say: This is what it looks like. This is the way that will help you have joy and express love.

In a metaphor, a parable, we might say that God is at the gateway to his kingdom, and he invites us in. You are welcome to come in, he says, where there is no more pain or sorrow, or lying or cheating or selfishness.

And some people may say, I would like to have "no more pain," but can't I keep my selfishness? And God says, "No, they are two sides of the same coin. Your selfishness is the cause of pain. If you go through this gate, I will scrub all the selfishness out of you, so that you don't cause pain either for yourself or for anyone else." And it's possible that some people will be so in love with their selfishness that they will refuse to go in.

So, we do not want to be in love with our selfishness. Rather, we need to see selfishness as one of our enemies, an attitude that can rob us of joy and peace. It is part of the sin that so easily besets us – it is an enemy that keeps us in slavery – it is an enemy we need to be liberated from. It is an enemy that Christ has already defeated on the cross, and he wants us to share in that victory, and it is done though the Holy Spirit living in us.

A Trinitarian understanding of our purpose in life helps us see the purpose of salvation, and the purpose of the commands we see in the Bible. Once we see where we are going, it is easier to see how God is bringing us there. Love is central to the whole picture, because love is the life of the Father, Son and Spirit, and we are participating in the divine nature, sharing in the life and love of the Triune God.

As images of God, we want our life to be characteristic of *the age to come,* patterned after the life that God himself has. We are images of God and representatives of God, and we should want to live in the way that he does. This life is representative of God himself, a fulfillment of the image that we are supposed to be. And in the age to come, we will forever be images of God, children of God, completely and perfectly.

VII. Conclusion

The doctrine of the Trinity has enriched our understanding of many other doctrines, and we will no doubt continue to learn more about it as we grow in grace and knowledge. And it makes sense, that God's nature is reflected in everything that God does, and that means it affects all our other doctrines, because our doctrines are based on what God is doing in the people he has created.

We see God's *love* throughout the story, from before creation and in the cross of Christ, and on into eternity in the future. We see the Father, Son and Spirit in creation, in salvation, and in eternity. God wants to live with us, and us to live with him, in love, forever and ever, and in his love and grace, he has *given* this to us — and in our love for him, we enjoy learning about it. But we know that this is only the beginning of our understanding.

In 1 Corinthians 13:12, the apostle Paul says that right now, "we see only a reflection as in a mirror; then we shall see face to face. Now I know in part; then I shall know fully, even as I am fully known." We have knowledge, but our knowledge is *partial,* and we look forward to learning more. We rejoice that God knows us fully, and we can be confident that he will continue to draw us toward himself, so that on some future day, we will see him face to face and know him fully, sharing in his life and love forever and ever.

Michael Morrison

QUESTIONS & ANSWERS
ABOUT TRINITARIAN THEOLOGY

Let's address several questions and objections.

Q. Are you saying there is no difference between a Christian and a non-Christian?

A No. We are saying that because of who Jesus is and what he has done, all humans—believers and non-believers—are joined to God in and through Jesus, through his human nature. As a result, God is reconciled to all people, all have been adopted as his dearly loved children. All, in and through Jesus, are included in the Triune love and life of God: Father, Son and Spirit.

However, not all people acknowledge who Christ is and therefore the truth of who they are in Christ. They have not yet put repented and put their trust exclusively in Christ, are not believers. They are not personally living in relationship with him and receiving the abundant life he gives.

One way to speak of the distinction between believers and non-believers is to say that all people are included in Christ (objectively) but only believers actively participate (personally) in that inclusion.

We see these distinctions spoken of throughout the New Testament, and they are important. However, we must not take these distinctions too far, creating some kind of separation or opposition, and think of non-believers as not accepted by and not loved by God. To see them in this way would be to overlook the great truth of who Jesus Christ is and what he has done already for all humanity. It would be to turn the "good news" into "bad news."

When we see all humanity joined to Christ, some of the categories we might have held in our thinking fall away. We no longer see non-believers as "outsiders" but as children of God in need of personally acknowledging how much their Father loves them, likes them, and wants them. We approach them as brothers and sisters. Do they know who they are in Christ? Do they live in personal communion with Christ, No—and it is our privilege to tell them of God's love for them that they might do so.

Q If all are reconciled already to God in Christ, why does Scripture say so much about repentance and faith?

A In the New Testament, the Greek word translated "repentance" is *metanoia*, which means "change of mind." All humanity is invited and enabled by the Spirit to experience a radical change of mind away from sinful egoistic self-centeredness and toward God and his love experienced in union with Jesus Christ through the Holy Spirit.

Notice Peter's invitation to this change of mind in Acts 2:38-39: "Repent and be baptized, every one of you, in the name of Jesus Christ for the forgiveness of your sins. And you will receive the gift of the Holy Spirit. The promise is for you and your children and for all who are far off—for all whom the Lord our God will call."

God does not forgive people in exchange for their repentance and belief. As Scripture proclaims, forgiveness is an unconditional free gift that is entirely of grace. It is a reality that exists for us even before we enter into it in our experience. We repent because we are forgiven.

The gospel truth—the truth about Jesus and about all humanity joined with God in Jesus—is that God has already forgiven all humanity with a forgiveness that is unconditional and therefore truly free: "Therefore," invites Peter, "repent and believe this truth—and be baptized by the Spirit with the mind of Jesus—which involves supernatural assurance that we truly are the children of God."

Repentance is a change of mind and heart; it involves coming to acknowledge who Jesus is for us and who we are in him, apart from anything we have done or will yet do. Through repentance, which is God's gift to us through the Spirit, our minds are renewed in Jesus and we turn to him and begin to trust him.

The Spirit moves us to repent because our forgiveness has already been accomplished in Christ, not in order to be forgiven. We repent because we know that, in Jesus, our sins have already been forgiven, and that, in Jesus, we are already a new creation. In this repentance, we turn away from the alienation within us as the Spirit baptizes our minds in Jesus' acceptance and in the assurance that comes with it.

Q Why does Paul say that if you don't have the Spirit, you don't belong to Christ?

A Romans 8:9 says, "You, however, are not in the realm of the flesh but are in the realm of the Spirit, if indeed the Spirit of God lives in you. And if anyone does not have the Spirit of Christ, they do not belong to Christ."

The sentence "And if anyone does not have the Spirit of Christ, they do not belong to Christ" is not meant to be lifted out of context and turned into a proof that some people do not belong to God. In the context of this passage, Paul is addressing believers; he is not making a statement here about non-believers. He is warning disobedient believers who are refusing to submit to the Holy Spirit in their lives. In effect, he is saying, "You say that the Spirit of God is in you, and you are right. However, your life should be reflecting the presence of the Spirit of Christ. Your actions do not demonstrate that you really do belong to Christ as you claim to. I don't dispute that. But if you do, then on that very basis act in accordance with that reality."

As Paul says to believers in verse 12, "We have an obligation—but it is not to the flesh..." (see verses 10-17).

Q If the world is reconciled, why would Jesus say that he doesn't pray for the world?

A In John 17:9, Jesus says: "I pray for them [his disciples]. I am not praying for the world, but for those you have given me, for they are yours."

Just because Jesus said in one instance that he was not praying for the world, but instead for his disciples, does not imply that he never prayed for the world. It is just that right then, his emphasis was on his disciples. He is praying in particular for them, focusing on them.

It is also important to understand how John uses the word "world" (*kosmos* in Greek) in the flow of his Gospel. At times the word can refer to all people (who are all loved by God; see John 3:16) while at other times it can refer to the worldly "system" that is fallen and hostile toward God.

It is apparently this system that Jesus has in mind in John 17. Since this fallen system or world resists God, Jesus' prayer does not include it. He is not praying for the world in its current fallen form, rather, he is praying for a group of people whom he can use to declare his love in this fallen world.

Later on in his prayer, Jesus does turn his attention specifically to those who are not yet his disciples. He prays "also for those who will believe in me through their message." And what he prays for them is that they, along with those who are already believing, "may be one, Father...so that the world may believe that you have sent me" (John 17:21). This aligns with the Gospel of John's message (3:16): God loves the whole world and wants to save everyone.

Q If all are reconciled already to God, why does Scripture speak of hell?

A Scripture speaks of hell because it is the natural consequence of rebellion against God. When we cut ourselves off from God and refuse his mercy, grace and forgiveness we are rejecting communion with him and cutting ourselves off from the very source of our life. Christ came to prevent that from happening. Grace enters in and disrupts the natural course of a fallen creation. Being created for personal communion with means we must be receptive to what he has done for us in Christ. All are included in what Christ intends for everyone, but we can refuse our inclusion. We are reconciled to the Father, but we can refuse that to receive that reconciliation and live as if God had not reconciled us to himself.

However, such refusal does not negate what God has done for all humanity in Christ.

In *The Great Divorce,* C.S. Lewis wrote:

> There are only two kinds of people in the end; those who say to God, "Thy will be done," and those to whom God says, in the end, "Thy will be done." All that are in hell, choose it. Without that self-choice there could be no hell. No soul that seriously and constantly desires joy will ever miss it. Those who seek find. To those who knock it is opened.

Q Why does the Bible talk about people whose names are not in the book of life?

A Revelation 13:8 says, "All inhabitants of the earth will worship the beast—all whose names have not been written in the Lamb's book of life, the Lamb who was slain from the creation of the world."

Revelation 17:8 says, "The inhabitants of the earth whose names have not been written in the book of life from the creation of the world will be astonished when they see the beast."

We need to consider the literary context of these statements in Revelation. John writes using a literary genre (style) known as apocalyptic. This genre, which was commonly used by Jewish writers in John's day, is highly symbolic. There is not a literal "book of life." The "book of life" is a figure of speech, a symbolic way of referring to those who are in allegiance with the Lamb. These verses in Revelation refer to people who reject the new life that Christ has already secured for them.

Q Why does Peter say it is hard to be saved?

A First Peter 4:17-18 says: "For it is time for judgment to begin with God's household; and if it begins with us, what will the outcome be for those who do not obey the gospel of God? And, 'If it is hard for the righteous to be saved, what will become of the ungodly and the sinner?'"

The point of verses 17-18 is found in verse 19: "So then, those who suffer according to God's will should commit themselves to their faithful Creator and continue to do good."

Peter has been encouraging persecuted believers to live in accord with their identity as children of God and not like those who live in debauchery and idolatry (verses 1-5). The difficulty is not in Jesus' power to save but for those believing to live faithfully through times of the suffering of persecution. The difficulties involved in being saved call for perseverance. And in any case Peter does not say that salvation is impossible for anyone. (See also Mark 10:25-27, where Jesus replies to his disciples query as to how anyone could be saved if it was difficult for the wealthy. Jesus answered, "For mortals it is impossible, but not for God; for God all things are possible," NRSV).

As part of his argument, he points out that persecution is participation in the suffering of Christ, and therefore if believers are to suffer, they should suffer for their faith and godly behavior instead of suffering for sinful and ungodly behavior (verses 12-16). His point is that believers, who know that Jesus, the Savior, is the merciful Judge of all, should not be living in the same base and evil ways as those who oppose Christ even under the threat of persecution.

It is actually impossible for anyone to be saved—were it not for Christ. Christ has done what is impossible for humans to do for themselves. But those who reject Christ are not participating in Christ's suffering; they participate in their own suffering as they reap what they sow. And that experience is a far more difficult path to be on than the narrow one of those who know Christ and can have fellowship with him even in their sufferings.

Q What is everlasting contempt and destruction?

A Daniel 12:2 reads, "Multitudes who sleep in the dust of the earth will awake: some to everlasting life, others to shame and everlasting contempt."

2 Thessalonians 1:6-9 says,

> God is just: He will pay back trouble to those who trouble you and give relief to you who are troubled, and to us as well. This will happen when the Lord Jesus is revealed from heaven in blazing fire with his powerful angels. He will punish those who do not know God and do not obey the gospel of our Lord Jesus. They will be punished with everlasting destruction and shut out from the presence of the Lord and from the glory of his might.

Both of these passages refer to the time of the final judgment when Jesus is "revealed" (sometimes referred to as the Second Coming or Jesus' "return in glory"). This is the time when all humans will see clearly who Jesus is and thus who they are because of who he is and what he has done. And this "revealing" presents to them a choice—will they say "yes" to their belonging to Christ, or will they say "no"?

Their decision neither creates nor destroys their inclusion, but it does determine their attitude toward it—whether they will accept God's love for them and enter the joy of the Lord, or continue in alienation and frustration (and thus in shame and everlasting contempt and destruction) The destruction is a self-destruction as they refuse the purpose for which they have been made, and the redemption that has already been given to them. They refuse to submit to God's righteousness through repentance and so refuse to receive his life, thereby effectively cutting themselves off from it.

In the Judgment, everyone will face Jesus, the Judge who died for all, and they will have to decide whether they will trust him and count on his being judged in their place. Those who trust their Savior agree with the judgment of God as to what is evil and must be done away with. They humbly receive the joy of the life God has given them in Christ. Those who reject him continue in their hostility and the hell that goes with their living in denial of the truth and of reality of their sin and of Christ's salvation for them.

Q What about the "narrow gate"?

A Jesus says in Matthew 7:13-14: "Enter through the narrow gate. For wide is the gate and broad is the road that leads to destruction, and many enter through it. But small is the gate and narrow the road that leads to life, and only a few find it."

Jesus describing what is happing in the present. A clearer translation is: "many are entering" and "only a few are finding it." In his day, at that time, most were living on the "broad road" of destruction. What Jesus offers here is descriptive not prescriptive. It does not say what Jesus wants nor what God intends. In fact, this is a warning and warnings are given to prevent the negative outcome from occurring. No parent says to their child, "Watch out, a car is coming!" because they hope the child gets run over! And Jesus gives the reason for the need to be warned: under fallen conditions the way to destruction is wide, inviting and easy to follow, or we can simply be swept along into it. The narrow way to life can be easy to miss, may seem difficult to follow and takes our being deliberate and intentional. There were only a "few" who had at that time embraced the truth that is in Jesus—and it is he who is "the narrow gate." But Jesus wants to turn that around so that there are many, not a few, who enter into the life that Jesus has for them. So he gives this warning out of his love for them.

Jesus addresses a similar issue in Matthew 7:21-23: "Not everyone who says to me, 'Lord, Lord,' will enter the kingdom of heaven, but only the one who does the will of my Father who is in heaven. Many will say to me on that day, 'Lord, Lord, did we not prophesy in your name, and in your name drive out demons and in your name perform many miracles?' Then I will tell them plainly, 'I never knew you. Away from me, you evildoers!'"

These people have done miracles, and in doing so have deceived many. They claim to know Jesus. Although Jesus obviously knows them (he is omniscient), he does not see himself in them with regard to their actual faith or behavior, and so he proclaims, "I never knew you." That is, I don't recognize you as a follower of mine. We haven't been in relationship, in communion, with one another despite what you were doing.

Q But don't we become God's children only at the point of belief?

A John 1:12-13 says, "Yet to all who did receive him, to those who believed in his name, he gave the right to become children of God—children born neither of natural descent, nor of human decision or a husband's will, but born of God."

We have already seen in Scripture that God has provided for everyone in the vicarious humanity of Jesus. When he died, we all died; when he rose, we rose. Our human natures have been regenerated in him. Therefore all humans are, from God's perspective, already adopted into his family. In Jesus, God gives people that "right" long before they accept it and live in it. They have an inheritance, as Paul puts it.

If we say that we don't have a right to become the children of God until after and unless we believe, then we end up denying what John goes on to say: that it doesn't come from natural descent or from human decision. Such an understanding would make our having the right be dependent upon our decision!

Those who believe in and accept Jesus as their Lord and elder brother, enter into and begin to experience the new life as children of God. But that place in God's family has been theirs all along, the new life that has been "hidden with Christ in God" (Colossians 3:3). In other words, what has been objectively true for them all along in Jesus, becomes subjectively and personally experienced by them when they become believers. They begin taking up their right and living as the children of God.

Q Is this universalism?

A No, not in the sense that every person ultimately will be saved (or enter into or receive their salvation) regardless of whether they ever trust in Christ. There is no salvation outside of Jesus Christ (Acts 4:12). Those who somehow absolutely refuse to enter into their salvation, receive it by repentance and faith in what Christ their Savior has done for them, have refused the benefits of their salvation, refused their inheritance, repudiated the "hope laid up for [them] in heaven" (Col. 1:5).

Jesus' atonement has universal intent (Romans 5:18). He died for all and he was raised for all because God so loved the world. He is the "Lamb of God, who takes away the sin of the world" (John 1:29). Scripture shows that God, in Christ, has reconciled all humans to himself (Colossians 1:20; 2 Corinthians 5: 19), but he will never force any person to embrace that reconciliation. Love cannot be coerced.

A relationship of love as the children of God could never be the result of a cause-effect mechanism. God wants sons and daughters who love him out of a joyful response to his love, not zombies who have no mind or choice of their own. As has been revealed in Jesus Christ, God is love in his innermost being, and in God the Persons of the Trinity relate to one another in the truth and freedom of love. That same love is extended to us in Christ that we might share in it, and in nothing less.

To hope that all people will finally come to Christ is not universalism—it is simply Christian and reflects the heart of God (1 Timothy 2:3-6; 2 Peter 3:9). If God calls us to love our enemies, does God himself do less? If God desires that all turn and be saved, can we do anything less?

This does not mean we can profess that every person will finally come to faith and receive their salvation. However this does mean that, given who God is and what he has done for us in Christ, we ought to be more surprised that some may somehow actually come to reject the truth and reality of their salvation than to find many in the end turning to Christ to receive his forgiveness and eternal life as his beloved children.

Q If we are reconciled already, why struggle to live the Christian life?

A Some people do not like the idea that others who do not work as hard as they do will end up with the same reward as they (see parable of the laborers in the vineyard, Matthew 20:12-15). But this concern overlooks the truth that no one, no matter how hard they work, deserves salvation. That is why it is, for everyone, a free gift.

However, in Scripture we learn that is why God doesn't want us to live that way. Consider the following passages:

No one can lay any foundation other than the one already laid, which is Jesus Christ. If anyone builds on this foundation using gold, silver, costly stones, wood, hay or straw, their work will be shown for what it is, because the Day will bring it to light. It will be revealed with fire, and the fire will test the quality of each person's work. If what has been built survives, the builder will receive a reward. If it is burned up, the builder will suffer loss but yet will be saved—even though only as one escaping through the flames. (1 Corinthians 3:11-15)

Galatians 6:7-8: "Do not be deceived: God cannot be mocked. People reap what they sow. Whoever sows to please their flesh, from the flesh will reap destruction; whoever sows to please the Spirit, from the Spirit will reap eternal life."

We are joined to Christ in order to live in fellowship with Christ. We are united to Christ in order to participate with him in all he does. It makes no more sense to say that since we belong to Christ there is no point in living the Christian life, than to say, since a man and woman are married, there is no point to them living together. No. They are married in order to live together. We are joined to Christ in order to live with him.

Q How do we explain John 6:44?

A John 6:44 says, "No one can come to me unless the Father who sent me draws them."

The Jewish religious leaders were seeking to deflect Jesus' seemingly outrageous claim: "I am the bread of life that came down from heaven" (John 6:41). This statement was tantamount to claiming divine status.

Jesus' reply to the Jewish leaders' complaint concerning this claim was that they "stop grumbling" (verse 43) and realize that "no one can come to me [the bread of heaven] unless the Father who sent me draws them..." (verse 44). Jesus' point is that the people would not be responding to him, except that God was making it possible for them to do so. If they really knew God they should recognize that people were coming to the Son according to the will and purpose of the Father. What they see happening in Jesus' ministry is not evidence that Jesus is a blasphemer, disobeying the will of God, but rather that God the Father is accomplishing his will through Jesus, his faithful Son.

In this passage, Jesus is not limiting the number of people who are drawn to him; he is showing that he is doing the Father's work. Elsewhere he says: "When I am lifted up, I will draw all people to myself" (John 12:32). And since Jesus does only what his Father wants, John 12:32 shows that the Father indeed draws all people to Jesus.

Q How does this theology compare to Calvinism and Arminianism?

A In comparing and contrasting Christian theologies, we are talking about different approaches or understandings among Christian brothers and sisters who seek to serve the same Lord and thus share the same faith. Thus, our discussion should reflect respect and gentleness, not arrogance or hostility.

Calvinism is a theology that developed from the teachings of the Protestant reformer John Calvin (1509-1564). Calvinism emphasizes the sovereignty of God's will in election and salvation. Most Calvinists define God's "elect" as a subset of the human race; Christ died for only some people ("limited" or "particular" atonement"). Those elect for whom he did die, however, were truly and effectively saved in the finished work of Christ, long before they became aware of it and accepted it. According to Calvinist doctrine, it is inevitable that those Christ died for will come to faith in him at some point. This is called "irresistible grace."

Trinitarian theology's main disagreement with Calvinism is over the scope of reconciliation. It's objection is based on the fundamental fact of who Jesus is and that he is one in will, purpose, mind, authority and act with the Father in the Spirit. The whole God is Savior and Jesus is the new Adam who died for all. The Bible asserts that Christ made atonement "not only for our sins, but for the sins of the whole world" (1 John 2:2). And while Trinitarian theology rejects the restrictive extent of "limited atonement" and the determinism of "irresistible grace," it agrees with Calvinism that forgiveness, reconciliation, redemption, justification, etc. were all accomplished effectively by what Christ did. And these gospel truths have been secured for us irrespective of our response to them.

Arminianism derives from the teachings of another Protestant reformer, Jacob Arminius (1560-1609). Arminius insisted that Jesus died for all humanity, and that all people can be saved if they take necessary, personal action, which is enabled by the Spirit. This theology, while not ignoring God's sovereignty, gives a more central or key role to human decision and free will. Its premise is that salvation, forgiveness, reconciliation, redemption, justification, etc., are not actually effective unless a person has faith. For only if God foresees a person using their free choice to receive Christ, does he then elect them. Those whom he foresees rejecting his salvation, he condemns. So like the Calvinist, in the end God wills the salvation of some and the condemnation of others.

Trinitarian theology differs from Arminianism over the effectiveness of the reconciliation. Atonement, or at-one-ment between God and humanity, is only a hypothetical possibility for Arminians; it does not become an accomplished actuality unless God foresees someone's decision of faith. In this view God, on the basis of his foreknowledge of an individual's acceptance or rejection, then accepts or rejects that person. Trinitarian theology, however, teaches that the atonement and reconciliation represents the heart and mind of God towards all and is objectively true in Christ, even before it has been subjectively accepted and experienced and remains true even if some deny it. God has one ultimate will or purpose for all, realized from the Father, through the Son and in the Spirit.

While Calvinism and Arminianism emphasize different aspects of salvation theology, Trinitarian theology has attempted, as did Church Fathers Irenaeus, Athanasius, and Gregory, to maintain in harmony the wideness of God's love emphasized by Arminians with the unconditioned faithfulness of God emphasized by Calvinists. But strictly speaking, the Incarnational and Trinitarian theology of GCI aligns neither with traditional Calvinism nor Arminianism. It emphasizes the sovereignty of God's Triune holy love that calls for our response. His sovereign will is expressed in accord with God's being a fellowship of holy love. Its center is the heart, mind, character and nature of God revealed in the Person and Work of Jesus Christ, the Incarnate Savior and Redeemer. God's sovereignty is most clearly and profoundly shown in Jesus Christ. The place and importance of human response to God's grace is also shown in Jesus Christ who makes a perfect and free response to God in our place and on our behalf as our Great High Priest. Our response then is a gift given by the Holy Spirit by which we share in Christ's perfect response for us in our place and on our behalf.

Q What is perichoresis?

A The eternal communion of love that Father, Son and Spirit share as the Trinity involves a mystery of inter-relationship and interpenetration of the divine Persons, a mutual indwelling without loss of personal identity. As Jesus said, "the Father is in me, and I in the Father" (John 10:38). Early Greek-speaking Christian theologians described this relationship with the word *perichoresis,* which is derived from root words meaning around and contain. Each person of the Trinity is contained within the others; they dwell in one another, they envelop one another.

WHAT'S SO SPECIAL
ABOUT TRINITARIAN THEOLOGY?

Learning more about the nature of God has dominated my Bible study for the last decade and I find it to be more and more fascinating. Having the correct perspective of who God is cannot be overestimated. Viewing his sovereignty over eternity and the nature of his being orders all of our doctrinal understandings.

I love the following quote from Charles Haddon Spurgeon, England's best-known preacher for most of the second half of the 19th century:

> The highest science, the loftiest speculation, the mightiest philosophy, which can ever engage the attention of a child of God, is the name, the nature, the person, the work, the doings, and the existence of the great God whom he calls his Father. There is something exceedingly improving to the mind in a contemplation of the Divinity. It is a subject so vast, that all our thoughts are lost in its immensity; so deep, that our pride is drowned in its infinity.

I am sometimes asked, "What's so special about Trinitarian theology—don't most orthodox churches believe in the Trinity?" Yes, they do. In fact, belief in the Trinity is considered the hallmark of authentic Christian doctrine. It was our acceptance of the Trinity that brought our denomination "in out of the cold," allowing us to break free from being considered a cult.

As I studied what various churches believe about the Trinity, I observed that while most consent to the doctrine, it does not have a central role in their faith. Many consider the Trinity to be an abstract idea, of interest to theologians but not really of much use to the rest of us. This is sad because when the Trinity is not at the center, shaping all other doctrines, strange ideas and distortions arise. For example, those who proclaim a health/wealth/prosperity gospel tend to view God as a divine "vending machine." Others tend to view God as a mechanistic version of fate who has determined everything from before creation—including who will be saved and who will be damned. I find it particularly hard to accept a God who creates billions of people just for the purpose of condemning and damning them for eternity!

Trinitarian theology puts the Trinity at the center of all doctrinal understanding, influencing everything we believe and understand about God. As theologian Catherine LaCugna wrote in her book *God for Us*:

The doctrine of the Trinity is, ultimately…a teaching not about the abstract nature of God, nor about God in isolation from everything other than God, but a teaching about God's life with us and our life with each other. Trinitarian theology could be described as par excellence a theology of relationship, which explores the mysteries of love, relationship, personhood and communion within the framework of God's self-revelation in the person of Christ and the activity of the Spirit. [Note: While I appreciate much of what is in this book, I don't agree with all of it.]

We know of this triune life of God from Jesus who is God's self-revelation in person. It should be our rule that anything we say about the Trinity must come from Jesus' life, teaching, death, resurrection, ascension and promised return.

I have seen many diagrams that attempt to explain the Trinity. The best of them fall short and some are confusing. It is, of course, impossible to explain the nature of God in a diagram. However, a good one can help us grasp some aspects of the doctrine. You may find helpful the diagram shown at right. It summarizes early church teaching, pointing out that correct biblical understanding concerning the nature of God upholds three essential beliefs about God. It also indicates that we end up denying that God is Triune when even one of these beliefs is rejected.

The three sides of the triangle in the diagram represent these three essential beliefs, and the point of the triangle across from each side represents the corresponding error when that particular belief is denied:

- Denial of the *Three Persons* results in *Modalism* (sometimes referred to as the Oneness teaching), the erroneous belief that God appears to us in three ways or modes, wears three hats, acts in three different roles or just has three different names.

- Denial of the *Equality of Persons* results in *Subordinationism*, the erroneous belief that one of the divine Persons is less than fully and truly God.

- Denial of *Monotheism* (the idea of the Unity of God) results in *Polytheism*, the erroneous belief in two or more separate gods (including the error of tri-theism—a belief in three gods).

When we are careful to uphold all three of these essential beliefs about God, we avoid the corresponding false teachings and thus bear faithful witness to the glorious mystery of the Trinity.

I thank God daily for answering our many prayers to reveal to us greater truth. His revealing himself to each of us as the Triune God was a miraculous moment for each one of us.

Joseph Tkach

essential belief

denial

polytheism

equality of persons

three persons

monotheism

modalism

subordinationism

V = rejection of corresponding opposite belief

Trinity

ie modalism – disbelief in the three persons

V
denial of the essential belief

– essential belief

BEWARE THEOLOGICAL LABELS

As our understanding of who God is (our theology) developed, we began using the term "Incarnational Trinitarian Theology" to identify and summarize our understanding. However, use of that term (and others like it) might cause some problems. First, it might confuse some who are not trained in theology. Second, it might be used by some who do not understand it well. Third, it might be overused and thus become cliché. Last, it might become a denominational label that could lead some to misunderstand what we actually believe and teach.

It is helpful to think of Incarnational Trinitarian Theology as describing *how* we believe rather than merely *what* we believe. Of course, all orthodox Christians accept the doctrines of the Trinity and the Incarnation. But for us, they are more than two doctrines on a list of many—they are the heart of our faith and worship.

Why is that not so for all Christians? Partly because these truths are deep mysteries beyond our fallen human imaginations. Also, these doctrines at times are poorly taught or not taught at all. Thus it is easy to drift away from this defining core and begin to emphasize secondary (even tertiary) issues. When that happens, everything becomes distorted.

This was seen clearly in the way Jewish religious leaders resisted Jesus. Those leaders looked to Scripture as a source of truth, but disagreed about its details. Nevertheless, they were united against Jesus. And so Jesus told them, "You have your heads in your Bibles constantly because you think you'll find eternal life there. But you miss the forest for the trees. These Scriptures are all about me! And here I am, standing right before you, and you aren't willing to receive from me the life you say you want" (John 5:39-40, *The Message*). Note how Jesus placed himself at the center as the living key to interpreting Scripture. He himself was the source of their life. If they would accept and understand that, they would put their petty disagreements in perspective and come together in acknowledging him as Messiah. Instead, they saw him as a heretic and plotted to kill him.

As Christians today, we can make the same mistake. Even if we accept Jesus as Lord and Savior, we can sideline the fundamental truths that define who he is. The result is the fragmenting of Christianity into competing "schools" of thought with their own doctrinal distinctives. This leads to a "my Christianity is better than yours" mentality. Though the distinctives may be accurate, they emphasize peripheral matters. The result is that the reality of who God is and what he has done for us in his Son is diminished, if not lost. Division within the Body of Christ results.

That is why we need to avoid using labels in ways that imply that we are setting ourselves apart as having a Christianity that is superior in comparison to others. The reason we use a label at all is to remind ourselves (and others, if they are interested) of the focus of our renewal—the reality of what is revealed in Jesus Christ according to Scripture.

Also, in using a label, we must avoid implying that we are slavishly beholden to some systematic theology or to certain theologians—even those identified as Incarnational or Trinitarian. There are approximately 50 systematic theologies extant today. However, there is no single concrete, uniform, particular school of thought called "Trinitarian Theology."

For example, Barth, the Torrance brothers and Thomas Oden drew on many other theologians throughout the ages and on the writings of the early church councils. Rather than seeking to establish a new theology, they were seeking to serve Jesus Christ and to build up his church through their teaching and research. Yes, they might be described as "Incarnational Trinitarian Theologians" because they saw that these particular elements of Christian faith were being neglected or even forgotten. They discerned that the church needed to get back on the central path of Christian faith.

When we use the term, "Incarnational Trinitarian Theology," we are referring to the fact that Jesus is the lens through which we read and interpret the Bible and how we have come to know God. Consequently, any other doctrinal points should flow from and fit with the Trinitarian nature of God. Our role in the administration of our denomination is to pass on the best formulations of Christian theology that we can find—especially on the major issues. We are blessed to incorporate the ideas of the great theologians of Christian history and we can learn from those alive today. But we do not do so slavishly and biblical revelation always has the controlling authority.

So, when we say that we believe and teach Incarnational Trinitarian Theology, we are describing how we understand and believe Scripture based upon Jesus as the centerpiece of God's plan for humanity. It is perhaps more like your computer's operating system rather than one of many programs you load into it. Individual doctrines are like the software applications, which must be able to interface with the operating system if they are to work properly. But it's the operating system that orders, organizes, prioritizes and produces all other useful results.

The focus of our renewal as a denomination has been the very theological issues that have been central to historical, orthodox Christianity. We are not the only branch of the church that neglected or even misunderstood the

doctrines of the Trinity and the Incarnation. We hope that we might benefit other parts of the Body of Christ with what we have learned. It is in this spirit that we offer our *Speaking of Life* and *You're Included* videos. If you have not viewed them, I urge you to do so. They will help us all keep the Center in the center, feed our continuing renewal in the Spirit, and enable us to join with all Christians down through the ages in giving witness to the glory of our triune God: Father, Son and Holy Spirit.

Joseph Tkach

ANSWERING QUESTIONS ABOUT OUR THEOLOGY

The label, "Incarnational Trinitarian Theology" should be understood as *descriptive* rather than as *prescriptive* of our doctrinal statements. Our critics sometimes want to regard this label as being prescriptive, but that is not the case. Also, it is not the case that our theological perspective is Barthian or Torrancian or whatever. At best, such labels are only partially descriptive. Any similarities are definitely not prescriptive.

What is prescriptive for us is the reality of who God has revealed himself to be in Jesus Christ according to Scripture. Our theological formulations are derived from and meant to point faithfully to that reality, which exceeds what can be contained in our theological understandings.

When we quote any theologians positively, or even when the historic Christian Creeds are referenced, they are being used as illustrative of our own theological position, not as a source or final norm of it. They show that other members of the Body of Christ at other times and places grasped the biblical revelation in a way similar to how we have come to understand it. It demonstrates that we are concerned not to be esoteric or eccentric in our teaching and that we believe that other members of the Body of Christ can be helpful to us, saying at least as well, if not better than ourselves, how we also understand God's Word.

Given what is noted above, the label "Incarnational Trinitarian Theology" is not meant to indicate that we hold to a special (or superior) form of Christianity. It indicates that the center and heart of our faith and worship corresponds to the center and heart of the revelation of the gospel itself— just as the whole of the historic, orthodox church has done down to this day. This label reminds us of the core reality of who God is and has revealed himself to be in and through Jesus Christ, according to Scripture. It also represents the nature of our renewal and restoration to true Christian faith which we have come to share with all the Christian church. If others have been pushed or pulled off-center we hold out to them these foundational truths, from which flow all other Christian doctrines, that they too might be renewed and restored in their faith and worship.

Some critics say we don't make distinctions between believers and non-believers because of the way we speak of God having a oneness of mind, heart and purpose towards all. Though it is not true, they say we affirm universalism. Why do they come to this wrong conclusion? Because they make inferences from our statements about God to our views about his creatures. "If God regards all the same way, then all must regard God the same way." But we do not come to our understanding through logical inferences made from one single affirmation about God. That would amount to both bad theology and bad logic. No simple logical inference is ever *necessarily* true, most especially when moving from God to talking about creatures.

It seems that their critique of our theology is a mirror-image of how their own theology works. Seeing a difference between believers and non-believers, they then imagine a corresponding difference in God. Again, they make a simple logical inference, but this time in the reverse direction: from a description of the differences among humans to what God then must prescribe for that difference among human persons. We do not reason in that way. Doing so would, in our view, constitute mythological projection, which is idolatry. Doing so would mean concluding something about what God prescribes from a description of individual creatures or a class of them. John Calvin made this mistake in reasoning in his polemical writings about predestination. Thankfully, he did not succumb to that faulty reasoning in most of his writings on theology (in his *Institutes* and elsewhere).

Typically, the difference between our viewpoint and that of those who criticize it, is that we start with God's self-revelation as the criterion for our statements about God ("only God reveals God"). We do not start with our own, or even the Bible's descriptions of how humans respond differently to God and then logically infer something about who God is and what God wants for his human creatures. Descriptions of human creatures and even of their potential eternal ends, either by means of our own observations or by reference to isolated biblical passages interpreted out of context, do not prescribe for us a definitive revelation of who God is and what he wants. Jesus Christ alone, according to divine revelation (Scripture) alone, prescribes for us our trust in and understanding of God's heart, mind, purposes and character. On that basis, we conclude that God is a redeemer who has a redemptive nature and heart, does not want any to perish, but wants all to repent and receive eternal life. That is, God is identical in character to Jesus Christ who is Lord and Savior.

Some condemn or dismiss our theological stance, typically labeling it as Universalism, Aminianism or Calvinism. However, we have no need to be aligned with a particular school of theology. Though each school has understandings deserving our consideration, each also has significant weaknesses that obscure important, even crucial elements of the biblical revelation. Those weaknesses have not only been identified by us but have been brought to light in the ongoing discussions and debates down through the history of the church. While we share faith in the same realities as do all Christians, our theological understanding and articulation does not fall neatly along the lines drawn in the typical Universalist-Arminian-Calvinist debates.

Those who are satisfied with one of these primary theological traditions and insist that these are the only options, likely will not be able to properly hear our theological testimony or grasp its source and norm the way we do. Their critiques likely will assume that we have bought into the one or two theological options which they have rejected—ones that might include being "incarnational" or "Trinitarian." While we can offer our reasons for why and how we understand the Christian faith the way we do, we don't have to accept any labels nor defend the one we use. We are simply trying to be as faithful as we can in understanding and explaining the biblical revelation. We hold out our convictions first to our own members for their benefit and second to others in trust—hoping that others might be renewed and blessed as we have been as the Lord has corrected and restored us.

It was not a particular theology or theologian who transformed Grace Communion International. Rather it was Jesus Christ speaking through his Holy Word who revealed to us the true nature and character of God. Grace Communion International was grasped by the gospel of Jesus Christ, as our Lord placed himself at the center of our worship and faith. If the label, "Incarnational Trinitarian Theology" properly *describes* that transformation, then we accept it. However, we have no need to defend a label, for it *prescribes* nothing.

Gary Deddo

STRONG THEOLOGY
VS. WEAK THEOLOGY

One of the best definitions of theology is the one ascribed to Anselm of Canterbury (1033-1109), who called it "faith seeking understanding." The converse of this — "understanding seeking faith" is known as apologetics. Pursued properly, both disciplines can lead us to dig deeper and deeper, coming to appreciate more and more the simple, yet profound statement that "God is love."

But just digging deeper does not guarantee that our conclusions will be good. We need to dig in the right direction. As we are reminded in 2 Timothy 3:7, it is possible to be "always learning but never able to come to a knowledge of the truth."

Theology has been described as being weak or strong based upon its arrangement and understanding of various doctrines and/or a specific understanding of the attributes of God. When I first heard this, I thought of it in terms of correct and incorrect doctrine. However, the more I think about it, I realize it is more than that. Doctrine is only one ingredient of authentic Christianity. It is important, to be sure — it is essential that the church teach right doctrines. However, doctrine is not all that we must include in our worship of our Creator, Savior and Sanctifier. Doctrine does not save us. No matter how much we know, Paul reminds us that it doesn't do us any good if we don't have love (1 Corinthians 13:2).

I first realized a distinction when, with Dr. J. Michael Feazell, I attended a large evangelistic conference several years ago. In one session it was noted that there was a tremendous evangelical opportunity to be had in the wake of the attacks we now refer to as *9/11*. The presenter suggested that we celebrate the firefighters, police officers and other heroes who saved the lives of others, sometimes losing their own in the process — a powerful analogy of what Jesus has done for humanity.

During a later talk, a serious contradiction became apparent, although most seemed oblivious to it. Another presenter, in order to motivate us to evangelism, emphasized that unless someone had made a conscious decision for Christ, God would send them to hell forever. Mike, putting the two presentations together, elbowed me and said, "So, how do you celebrate a hero who gave his life to save others but who had been sent to hell forever because he had not accepted Jesus as his Savior? What is there to celebrate about a hero who is now burning in hell?"

"That's the problem with a weak theology," I replied.

Our theology defines how we understand God's nature, character, heart, mind and purpose. It fills out for us how God views us and others and what kind of relationship he wants with us.

Strong theology has a clear and coherent grasp of who God is and what God wants for us: God is exactly like Jesus all the way down. He is the fullness of deity, bearing the stamp of the character of God. He is the visible image of the Father and the Spirit. In Jesus, what you see is what you get.

Weak theology, however, presents God in bits and pieces, often leaving us with a view of a God who is of two minds, or who has two different wills, or even two different sides to his character. Sometimes Jesus is presented as one "side" of God who wants to save us by grace and the Father as the other "side" who wants to condemn us under the Law. This God has two wills, two purposes, two attitudes towards his creation and so has two kinds of relationship with us. This God is *for* some of us, but *against* others.

Weak theology leaves us with two minds toward others. We're supposed to love others, even our enemies, and present the Gospel to them and encourage them to surrender their lives to Christ who died for them. But if we believe God only loves some and will only call some to himself but is against others and just as happy to send them to hell, it's hard, if not impossible, to have the same attitude and hope for all. We are left with the sense that we're not being totally truthful when we present the Gospel as if it's for everyone.

While it is true that some may somehow reject the Gospel of grace no matter what we or even God does for them, perhaps for all eternity, God's revelation to us of his single mind, will and purpose for all is made clear by Paul:

> For God was pleased to have all his fullness dwell in him, and through him to reconcile to himself all things, whether things on earth or things in heaven, by making peace through his blood, shed on the cross (Colossians 1:19-20).

Weak theology undermines this vital truth leaving us with the impression that Jesus only shows us one side of God, not the fullness of God and that God is interested only in reconciling some things, not everything. Weak theology can lead to an "us vs. them" elitist mentality where, after the evangelistic meeting is over, we minister to those on the "inside" far differently from those on the "outside."

While weak theology leads us down this dark and conflicted path of exclusivism, strong theology affirms that God loves everyone profoundly and places love above all other gifts from God:

> If I have the gift of prophecy and can fathom all mysteries and all knowledge, and if I have a faith that can move mountains, but do not have love, I am nothing (1 Corinthians 13:2).

While weak theology leads us to erect barriers between people, strong theology understands that God, who is no respecter of persons, "*wants all men to be saved and to come to a knowledge of the truth*" (1 Timothy 2:3-4). Led by this truth, we are encouraged to join with Paul in tearing down barriers that divide people from God and one another:

> Though I am free and belong to no one, I have made myself a slave to everyone, to win as many as possible. To the Jews I became like a Jew, to win the Jews. To those under the law I became like one under the law (though I myself am not under the law), so as to win those under the law. To those not having the law I became like one not having the law (though I am not free from God's law but am under Christ's law), so as to win those not having the law. To the weak I became weak, to win the weak. I have become all things to all people so that by all possible means I might save some. I do all this for the sake of the gospel, that I may share in its blessings (1 Corinthians 9:19-23).

While weak theology includes or excludes people from coming under God's reconciling work based upon their performance, strong theology recognizes that Jesus' atonement has pre-qualified everyone for salvation. Note Paul's words to the Christians in Colossae:

> Giving thanks to the Father, who has qualified us to share in the inheritance of the saints in light. For He rescued us from the domain of darkness, and transferred us to the kingdom of his beloved Son, in whom we have redemption, the forgiveness of sins (Colossians 1:12-14, NAS).

To sum it up, whereas weak theology begins with bad news, hoping to convince (or frighten) people into hoping there is good news, strong theology starts and ends with the Good News for all:

> God so loved the world that he gave his one and only Son, that whoever believes in him shall not perish but have eternal life. For God did not send his Son into the world to condemn the world, but to save

the world through him (John 3:16-17).

Strong theology is profoundly and consistently evangelical, while weak theology is a pretender. As we dig deep into theology, it is important that we dig in the proper direction.

Joseph Tkach

FOUNDATIONS OF THEOLOGY FOR GCI

By Joseph Tkach, J. Michael Feazell, Dan Rogers, and Michael Morrison
Transcript of a video presentation

Joseph Tkach: Acts 17:11 tells us that the Bereans "…examined the Scriptures every day" to see if what Paul said about Jesus was true. The Bereans were engaged in theology — studying to know God.

The English word "theology" comes from two Greek words, *theos* and *logia* — meaning "God" and "knowledge." Theology is what we as Christian believers do — we involve ourselves in "God knowledge" or "God study" seeking to know God as fully as we can. Theology is simply the study of God.

What we believe, and what a Christological, or Trinitarian, theology is all about, is that theology itself needs to emerge from God's own witness to himself in Scripture.

Michael Morrison: The idea of studying theology, or even thinking about theology, can be frightening to many people. But really, everyone has a theology, whether they know it or not. Even atheists have a theology.

A college student once admitted to the college chaplain that she did not believe in God. The chaplain was curious, and so he asked: "Well, what sort of god is it that you don't believe in?" She described an old man in the sky, someone who is just looking for people to do something wrong so he can zap them. And the chaplain replied, "Well, if that's what you mean by the word god, then I'd be an atheist, too. I don't believe in that kind of god, either."

JT: A person's theology is really just their beliefs about God. Some people think that God is an angry judge; others believe that he is like a grandfather who means well but can't do much. Others see him as a cosmic concierge who exists to grant us our every desire. Some people think of God as far off and unknowable; others think of him as near and accessible. Some people think God never changes his mind; others think that he is always changing in response to the prayers of his people. How people view God affects how they read and interpret the Bible.

MM: When Paul tells us that Adam brought condemnation on everyone, and that Jesus brought justification for everyone, then we have to think about what that means about humanity and about Jesus and about salvation. When Paul says that we were baptized into Christ's death, or when Jesus says, "If you have seen me you have seen the Father," we need to think about what that means — and that's theology.

A study of theology helps us learn to put all our various doctrines or beliefs or teachings together, to see if they are consistent with one another, or if they seem to contradict one another. But we don't do theology just according to what sounds good to us. We are not the authority — God is. If he didn't reveal himself to us, then we wouldn't know anything for sure about him. But he has revealed himself to us, and in two ways — in Scripture, and in Jesus — and we know Jesus through Scripture as well. So Scripture should provide our foundation for theological thought.

J. Michael Feazell: At the heart of all our doctrines and beliefs in our denomination is the Bible. And yet, as is clear even from our own history (not to mention the history of the Christian church in general), people do not agree on how the Bible should be interpreted. A person's theology, or their perspective on who God is and how he relates to humanity and how humanity relates to him, is like a lens though which people interpret what they read in the Bible. What we believe, and what a Christological, or Trinitarian, theology is all about, is that theology itself needs to emerge from God's own witness to himself in Scripture. And God's own witness to himself in Scripture is Jesus Christ. "If you have seen me," Jesus said, "You have seen the Father."

Dan Rogers: In Jesus, God fully revealed himself to humanity. Karl Barth once said you really can't do theology. If theology is the study of God, the knowledge of God, how can the human mind ever study God? Well, there is a way — as he then pointed out. God fully revealed himself in Jesus Christ.

JT: In our denomination, our theology is what gives cohesion and structure to our beliefs and establishes priority for our doctrines. It has developed over the years as we have worked through various doctrinal issues, all the while being careful to maintain a Bible-based understanding of who God is and how he relates to humanity.

MF: God is known by faith, and by that we mean that we know God not merely as we hear about him through the Scriptures, but as we actually put our trust in him. In that obedient life, the Spirit engages us to think about and reflect on what God reveals about himself. That is why a Christological, or Christ-centered, theology is so important, so that we have the right starting place for our journey of growing in the grace and knowledge of God.

JT: As our theology developed, we found the writings of Thomas and James Torrance and Karl Barth to be especially helpful because of their intense focus on the biblical revelation of God through Jesus Christ.

MM: We have a Christ-centered, or Trinitarian, theology. That means not only that we accept the doctrine of the Trinity, but that this doctrine lies at the heart of all other doctrines. The central Bible truth that Jesus Christ is God in the flesh, that he and the Father with the Spirit are one God, forms the basis for how we understand everything we read in Scripture.

In John 14, the apostle Philip asked Jesus, "Lord, show us the Father." Jesus replied, "If you have seen me, you have seen the Father. I am in the Father, and the Father is in me." In other words, Jesus reveals to us what the Father is like. Jesus shows us a God who is love, is compassion, is patience, kindness, faithfulness, and goodness. God is like that all the time.

Some people imagine that the Father is angry at humanity and really wants to punish everyone, but that the Son intervened for us and paid the price to save us from his Father's wrath. That's quite confused, because the Bible says that the Father is just like Jesus. The Father loved the world so much that he sent his Son to save the world. It's not like Jesus was working behind his Father's back — no, it's just the opposite: the Father was working in and through Jesus. The Father is just as eager to save humanity as Jesus is.

When Jesus was born, he was Immanuel, which means "God with us." When the Word became a human being, he showed us that God is present with humanity, and he is working for humanity. We are his creations, and he doesn't want to let us go to ruin. When God came in human flesh, he, as a representative of humanity, was able to do what other humans had not been able to do. As the perfect human, Jesus offered God perfect worship, and a perfect sacrifice, and God accepted this worship that was offered on behalf of the human race. Just as in Adam we are all condemned, so also in Christ we are all acquitted, and accepted, and welcomed into the love and fellowship of the Trinity.

DR: As we study Jesus, we begin to see God and his relationship with us as his creation — with humanity. So we began to view the Scriptures through that lens, and we noticed that many others had done likewise; men such as Athanasius and in our modern times theologians like Karl Barth had looked through this same lens, and we began to interact, to participate in a dialectical discussion with the writings and the thoughts of these great Christians from ages past. As we did, we began to focus more and more and more on a certain theology, the theology of adoption, the theology of God's love for humanity. How God wanted to take us into himself and share his life with us because he is a God of love — a God who gives, and a God who shares.

JT: Thomas Torrance is widely considered to be one of the premier Christian theologians of the twentieth century. He was awarded the Templeton Foundation Prize for Progress in Religion in 1978, and his book, *Theological Science,* received the first "Collins Award" in Britain for the best work in theology, ethics, and sociology relevant to Christianity for 1967-69.

Torrance founded the *Scottish Journal of Theology* and served as moderator of the General Assembly of the Church of Scotland in 1976-77. He served for more than 25 years as chair of Christian Dogmatics at the University of Edinburgh, and is author of more than 30 books and hundreds of articles.

Torrance, following in the theological tradition of Athanasius and Gregory of Nazianzen, is a leading proponent of what is called Trinitarian theology: theology rooted in God's own revelation of himself through the Scriptures in the person of Jesus Christ. In the Scriptures, human life and human death find their meaning only in the life and death and resurrection of Jesus Christ, the Son of God, who in becoming human for our sakes has brought humanity into the eternal joyous fellowship of the Father, Son and Spirit. Because Christ has done in our place and on our behalf everything needed for our salvation, all that remains for us is to repent and believe in him as our Lord and Savior.

MF: When we take seriously passages about the width and breadth of God's gracious and powerful reconciling work in Jesus Christ, such as Colossian 1:19-20, some people respond with "You're just teaching universalism." Colossians 1:19-20, as you probably know, says: "God was pleased to have all his fullness dwell in him, and through him to reconcile to himself all things, whether things on earth or things in heaven, by making peace through his blood, shed on the cross."

Well, Paul wrote the passage, not us, not Karl Barth, not Thomas Torrance. Barth, responding to accusations that he was teaching universalism said, "…there is no theological justification for setting any limits on our side to the friendliness of God towards humanity which appeared in Jesus Christ." We have no reason to make apologies for the wideness of God's grace. Paul also wrote, in 1 Timothy 2:4, that God "…wants all men to be saved and to come to a knowledge of the truth."

Still, as Barth pointed out, God declares an eternal "No" to sin, and God's "No" is the power of God by which evil is overthrown and negated, and its power and future denied. God rejects and opposes all opposition to himself, and yet in Jesus Christ, God's elect, all humanity is indeed elect and reconciled, as Colossians says.

But kingdom life is none other than a life of faith in Jesus, not a life of unbelief. That means that even though all humanity is elect in Christ, unbelieving elect aren't living a kingdom life; they aren't living in the joy of fellowship with the Father and the Son and the Spirit. So if it were to be that everyone would ultimately enter into the life of the kingdom, and that is not something we are given to know, but if it were to be, it would only be after repentance, which is turning to God, and faith in Jesus Christ. "Now this is eternal life," Jesus said in a prayer to the Father, "that they may know you, the only true God, and Jesus Christ whom you have sent." There is no salvation outside of a life of faith in Jesus Christ.

That's what hell is all about—life outside the fellowship of the Father, Son and Spirit—life, if you can call it that, in the dark, outside the king's banquet, being left to the miserable fruit of one's own self-centeredness. Call it fiery, call it outer darkness, call it weeping and gnashing of teeth — the Bible uses all those metaphors in describing the existence of those who refuse to embrace his grace and love, that amazing grace and love God has even for his enemies.

JT: The Bible confronts us with a wonderful, amazing, reconciliation in Christ that is so broad as to encompass not only all things on earth, but even all things in heaven, Colossians tells us in no uncertain terms. Yet God calls on humanity to receive, to accept, that grace he so powerfully bestows on all humanity in Jesus Christ. But for those who refuse it, who persist in their rebellion, and in their rejection of God's grace for them, hell is what remains for them. As Robert Capon puts it, God will not allow them to spoil the party for everyone else.

MM: Ancient Greek philosophers reasoned that since God is perfect, that must mean that he never changes, and that he never has any feelings, because if he would ever change, then that would mean that he wasn't perfect before the change.

So they thought of God as static, the so-called "unmoved mover" who made everything happen, but who could not ever change course, because to do so would call his perfection and his power into question. This kind of God would never dirty himself by getting involved with people and their problems. He was far off, watching, but not directly and personally involved. This concept of God has often affected even how Christians think about God.

But the Bible reveals a different sort of God — one who is not constrained by the limits of a philosopher's logic. God is completely sovereign — he can do whatever he wants to do — and he is not limited by any external rules or ideas or human logic. If he wants the eternal Word to become a human being, then he does it, even though it constitutes a change. The God of the Bible is free to be whoever he wants to be — free to become what he was not before: the Creator; and free to create human beings who would be free, who could go astray, and God is even free to become one of those human beings in order to rescue humanity from its rebellion and alienation.

In this theological thinking, it is not our logic that is in charge — God is the one in charge, and our task, our desire, is to try to understand God not the way that we might reason him out to be by our finite forms of logic, but rather to seek to understand God the way that he has actually revealed himself through the Bible in the person of Jesus Christ.

Throughout church history, people have defined theology as "faith seeking understanding." We believe, and now we want to understand as much as we can about what we believe. It's like we've fallen in love with someone, and we want to find out as much as we can about that person. Theology is faith, trying to understand more about the God who loves us. And we must seek that understanding in the context of God's own revelation of himself as Father, Son and Spirit revealed to us perfectly in Jesus, the Son of God made flesh for our sakes.

JT: When it comes to theologies, it is not so much a matter of a particular theological perspective being totally "right" or totally "wrong." It is more a case of how adequate a particular theology is in fully addressing believers' biblical understanding of God and how God relates to humanity. We have found that of all approaches to Christian theology, Christo-centric, or Trinitarian, theology reflects and adheres most faithfully and carefully to what God reveals about himself and humanity in the Bible.

We should keep in mind that theology is a journey, not a destination. We will always be seeking as clear and adequate a theological vision as we can in order to soundly convey the biblical vision and understanding God has given us over 15-plus years of doctrinal reformation. Theology includes the task of seeking adequate thought-forms to convey doctrinal truths in a rapidly changing world.

MF: Many people today, even believers, are afraid: They're afraid of their standing with God, worried that they're not measuring up, that they're not doing enough, worried that their sins and failures have cut them off from God's love. That's what theologies that start from ideas of, say, holiness, or of judgment, cause. So instead of taking confidence in Jesus, and knowing that Jesus has already done for them everything God requires of them, instead of knowing that Jesus is their perfection, their obedience, their faithfulness, they suffer under a burden of guilt and anxiety.

When we know that it isn't our righteousness but Jesus' righteousness that has already put us in good standing with God, then we are freed from ourselves and our sinfulness to trust in Jesus and to take up our cross and follow Jesus as we could never be free to do when we're afraid that God is mad at us. A sound, biblically rooted theology will always start with and be centered in Christology, because in Scripture we are confronted with a God who chooses to be God in Jesus, with Jesus and for Jesus. If we let the Bible forge our theology, we cannot look outside of Jesus to understand who God is, or to define God.

MM: In Jesus we meet God as God really is, the way God himself has revealed himself to be, as the God who is for us, because he is for Jesus. We find that the Father loves us unconditionally, that he sent Jesus not out of anger and a need to punish someone, but out of his immeasurable love and his unbending commitment to our redemption. The love we see in Jesus is none other than the love of the Father, because the Father is in the Son and the Son in the Father and they are one. That means that when we know Jesus Christ, we know God the Father.

MF: In Jesus, God reveals himself as our Creator and our Judge, and also as our Reconciler and Redeemer. In other words, the God who made us and whom we stand under as our Judge is also the one who reconciles and redeems us. That means we can believe him and trust him instead of being afraid of him and hiding from him. In Jesus, we are free for obedience and faith because we aren't relying on our own obedience and faith, but on his. That takes our minds off ourselves and rests them in Jesus.

JT: In Trinitarian theology, which is centered on Jesus as God's perfect revelation of himself, we see that 1) God is free in the fullness of his divine love and power to be with us and for us and 2) that humanity, secure in God's grace manifest in Jesus, is free to be with God and for God. That is because Jesus is both the fullness of God and the fullness of humanity, exactly as God reveals himself in the Bible.

MM: The Christian life is a response to God's grace. It is letting God's grace work in us, change us, and shine through us. Paul said, "It is not I who live, but Christ lives in me." His grace works in us, and as we are united to Christ, we have a new life, and we walk in newness of life, in a new way — a way that is being transformed by Christ in us.

We are not working our way into salvation, or trying to obey Jesus in order to be a child of God. No, by grace God has already said that we are his children. That is who we are, and that does not change. God says to us, "You belong to me. Now, I invite you to live a new way, a better way, a way that gives meaning and purpose to life. I invite you — I urge you — to join and enjoy the life of love — the way that has worked for all eternity. I invite you to the banquet, to the party, to the never-ending fellowship of the Father,

Son, and Holy Spirit."

DR: As we began to look at certain doctrines, every doctrine was viewed through the lens of Jesus Christ. As time has gone by, we have seen that our statement of beliefs has held up very well and we are coming more and more into a fuller and fuller understanding of the implications of this theology of adoption, of God as Trinity and as God fully revealed in the person of Jesus Christ.

JT: The articles and Statement of Beliefs posted on our website express the official doctrines of our fellowship and discuss our theological vision. We are adding high quality biblical studies, Christian living and theological material to our website continually.

Christo-centric, or Trinitarian, theology originates as far back as the early Church Fathers with Irenaeus, Athanasius and the Cappadocian Fathers. Some of the greatest theologians in modern history have devoted their life's work to explaining the relationship between God's triune nature and his redemptive work on behalf of humanity.

It is important that our preaching and teaching reflect sound theology, and that it remain rooted in the good news, the biblical revelation of Jesus Christ as the incarnate Son of God in whom we live and move and have our being.

Theologians whose work has been of special help to us in understanding and articulating a sound, Bible-based theology would include Karl Barth, Thomas and James Torrance, Michael Jinkins, professor of pastoral theology at Austin Presbyterian Theological Seminary, Ray Anderson, professor of theology and ministry at Fuller Theological Seminary, Colin Gunton, Robert Capon, Gary Deddo, C. Baxter Kruger, Donald Bloesch, Michael Green and others. We have also found the writings of C.S. Lewis of particular value, although Lewis was not a theologian, per se.

Although it is not likely that you or I would necessarily agree with every single statement in any particular book, we are able to recommend a number of books on theology that we believe provide a sound and faithful reflection of biblical doctrine. These would include such books as:

Invitation to Theology by Michael Jinkins
The Mediation of Christ by Thomas Torrance
Dogmatics in Outline by Karl Barth
Worship, Community & The Triune God of Grace by James Torrance
The Christian Doctrine of God: One Being Three Persons by T.F. Torrance
The Trinitarian Faith by Thomas Torrance
Theology, Death and Dying and *Judas and Jesus: Amazing Grace for the Wounded*

Soul by Ray Anderson
On the Incarnation by St. Athanasius
The Christian Foundations Series by Donald Bloesch
The Parables of Judgment, The Parables of Grace, and The Parables of the Kingdom
    by Robert Capon
The One, the Three, and the Many by Colin Gunton
Across All Worlds and *The Great Dance* by Baxter Kruger
The Promise of Trinitarian Theology by Elmer Colyer
How To Read Thomas F. Torrance by Elmer Colyer
The Humanity of God by Karl Barth
Mere Christianity by C.S. Lewis
The Great Divorce by C.S. Lewis

This is by no means a complete list, but it's a good start. I should stress that most pastors will find Michael Jinkins' *Invitation to Theology* especially helpful as a one-volume, easy-to-read, basic theology text.

I want to take this and every possible occasion to thank all of you who labor in the gospel for your faithful work and to let you know how much all of us here in Glendora appreciate your service in Christ to his people.

May God bless and keep you always in his faithful embrace.

THE WRITTEN WORD OF GOD

How do we know who Jesus is, or what he taught? How do we know when a gospel is false? Where is the authority for sound teaching and right living? The Bible is the inspired and infallible record of what God wants us to know and do.

A witness to Jesus

Perhaps you've seen newspaper reports about the "Jesus Seminar," a group of scholars who claim that Jesus didn't say most of the things the Bible says he did. Or perhaps you've heard of other scholars who say that the Bible is a collection of contradictions and myths.

Many well-educated people dismiss the Bible. Many other equally educated people believe it is a trustworthy record of what God has done and said. If we cannot trust what the Bible says about Jesus, for example, then we will know almost nothing about him.

The Jesus Seminar began with a preconceived idea of what Jesus would have taught. They accepted the sayings that fit this idea, and rejected the sayings that didn't, thereby, in effect, creating a Jesus in their own image. This is not good scholarship, and even many liberal scholars disagree with the Seminar.

Do we have good reason to trust the biblical reports about Jesus? Certainly—they were written within a few decades of Jesus' death, when eyewitnesses were still alive. Jewish disciples often memorized the words of their teachers, so it is quite possible that Jesus' disciples preserved his teachings accurately. We have no evidence that they invented sayings to deal with early church concerns, such as circumcision. This suggests that they are reliable reports of what Jesus taught.

We can also be confident that the manuscripts were well preserved. We have some copies from the fourth century, and smaller sections from the second. This is better than all other historical books. (The oldest copy of Virgil was copied 350 years after Virgil died; of Plato, 1,300 years.) The manuscripts show that the Bible was copied carefully, and we have a highly reliable text.

Jesus' witness to Scripture

Jesus was willing to argue with the Pharisees on many issues, but he did not seem to argue with their view of the Scriptures. Although Jesus disagreed on interpretations and traditions, he apparently agreed with other Jewish leaders that the Scriptures were authoritative for faith and practice.

Jesus expected every word in Scripture to be fulfilled (Matthew 5:17-18; Mark 14:49). He quoted Scripture to prove his points (Matthew 9:13; 22:31; 26:24; 26:31; John 10:34); he rebuked people for not reading Scripture carefully enough (Matthew 22:29; Luke 24:25; John 5:39). He referred to Old Testament people and events without any hint that they were not real.

Scripture had the authority of God behind it. When Jesus answered Satan's temptations, he said, "It is written" (Matthew 4:4-10). The fact that something was written in Scripture meant, for Jesus, that it was an indisputable authority. The words of David were inspired by the Holy Spirit (Mark 12:36); a prophecy was given "through" Daniel (Matthew 24:15) because its real origin was God.

Jesus said in Matthew 19:4-5 that the Creator said in Genesis 2:24: "A man will leave his father and mother and be united to his wife." However, Genesis does not describe this verse as the words of God. Jesus could say that God said it simply because it was in Scripture. The assumption is that God is the ultimate author of all of Scripture.

The evidence throughout the Gospels is that Jesus viewed Scripture as reliable and trustworthy. As he reminded the Jewish leaders, "the Scripture cannot be broken" (John 10:35). Jesus expected it to be valid; he even upheld the validity of old covenant commands while the old covenant was still in force (Matthew 8:4; 23:23).

Witness of the apostles

The apostles, like their teacher, considered Scripture authoritative. They quoted it repeatedly, often as proof of an argument. The sayings of Scripture are treated as words of God. Scripture is even personalized as the God who spoke to Abraham and Pharaoh (Romans 9:17; Galatians 3:8). What David or Isaiah or Jeremiah wrote was actually spoken by God, and therefore certain (Acts 1:16; 4:25; 13:35; 28:25; Hebrews 1:6-10; 10:15). The law of Moses is assumed to reflect the mind of God (1 Corinthians 9:9). The real author of Scripture is God (1 Corinthians 6:16; Romans 9:25).

Paul called the Scriptures "the very words of God" (Romans 3:2). Peter says that the prophets "spoke from God as they were carried along by the Holy Spirit" (2 Peter 1:20). The prophets didn't make it up—God inspired them, and he is the real origin of their words. They often wrote, "the word of the Lord came..." or "Thus says the Lord..."

Paul also told Timothy that "all Scripture is God-breathed and is useful for teaching, rebuking, correcting and training in righteousness" (2 Timothy 3:16). It is as if God breathed his message through the biblical writers.

However, we must not read into this our modern ideas of what "God-breathed" has to mean. We must remember that Paul said this about the Greek Septuagint *translation* (the Scriptures that Timothy had known since childhood—v. 15), and this translation is in some places considerably different than the Hebrew original. Paul used this translation as the word of God without meaning that it was a perfect text.

Despite its translation discrepancies, it is God-breathed and able to make people "wise for salvation through faith in Christ Jesus" and it is still able to equip believers "for every good work" (v. 17).

Imperfect communication

The original word of God is perfect, and God is certainly able to cause people to state it accurately, to preserve it accurately and (to complete the communication) make us understand it accurately. But God has not done all this. Our copies have grammatical errors, copyist errors, and (far more significantly) humans always make errors in receiving the message. There is "noise" that prevents us from hearing perfectly the word God inspired to be written in Scripture. Nevertheless, God uses Scripture to speak to us today.

Despite the "noise" that puts human mistakes between God and us, the purpose of Scripture is accomplished: to tell us about salvation and about right behavior. God accomplishes his purpose in Scripture: he communicates his word to us with enough clarity that we can be saved and we can learn what he wants us to do.

Scripture, even in a translation, is accurate for its purpose. But we would be wrong to expect more from it than God intended. He is not teaching us astronomy or science. The numbers in Scripture are not always mathematically precise by today's standards. We must look at Scripture for its purpose, not for minor details.

For example, in Acts 21:11, Agabus was inspired to say that the Jews would bind Paul and hand him over to the Gentiles. Some people might assume that Agabus was specifying who would tie Paul up, and what they would do with him. But as it turns out, Paul was actually rescued by the Gentiles and bound by the Gentiles (21:30-33).

Is this a contradiction? Technically, yes. The prediction was true in principle, but not in the details. Of course, when Luke wrote this, he could have easily doctored the prediction to fit the result, but he was willing to let the differences be seen. He did not think that people should expect precision in such details. This should warn us about expecting precision in all the details of Scripture.

We need to focus on the main point of the message. Similarly, Paul made a mistake when he wrote 1 Corinthians 1:14 — a mistake he corrected in verse 16. The inspired Scriptures contain both the mistake and the correction.

Proof of the Bible

No one can prove that all of the Bible is true. They may show that a particular prophecy came true, but they cannot show that the entire Bible has the same validity. This is based more on faith. We see the historical evidence that Jesus and the apostles accepted the Old Testament as the word of God. The biblical Jesus is the only one we have; other ideas are based on guesswork, not new evidence. We accept the teaching of Jesus that the Holy Spirit would guide the disciples into more truth. We accept the claim of Paul that he wrote with divine authority. We accept that the Bible reveals to us who God is and how we may have fellowship with him.

We accept the testimony of church history, that Christians through the centuries have found the Bible useful for faith and practice. This book tells us who God is, what he did for us, and how we should respond. Tradition also tells us which books are in the biblical canon. We trust that God guided the process so that the end result accomplishes his purpose.

Our experience also testifies to the accuracy of Scripture. This is the book that has the honesty to tell us about our own sinfulness, and the grace to offer us a cleansed conscience. It gives us moral strength not through rules and commands, but in an unexpected way—through grace and the ignominious death of our Lord.

The Bible testifies to the love, joy and peace we may have through faith—feelings that are, just as the Bible describes, beyond our ability to put into words. This book gives us meaning and purpose in life by telling us of divine creation and redemption. These aspects of biblical authority cannot be proven to skeptics, but they help verify the Scriptures that tell us these things that we experience.

The Bible does not sugar-coat its heroes, and this also helps us accept it as honest. It tells us about the failings of Abraham, Moses, David, the nation of Israel, and the disciples. The Bible is a word that bears witness to a more authoritative Word, the Word made flesh, and the good news of God's grace.

The Bible is not simplistic; it does not take the easy way out. The New Testament claims both continuity and discontinuity with the old covenant. It would be simpler to eliminate one or the other, but it is more challenging to have both. Likewise, Jesus is presented as both human and divine, a combination that does not fit well into Hebrew, Greek or modern thought. This complexity was not created through ignorance of the philosophical problems, but in spite of them.

The Bible is a challenging book, not likely to be the result of fishermen attempting a fraud or trying to make sense of hallucinations. Jesus' resurrection gives additional weight to the book that announces such a phenomenal event. It gives additional weight to the testimony of the disciples as to who Jesus was and to the unexpected logic of conquering death through the death of the Son of God.

Repeatedly, the Bible challenges our thinking about God, ourselves, life, right and wrong. It commands respect by conveying truths to us we do not obtain elsewhere. Just as the proof of the pudding is in the eating, the proof of the Bible is in its application to our lives.

The testimony of Scripture, of tradition, of personal experience and reason all support the authority of the Bible. The fact that it is able to speak across cultures, to address situations that never existed when it was written, is also a testimony to its abiding authority. The proof of the Bible is conveyed to believers as the Holy Spirit uses it to change their hearts and lives.

Inerrancy and Infallibility

Some evangelical Christians believe that Christians should call the Bible inerrant; others prefer to call the Bible infallible. Although in normal usage these words would mean practically the same thing, in theology they are used for different concepts.

Inerrant usually means without error in theology, history or science. *Infallible* (sometimes called limited inerrancy) refers to doctrine; it does not insist on scientific and historical accuracy, since those are outside of the Bible's purpose.

Some believe the Bible is inerrant; others prefer the term infallible. We use the less-specific word, *infallible*. On that we can all agree, since people who believe in inerrancy also believe that the Bible does not fail in its purpose: to teach us about salvation.

John Stott, who accepts inerrancy, nevertheless lists "five reasons why the word *inerrancy* makes me uncomfortable":

> First, God's self-revelation in Scripture is so rich—both in content and in form—that it cannot be reduced to a string of propositions which invite the label 'truth' or 'error.' 'True or false?' would be an inappropriate question to address to a great deal of Scripture. [Commands are neither true nor false.]
>
> Second, the word *inerrancy* is a double negative, and I always prefer

a single positive to a double negative. It is better to affirm that the Bible is true and therefore trustworthy....

Third, the word inerrancy sends out the wrong signals and develops the wrong attitudes. Instead of encouraging us to search the Scriptures so that we may grow in grace and in the knowledge of God, it seems to turn us into detectives hunting for incriminating clues and to make us excessively defensive in relation to apparent discrepancies.

Fourth, it is unwise and unfair to use *inerrancy* as a shibboleth by which to identify who is an evangelical and who is not. The hallmark of authentic evangelicalism ... is not whether we subscribe to an impeccable formula about the Bible but whether we live in practical submission to what the Bible teaches....

Fifth, it is impossible to prove that the Bible contains no errors. When faced with an apparent discrepancy, the most Christian response is neither to make a premature negative judgment nor to resort to a contrived harmonization, but rather to suspend judgment, waiting patiently for further light to be given us (*Evangelical Truth,* pp. 61-62).

There is an additional problem with the word *inerrant:* It must be carefully qualified. Even one of the most conservative statements about Scripture admits that the Bible contains grammatical irregularities, exaggerations, imprecise descriptions, inexact quotations, and observations based on a limited viewpoint ("The Chicago Statement on Biblical Inerrancy," Article XIII, printed in Norman L. Geisler, editor, *Inerrancy,* Zondervan, 1979, page 496).

In other words, *inerrant* does not mean "without error of any kind." Further, inerrancy applies only to the autographs, not to the copies that we have today. These qualifications seem to drain *inerrancy* of much of its meaning. When pages have to be written to explain what the word does *not* mean, perhaps we need a different word. The main point, as Millard Erickson says, is that "the Bible's assertions are fully true when judged in accordance with the purpose for which they were written" (*Introducing Christian Doctrine,* p. 64). That is a wise qualification.

Tips on biblical exegesis

We have sought to address typical questions and objections that arise as people consider Trinitarian theology. No doubt, there are other verses that bring similar questions or objections. What we have sought to do in this booklet is to demonstrate a Trinitarian, Christ-centered approach to reading and interpreting all passages of Holy Scripture.

Some object to the idea of interpreting Scripture. They say, "I just let the Bible say what it means." This idea, though admirable, is not accurate, nor possible. The act of reading is, necessarily, an act of interpretation. So the issue is not whether to interpret; it is this: What criteria do we use in interpreting as we read?

We always bring to Scripture certain ideas and advance assumptions. What we are urging here is that we come to Scripture with the truth of who Jesus Christ is as the beginning point and the ongoing criterion by which we read and interpret the Holy Scriptures. Jesus must be the "lens" through which all Scripture is read.

Therefore, in reading Scripture, we recommend thinking about the following questions:

- How does this passage line up with the gospel, which answers its central question, "Who is Jesus?"

- Is this passage referring to the universal, objective salvation of all humanity in Jesus, or is it referring to the personal, subjective experience of accepting or rejecting that salvation?

- What is the historical, cultural, and literary context?

- How is this passage worded in other translations? Other translations can sometimes help us see passages from different perspectives. It's also helpful to check Greek lexicons and other translation helps, because some of the richness and subtleties of the Greek New Testament are lost in translations into other languages.

For a guide to biblical exegesis, you may find it helpful to consult *How to Read the Bible for All Its Worth,* by Gordon D. Fee and Douglas Stuart (Zondervan, 1981, 1993, 2014) or *Elements of Biblical Exegesis: A Basic Guide for Students and Ministers,* by Michael J. Gorman (Baker, 2010). See also the free book *A Guided Tour of the Bible,* by John Halford and Michael Morrison, at https://www.smashwords.com/books/view/139409.

For further reading

Achtemeier, Paul. *Inspiration and Authority.* Hendrickson, 1999.

Arthur, Kay. *How to Study Your Bible.* Harvest House, 2001.

Marshall, I. Howard. *Biblical Inspiration.* Eerdmans, 1982.

McQuilken, Robertson. *Understanding and Applying the Bible.* Moody, 1992.

Mickelsen, A.B. and A.M. *Understanding Scripture.* Hendrickson, 1992.

Stott, John. *Understanding the Bible.* Zondervan, 1999.

Thompson, Alden. *Inspiration.* Review & Herald, 1991.

Thompson, David. *Bible Study That Works*. Evangel, 1994.

Veerman, Dave. *How to Apply the Bible*. Tyndale, 1993.

Wright, N.T. *The Last Word: Scripture and the Authority of God*. Harper, 2006.

Michael Morrison

INSPIRATION, AUTHORITY, AND RELIABILITY OF SCRIPTURE

Inspiration

Affirmation: We accept the Bible as the inspired Word of God. The writers were inspired, moved by the Holy Spirit (2 Peter 1:21), and the resultant writings are inspired, as if breathed or spoken by God (2 Timothy 3:16). The Bible is therefore useful as a guide to salvation through faith in Christ, and sufficient for doctrine, correction, moral and ethical instruction (2 Timothy 3:15-17).

The New Testament affirms the inspiration of the Old Testament, especially in its function of pointing to Jesus Christ (Luke 24:44; John 5:46; Acts 10:43). Jesus used the Old Testament as thoroughly reliable words of God (Matthew 5:18; Mark 12:35; John 10:35). The sayings of Jesus are accepted as of divine authority (Matthew 24:35; Mark 8:38; John 6:63), and the letters of Paul are also considered Scripture (2 Peter 3:15-16). The early church quoted the New Testament in the same manner as the Old, treating all these writings as God-given words.[1]

Biblical authors were inspired, and the writings are inspired, but the Bible does not give many details about *how* God worked with humans to produce these documents. Numerous passages claim to be quotes directly from God (e.g., Exodus 20:1-17); others claim to be the result of ordinary research (Luke 1:1-4); some appear to be private letters (Philemon). Regardless of the method of inspiration, all these writings are considered canonical Scripture — an authoritative message from God to humans. The Bible reveals truths about God and about what God does so that we may know God and have a relationship with God.

But grammatical irregularities and stylistic differences indicate that God did not dictate every word. Rather, God allowed the divine message to be given in the phraseology of the human authors. Just as Jesus was God in human form, the Bible is God's word in human words.

Since the Bible is written with human words and grammar, people are able to understand much of the message. But they do not necessarily understand that the message is *true,* because spiritual truths are understood only with divine intervention (1 Corinthians 2:6-16). The written Word of God becomes an effective Word of God only when the Holy Spirit enables a person to understand spiritual truths contained in it.[2] The effectiveness is not in the grammatical details (which can be understood even by atheists) — it is in the message being conveyed and the God-given willingness to submit to it.

Further details concerning the reliability of Scripture will be discussed below.

Authority

Affirmation: God has all authority, and we accept the Bible as the primary authority by which God communicates to us what God wants us to believe and to do. The New Testament clarifies and sometimes supersedes the Old Testament guidance on faith and life. The primary purpose of the Bible is its message about salvation, and that is its primary sphere of authority. It is a sufficient guide that tells us how we are given eternal life with God. Those who believe the biblical revelation about God's grace and Jesus Christ are saved; those who do not believe are not saved (John 3:18; 14:6; Acts 4:12; 1 John 5:11-12). This message of salvation is essential.

The Bible also reveals divine commands and principles regarding the way we ought to live. A genuine faith in Christ as Lord and Savior transforms our lives and minds, with the result that our lives are brought progressively into greater submission to the will of God. Biblical instructions give us authoritative guidance on the will of God concerning how we should live and think and interact with one another.[3]

The Bible is an authoritative revelation of truths about God, and we want to worship our Creator with as much understanding as possible. Moreover, we want to obey God's commands, not only to honor God but also because we believe that our all-wise and perfectly loving Creator has given us the best possible commands and guidance for life. Therefore, we want to understand the written message of God as best we can. But this is not always easy.

Humans are limited beings, and our minds are corrupted by sin, so even at our best we know only in part (1 Corinthians 13:12). Thus we find that the authority of God in the Bible is not only mediated by human language but also by our ability to understand its truths. Although our understanding is imperfect, the Bible is the standard by which our misunderstandings are corrected. God is able to give us sufficient understanding of biblical truths for us to have a saving relationship with God.[4]

Biblical interpretation is complicated by the fact that the Bible is written in many literary styles. Some passages are didactic, prescriptive, and concrete; others are narrative, imaginative and/or poetic. To communicate one spiritual truth, figures of speech may be used that may obscure other equally important truths revealed in other passages. Some commands are historically conditioned and others are timeless. To help us understand and submit to the authority of biblical principles, we humbly seek the guidance of the Author, and study the Scriptures. As well as seeking the guidance of the Spirit, we use reason to understand each biblical passage and point, and to discern what teachings are normative for us today.

Our ability to understand and to reason is shaped in part by our personal experiences and the traditions that have shaped our presuppositions. Reason, tradition, and experience should be subservient to Scripture; they should not contradict biblical authority. Nevertheless, because of different traditions and experiences, equally sincere people come to different conclusions about what the Bible teaches. Therefore we confidently teach our understanding of the Bible and simultaneously respect those who submit to biblical authority in different ways.

Reliability

Affirmation: The Scriptures are a trustworthy guide for our relationships with God and with other humans. They give truth about faith, worship, salvation, morals and ethics (2 Timothy 3:15-16). But biblical commands cannot be applied simplistically, because some are superseded and some apply only in limited situations. We seek the illumination of the Holy Spirit and ask God to guide our reasoning and our use of tradition and experience so we might understand how to apply biblical principles.

The further we go from the stated purposes of the Bible, the less the Bible says about the subject and the less likely we are to have a complete statement about the subject. Statements about history and science are of special interest.

Historians find the Bible to be an accurate record of many ancient events, more reliable than other ancient writings. But its standard of accuracy is looser than the expectations of modern science and history, as can be discerned from parallel accounts in Scripture. The same event can be attributed to Satan or to God (2 Samuel 24:1; 1 Chronicles 21:1), to Jesus in vision or to Ananias (Acts 22:14-15; 26:16-18). Paul's companions stood and heard, but they also fell down and did not hear (Acts 9:7; 22:7, 9).

Most alleged discrepancies in the Bible are easily resolved, but these parallel accounts show that we must be cautious about taking biblical statements at face value. Even if we do not have a parallel account, it is hazardous to assume that unnamed intermediaries, for example, were not involved. This means that some biblical statements are true, but imprecise and incomplete, and therefore not a basis for a modern history. They may be used only with caution. Although biblical comments about salvation require the historical truth of certain *events,* such as the resurrection of Jesus, our faith does not require that we accept every biblical comment as historically or scientifically precise. [5]

Even one of the most conservative statements about Scripture admits that the Bible contains grammatical irregularities, exaggerations, imprecise descriptions, inexact quotations, variant selections, observations based on limited viewpoint, and free citations of the Old Testament.[6]

When Scripture talks about the sun rising (Matthew 5:45), its purpose is not to make a statement that the sun moves around the earth. When it calls a mustard seed the smallest seed (Matthew 13:31-32), it is not making a botanical claim. Genealogical lists may be incomplete (Matthew 1:8; 2 Chronicles 22-24), and the length of kings' reigns may be misinterpreted due to co-regencies.[7] Narrated events may be out of sequence (Matthew 4:18-22; 8:14; Luke 4:38-5:11), predicted events may not be fulfilled in every detail (Acts 21:11, 32-33; 27:10, 22), etc. Such irregularities encourage us to focus on the broad picture and the overall meaning, not tangential details.[8]

The truthfulness of the Bible should be evaluated according to its own "usage and purpose."[9] However, the Bible's purpose rarely includes details of history and science.[10] Further, the Bible's demonstrable flexibility in word usage makes it unwise for us to insist on one meaning of a word when other meanings are possible. God inspired the ambiguities as well as the clear statements. Some things we need to know, and others we do not. God is not primarily concerned with whether we understand astrophysics, botany, and chronology. We err if we try to use his inspired book for purposes it was not designed for.

Christians come to different conclusions about the reliability of the Bible. Many insist that the Bible is more reliable in history and science than we do. We respect that view, for it is close to our own, but we do not think it theologically or biblically required. Other Christians insist that the Bible is less reliable than described herein. We respect their faith in Christ, but we repeat our belief, in summary, that the Bible is the inspired Word of God, authoritative and reliable in matters of faith, worship, morals, and ethics. We encourage all Christians to focus on these central and stated purposes of the Scriptures we have in common.

Endnotes

[1] The testimony of the Bible to itself is summarized in I. Howard Marshall, *Biblical Inspiration,* Grand Rapids: Eerdmans, 1982, pages 19-30.

[2] Revelation is both propositional and personal. See Marshall, pages 12-15.

[3] Some parts of the Bible are more authoritative than others (for example, commands about circumcision and holy kisses are less authoritative) and do not function as a word of God in the same way other verses do. Marshall says, "The Bible…presents a progressive revelation, parts of which are now superseded in the light of what followed" (58). The Old Testament must be used on the basis of general principles, which suggests a similar approach for the New Testament, too.

[4] Any attempt to know God or Christ without reliance on Scriptural propositions is subjective. "In subjectivism each man is his own authority, and if each man is his own authority there is neither truth nor authority" (Bernard Ramm, "The Pattern of Religious Authority," in Erickson, *Readings in Christian Theology, Volume 1: The Living God,* 1973, page 260).

[5] I am not addressing the question whether there are any historical and scientific errors. I do not yet know a resolution for several passages: Luke 2:1-2, Mark 2:26, Mark 15:25 compared with John 19:14, and Mark 15:65 compared with Luke 22:63. Marshall writes, "One may wish to suspend judgment, which is a perfectly legitimate thing to do…. The Bible does contain what may be regarded as error and contradictions by modern standards but which are not in fact contrary to its own standards and purpose" (89, 71). James Orr writes, "'Inerrancy' can never be demonstrated with a cogency which entitles it to rank as the foundation of a belief in inspiration. It must remain to those who hold it a doctrine of faith; a deduction from what they deem to be implied." (in *Readings in Christian Theology,* 245.)

[6] International Conference on Biblical Inerrancy (ICBI), "The Chicago Statement on Biblical Inerrancy," Article XIII. Printed in Norman L. Geisler, editor. *Inerrancy.* (Grand Rapids: Zondervan, 1979), 496. The analogy of Jesus, the Word made flesh, may offer a parallel. We accept his statements about God and salvation as completely true, and his life as perfectly sinless, but this does not necessitate that he never made a measurement mistake in his carpentry work. Likewise, the Bible may contain grammatical and other irregularities.

[7] Dewey Beegle, in *Readings in Christian Theology,* 297-299, citing Edwin Thiele.

[8] "One practical purpose for allowing the differences in parallel passages may be to give us a subtle clue that those are the kinds of things not worth quarrelling over!" (Alden Thompson, *Inspiration,* Hagerstown, Maryland: Review and Herald, 1991, 70). Free citations of the Old Testament suggest that *meaning* is more important than individual words, but a problem still arises when the New Testament gives a different meaning to an Old Testament passage.

[9] ICBI, Article XIII. Actually, the qualifications in Article XIII make it difficult to accept some of the other articles, such as XI and XII, which say that Scripture never misleads us in matters of history and science. Galileo would disagree! As James Dunn says, "Having recognized that God's honour is not compromised by use of irregular grammar, etc., why is it so difficult to accept that his honour can be equally unaffected if he chooses to use equivalent irregularities in historical and scientific detail?" ("The Authority of Scripture According to Scripture," *Churchman* 96 [1982] 120.)

[10] "The Bible...nowhere claims to give instruction in (for instance) any of the natural sciences...and it would be an improper use of Scripture to treat it as making pronouncements on these matters" (J.I. Packer, *"Fundamentalism" and the Word of God,* Grand Rapids: Eerdmans, 1958, 96). Perhaps we could say that all "scientific" statements in the Bible are (to use a word used by ICBI) phenomenological, observations based on a limited viewpoint, and therefore the concept of inerrancy is irrelevant for them.

Michael Morrison

TIMELESS TRUTHS IN CULTURAL CLOTHES: THE AUTHORITY OF SCRIPTURE

Most Christians accept the Bible as authoritative, as a book that gives reliable spiritual guidance. If we took a survey of Christians, asking them, "Do you believe the Bible?," most of them would say, "Yes" — or at least they would try to say yes to some portion of the Bible, such as the New Testament, or the teachings about loving one another. They *want* to say in some sense that they believe the Bible, that they accept it as an authority in their faith.

Protestants in particular respect the Bible as the basis for the Christian faith — the basis for their beliefs about God, Jesus, salvation and the church. Even though they may not have read the Bible, they tend to assume that it is true. Their faith in Christ leads them to accept the book that tells them about Christ. A preacher can say, "The Bible says…" with the expectation that the audience will give favorable weight to a biblical citation. The general tendency is for Christians to trust the Bible.

Some Christians view the Bible skeptically, but this is a more intellectually challenging (and therefore less common) position. It is not immediately apparent to new believers how a person can combine trust and mistrust — faith in Christianity with skepticism about the book that has been the traditional basis of that faith. They might view it as like sawing off the limb on which one's ladder is resting.

Limits to belief

Of course, even believing Christians do not automatically believe everything that the Bible says. For example, if the preacher says, "The Bible says to destroy houses with persistent mildew," most Christians would not take it very seriously. Although the Bible does indeed say that (Leviticus 14:43-45), most Christians would not accept it. Their reasons might vary in sophistication: 1) That would be foolish. 2) No other Christians believe that, so it can't be right. 3) Jesus never said anything like that. 4) That has nothing to do with going to heaven. 5) Old Testament laws don't apply to Christians.

Most Christians reject the teaching about mildew. They are using a filter on the Bible — a filter that in most cases they haven't thought much about. They say they accept the Bible as an authority for their beliefs and practices, yet they do not accept part of the Bible. In this case, the common sense of most Christians functions as more authoritative than the original meaning of Scripture.

I am not saying that houses should be destroyed. Nor am I saying that we should routinely ignore the Bible and follow our common sense. We do not have to choose between such extremes. But Christians should think about the *kind* of authority the Bible has. If we openly disobey some of its teachings, then in what sense can we say that it is authoritative? Whether we like to think about such tensions or not, we do not read far in the Bible before we are faced with the issue. Why do we stand on some parts of the Bible, but not others? To use the ladder analogy again, we want to be sure that our ladder is resting on the correct branch, a branch that will not be broken by the winds of additional thought.

Let's use a New Testament example. Paul says four times, "Greet one another with a holy kiss" (Romans 16:16; 1 Corinthians 16:20; 2 Corinthians 13:12; 1 Thessalonians 5:26), and Peter also says it (1 Peter 5:14). Nevertheless, the vast majority of Christians who claim to accept the Bible as authoritative do not accept this command as required for Christians today. They greet one another, but not with a holy kiss. Why? Nothing in Scripture says that we can ignore what Peter and Paul wrote. There is no "Third Testament" to tell us that this part of the New Testament is obsolete. So the question remains: How can we say that the Bible is authoritative, and yet consider parts of it as not authoritative? In what way is the authority of the Bible *limited?*

Accidents of history

Christians often call the Bible the Word of God. They view it as revelation from God to humans. The writers "spoke from God" as they were "carried along by the Holy Spirit" (2 Peter 1:21). The Old Testament Scriptures were "God-breathed" (2 Timothy 3:16). The New Testament is believed to be inspired in the same as was the Old.

But the Bible is not the supreme revelation of God — Jesus Christ is. The letter to the Hebrews begins by noting that difference: "God spoke to our ancestors through the prophets at many times and in various ways, but in these last days he has spoken to us by his Son, whom he appointed heir of all things, and through whom also he made the universe" (Hebrews 1:1-2). Jesus, the Son, reveals God perfectly: "He is...the exact representation of [God's] being" (v. 3). "In Christ all the fullness of the Deity lives in bodily form" (Colossians 2:9). Jesus reveals God so well that whoever has seen Jesus has seen the Father (John 14:9).

But this supreme revelation of God came in a very specific form. His hair was a certain color, his skin was a certain color, he wore a certain style of clothes and spoke specific human languages. He was a male Jew living in

Galilee and Judea at a particular time in history. So, is this what the Father looks like? Are we to identify a particular style of clothing and language as more God-like than other styles? No, those things do not reveal God to us — they are accidents of history. In speech, dress, and personal appearance, Jesus probably looked much like Judas Iscariot — and in such incidentals, Jesus reveals no more to us about God than Judas does.

Jesus, the supreme revelation of God, came to us in a specific cultural form, and when we discuss the way in which Jesus reveals the Father, we must distinguish between form and substance, between culture and principle. Sometimes it is easy to distinguish Jesus from his culture. But in other cases, Jesus participated in his culture — he went to Jerusalem for Jewish festivals, he told someone to follow a Jewish ritual, he told Peter to pay a tax, he told stories about kings and vineyards, he ate fish and drank wine, and called God *Abba* (John 7:14; 10:22; Matthew 8:4; 17:27; Luke 24:43; Mark 14:36). Did he do these things by conviction, or by custom? Are Christians today to follow his example in these things, or do we overlook them as cultural accidents?

Jesus must be seen within his culture. We do not go to the extreme of imitating everything Jesus did, nor do we go to the other extreme of ignoring everything. We call Jesus our Lord, and we feel that we should obey his teachings, but we also make various exceptions. We do not "sell everything" and give it all to the poor (Luke 18:22). Some of Jesus' teachings were limited to a particular time and place, even a particular person. Even though Jesus has supreme authority, we filter his teachings. We want to ensure that we are responding to the right teachings, not a command intended for someone else. We want to make sure that our ladder is resting against the correct branch of the tree.

Scripture likewise limited

Jesus, the supreme revelation of God, must be interpreted with some allowance for the specifics of his culture. How much more so must the Bible, a less direct revelation! Each writing was given at a particular time and place, in a particular language with words of a particular nuance. Sometimes the text addresses one specific situation *only*. We do not need to obey all the commands God gave to Noah, or to Abraham, or to Moses, or even to Jesus' disciples or to the believers in Corinth.

The command, Bring my cloak and parchments (2 Timothy 4:13), was given to a specific person. So was the command, Use a little wine because of your stomach (1 Timothy 5:23). The same letter says, "No widow may be put on the list of widows unless she is over sixty" (v. 9). Such commands are rarely obeyed now, even by those who say they accept the Bible as authoritative.

Clearly, Scripture is not a collection of timeless truths. Although *some* of its truths are timeless, others parts of the Bible are designed for a specific situation in a specific culture, and it would be wrong for us to take them out of that context and impose them on modern situations. First-century men were advised to pray with their hands raised (1 Timothy 2:8). Slaves were advised to submit even to harsh masters (1 Peter 2:18). Virgins were advised to remain virgins (1 Corinthians 7:26). Women were told how to dress when they prayed (1 Corinthians 11:5), and men were given advice regarding hair length (v. 14). Similarly, people were told to greet one another with a kiss.

These behaviors were appropriate in first-century Mediterranean culture, but are not necessary in Western culture today. Just as the New Testament was written with Greek words, but we not have to repeat those Greek words in our worship, so also the New Testament was written with a particular culture in mind, but we do not have to repeat all the cultural details. Just as we recognize that the command to destroy mildewed houses was given to a specific people at a specific time, and does not apply to us today, we can also recognize that the command to kiss one another was also given to a specific people at a specific time, and *we* are not those people. Despite the fact that the command is given five times in the New Testament, it is not a command for us today.

The apostle Paul used one style of message in the synagogue and a different style at the Areopagus. If he could speak in our culture, he would change his style again (1 Corinthians 9:19-23). He might cite Old Testament scriptures in a different way, or different scriptures, or at least give a longer explanation of how the verse is relevant to his argument. Parables might refer to urban life more often than to agricultural customs. Advice about slavery would not be included; modern situations would be addressed. The Bible was written *in* a different culture and *for* a different culture. Its truths were given with words and styles shaped by the culture it was given in.

Now, we must also acknowledge that Scripture itself does not warn us when a culturally-specific command is being given. When we read, we do not know in advance which verses are going to be culturally conditioned, so we cannot rule out the possibility in advance. We have to consider the possibility for *all* verses. This may complicate our approach to Scripture, but it is unavoidable, for this is the way Scripture was inspired. It came with certain extraneous details, just as Jesus had certain personal details about himself that were not essential to his revealing God to us.

Of course, *everything* in Scripture had an original setting, but we do not conclude that the Bible had value *only* in its original setting. It continues to have value. Although the New Testament declares much of the Old Testament obsolete (Hebrews 8:13), it also says that the Old Testament continues to be useful for Christian doctrine and training in righteousness (2 Timothy 3:16). The NT often quotes the OT not just as a reference to ancient history, but for a principle that continues to be important for Christians. The NT is not advocating a wholesale use of old covenant laws, but it is saying that the OT has a less specific but no less important usefulness, a usefulness rooted more in principles and concepts than in specific laws or specific words.

Why have I spent so much time on the Old Testament? Because, when the NT speaks of the inspiration and authority of Scripture, it has the *Old* Testament in view. Our understanding of inspiration for both OT *and* NT is built on scriptures that are about the OT. The New Testament is inspired in the *same* way as the Old Testament. Just as with the OT, the authority of the NT is not in the specific cultural situations it happens to mention, but in the principles and concepts that lay behind the writings.

We not here attempting to show anyone *how* to distinguish cultural details from timeless truths. In some cases the difference will be obvious. In other cases it will take more work to determine whether a teaching applies in other cultures, and in some cases it will be debatable. The point we wish to make now is simply that a discrimination is necessary. There *are* obsolete instructions in the New Testament. The authority of the New Testament must be sought not in a literalistic application of every word (e.g., kiss), but in the level of principles (e.g., greet with affection).

Let me use the analogy of the ladder again. Many new Christians see that the tree is solid and well-rooted. They assume that all its branches are equally solid — even the smallest twigs — and they place their ladder against the tree without realizing that those twigs were never designed to carry such weight. Small branches may support the ladder for a while, but when a wind or an extra weight comes along, the ladder becomes unstable and possibly dangerous. Let me suggest a safer approach: New Christians need to begin at the trunk of the tree, and move out on branches only after testing them for stability. Some parts of the Bible (mildew, kisses, clothing styles) are good for decoration, as it were, but not for support. They are useful, but not always in the way we assume. They were inspired for one purpose, and we go wrong if we try to make them serve a different purpose. We need to focus on the purpose.

Authority of Scripture

So far, I have shown that Scripture has limitations, in particular the fact that it was written in and *for* other cultures. Some people use that fact to dismiss large portions of the Bible, perhaps Scripture itself. We have shown that biblical authority must be qualified in some way, but we do not jump from there into the opposite ditch, to say that it has no authority at all. We are not forced to choose between all or nothing.

Let me mention some evidence that supports biblical authority. First, Scripture itself claims to be inspired by God. Writers such as Paul claimed to write with authority derived from his commission from God. God is the ultimate authority; Scripture is a derivative authority, but an authority nonetheless because it comes from God and testifies about Christ. This is a faith claim, not a proof. There is no way to prove the Bible's authority beyond all question; not even Jesus convinced everyone.

Tradition supports biblical authority. Christians throughout the centuries have found these writings to be useful and reliable, for both faith and practice. These books tell us what sort of God we believe in, what he did for us, and how we should respond. The biblical Jesus is the only one we have; other reconstructions are based more on presuppositions than on new evidence. Tradition also tells us which books are in the Bible; we trust that God ensured that the right books were included. Since God went to the extreme of revealing himself in flesh, we believe that he would also ensure that the revelation be sufficiently preserved. This cannot be proved, but is based on our understanding of what God is doing with us.

History also shows that Scripture has been useful as a corrective to abuses within the church (for example, abuses in the Middle Ages) and within society (for example, slavery and Nazism). The fact that a moral authority is needed does not prove that the Bible *is* that authority, but history at least shows that the Bible was useful in reforming the problems, and its usefulness came because people accepted it as an authority.

Personal experience also helps us understand that the Bible has authority. This is the book that has the honesty to tell us about our own depravity, and the grace to offer us a cleansed conscience. It gives us moral strength not through rules and commands, but in an unexpected way — through grace and the ignominious death of our Lord. The Bible testifies to the love, joy and peace we may have through faith — feelings that are, just as the Bible describes, beyond our ability to put into words. This book gives us meaning and purpose in life by telling us of divine creation and redemption. These aspects of biblical authority cannot be proven to skeptics, but they help authenticate the writings that tell us these things we consider true.

The Bible does not sugar-coat its heroes, and this also helps us accept it as honest. It tells us about the failings of Abraham, Moses, David, the nation of Israel, and the twelve disciples. The Bible is a message of grace, and grace resists manipulation. Although some use Scripture as a weapon, the Bible itself gives the message that undercuts such misuse of its authority. The Bible is a word that bears witness to a more authoritative Word, the Word made flesh, and the good news of God's grace.

The Bible's complexity is impressive. It is not simplistic; it does not take the easy way out. The New Testament claims both continuity and radical discontinuity with the old covenant. It would be simpler to eliminate one or the other, but it is more thought-provoking to have both. Likewise, Jesus is presented as both human and divine, a combination that does not fit well into Hebrew, Greek or modern thought. This complexity was not created through naïveté of the philosophical problems, but in spite of them. The Bible is a challenging book, not likely to be the result of peasants attempting a fraud or trying to make sense of hallucinations.

It is evident that the disciples firmly believed Jesus to have been resurrected, and the most likely explanation for their belief is that Jesus was actually raised from the dead. (Fraud, hallucination, and mistake are other options, but all are implausible.) Jesus' resurrection then gives additional weight to the book that announces such a phenomenal event. It gives additional weight to the testimony of the disciples as to who Jesus was and to the unexpected logic of conquering death through a death.

Repeatedly, the Bible challenges our thinking about God, ourselves, life, right and wrong. It commands respect not so much through outright command, but by conveying truths to us we do not obtain elsewhere. The testimony of Scripture, of tradition, of personal experience and reason, all support the authority of the Bible — yet it is an authority given in a particular historical context. The fact that it is able to speak across cultures, to address situations that never existed when it was written, is also a testimony to its abiding authority. Its timeless truths are given to us in cultural clothes.

Bibliography

The literature on biblical authority is enormous, often technical, and often contradictory. I recommend here a few introductory books. Perhaps one of these titles will pique your interest, should you want to explore this subject a little more:

Achtemeier, Paul. *Inspiration and Authority*. Hendrickson, 1999.

Green, Joel. *Seized by Truth: Reading the Bible as Scripture.* Abingdon, 2007.

Marshall, I. Howard. *Biblical Inspiration.* Eerdmans, 1982.

McKnight, Scot, ed. *Introducing New Testament Interpretation.* Baker, 1989.

McQuilken, Robertson. *Understanding and Applying the Bible.* Moody, 1992.

Mickelsen, A.B. and A.M. Mickelsen. *Understanding Scripture.* Hendrickson, 1992.

Stott, John. *Understanding the Bible.* Zondervan, 1984, 1999.

Thompson, Alden. *Inspiration.* Review & Herald, 1991.

Wright, N.T. *Scripture and the Authority of God.* HarperOne, 2011.

Michael Morrison

SCRIPTURE: GOD'S GIFT

By Gary W. Deddo

The Christian church down through the ages has always regarded the Bible as indispensable for its worship, devotion and life. Its very existence is bound up with it. The church would not be what it is without it. Holy Scripture is part of the air it breathes and the food it eats.

I learned of the importance of the Bible as a young child and was encouraged and taught to read it and memorize it. I studied it both on my own and with others—I'm glad I did, now years later. The study of the Bible has always been an essential part of my ministry in serving others, whether it was teaching it, preaching from it, studying it with small groups of other Christians, or referring to it when counseling others.

When I attended seminary, my primary focus was the study and interpretation of Scripture. It was so important to me that I was willing to try to learn Hebrew and Greek to see if I could understand Scripture better!

Along the way, I learned that there were various ways the nature and place of Scripture was understood, and various ways to make use of it. Some of these seemed better than others, while some seemed to lead to the misuse of Scripture, or even to making it irrelevant. I read books and took courses to sort out these issues, hoping I could find some wisdom in all this – not only to help me, but to pass on to others.

Scripture is so essential to the Christian faith that most denominations have an official statement concerning the importance and place of Scripture. Grace Communion International is no exception. These summaries can be a good place to start reflection on the nature, purpose and right use of Scripture. GCI's statement is brief, to the point and fairly comprehensive:

> The Holy Scriptures are by God's grace sanctified to serve as his inspired Word and faithful witness to Jesus Christ and the gospel. They are the fully reliable record of God's revelation to humanity culminating in his self-revelation in the incarnate Son. As such, Holy Scripture is foundational to the church and infallible in all matters of faith and salvation.

Let's explore what's behind this theological summary of our understanding of Scripture. We do so not so we can enter into endless debate or prove ourselves superior to other Christians who might have a different view. And I don't think we simply want a theory about it. We seek understanding of Scripture because we highly value it and want to honor and make proper use of it. We want to handle it well so we can get the most out of it. Holy Scripture itself encourages us to do these very things. We also can recall that others in church history have benefited greatly through a deep understanding of Scripture and how to interpret it. But in the end, I think we want to grasp and use it well because we hope to get to know even better the God of the Bible in whom we put our faith.

By God's grace

Many of us have sung the childhood song that says: "Jesus loves me, this I know—for the Bible tells me so." And that's true enough. However, there's a different way to sing that verse that is also true: "Jesus loves me this I know—*so* the Bible tells me so!" This second way is reflected in the GCI statement that the Bible is God's gift to us, a gift of grace and therefore of his love. Because God loves us in and through Christ, he has graciously provided us his written Word.

God didn't have to do so, but his love for us, his creatures, has moved him to provide us with his Word in written form. God's love for us comes first, then follows his provision of the Bible. We wouldn't really be able to know and love God if God hadn't first loved us and communicated to us through his written Word. God gives us his word in Scripture because he loves us and wants us to know that he does. We should always remember that the Bible is God's gracious gift of love to us.

God continues to empower his Word

But that's not the end of it. Human words in and of themselves don't have the capacity to reveal to us the truth and reality of God. Human words are just that, human. They derive primarily from our human experiences. But God is not a creature and can't be simply grasped in creaturely terms, concepts and ideas. Words, when referring to God, don't mean exactly the same thing as when they refer to creation. So we can say we "love" and we can say God "loves." But God's love far exceeds our love. We use the same word, but we don't mean the same thing when we use it of God compared to when we use it of ourselves. Yet our love can be a dim mirror image of God's love. So God himself has to sanctify, make holy and adequate, our mere human words so we can use them to accurately and faithfully refer to the God of the Bible and not lead us into misunderstandings of God and his ways.

The God of the Bible is active and continually gracious to us by superintending our reading and interpretation of Scripture, helping us to see how they uniquely make God and his ways known to us. He has not become mute since the Bible came into existence. God continues to speak in and through his written Word, enabling it to refer to him and not just to creaturely ideas or realities. The God of the Bible continues to speak his word to us through this gift of written revelation.

If God ceased to be personally involved and stopped empowering the written word to accomplish the miraculous feat of enabling us to know him, then God would not be truly known. We would simply have human and creaturely ideas about God to consider and nothing more. The result would likely be not much better than the ancient Greek and Roman mythological gods.

Inspired by the Spirit

If we ask, "How has God spoken and made himself known to us?" it turns out that this work involves the whole of God, that is, the Father, Son and Holy Spirit. The word "inspired" means "God breathed." The Holy Spirit is identified as the wind or breath of God. By the Spirit of God, certain people down through the ages were called, appointed and specially enabled to speak authoritatively for God. They were "inbreathed" by the Spirit. *How* exactly the Spirit works we do not and cannot know. But we have been told that the Spirit can and has empowered first the prophets of the Old Testament and then the apostles of the New Testament.

The Spirit seems to take into account everything about a particular prophetic or apostolic author and graciously makes use of them. The Spirit incorporates their language, culture and social-political background as well as their own relationship with God into his communicative purposes. The Spirit uses the human elements of the selected prophets and apostles. But the Spirit uses these elements in a way that enables them to refer far beyond creaturely realities. The Spirit takes charge of them in a way that gives those words a capacity to communicate that they could never have on their own.

So by the Spirit, Scripture as a whole serves as a written form of communication that God can continually use to make himself and his ways known to his people down through the ages. If the Spirit was not at work with these individuals, we would not have any authoritative and trustworthy access to God's word. So we can thank God for choosing certain individuals down through the ages and, by his Spirit, inspiring them to speak faithfully for him.

Providential preservation

We have these written words because they have somehow been preserved for us down through the ages. This too must be regarded as the gracious work and gift of God. Because of his great love for us the God of the Bible not only kicked things off by selecting and inspiring certain individuals, but also by overseeing them being handed on and finally collected together. We call this form of God's grace his providence.

Apparently an aspect of God's providential oversight also included some inspired editing of preexisting material. God providentially maintained contact with his written word and with the process by which it was canonized (brought together in an authoritative collection). Of course if the God of the Bible wanted us to have a written witness to his Word, then we shouldn't be surprised that God would also have to anticipate and secure its preservation down through the ages (you do, after all, have to be pretty smart to be God!).

The Self-Revelation

The gracious gift of revelation as it traces through history does reach a crucial high-point. All the prophetic words prepare for and look forward to the self-revelation of God in Jesus Christ, the Incarnate Son of God. And all the apostolic writings look back to the time and place where God himself, as himself, reveals and interprets himself in and through Jesus Christ.

In Jesus, we don't have simply another inspired word about God, but the Living Word of God himself, in person—in time and space and in flesh and blood. So Jesus tells us that he is, himself, the Way, the Truth and the Life. He does not show us a way or tell us about the truth or give us things that lead to life. He himself is these things. Thus God's gracious revelatory work reaches a qualitatively different level with the birth of the Word of God in human form. And, as it turns out, the written word of God's Spirit-inspired prophets and apostles point to the fulfillment of their own word with the coming of the Living Word.

John the Baptist, as the last of the prophets and representative of them all, serves as an authoritative witness when he points to Jesus as being the Light, the Lamb of God who takes away the sins of the world, the Messiah and the Son of God (John 1:8; 29-34). John proclaimed that Jesus came before him and is the one who baptizes with the Spirit. Therefore John said he must decrease and Jesus increase, for Jesus is the center of the center of God's revelatory work and thus stands at the very center of Holy Scripture.

Faithful and infallible

The written word, derives its authority and faithfulness from the Father, through the Son and in the Spirit. Because God is the living and speaking God, we have a written word that puts us in touch with the Living Word of God, all by the Spirit. The Bible's authority is established and maintained by a living and real connection of God to the Bible. Scripture can serve as it does because it remains connected to the infallible God. The Bible's authority and faithfulness is not in itself, apart from God, but in its actual, continuing connection with the Father, Son/Word and Spirit. So when we read or listen to the Bible, we can expect to hear the living, triune God speak to us once again.

DISCERNING THE FOCUS OF SCRIPTURE

In the previous chapter, we considered how Scripture is a gift of the living and speaking God. But this gift is not one that becomes separated from the giver. By the Spirit God spoke through the prophets and then the apostles. But God continues to speak by the same Spirit through those God-breathed written words. In fact if God fell mute, and ceased to actively communicate to us in and through those written words, we would not have a true and authoritative word from God by which he makes himself known. But the living and speaking God of the Bible does not remain at a deistic distance, winding up his Bible and then sending it out to mechanistically convey information about God.

The very nature of God is to communicate himself, making himself known, so that we might communicate with him as his children and so share in holy loving communion.

One further point, made in chapter 1, confirms all this. God's personal act of communication is in and through his Son, the Living Word. The whole of the written words of the prophets and apostles direct our attention to the Living Word, Jesus the incarnate Son of God. This Jesus is God's own self-communication, his own self-revelation to us. Jesus does not give us words from God, he is himself God's Word to us. He expresses the very character of God as a speaking and communicating God. To hear Jesus is to hear God himself speaking to us, directly, in person, face-to-face.

So Jesus is at the center of the written word, Scripture. But he is behind all the words, the whole of the Bible, as its source, as the speech of God to us. He is the original Word and the final Word of God, the Alpha and Omega. In other words, by the incarnation of the Word of God the author of the written word of God has come into the play, he has shown up in the person of Jesus. And as the author, Jesus himself indicates that he is at the center and behind it all. So when the Pharisees attempt to use Scripture (and their interpretation of it against Jesus), he confronts them and says: "You search the scriptures because you think that in them you have eternal life and it is they that testify on my behalf. Yet you refuse to come to me to have life" (John 5:39-40, NRSV throughout). Jesus has to tell them that he is the author [Lord] of the Sabbath (Luke 6:5) and that they are in no place to judge him by their pre-understanding of the Sabbath. When the author of Scripture shows up, we have to stop interpreting Jesus in terms of our pre-understandings of Scripture and interpret the written words in terms of Jesus, the Living Word.

Through his interaction with the men on the road to Emmaus after his resurrection, Jesus instructs us how to approach the written word of God. To help these disciples understand who he was and what he had gone through, this is what he did: "Then beginning with Moses and all the prophets, he interpreted to them the things about himself in all the scriptures" (Luke 24:27). A bit later he explained to them: "'These are my words that I spoke to you while I was still with you—that everything written about me in the law of Moses, the prophets, and the psalms must be fulfilled.' Then he opened their minds to understand the scriptures" (Luke 24:44-45).

The written word of God is to be interpreted in the light of the Living Word, for the purpose of the written word is to direct us to the Living Word so that we might know who God is and what he has done for us. When we approach all of Scripture with Jesus himself as the interpretive key to it all, then we hear the word of God as it was meant to be heard. Thomas F. Torrance used to explain it this way: It's like reading a murder-mystery for the second time. The first time we're looking for clues as to "who-done-it." But not everything is clear. Some things make sense others don't. Some things seem significant, others seem trivial. But in a well-crafted murder mystery there will be plenty of clues—so many clues that when it finally is revealed who committed the crime, we are somewhat surprised but also satisfied that it makes sense. We say, "Yes there were clues all along. We just didn't know which ones to pay attention to and didn't see how they 'added up.'"

Now, what would happen if we were to read the murder mystery for a second time? Now knowing "who-done-it," those early clues would not be irrelevant. Rather we would see how truly significant they were. We would be able to sort out the irrelevant clues from the meaningful ones. Those clues would stand out as even more extraordinary. "No wonder suspect A said X. No wonder suspect B did Y." We would see what they mean; how they point to who committed the crime. We would end up valuing those clues as foreshadowings even more than on the first reading.

And that's much what it's like when properly reading the Bible. Knowing it all leads to what God has done in Jesus Christ, we don't set that recognition aside. Rather we interpret the whole of the written word in terms of its center, the Living Word of God. In that way, the whole of Scripture is properly interpreted; the gift of God is properly received.

Another way to say all this is that the Bible itself tells us whose Scripture this is. We know who the author is. We know where the Bible came from. It is not anonymous. So another analogy would be that reading the Bible is like reading a letter from someone you know and who knows you, not like getting junk mail from someone you don't know and who doesn't know or care about you. Reading these two types of mail are entirely different experiences, aren't they? Sometimes when I've gotten letters (or emails) from those I know well, as I read what they wrote, I can almost hear their voices. I know just how they'd say it. It sounds "just like them." Reading the Bible should be like that. The more we get to know the heart, mind, purpose and attitudes of Jesus, the more we'll hear his voice throughout all of Scripture and see how it points to him the Son, and to his mission as the self-revelation of the Father and the Spirit.

When reading and trying to understand Scripture out of the center of knowing whose scripture it is, another aspect of a proper approach becomes apparent. The primary purpose of all of Scripture is to reveal to us who this God is. That is, central to the message of all the biblical writers is to convey to us the nature, character, purpose and attitudes of our Creator and Redeemer God. They want us above all to know not just that some kind of god exists, but which God in particular and what this God is like. And they want their hearers to know who God is because the God they know wants to be known and is working though them to accomplish just that.

But the revelation that God is accomplishing is not just aimed at a kind of abstract, impersonal information. It is knowledge that reveals a God who has created us for relationship, communication and holy love. Knowing this God involves interaction of faith, trust, praise, adoration, worship and so fellowship and communion, which includes our following in his ways; that is, our obedience. And this interaction is not just a "knowing about" but a knowing in a sense similar to how we hear of Adam "knowing" Eve and so conceiving a child. By God's acts of revelation, we come to know deeply who this God really is. Love for this God, the worship of this God, trust or faith in this God are our responses to who this God is. True knowledge of God that is accurate and faithful leads to true worship and living trust in God.

Throughout the Old Testament, the most often and widely repeated description of God's nature and character is his "steadfast love." In the Psalms alone, the Lord's steadfast love is highlighted nearly 120 times. Psalm 136 uniquely proclaims God's steadfast love in the refrain of all its 26 verses. An expanded but slightly more comprehensive description found across the Old Testament echoes what the Lord revealed of himself to Moses: "The LORD, the LORD, a God merciful and gracious, slow to anger, and abounding in steadfast love and faithfulness." The Old Testament prophets constantly held out to their hearers the nature and character of God, the only one worthy of their faithfulness and worship. However, the fullness of what God's steadfast love means does not come into full view until we see it embodied and lived out in the incarnation, life, death, resurrection and ascension of Jesus with his promise to return.

Jesus himself made inquiring about and knowing who he was of paramount importance. His teachings and actions are designed to raise the question: "Who then is this?" His parables prompted his hearers to inquire more deeply. And of course, Jesus even confronts his own disciples with this question at two levels: "Who do people say that I am?" and then even more pointedly "Who do you say that I am?" (Mark 8:27, 29). Jesus himself makes the question of *Who* central. We must do the same if we are to hear the Word of God (Living and so written) as it was meant to be heard.

What is disclosed in Jesus and preserved for us in the responses of the apostles and their writings is that God is not just graciously loving towards us, but is Father, Son and Holy Spirit who have their being in triune holy loving from all eternity, before there ever was a creation. Jesus is who he is in his eternal relationship of holy love to the Father and eternal Spirit. That is the deepest level of God's self-revelation, where we discover who God is in God's inner and eternal triune life.

So we should approach our Bible study with our primary goal being listening and learning from Scripture who our triune God is as revealed to us in Jesus Christ. We can then rightly interpret Scripture out of that center. This approach means that other questions we might like to ask first, or about which we might be anxious, will be secondary. For Scripture, with Jesus at the center, not only provides us with certain answers, it tells us what the right questions are! So the questions of *What?*, *Where?*, *When?*, *Why?* or *How?* must be made relative to the question of *Who?* For it is the key to all these other questions.

We now have laid out the basic orientation for our understanding of Scripture and how best to approach it. We will consider some further implications for listening to the Word of God in the next chapter.

APPROACHING SCRIPTURE REVERENTLY WITH PRAYER BY FAITH

Since, as we have been discussing, Scripture is the gift of God, where God has graciously promised to speak to us through his living Word, what, then, are some guidelines for approaching it? I think the first thing needing to be said is that we must approach it reverently with a desire to be addressed, to hear a word from God. This attitude is probably best demonstrated when we start with prayer to God, the God of the Bible. In prayer we acknowledge that we look for and anticipate receiving a word from God himself, that is, hearing from the Living Word through the written word by the Spirit. It shows we are ready to listen, to hear. And we express in prayer that we want to hear what the Lord has to say to us. That is, we listen as his children, as his sheep, not as one of his advisers or as an engineer might seek impersonal information about some empirical object or law of physics perhaps to use for some other purpose.

In prayer, we also acknowledge that we depend upon the Lord and his grace to speak in a way that we can receive. That is, we listen by faith, as we trust that the Lord does speak and knows how to get through to us, the dumb sheep! Listening to Scripture as God's holy word is an act of faith in the God whose word it is. We read or listen to Scripture by faith in the grace of God, just as we do in every other response of ours to God. We listen and study Scripture by faith.

This means that we do not put our trust in our techniques for studying the Bible no matter how simple or how sophisticated they are. And we aren't just mining for data, for information, for formulas or principles or for truths that we can possess or use for our own ends or purposes. In prayer we place ourselves before the living Lord trusting that he will make himself known to us and enable us to hear and follow him wherever he takes us. Faithful prayer to the Living God of the Bible is essential for our preparation for listening to Scripture.

God's agenda, not ours

Second, listening to Scripture as God speaking to us means letting it set the agenda for us, according to the nature and purposes God has for giving us the gift of his word. This means that we'll come to Scripture not to give us, first, exactly what we're looking for, such as answers to our current or even pressing questions, but to show us what the right questions are and what issues have priority in God's view. We will not force Scripture to answer questions that it is not designed to answer nor give priority to some concern or issue we have that does not match with the priorities and central matters of Scripture itself. We'll be open to having our mind reshaped to reflect the mind of Christ and what he views as of first-order importance.

The primacy of the WHO? question

And what is the central thrust of biblical revelation? It is to make known the identity, character, heart, purpose and nature of God. Scripture is primarily designed to answer the question, "Who is God?" So our primary question in reading and listening to Scripture ought to be, "Who are you, Lord?" That's the first and most important question that ought to be on our hearts and minds as we study Scripture. No matter what passage we're dealing with, our primary concern ought to be: "What is God telling me about himself in this passage?"

We'll need to put in second place our questions of *What? How? Why? When?* and *Where?* In fact, these questions can only be rightly answered by putting the *Who?* question first. In many church settings the most difficult question needing to be put on the back burner is this: "What am I supposed to be doing for God?" We are so anxious to discover what God wants us to do for him that we often overlook the most foundational aspect of Scripture which involves revealing, clarifying and reminding us of God's nature, character, heart, purpose and aim. It's far more important to know *who* it is we're obeying, than to attempt to do the right thing. In fact, we can't even accurately discern *what* God wants us to do, and in what way to do it, unless we act out of knowing and trusting in this God according to *who* he is. Only then will our attitude and motives and the character of our actions match or bear witness to God's own character. Only then will we find that his commandments are not burdensome and that his yoke is easy and his burden is light. So we need to read the Bible and listen to preaching in order to see more deeply into who God is.

I should also add that the greatest and most damaging deception we can fall into is being misled about the nature and character of God. Being misled or deceived about who God is undermines our faith, which is in turn the foundation of our whole response to God. With our faith or trust in God undermined or twisted, all the rest will collapse too: our worship, our prayer, our listening to Scripture, our obedience, our hope and our love for God and for neighbor. Our faith is a response to who we perceive God to really be. When that is properly aligned, then the Christian life is enlivened and energized even under difficult situations. When it is distorted, we then attempt to run the Christian life with ropes tangled around our feet. So being reminded daily of the truth of who God is must be our top priority—matching the priority of the structure and aim of both the written and the Living Word of God.

Jesus Christ, the Center of the center

Third, as we do so, we'll have as the center and norm of our knowledge and trust in God all of what Scripture says about Jesus Christ. Oriented to this living Center of the center, we'll want to see how the Old Testament points and prepares us to recognize him. Jesus Christ is God's answer to the *Who* question—in person, in time and space, in flesh and blood—that ancient Israel sought to know. In Jesus Christ, "What you see is what you get." In him the whole God is personally present, active and speaking. Jesus is the interpretive key to all of Scripture, for in him we see and hear the heartbeat of God. We watch and hear the motions of his heart and mind, even his Spirit, the Holy Spirit. The light we find shining forth from the face of Jesus sheds light on all of Scripture, for in him the God of the whole Bible has personally revealed himself.

So we ought to read and interpret Scripture in a way that through it all, in one way or another, we come to see how it points towards and finds its fulfillment in Jesus Christ. Think of this as a process much like reading a murder mystery novel for the second time. The first time through, at the end, you finally come to discover "who done it." The second time through is a much different experience. You can see in a new light how all the clues early on in the mystery pointed to "who done it." You appreciate the clues (and recognize the false leads) even more the second time through. But the clues are not the solution. Their value is how they indicate or are signs pointing to the resolution of the mystery.

This means that central to our study and understanding of the whole Bible should be the person and acts of Jesus. This calls for giving a certain priority to and focus on the Gospels. This does not mean narrowing our attention simply to the words or teaching of Jesus, as some "red letter" Bibles might tempt us to do. Rather, this means placing at center stage all of what the Gospels tell us about who Jesus is. This will include his own words, actions and self-interpretations (think, for example, of all the "I am" statements in John), but also make use of those texts that answer most directly who Jesus is, not only in the Gospels but also throughout the rest of the New Testament.

Who Jesus is in relationship
to the Father and the Holy Spirit

As we prayerfully begin to listen to Scripture concentrating on the *Who* question as answered by God himself in Jesus, you'll find that the primary way Jesus is identified involves his relationship to God the Father and God the Holy Spirit. The answer to the *Who?* question is intrinsically bound up with grasping the nature, character, purpose and aim of Jesus *in relationship* with the Father and Spirit. For Jesus primarily and consistently identifies himself by means of those relationships. He is the one sent from the Father, the one who has been eternally with and eternally loved by the Father. He is the One who has the Spirit and who has come to give us his Holy Spirit.

The highest concentration on the importance of Jesus' relationships with the Father and Spirit comes in the Gospel of John, reaching the apex in John 17. To know Jesus is to know the Father. To know the Father means recognizing who Jesus is. Interacting with Jesus means dealing directly and personally with the Father and the Spirit.

So in our Bible study and preaching we must pay attention to the quality and nature of Jesus' relationship and interactions with the Father and Spirit. For he is, in his being, the Son of the Father, one with his Spirit. Pay special attention to anywhere in Scripture where we're given insight into the relationships of the Father, Son and Spirit. For in those relationships we will see and hear most directly, personally and concretely who the God of the Bible is. And in returning to that living Center of the center, again and again we'll find our faith nourished and growing with a life of joyful obedience flowing out of it.

With the Center of our prayer, faith, devotion and worship set, as a kind of North Star, everything else regarding listening to and studying the Lord's Scripture gets properly oriented.

RULES FOR INTERPRETING SCRIPTURE

As I said at the end of the previous chapter, "With the Center of our prayer, faith, devotion and worship set, as a kind of North Star, everything else regarding listening to and studying the Lord's Scripture then gets properly oriented." So now, let's explore some of those more general implications that can be expressed as certain kinds of rules, which keep us navigating in alignment with our North Star.

Interpret parts in light of the whole

As you know, Jesus is identified in Scripture as the First One and as the Last One. He is also identified as the living Word of God or the *Logos* of God. We could say that Jesus is and speaks both the first word to creation and is and has the last word about creation. Everything was set in motion by him and the ultimate destiny of everything is established in relationship to him, its rightful inheritor.

Perhaps we don't often think of it, but recognizing this about Jesus, our risen and ascended Lord, has implications for our hearing and studying of Scripture. In the past it has been put this way: always interpret the various parts of Scripture (verses, paragraphs, chapters, books, etc.) in terms of the whole of Scripture. No part of Scripture ought to be understood simply on its own, but only in the context of the whole. Some have said that every part of Scripture ought to be interpreted in terms of the fullness of its meaning (its *sensus plenior*).

You may have heard the good advice to not take verses "out of context." That's right. The context includes not only the verses immediately surrounding a certain text, but the chapter, the whole book in which it appears and, in the end, the whole of Scripture. Many false teachings down through the ages and even in our contemporary situation come from taking a passage out of context and then concluding what it means on its own. In reality we can then easily substitute our own context for the actual context provided for us by the whole of Scripture. Our context then becomes the interpretive North Star. So there is no substitute for taking a lifetime to study the whole of Scripture, that is, considering "the whole counsel of God."

But the whole turns out to be not just all the books and verses of the Bible. It turns out that the whole includes Who is before, behind, surrounding and standing at the end of Scripture. This whole is what the Bible says as a whole about who God is. As the *Logos* of all things, including Scripture, Jesus Christ contains it all. So the whole involves all of what we learn through the whole history of revelation preserved in Scripture. And every part must be grasped in a way that it contributes to the whole (of who God is in Christ) and how the whole includes the parts. That "rule" will help us properly hear and interpret the meaning of Scripture as we listen to its various parts, for it all comes from one and the same whole God, Father, Son and Holy Spirit. It ought to all sound like it belongs to one and the same God personally known in Jesus Christ.

Interpret the unclear in light of the clear

Another "rule" often recommended in past ages of the church that will help us stay oriented to the North Star is to "interpret unclear passages in terms of the clear." This is a good guideline. Much false teaching has derived from a fascination with the unclear, the obscure, or the opaque passages of Scripture. Teachers can take advantage of those cases because, given the ambiguity of their meaning, lots of meanings can be made to seem plausible. They're not clear enough on their own to rule out a range of speculative understandings. So someone who can give a logical argument can often be persuasive, often actually reading in their own meaning. The rule to make use of clear passages to sort through the various options for interpreting the meaning of difficult parts guards against this danger. We especially should not let the unclear passages, and some particular understanding of them, be used to reinterpret the clearer passages!

But we can take this rule a step farther. Who or what is the clearest expression of the heart, mind, will and character of God? Jesus Christ. He is the Light of all light. All Scripture, in the end, should be understood in his clear Light. He alone shows us the face of God in person.

Let's look at an example. The Pharisees of New Testament times had an understanding of God's Law, the Torah. When Jesus came along they accused him of violating what they considered the highest priority of that Law, namely the keeping of the Sabbath. And they had worked out logically what must be implied in keeping the Sabbath. They interpreted Jesus and his actions in terms of their pre-understanding of the Law of God. How did Jesus respond to their accusations? Did he simply say, "I came to give you another interpretation of how the Law should be applied"? No, he said, "For the Son of Man is Lord of the Sabbath" (Matthew 12:8). The Pharisees gave priority to their understanding of the Law, and interpreted Jesus in terms of it. But Jesus countered by telling them who he was in relationship to the Law and so said, "I created the Law, I gave it its meaning, I know how it is to be honored and when it is being violated. Interpret the Law in terms of me, its Lord, not me in terms of the Law. It is my servant. I am not its servant, to be judged by it."

So Jesus puts the Pharisees at a crisis point. Will they recognize Jesus as the Living Lord, the Lord of the Law or will they continue to use the Law as "lord" to interpret and judge Jesus? What or who is the whole and what or who is the part? What or who is the clear and what is relatively obscure? We may not regard the Law as the Pharisees did, but we may have other truths or attitudes or viewpoints that we assume and use to interpret or understand Jesus and who God is. Recognizing Jesus as the Center of the center will challenge us to view everything in terms of his interpretation of things, in his light.

We can sum up: we interpret the parts in terms of the whole and the unclear in terms of the clear, and all in terms of Jesus Christ!

Interpret the Old Testament in light of the New

Another implication that has been identified in the past is to interpret the Old Testament in terms of the New Testament. This too is a good "rule" we can follow and further expand. Jesus is the fulfillment of the revelation and provision of God. That is, he is the self-revelation and the self-giving of God for us and for our salvation. He fulfills all the promises of God set up and signaled in the Old Testament. The promises are to be understood in terms of the fulfillment, not the other way around.

But the Old Testament is about more than the promises themselves. It involves an ongoing relationship and interaction of God with Israel over roughly a thousand years, including interaction with numerous prophets at various points in the history of that relationship. God was taking Israel somewhere and Israel knew it. God had not given them the final word. They looked forward to having his Spirit poured out on all flesh (Joel 2:28) being given to reignite life in the dry bones (Ezekiel 37:5) and having new hearts (Ezekiel 11:19; 36:26). They looked forward to the time of God's peace or shalom when they wouldn't have to prepare for war anymore and not have blood on their hands (Isiah 2:4; Joel 3:10; Micah 4:3). They anticipated the completion of the sacrificial worship where they could be in the very presence of the living God and then truly live! The Old Testament revelation included the proclamation that there was much more to come, that God was not finished making himself known and providing everything for them. Even at the conclusion of the last words of the prophets, they knew they were not at the end of the story. The climax had not yet been reached.

The fact that God's revelation involves a history of interacting with Israel and speaking through selected prophets means that we should interpret any passage in terms of where it comes in the story as it leads up to or down from God's self-revelation and self-giving in Jesus Christ. This rule of interpretation is especially important for particular ethical or liturgical directives given to ancient Israel. What God commands of Israel in a particular instance is not God's final or eternal word.

For instance while the "eye for an eye and tooth for a tooth" saying was far more compassionate than the code of revenge practiced by the surrounding ancient near eastern cultures of the time, it was not God's final word to his people. Rather, the final word is embodied in Christ who loved his enemies to the end and directed us to do the same. So interpretation should take into account where in the story we find the actions, attitude or instructions given. God fills out and clarifies his revelation through a history of interaction with his people, so not every word in the Bible is God's last word on the subject. Providentially, there are many places in the New Testament where significant change or discontinuity, is explicitly spelled out, such as keeping of the Sabbath.

This does not mean that everything said in the Old Testament will necessarily be radically reinterpreted later on. Some insight or instruction may remain largely unchanged, such as principles we identify as broad moral instructions that are linked to our human nature and take into consideration our fallen condition. About rather permanent and universal features of humanity such as marriage, sexual morality and the relations of parents and children that abide throughout history and across differing cultural contexts, we would expect significant continuity of teaching. The New Testament often does spell out particular continuities and redemptive development of expression.

Even if there are some practical or particular differences, at the level of fundamental principles that reflect God's character we should expect to see some continuity between earlier and later application of that same principle in the New Testament. There seems to be a redemptive development in the way God's more general purposes are to be applied in the life of the church after the fulfillment of God's will is accomplished in Christ as compared to before this fulfillment. An example would be that although Israel is directed at times to go to war, she was instructed not to be vengeful and to look forward to a time when her swords would be beaten into plowshares. The Christian church is called to continue along that trajectory to finally be peacemakers and to not regard any human being as their ultimate enemy, but rather forgive and seek reconciliation and restoration.

The issue of slavery seems to fall along the same lines. What was allowed to Israel is no longer to characterize the Christian church. So Paul directed Philemon to emancipate his slave Onesimus (Philemon 16-17). Slavery is a practice that was "passing away." So such instructions as were given Israel cannot be directly picked up by the church now with no regard for our occupying a different place in the story than was ancient Israel. The God of the Bible is a God of life, not death; a God of freedom, not slavery; a God of love, reconciliation and redemption and not enmity and revenge. While we certainly can find signs of these characteristics in the Old Testament, at times some significant ambiguity appears along the way in God's history of interaction with Israel. We now, however, live to bear witness to the clear and complete fulfillment of God's Word in Christ, not to its foreshadowing and preparation. In this way, we interpret the Old Testament in terms of the New.

There we have several guidelines for properly interpreting Scripture with Jesus Christ the Living Word at the center of the Written Word. In the next two chapters we'll continue to offer some more guidelines to help us stay oriented to our North Star.

REALITY AND
THE MEANING OF SCRIPTURE

This chapter covers several more aspects of listening to, studying and interpreting Scripture that honors its God-given nature and purpose. As we examine these, perhaps we'll find some bad habits that need to be unlearned.

Discovering the meaning that is there

Often when we hear Scripture read or preached or study it for ourselves, we approach it thinking we're going to "try to make sense of it." But I don't think that's really the best way to put it. Rather, we come to realize that as God speaks to us in Scripture it reads us, it makes sense of us! God's Word sheds light on our lives. God's Word is living and active and not a passive collection of data that we probe, organize, arrange and apply and then announce what *we've* made of it. Rather, as we listen to Scripture, we are acted upon by the Word and the Spirit. It comes with its own meaning and sense. So, we don't give it meaning and make sense of it. We *discover* its meaning and sense.

Listening to and studying Scripture is a matter of discovery, not creativity, innovation or theorizing. So hearing Scripture in a way that fosters faith calls for a receptiveness on our part, allowing it to tell us. We do not sit in critical judgment upon it, deciding ahead of time what we will or won't hear or whether we will or won't live by it. St. Augustine long ago realized there was a huge difference in approaching Scripture as *users* compared to being *receivers* who are prepared to enjoy and live under the Word we hear. He advised, just like the book of James does, that we take the posture of hearers of the Word of God, receiving and even delighting in it.

Receptivity, the proper subjectivity

We don't have to guess or sort through a lot of hypothetical options to discover what particular attitude of receptivity we should have towards God's Word. First, Jesus, in his own responsiveness to his Father and the Spirit, demonstrates the proper personal and internal (subjective) orientation we are to have to the Word. Second, the apostles whom Jesus chose, including Paul, embodied the spirit of responsiveness that reflected Jesus' own receptivity. These apostles were not chosen merely because they could be relied upon to convey accurate information (facts). They were appointed because they had the right kind of receptivity (subjective orientation) to the truth that they were given. If we are to hear the Word of God, we must stand in their place, taking up their attitude of receptivity. We have to have ears to hear in order to grasp what they are saying—to hear what they heard.

Often we think that the biblical revelation given to us by its authors is simply a collection of data, information that sits objectively there on the page, neutrally and in that sense objectively (we say). We then take over that "data," mining it for ourselves with whatever subjective orientation we please, including the attempt to rid ourselves of any subjective element at all. But the biblical preservers of revelation do not simply offer objective information that we then decide how or whether to appropriate or receive. No, the biblical revelation includes the revelation of the nature of its own proper receptivity, its own orientation and attitude. And that subjective aspect is embodied in Jesus and his apostles and is also conveyed in their preserved writings. Revelation as revelation cannot be gained apart from this particular kind of receptivity because it is included in it.

And this subjective orientation is not neutral or abstractly objective. The receptive orientation of the biblical writers is one of trust, readiness to repent, a desire for reconciliation and confidence in the power and faithfulness of God to redeem, renew and put right all things. Revelation itself includes both objective and subjective elements perfectly coordinated with each other. How the revelation is received is perfectly harmonized with what is revealed. In fact, the revelation cannot be grasped at all except in and through that particular subjective orientation. God does not approach us neutrally, but passionately and redemptively. So we cannot approach God neutrally and dispassionately if we are to really receive the content and benefits of his revealed redemption. And that receptivity which is resident in Jesus and resonant in the apostles is given to us as a gift of the Spirit so that we might receive the revelation of God that the apostles of Jesus Christ passed on to the whole church for all time.

The false objectivity of abstract thinking

So much of the information we get, some of which is called scientific, is abstract. It is disconnected from the source of the information, from the object being investigated. Such input can seem to be simply words, concepts, ideas, principles or numbers and mathematical formulas. Sometimes the information comes to us as a line of argument made up of a chain of logical connections. To use an analogy, it would be like studying the wake made by a boat that has long since passed by, but not learning much about the boat itself—which is really what we want to know. Such information rarely helps us relate to or interact with the object, the reality itself, since it's only indirectly connected to it. We're looking at the effects of something, not the source or cause of the effects.

Often in Christian teaching we're led to consider evidences of something (the wake, the effects) but aren't directed to think about the reality itself (the boat, cause or source of the effects). For example we might be presented evidences for the empty tomb, or for the possibility of Jesus' miracles, but not give much consideration to Jesus himself. Following that path we may learn something *about* him, but we don't get to know Jesus *himself*.

This rather abstract approach is often what we get from "experts." Sometimes we are impressed by the knowledge and insight they impart. But at other times, their abstract information and principles annoy us and leave us cold. It can seem that such information has nothing practical to do with life. We suspect that what they are sharing is the product of overactive minds fueled by over-sized egos!

Though not always, this abstract approach is often characteristic of theological or philosophical thinking, which provides *ideas* or *concepts* about God. Doctrine then becomes a mere collection of ideas or concepts to believe in (or not!). This reduces Christianity to merely understanding Christian ideas—ideas undoubtedly derived from the Bible. But this abstracting and conceptualizing approach sets us up for the disaster that is common in modernity and postmodernity (two periods now existing side-by-side). The modern mindset tends to regard faith as bias that distorts any true knowledge of the reality. The postmodern mindset tends to see faith, like all forms of knowing, as governed by personal/subjective factors (such as race, gender, class, etc.). With this postmodern perspective, all knowing collapses into self-knowing, agnosticism or, more often, a knowledge controlled by the will-to-power.

A biblically-formed mindset acknowledges these barriers to knowing truth, including knowing God. From the biblical perspective, we fallen humans are seen as idolaters who create gods in our own image in order to justify ourselves and our own kind. The prophets of Israel spoke out against this idolatry, which is our attempt to recreate God in our own image or images that we can control and use. The golden calf in Moses' time is an example. All of Scripture teaches that God cannot be found by sheer human effort and that we will only end up deluded by the results of such misguided efforts. Jesus declared, "No one knows the Son except the Father, and no one knows the Father except the Son" (Matthew 11:27). As the early church used to put it: "Only God knows God." But that does not mean God cannot be known, for it does not rule out God's being smart and motivated enough to figure out how to make himself known. So the early church saying went on: "And only God reveals God." And that is what Jesus goes on to say,

"…and those to whom the Son chooses to reveal him."

The God of the Bible can and wants to make himself known. He's the Good Shepherd who knows how to get through to the dumb sheep. God's act of self-revelation is required if we are to know God himself, personally and deeply (*epignosis* is the Greek word used in the New Testament, parallel to Adam "knowing" his wife Eve).

Revelation, especially the *self*-revelation of God in Christ, that was borne witness to by Jesus' personally selected apostles and the working of the Spirit, can't be approached in either the modern or postmodern way, by either eliminating the subjective element or declaring that it always in every case hides or distorts the truth. Knowing God in his act of self-revelation calls for a particular subjective orientation that correlates with the nature and purpose of the revelation, namely being reconciled to God. It calls for humility and a mustard seed's worth of faith/trust to get the ball rolling. We have to be willing to orient our ways of knowing, both its objective and subjective elements, to the nature of the revelation. Knowing God calls for a readiness to repent and a desire to be reconciled to God. God's self-revelation rules out the twin errors of either attempting to remove all subjectivity (a false objectivity) or assuming that any subjective stance we might prefer would suffice (a false subjectivity).

Listening in this way to the Living Word through the Written Word by the Spirit puts us into contact with the reality itself, with the living God. In and through Scripture, with Christ at the center, we're not being given information *about* God, but hearing a Word *from* God who makes himself known as Lord and Savior through the medium of those witnesses preserved for us. If we approach Scripture as simply a set of concepts, ideas or principles about God and his ways, we will be missing the boat! Scripture, by the Word and Spirit, does not primarily enable us to know *about* God or his will for us, but to know God, *himself*, in person. That is the case because God is a Living God and a speaking God and has not become mute since the days of Jesus. Listening to and studying Scripture with humility and trust/faith in the God of the Bible is a vital aspect of our living in actual relationship, communication, and communion with God. If we miss this we miss receiving the gift of God.

Taking the Bible realistically

Now some in the church and its various seminaries have attempted to correct such an abstract approach to the Bible by emphasizing that we take the Bible "literally." Their aim is to achieve a more "objective" approach. Others have recommended that we fix the problem on the subjective side of things by taking Scripture more seriously, more imaginatively, in a more narrative way. Or those seeing the problem on the subjective side might gravitate toward interpreting it more ethically (either personally or socio-politically), more pragmatically or with greater conviction, courage and commitment. While well-intentioned, these commendations seem to me to fall short of what is hoped for and don't align as closely with the actual nature and character of God's Word as we might think.

There are other theologians, most notably Thomas F. Torrance, who said what is needed is that we take the Bible *realistically*. When we listen to or study Scripture we are hearing from those who, by the inspiration of the Spirit of Jesus, are telling us about the *reality* of who God is and what God has done, is doing and will do. Scripture tells us about the nature of reality, reality we *can* have contact with and can access, for example creation, and also reality that we ourselves *cannot* directly access but that can contact us, e.g. the Living Word by the Spirit. The words of Scripture, then, point to, inform us and put us into contact with the reality of who God is and who we are in relationship to him and to creation. By them the Living God tells us what is the real situation. In listening to Scripture we are getting to know God *himself* because God is able to use, by the Spirit, the created medium of divinely appointed human communication to speak again to us through it. When interacting with Scripture, we're dealing with the "boat" itself, not the wake it leaves behind.

So the question we ought to ask in reading any text of Scripture is this: "What reality is this passage telling me about?" This ought to be the central and controlling question whether it's a historical event or a didactic teaching, a narrative or parable, a simile, a metaphor or symbol, a historical person or a hypothetical and representative character. Of every passage we need to ask these questions: What am I being told about the nature of reality, of God, of human nature, of our relationship with God, of right relationship with each other? Of course by "reality" we do not mean simply that which human creatures can see, taste, touch, measure, weigh and calculate. Those features only have to do with empirical realities, part of what we call *nature* considered as causal and mechanical and impersonal things. But Scripture puts us in touch with realities that cannot be investigated by empirical means. The most important reality is the nature, character and reality of God the Father and God the Holy Spirit and what he has done for us in Jesus. These are not natural or earthly realities at all. The Living and Speaking God continues to reveal the true nature of these realities through his Written Word with the Living Word as its center.

Faith comes by hearing

How do we discover these, to us, invisible realities if we can't see them, touch them, weigh them or experiment with them? The answer is that we *hear* about them from reliable, personal sources or authorities. We encounter their objective reality through being told about them by those who know. We can know about things we cannot empirically explore by being told about them. By having ears to hear we can *see* with spiritual eyes (the eyes of our heart; Ephesians 1:18, Acts 26:18). Jesus' eternal relationship with the Father and the Spirit is an example of such a reality. Other examples are the prophetic words from Jesus and his apostles about God's future intentions for his creation, namely, that God will give us a renewed heavens and earth and that every tear will be wiped away by God's final restorative working. By means of hearing from those who know, we can know and also interact with creaturely and divine realities that cannot be seen and cannot be empirically discovered. Speaking and hearing can be an objective event that conveys to us and thus puts us into contact with a divine transcendent reality. By the Spirit, this encounter corrects our wrong notions and arrogant attitudes. We can know, love, trust, obey and pray to God himself, who speaks an objective word to us in and through his Word.

So we listen to Scripture as a way of getting to know and interact with divine and creaturely reality, not just to have correct truths, ideas, concepts, ideals or doctrines. By hearing we come into contact with the truth and reality of who God is and who we are and discover the true nature of created things. Taking all of Scripture realistically tells us who and how things really were, are and will be.

The meaning of Scripture

Another connection that probably needs to be made, although it perhaps sounds self-evident when articulated, is that what the Bible means is the reality to which it refers. The words of the Bible point beyond themselves by referring to and, by the Spirit, disclosing to us the reality itself, e.g. who God is. The words of the Bible have their significance (they signify or point to) actual realities. So when we take Holy Scripture realistically we are in fact asking after the meaning and significance of the words. The words don't refer to or mean other words or ideas. The words refer beyond themselves and indicate realities that are far greater than the words themselves. The realities cannot be reduced to the words, but faithful and accurate words authorized by God through the Spirit can indeed put us in actual contact with the reality. We want to know what realities the words point to, for that reality is their meaning. We are not attempting to find or create or give meaning to Scripture or make the Bible meaningful to us or others. Rather, we're discovering the meaning and significance it already has as we recognize the realities to which the words point and, by the Spirit, put us into contact with. That's what God's revelation intends to do and can do, that is its meaning.

Meaning beyond the words through the words

An implication of Scripture's meaning is that the fullness, meaning and significance of the reality exceed the words used to point to it. Even words that are indispensable for discovering and relating to the reality, like biblical revelation, can never substitute for the reality itself. The reality of God especially cannot be reduced to words, even biblical words. But those inspired words are not arbitrary or dispensable. They are the gift of God, the God-given means empowered by the Spirit to refer us to and reveal those realities. The Bible is like an absolutely unique and authoritative map that is essential to guiding us to our destination—which is not a point on the map itself, but an actual location in reality. So the meaning of the texts will always be found beyond the words themselves, although never discovered in any authoritative way except in and through the words spoken to us. That is why Scripture is indispensable to the Christian church, though we don't worship the Bible. We don't pray to the Bible and we don't believe that the Bible will, on the last day, raise us from the dead. The object of our worship, love and faith is not the Bible, but the God who speaks to us uniquely through his written Word.

Our own words (in writing, preaching and teaching), including our doctrines, ought to be evaluated by how well they point to the same reality that Scripture itself points to. And we don't want to be drawn into arguments about our words or those used by others. Rather, we listen for their meaning—the reality to which they point—realizing that words fall short of the transcendent and divine reality itself. We look for the most faithful words we can find, often with the help of others, in faith hoping to add our non-authoritative witness and testimony to the reality that the words of Scripture point to authoritatively.

These points about reality and the meaning of Scripture are large overarching concerns. But if Scripture is taken to offer simply concepts or ideas about God, or if we think our job is to make sense of it, or think the meaning of the words of Scripture are simply other words or ideas, we'll go off in an unhelpful and confusing direction that will not easily contribute to our faith relationship with its Giver.

There are still a few more detailed, nitty-gritty suggestions we can touch on to wrap up this series on listening to and studying Scripture. We'll take them up in the next chapter.

CONCLUDING PRINCIPLES

We conclude this series with several principles that help us interpret Scripture in ways that honor its God-given nature and purpose.

The written form of biblical texts

God's gift comes to us in the form of writings that were preserved down through the ages in the form of written texts in human languages. To honor Scripture is to honor the *form* in which is it given to us not just the content. Thus to pay careful attention to the Bible, we have to take into consideration its historical, linguistic and literary forms. Our methods have to be able to attune us to the communication offered in those forms. But the methods used to engage the forms of communication cannot be allowed to take over and determine what we are able or are allowed to hear. That's how modern biblical studies and criticism have often gone wrong. However, we can selectively use methods attuned to the form of Scripture in ways that enable us to hear the words as references to the realities that disclose to us its meaning and significance. Methods that impose their own meanings and significance must be set aside; otherwise we are granting them final authority over Scripture, placing our ultimate trust in them and not in the living Word of God.

What are some implications of recognizing the importance of the form of biblical revelation? First, a knowledge of the biblical languages can be helpful for those translating it into other languages (missionary translators), for those translating it into other historical-cultural contexts (pastors and teachers) and for those who equip others to communicate the biblical message and meaning. A familiarity with the customs, the culture, the time period of history and the original audience addressed at the time the various texts were written is also useful. A grasp of the various literary forms used and how they function as means of communication (e.g. history, wisdom literature, letters, gospels, apocalyptic etc.) also helps us better listen to God's Word. Much of scholarship is devoted to these elements of biblical studies. There are a number of good books that assist us in discerning the genre of the various biblical writings and how to approach them.

Methods must serve the message and meaning of the texts

However, the methods have to always be in service of and subservient to the message and the meaning (realities to which they refer) of the biblical revelation. Whatever methods we use should not: 1) impede our hearing the

message or 2) call into question the ʳ
realities or 3) impose their own philⁱ
can expect to know or hear before ʳ
sense of objectivity (which promotⁱ
between us and the object of revⁱ

Those methods that do so
repented of. For in those case
primary object of trust, the aⁱ
assumptions about reality. They wiⁱⁱ,
reality and therefore serve as conceptual idoⁱₛ
lords over the Word of God.

And they may do this all under the cover of our assumeᵈ ₁
have and need for "knowing good and evil." (Just what the serpenₜ ⸱
Adam and Eve to think they needed.) But such dangers need not rule ouₜ ⸱
proper use of methods that are ordered to the nature and ends of the good
gift of Scripture. We honor the creaturely form of Scripture when our
methods correspond to it rather than rule over it. And such methods will pay
careful attention to the genre of the various biblical texts as well as the
language and historical and cultural background. A resource such as the *IVP
Bible Background Commentary* provides such information to assist anyone on
any passage of Scripture.

Whole literary units

Another simple implication is that the form of biblical revelation is for
the most part conveyed to us as whole literary pieces. The books of the Bible
were written, collected and arranged as whole pieces. Thus, harkening back
to what we said about interpreting the parts in terms of the whole and the
whole as made up of all the parts, we should always consider the whole of
the literary unit in which Scripture was written and preserved for us to
ascertain the meaning and significance of the various sub-units within.

Individual passages or even chapters should be interpreted in the light of
the whole book and the location and order in which each verse, paragraph or
section appears in the book. Failing to do so takes the parts out of context
and does not honor the coherent form in which God has given and preserved
his written word for us. On any topic, every book of the Bible must be taken
into consideration along with its particular location in the history of God's
revelation and in relation to its revelatory center in Jesus Christ. But that
process must start by studying the biblical books as whole units written or
collected and arranged as wholes. In that way we have many pointers, some
clearer than others, guiding us to know and properly relate to the realities that

disclose to us.

grace are the foundation
ratives of grace

ome alert to another bad habit that somehow has sneaked into interpretation that could use some corrective attention. We are er conviction that the Bible is primarily there to tell us what to do or how to do certain things for God. This is especially true for those have already become believing people, members of a church. This pull being obligated to do things for God becomes so strong that often we are rawn into bad habits of biblical interpretation. We end up not really hearing the Word and inadvertently distort what we hear. We end up thinking God is essentially a taskmaster and we are his slaves or worker-bees!

The problem arises when we take something that is simply declared to us so that we might trust in its truth and reality and then turn it into something we are to do, or accomplish or somehow make actual or real. In shorthand and using the terms of grammar, we turn *indicatives* of grace into *imperatives* (commands) of works.

For example, in the Beatitudes in Jesus' Sermon on the Mount (Matthew 5), we turn the indicatives that tell us that God has blessed certain folks (the poor in spirit, the meek, those who thirst for righteousness and those who are peacemakers) into commands telling us to try harder to become these things. But Jesus was not using imperatives to command his listeners to work harder at to do or become those things. Rather, he was indicating what God already has done in blessing his people. God blessed some listening to Jesus right then and there. Jesus was then inviting them (and us!) to recognize and marvel at what God had done by his Spirit in his people.

A little later in the Sermon, Jesus does give a command—he issues an unconditional imperative at the end of the Beatitudes: "Rejoice and be glad!" Yes that's what we are obligated to do for God! And why? Jesus tells us: because God has blessed his people so that some are meek, some are longing for righteousness, some are peacemakers. God is a blessing God…rejoice and be glad! But when the indicatives of this passage are twisted into imperatives, by the time we get to the actual imperative in the sermon, we're too burdened down with guilt to even hear Jesus' command. Or if we do hear, we don't obey. "Right," we say, "rejoice and be glad. No way! He can't be serious after haranguing us like that—disappointed that we're not doing all that we're supposed to do." When we follow that faulty line of reasoning, taking what we think might be the "harder road," we've dismissed the truth of Jesus' message about the blessings of God and missed the actual response he intends to elicit from us!

The Ten Commandments in perspective

I could multiply examples where people take a description in Scripture of what God has done or what he can be trusted for and convert that description (indicative) into an obligation or a command (imperative). This mistake comes from our anxiety to do things for God. The supposed commands are seen as conditions for getting God's approval or his blessing. But as you study Scripture, look to see if it isn't the case that underneath or behind every command there isn't some indication of who God is or what God can be trusted for, which supplies the very foundation and motive for those commands that are given. God does not need to be conditioned to be faithful to himself and his promises to us.

Let me give one more example. Let's go back to the Old Testament to the Ten Commandments given to Israel. Notice that it is not given until 430 years after God established his covenant with Abraham. It amounted to a promise: "I will be your God and you shall be my people." "Through you all the nations of the earth shall be blessed." But even Exodus chapter 20 does not begin with "Thou shalt nots." Note verse two: "I am the Lord your God who brought you out of Egypt, out of the land of slavery." This verse indicates who God is and what he can be trusted for. It points out that the God who commands is the kind of God who rescues, redeems, sets free, delivers and saves! Why would Israel have an interest in other gods? Did the frog god do such for them? Did the fly god? The Nile river god? The cow god? The sun god? No, all the gods of Egypt became curses and led to death, not life.

As long as Israel trusted their God to be true to his character as revealed and indicated in the great Exodus, they would not even be tempted to turn to these idols, much less make images of them! Who God is in his nature and character is the foundation and the freedom for obeying his commands that follow. When this God is obeyed by faith in his character as revealed in his acts of deliverance, his commands are easy to obey. They are difficult and perhaps impossible to obey only if and when we don't trust God to be true to his character, the same character we see revealed supremely and in person in Jesus Christ our Ultimate Deliverer.

Look for the indicatives of grace
upholding every command of grace

So the simple interpretive rule here is: always interpret the commands of God in terms of indicatives of God's grace and faithful character. Never grab a command apart from its foundation on the indicatives that reveal and remind us who God is. Whenever you find a command, stop and find the indicative of grace upon which it rests and then interpret them together. It should be somewhere nearby, either before or after the command. It might be the whole first half of the book, like Romans where chapters one through eleven lay out the grace of God and chapters 12-16 present the proper response to that grace. And certainly don't turn the indicatives of grace into an obligation of works. Doing so violates the form (grammar, in this case) and meaning of the words of Scripture. Don't let your guilt, fears and anxieties tempt you to turn a truth about God into an obligation to be laid on yourself or others.

Where do warnings come from?

Another bad habit I have run into and been guilty of myself in years past regards how we interpret the warnings in Scripture. For some reason, I don't know why, when reading the warnings in the Bible many have the habit of thinking that it indicates that God has a mean streak (should I say "spirit"?) and wants the horrible outcome spoken of to come to pass. So we might be tempted to think that Jesus wants and delights in sending away those not prepared for the wedding feast, or that he wants the rich man who mistreated Lazarus to suffer eternally, etc. After reading a warning we often conclude, "See, we knew there was a dark and unforgiving side of God—look at that warning right there in Scripture! He delights just as much in punishing, rejecting and being wrathful as in saving, reconciling and restoring."

But what is the meaning, the reality of these warnings? How should we interpret them in the context of all of Scripture and in light of the character of God revealed in our Lord and Savior Jesus Christ? First off, warnings are not the first word God gives. Warnings come as the last word offered to those who reject all the other words of promise and blessing that call for complete trust in and worship of God alone. And they are mostly directed at self-righteous and haughty religious people, not those who are unbelieving and not a part of the community of worshippers.

And then, what is the purpose or aim of a warning and why would someone give a warning? The purpose is to prevent the outcome pictured from happening! It is not given to assure that it does happen. It is given because the outcome is not wanted, is not desired but to be averted. It is given to help the very one being warned of the danger. Warnings are a sign of love, not rejection. Perhaps it is the last sign given, but nevertheless still one of love. If God didn't care or wanted the anticipated negative outcome to occur, there would no reason for him to issue a warning at all. Why even bother! But, no, warnings are the last words of love to prevent the potential outcome.

Other biblical teaching tells us that God does not delight in the punishment of the wicked (Ezekiel 33:11) and he wants no one to perish but to turn and repent (2 Peter 3:9). Jesus' own explanation that he came not to condemn the world but to save it (John 3:14-18) backs up this understanding of biblical warnings. We have Scripture that tells us in no uncertain terms how God regards the unbeliever, the unrepentant ones. God does not take delight in seeing his good creation come to ruin. Warnings are expressions of love when nothing else has worked. They are not threats God can't wait to carry out. So we ought to interpret biblical warnings in terms of the character of God shown in Christ and according to the purpose of warnings meant to prevent the potential disastrous outcome to those God loves.

Interpret deeds in the light of the interpretive words

And finally one last bad habit of interpretation to consider. In listening to and studying Scripture we can fall into the trap of interpreting an action of God or of God's people apart from the accompanying words that indicate its meaning. The revelation of God involves a Word-Deed event. Certainly, God does things and has his people do certain things. But the deeds cannot be understood apart from the word given that interprets it. Deeds do not interpret themselves.

The significance and meaning of a particular deed is revealed through words that explain what was behind that action. But often we read of God doing something, especially in the Old Testament but sometimes in the New, and immediately react and draw conclusions about what that deed must say about God or his purposes or mind. For example, we read that the Egyptians drowned in the Red Sea or that God hardened Pharaoh's heart. Or we read of Jesus driving out the money-changers from the temple, or cursing the fig tree, or warning those who have not repented, or instructing the disciples to shake the dust off their feet from those villages that refuse to welcome them. Instead of looking for the prophetic and apostolic interpretation of these deeds—seeking to understand what they point to and how they are fulfilled and perfected (brought to their right and true end or purpose)—we interpret them in the context of what we might mean if we were to do these things today (or perhaps what the worst and meanest person we can think of might mean by it!).

In making this mistake, we are substituting our imagined context for the biblical context and explanation. Although sometimes it's not obvious in every text, when the whole picture is assembled we find that the ultimate purpose of the text is redemption, reconciliation, deliverance—the salvation that is fulfilled in Jesus. Deciding on what a deed of God or his people means apart from God's character and words that interpret such deeds is another way of taking Scripture out of context—it is the grasping of an individual part that is disconnected from the whole. Deeds must never be understood apart from their revealed explanations.

While there are other words surrounding and interpreting for us those deeds mentioned above, I want to conclude by reminding us that Jesus Christ himself is the final Deed and Word of God. Jesus had to interpret his deeds even to his own disciples for them to know what they meant. This is especially true of the saving significance of his death and the hope of the resurrection. Without hearing his spoken words we would not know the meaning of his actions. Both must be taken together.

Jesus, God's final Word and deed

In fact, all the deeds of God in the Bible and other prophetic words should be interpreted in terms of who Jesus is, the Final Word-Deed. The Exodus and Pharaoh must be interpreted in terms of Jesus and his revelation of the heart and mind of God toward all his human creatures. He embodies and explains his very purpose to save. As the Son of God and the Son of Man he worked out that purpose by assuming our human nature as the second Adam and becoming the new head of the race.

So even Jesus' own deeds must be interpreted in terms of his own words, not in terms of our own words/thoughts/imaginations. In other words, all his deeds or work must be interpreted in the light of his person—in the light of who Jesus is. Said another way, we must interpret his works in terms of his person. And who is Jesus in his being and nature? He is the Son of the Father, our Savior, Redeemer and Reconciler. That's what the name Jesus means—the name given to him by his heavenly Father. All of Jesus' deeds indicate who he is as the eternal Son of the Father, become our Brother, Lord and Servant King in order to make us his beloved children. As God's final word and deed, Jesus is the key to interpreting every word and deed in Scripture—the written word belongs to Jesus and comes from him, God's

Living Word to us.

This is exactly what was occurring when Jesus stayed with those he met on the road to Emmaus following his resurrection: "And beginning with Moses and all the Prophets, he interpreted to them in all the Scriptures the things concerning himself" (Luke 24:27 *ESV*). You'll also recall Jesus' admonition to the Pharisees: "You search the Scriptures because you think that in them you have eternal life; and it is they that bear witness about me; yet you refuse to come to me that you may have life" (John 5:39-40 *ESV*).

Interpretation of Scripture is the church's responsibility

There is one last word to consider before we end this series. The task of interpreting Scripture is not the responsibility of isolated individuals but the task of the whole church, involving its various members with their gifts and callings, including those gifted as teachers and preachers. Proper interpretation of Scripture takes account of how particular passages of Scripture have been understood by many down through the history of the church and into our own times. We'll want to pay more attention to those teachers and interpreters who follow the kind of guidelines we have laid out in this series.

In presenting this series, I am indebted to many who have gone before me. I have not footnoted these references, but I could have. It is good to consult others before we make final determinations of what a given passage of Scripture means or what a collection of Scriptures add up to mean. We should look for precedents—paying attention to those who have been called by God to assist the church in listening to and understanding Scripture. We ought to be skeptical about esoteric interpretations that have little or no continuity with what the orthodox church as a whole has historically understood. This does not mean that deeper understanding could not be obtained as we stand on the shoulders of those who have gone before. But that understanding should be deeper and fuller than what has gone before, not a departure or wholesale discount of it.

God has many laborers working by faith to understand Scripture. We must not be so arrogant as to think that we alone, individually, can have an independent and final say. While the approach advocated in this series will not guarantee uniformity of interpretation throughout the church, it will help us avoid falling into traps, especially those already identified centuries ago! God gives his Word and his Spirit to the Church as a whole. We must not despise others who approach it with the same honor with which we regard it, for in doing so we would be rejecting some of the good gifts that God has given to the church in the past for our benefit today.

With those words then, I end this series with the hope that more questions have been answered than raised; more light shed than heat generated.

May the Lord himself sanctify all these words to you. Amen.

THE TRINITY: JUST A DOCTRINE?

Ask ten average Christians in ten average churches to explain the doctrine of the Trinity, and you'll probably get ten different explanations. Most Christians "accept" the Trinity as orthodox Christian doctrine. But they would be at a loss to explain why the doctrine matters, or how it affects their Christian lives.

As Catherine Mowry LaCugna explains in her introduction to *God For Us*, the Trinity is a doctrine that most people "consent to in theory but have little need for in the practice of Christian faith" (Catherine Mowry LaCugna, *God For Us*, p. ix).

LaCugna continues, "On the one hand, the doctrine of the Trinity is supposed to be the center of faith. On the other hand, as Karl Rahner [one of the most influential theologians of the 20th century] once remarked, one could dispense with the doctrine of the Trinity as false and the major part of religious literature could well remain virtually unchanged" (*ibid.,* p. 6).

Does it make any difference?

And no wonder. The doctrine is hard to understand, and most discussions about it are…well… boring. For the average Christian, the kind of people who have families to feed, jobs to get to, and lives to live, what difference does an ancient doctrine make anyway? God is God, isn't he? Isn't that enough? If he happens to be Father, Son and Spirit instead of just Father, well, fine, but that doesn't really change anything from our end, does it?

Actually, it does matter. It matters a lot, in fact—which is exactly what you'd expect us to say since, after all, why else would we be writing an article about an ancient, boring doctrine?

First, let's dispense with going through the biblical proof that the doctrine is correct. You can find that in a later chapter. Instead, let's spend some time talking about why the doctrine of the Trinity matters, and especially, why it matters to you.

Let's start by taking a look at the common idea that God is a single, solitary being "out there" somewhere, looking down on Earth, watching us, judging us. Bette Midler put it to music in the chorus to her tune "From a Distance" with the lyrics, "And God is watching us, God is watching us, God is watching us from a distance."

This God comes in three main flavors: first, vanilla, the one who just kind of wound up the universe and then stretched out in the heavenly gazebo for a few-billion-year nap. (Who knows, maybe he wakes up once in a while and does something nice, like the kind of God George Burns portrayed in the film *Oh God.*) Second, red hot cinnamon, the one who keeps careful tabs on everything everybody does, and since everybody blows it now and then, he gets madder and madder. His worshippers say he takes joy in watching people who offend him slowly roast but never quite get done. Third is apricot, the one who might or might not like you, depending on many things, none of which are all that clear to anybody. He's the one that Oakland Raiders fans pray to for touchdowns.

Sometimes this God comes in an alternate flavor, water balloon. You might think water balloon isn't a flavor, but it is. It's chewy, and the variety of colors is endless, but it always tastes watery. This God is more of an abstract principle than a supreme being, kind of a "spirit of everything" that you can try to get in touch with if you empty your head of all thoughts and sit still long enough without going to sleep. (I think that's where Burger King commercials come from.)

A God who wants to share

The God of the Bible is not like that. The God of the Bible is Father, Son and Holy Spirit—three Persons. (Keep in mind that the Father, Son, and Spirit are not "persons" in the same way we humans are. They are not three Gods, but one, and each "Person" of the Godhead is distinct, but not separate from the others.) These three divine Persons share perfect love, joy, unity, peace, and fellowship. It's important to know that because, when the Bible talks about us being "in Christ," it means that we get to take part in that divine kind of life. Just like Christ is the beloved of the Father, so we too, because we are "in him," are also the beloved of the Father.

That means that you are included in the household of God. It means you're not an outsider or a stranger. You're not even a respected guest. You're one of the kids, beloved of the Father, with free run of the house, the grounds, and the fridge.

The trouble is, you probably have a hard time believing that. You know what you're really like deep down inside, so you think God doesn't like you. How could he, you figure. You don't even like yourself. So based on your assessment of your "goodness/badness" ratio, you determine that God is more than likely mad at you, and *far* more than likely mad at all those other types you meet in traffic every day.

But the whole point of God letting us know through the Scriptures that he is Father, Son and Spirit, and not just "God out there somewhere," is so that we'd know he really does love us and we really are on the ins with him. And again, how do we know? Because Jesus, you know, "God with us," "God in the flesh," the one the Father sent not to condemn the world but to save it (John 3:17), is the Father's Son, and that means that the Son of God is now one of us. And as one of us, but still God, only God in the flesh now, he dragged the whole bunch of us home to the Father right through the front door.

No, we didn't deserve it and no, we didn't earn it. We didn't even ask for it. But he did it anyway, because that's the exact reason he made us in the first place—so he could share with us the life he has shared eternally with the Father and the Spirit. That's why he tells us he made us in his image (Genesis 1:26).

Showing us the Father

Salvation isn't about a change of location, floating off to some secret set of coordinates in the Delta Quadrant called heaven, as if that would solve all our problems. And it's not about a new super government patrolled by angelic cops who never miss an infraction of the divine penal code.

Salvation is about getting adopted into God's family—and learning how to live in it. And the Trinity is at the heart of it: The Father (Let's get technical—the First Person of the Godhead) loves us so much, in spite of our screw-ups, that he sent the Son (the Second Person of the Godhead) to do everything it took to bring us home (John 1:1, 14), and the Father and the Son sent the Spirit (the Third Person of the Godhead) to live in us, teach us and strengthen us in how to live in God's family so we can enjoy it like we were created to do, instead of being screw-ups forever.

In other words, the God of the Bible is not three separate Gods, where one, the temper-challenged, unpredictable Father, is so furious at humans that he just has to kill somebody in order to calm down, so the sweet, loving Son, seeing Dad about to lose it, steps up and says, "Okay, if you've got to kill someone, then kill me, but spare these people." The doctrine of the Trinity is important precisely because it keeps us from seeing God in such a ridiculous way, and yet, that is how a whole lot of people *do* see God.

If you want to know what the Father is like, just look at Jesus, because Jesus is the perfect revelation of the Father. Jesus told Philip, "Anyone who has seen me has seen the Father" (John 14:9). He told the crowd, "I and the Father are one." We know how the Father feels about us because we know how Jesus feels about us.

To summarize, God is not some isolated cosmic bean counter "out there" keeping tabs on us in preparation for Judgment Day, nor is he three Gods with very different ideas about how to deal with humanity. The God of the

Bible is one God who is three divine Persons, in perfect unity and accord, who love each other in perfect love and dwell in indescribable joy, and who created us for the express purpose of sharing that life with them through our adoption into Christ, who is eternally the beloved of his Father.

That's why the doctrine of the Trinity matters. If we don't understand God the way he reveals himself in the Bible, then we wind up with all kinds of messed up, funky and scary ideas about who God is and what he might be cooking up to do to us some day.

Reconciliation for everyone

You're still not convinced, are you? Well, try reading this one again: "...while we were yet sinners Christ died for us" (Romans 5:8). God did not wait for you to get good enough to bring you into his household. You can't get good enough, which is the reason he went after you to bring you home in the first place. When Paul says God saves sinners, he's talking about everybody, since that's what everybody is—a sinner. (By the way, if you're worried God might find out how rotten you really are and send a lightning bolt your way, take heart, he's known all along and loves you anyway.)

Paul makes the point even stronger in verse 10: "For if, when we were God's enemies, we were reconciled to him through the death of his Son, how much more, having been reconciled, shall we be saved through his life!"

Did you notice how Paul puts that reconciliation with God in the past tense? Jesus died for our sins—*past tense*. God does not count our sins against us—*period*. They've already been paid for. Jesus has already put us in good standing with God. All that remains for us now is to turn to God (repent), believe the good news (have faith), and follow Jesus (let the Holy Spirit teach us how to enjoy life in the new creation).

Jesus said, "If anyone would come after me, he must deny himself and take up his cross and follow me." When we think of God in any other way than the way he revealed himself in the Bible—as the Father, Son, and Spirit who created us and redeemed us and have made us to share their joy though union with Jesus Christ—we're going to find these words of Jesus daunting and discouraging.

But when we know God the way he reveals himself, we can say with all assurance of joy, "Therefore, there is no condemnation for those who are in Christ Jesus..." (Romans 8:1). "For God," Paul wrote to the Colossian church, "was pleased to have all his fullness dwell in him [Jesus], and through him to reconcile to himself all things, whether things on earth or things in heaven, by making peace through his blood, shed on the cross" (Colossians

1:19-20).

All humanity is included in that reconciliation, according to Paul. In the doctrine of the Trinity, God has shown himself to be the God who loves the world and who beckons every person to come to Christ and take part in the joy of life in the household of God. There is no person whom God does not want, whom God does not include, whom God does not love. And in Christ, following the Spirit's lead, we are all freed from the chains of sin to come to the Father whose arms are open wide to receive us, if only we will.

That's why the doctrine of the Trinity matters. Without it, we might as well join the Canaanites wondering whether Baal will flood out the crops with storms this year or burn them out with lightning. In Jesus Christ, God has taken up our cause as his own. God has, through the atoning work of Jesus, healed us from head to toe, mind and heart, and made us the Father's Son's best friends, no, much more than that; made us adopted children of the Father, brothers and sisters of our older Brother and full members of the household of God.

With Paul, we can only say, "Thanks be to God for his indescribable gift!"

Key points

- 1. God created all humans in his image, and he wants all people to share in the love shared by the Father, the Son and the Holy Spirit.
- 2. The Son became a human, the man Jesus Christ, to reconcile all humanity to God through his birth, life, death and resurrection and ascension. In Christ, humanity is loved and accepted by the Father.
- 3. Jesus Christ has already paid for our sins, and there is no longer any debt to pay. The Father has already forgiven us, and he eagerly desires that we turn to him.
- 4. We cannot enjoy the blessing of his love if we don't believe he loves us. We cannot enjoy his forgiveness unless we believe he has forgiven us.
- 5. When we respond to the Spirit by turning to God, believing the good news, and picking up our cross and following Jesus, the Spirit leads us into the transformed life of the kingdom of God.

J. Michael Feazell

IS THE DOCTRINE
OF THE TRINITY IN THE BIBLE?

Some people who reject the Trinity doctrine often claim that the word "Trinity" is not found in Scripture. Of course, there is no verse that says "God is three Persons" or "God is a Trinity." This is all evident and true, but it proves nothing. There are many words and phrases that Christians use, which are not found in the Bible. For example, the word "Bible" is not found in the Bible.

More to the point, opponents of the Trinity doctrine claim that a Trinitarian view of God's nature and being can't be proven from the Bible. Since the books of the Bible are not written as theological tracts, this may seem on the surface to be true. There is no statement in Scripture that says, "God is three Persons in one being, and here is the proof. . ."

However, the New Testament does bring God (Father), the Son (Jesus Christ) and the Holy Spirit together in such a way as to strongly imply the Trinitarian nature of God. Three Scriptures are quoted below as a summary of the various other biblical passages that bring together the three Persons of the Godhead. One Scripture is from the Gospels, another is from the apostle Paul and a third is from the apostle Peter. The words in each passage referring to each of the three Persons are italicized to emphasize their Trinitarian implication:

- All authority in heaven and on earth has been given to me. Therefore go and make disciples of all nations, baptizing them in the name [singular] of the *Father* and of the *Son* and of the *Holy Spirit* [Matthew 28:19].

- May the grace of the *Lord Jesus Christ*, and the love of *God*, and the fellowship of the *Holy Spirit* be with you all [2 Corinthians 13:14].

- To God's elect. . .who have been chosen according to the foreknowledge of *God the Father*, through the sanctifying work of *the Spirit*, for obedience to *Jesus Christ* and sprinkling by his blood [1 Peter 1:1-2].

Here are three passages in Scripture, one on the lips of Jesus, and the other two from leading apostles, each bringing together the three Persons of the Godhead in an unmistakable way. But these are only a sampling of other similar passages. Among others are the following: Romans 14:17-18; 15:16;1 Corinthians 2:2-5; 6:11; 12:4-6; 2 Corinthians 1:21-22; Galatians 4:6;

Ephesians 2:18-22; 3:14-19; Ephesians 4:4-6; Colossians 1:6-8; 1Thessalonians 1:3-5; 2 Thessalonians 2:13-14; Titus 3:4-6. The reader is encouraged to read each of these passages and note how God (Father), Son (Jesus Christ) and the Holy Spirit are brought together as instruments of our salvation.

Such passages show that the New Testament faith is implicitly Trinitarian. It's true that none of these passages say directly that "God is a Trinity. . ." or "This is the Trinitarian doctrine. . ." But they don't need to. As mentioned above, the books of the New Testament are not formal, point-by-point treatises of doctrine. Nonetheless, these and other Scriptures speak easily and without any self-consciousness of God (Father), Son (Jesus) and Holy Spirit working together as one. The writers show no feeling of strangeness in joining these divine Persons together as a unity in their salvific work. Systematic theologian Alister E. McGrath makes this point in his book *Christian Theology:*

> The foundations of the doctrine of the Trinity are to be found in the pervasive pattern of divine activity to which the New Testament bears witness.... There is the closest of connections between the Father, Son, and Spirit in the New Testament writings. Time after time, New Testament passages link together these three elements as part of a greater whole. The totality of God's saving presence and power can only, it would seem, be expressed by involving all three elements...[page 248].

Such New Testament Scriptures answer the charge that the Trinity doctrine was only developed well into the church age and that it reflects "pagan" ideas, and not biblical ones. If we look at Scripture with an open mind regarding what it says about the being we call God, it's clear that he is shown to be Triune in nature. The Bible reveals that the Father is God, Jesus the Son is God, and the Holy Spirit is God, and yet the Bible also insists that this is only one God. These biblical teachings led the early church to formulate the doctrine of the Trinity.

We can confidently say that the Trinity, as a truth regarding God's essential being, has always been a reality. Perhaps it was not completely clear in antiquity, including even in the Old Testament. But the Incarnation of the Son of God and the coming of the Holy Spirit revealed that God was Triune. This revelation was made in *concrete fact*, in that the Son and the Holy Spirit broke into our world at definite points in history. The fact of the Triune revelation of God in historical time was only later described in the word of

God we call the New Testament.

James R. White, a Christian apologist, says in his book *The Forgotten Trinity*: "The Trinity is a doctrine not revealed merely in words but instead in the very action of the Triune God in redemption itself! We know who God *is* by what He has *done* in bringing us to himself!" (page 167).

Paul Kroll

HOW MANY GODS
DOES GOD SAY THERE ARE?

Scriptures that show there is only one God

Some Bible passages are difficult to understand. Others are easy. The Bible has many plain, simple, straightforward, unambiguous verses, and these are the verses we should study first when we want to understand what the Bible teaches. Understanding the plain, straightforward verses then becomes our basis for understanding the more difficult verses. The plain verses become the foundation for the rest of our biblical understanding. We build on those.

By building such a foundation, we have something to go back to when we have difficulty understanding other verses. We can take the "difficult" verses and explain them within the context of the plain, straightforward ones. This assures us that our explanations and understanding conform with the foundational verses.

Rather than throw out or ignore those simple, straightforward verses, we should throw out the explanations that contradict them. In theological terms, this is the correct exegetical approach.

The Bible proclaims plainly and clearly that there is one and only one God. When the Bible says that God is one, the word *one* does not refer to a "God Family," but to one God. Let's begin by looking at passages in the Old Testament.

Old Testament verses

Deuteronomy 4:35: "You were shown these things so that you might know that the Lord is God; besides him there is no other."

Deuteronomy 4:39: "Acknowledge and take to heart this day that the Lord is God in heaven above and on the earth below. There is no other."

Deuteronomy 6:4-5: "Hear, O Israel: The Lord our God, the Lord is one. Love the Lord your God with all your heart and with all your soul and with all your strength."

Deuteronomy 32:39: "See now that I myself am He! There is no god besides me."

1 Samuel 2:1-2: "There is no one holy like the Lord; there is no one besides you; there is no Rock like our God."

2 Samuel 7:22: "How great you are, O Sovereign Lord! There is no one like you, and there is no God but you, as we have heard with our own ears."

2 Samuel 22:32: "For who is God besides the Lord? And who is the Rock except our God?"

1 Kings 8:60: "So that all the peoples of the earth may know that the Lord is God and that there is no other."

2 Kings 19:15-19: "Hezekiah prayed to the Lord: 'O Lord, God of Israel, enthroned between the cherubim, you alone are God over all the kingdoms of the earth. You have made heaven and earth. Give ear, O Lord, and hear; open your eyes, O Lord, and see; listen to the words Sennacherib has sent to insult the living God. It is true, O Lord, that the Assyrian kings have laid waste these nations and their lands. They have thrown their gods into the fire and destroyed them, for they were not gods but only wood and stone, fashioned by men's hands. Now, O Lord our God, deliver us from his hand, so that all kingdoms on earth may know that you alone, O Lord, are God.'..."

Psalm 18:30-31: "As for God, his way is perfect; the word of the Lord is flawless.... For who is God besides the Lord? And who is the Rock except our God?"

Psalm 83:18: "Let them know that you, whose name is the Lord — that you alone are the Most High over all the earth."

Isaiah 43:10, 13: "'You are my witnesses,' declares the Lord, 'and my servant whom I have chosen, so that you may know and believe me and understand that I am he. Before me no god was formed, nor will there be one after me. I, even I, am the Lord, and apart from me there is no savior.... Yes, and from ancient days I am he. No one can deliver out of my hand. When I act, who can reverse it?'"

Isaiah 44:6-8: "This is what the Lord says — Israel's King and Redeemer, the Lord Almighty: I am the first and I am the last; apart from me there is no God. Who then is like me? Let him proclaim it. Let him declare and lay out before me what has happened since I established my ancient people, and what is yet to come — yes, let him foretell what will come. Do not tremble, do not be afraid. Did I not proclaim this and foretell it long ago? You are my witnesses. Is there any God besides me? No, there is no other Rock; I know not one."

Isaiah 45:5-6: "I am the Lord, and there is no other; apart from me there is no God. I will strengthen you, though you have not acknowledged me, so that from the rising of the sun to the place of its setting men may know there is none besides me. I am the Lord, and there is no other."

Isaiah 45:18: "This is what the Lord says — he who created the heavens, he is God; he who fashioned and made the earth, he founded it; he did not create it to be empty, but formed it to be inhabited — he says: 'I am the Lord, and there is no other.'"

Isaiah 45:21-22: "Declare what is to be, present it — let them take counsel together. Who foretold this long ago, who declared it from the distant past? Was it not I, the Lord? And there is no God apart from me, a righteous God and a Savior; there is none but me."

Isaiah 46:9: "Remember the former things, those of long ago; I am God, and there is no other; I am God, and there is none like me."

As you can see, there is no question about the biblical fact that there is one and only one God, not two or more "Gods." God speaks in the singular, as "I," saying that he is the only God, and there is no other being that is even like him. That's why God commands us, "You shall have no other gods before me" (Exodus 20:3).

The idea of more than one being in a family of gods is condemned throughout the Scriptures. That was precisely the concept that the polytheistic nations surrounding Israel taught. Polytheistic is a word that refers to a belief in more than one god (*poly* = many; *theos* = god). The Bible teaches that there is only one God, a belief called monotheism, from *mono* (one) and *theos* (God).

A family is made up of more than one being. The pagan hierarchies of gods were made up of more than one "god being," and at the top of the hierarchy were usually a father god, a mother god and one or more son and daughter gods. The Bible condemns the concept of a family of gods.

New Testament

The Bible does not allow for the existence of two God Beings. It categorically denies it. Let's take a look at some New Testament passages.

Matthew 19:17: "'Why do you ask me about what is good?' Jesus replied. 'There is only One who is good.'" The parallel verse in Mark is 10:18: "'Why do you call me good?' Jesus answered. 'No one is good — except God alone.'"

Jesus quoted Deuteronomy 6:4 when he affirmed that there is one God. Answering the question about what is the greatest commandment, he said: "The most important one...is this: 'Hear, O Israel, the Lord our God, the Lord is one'" (Mark 12:29).

Mark 12:32-34: "'Well said, teacher,' the man replied. 'You are right in saying that God is one and there is no other but him. To love him with all your heart, with all your understanding and with all your strength, and to love your neighbor as yourself is more important than all burnt offerings and sacrifices.' When Jesus saw that he had answered wisely, he said to him, 'You are not far from the kingdom of God.'"

There is no other being that is worthy of worship (Matthew 4:10).

John 5:42-44: "I have come in my Father's name, and you do not accept me: but if someone else comes in his own name, you will accept him. How can you believe if you accept praise from one another, yet make no effort to obtain the praise that comes from the only God?"

John 17:3: "This is eternal life: that they may know you, the only true God, and Jesus Christ, whom you have sent."

Likewise, Paul taught that there is one God. He wrote:

Romans 3:29-30: "Is God the God of Jews only? Is he not the God of Gentiles too? Yes, of Gentiles too, since there is only one God."

Romans 16:27: "To the only wise God be glory forever through Jesus Christ! Amen."

1 Corinthians 8:4-6: "So then, about eating food sacrificed to idols: We know that an idol is nothing at all in the world, and that there is no God but one. For even if there are so-called gods, whether in heaven or on earth (as indeed there are many 'gods' and many 'lords'), yet for us there is but one God, the Father, from whom all things came and for whom we live; and there is but one Lord, Jesus Christ, through whom all things came and through whom we live."

Galatians 3:19-20: "The law was put into effect through angels by a mediator. A mediator, however, does not represent just one party; but God is one."

Ephesians 4:6: "One God and Father of all, who is over all and through all and in all."

1 Timothy 1:17: "Now to the King eternal, immortal, invisible, the only God, be honor and glory for ever and ever. Amen."

1 Timothy 2:5: "For there is one God and one mediator between God and men, the man Christ Jesus." Even while describing the role of Jesus Christ, who was God in the flesh, Paul still affirmed that there is only one God. When the Son became flesh, he did not cease to be God — he was God in the flesh (John 1:1, 14). But there was not, never has been, never will be, two Gods.

1 Timothy 6:13-16: "In the sight of God, who gives life to everything, and of Christ Jesus, who while testifying before Pontius Pilate made the good confession, I charge you to keep this commandment without spot or blame until the appearing of our Lord Jesus Christ, which God will bring about in his own time — God, the blessed and only Ruler, the King of kings and Lord of lords, who alone is immortal and who lives in unapproachable light, whom no one has seen or can see."

James wrote: "You believe that there is one God. Good! Even the demons believe that — and shudder" (2:19).

James 4:12: "There is only one Lawgiver and Judge, the one who is able to save and destroy."

Jude 25: "To the only God our Savior be glory, majesty, power and authority, through Jesus Christ our Lord, before all ages, now and forevermore!"

Contradictory truths?

The Bible gives us two facts that (on the surface) look contradictory. But they only *appear* to be contradictory because our minds are finite and limited, while God, our Creator, is infinite and unlimited. The Bible tells us there is one God. The Father is God. The Son is also God (John 20:28-29). He was eternally with God and also was God (John 1:1-2). The Father is God and the Son is God, but there is only one God. God is one in one respect, but plural in another respect.

The early church explained this by saying that God is one in *being,* but plural in *persons.* This is part of the Christian doctrine usually called the doctrine of the Trinity. This doctrine does not teach plural Gods, but only one. They are distinct, but not separate. There is no "family" of Gods.

God *has* a family (we are his children), but he is not a family in himself. People cannot be born into the "God family," because there is no such thing. We will never be God in the same way that God is God. Rather, we are partakers of the divine nature (2 Peter 1:4) — children of God, but never Gods. We are children by adoption, but in essence or being. We will always remain created beings. There can be only one God. We are born into God's family, but not the God family. We belong to God, but we will never be God,

This is not a matter of confusion, as some say. It is a matter of believing the Bible and realizing that God is greater than our finite imaginations can perceive. It is a matter of faith, because we believe the Bible.

The "average" Protestant or Catholic cannot explain God's nature. Some may even think that there are three God Beings in one Godhead, or a three-headed Being of some sort. But their misunderstandings do not affect the truth of the teaching. The Bible teaching is that there is one God who is the Father, the Son, and the Holy Spirit. It is not my idea, nor is it the idea of some fourth-century theologians. It is the teaching of the Bible.

The fourth-century theologians formulated a doctrine that denies certain unbiblical teachings about God that were in vogue at the time. One such teaching was the idea that the Son was a created being. Another heresy is the idea that the Father, the Son, and the Holy Spirit are not distinct but are really all the same — in other words, the idea that the one God is sometimes the Father, sometimes the Son, and sometimes the Holy Spirit, but not all three all the time. This was declared to be false.

God is not like a human

God transcends our world of time and space. He created time and space. He appears in it when he desires, but he is in no way limited to time and space. He does not need time and space to exist. However, we are able to think only in terms of creation, in terms of time and space. God is everything we can conceive of, but much more! He uses all sorts of concepts in the Bible to reveal himself to us, and he does it in terms we can understand — like King, Redeemer, Shepherd, Defender, Fire, Rock, Shelter. He is all those and more, and not just like any of them, because they are all part of the created world.

God does not have or need a "mighty arm," for example. God uses the human term, "mighty arm," because it is one we can understand, one that helps us understand something important about the power of God. But it is not a literal description of God. It is a metaphor.

God also speaks of his "right hand." Is that because his "right hand" is stronger or more skilled than his "left hand"? Of course not. He is conveying the fact that he is powerful, that he intends to do a particular thing, and that he is going to do it in a powerful way. Bible-believers should not take such descriptions literally and think of God as subject to time and space like ourselves.

This brings to mind Paul's statement in Romans 1:22-23: "Although they claimed to be wise, they became fools and exchanged the glory of the immortal God for images made to look like mortal man and birds and animals and reptiles." There are stone images, and there are mental images.

None of us would want to make God like a created thing, but if we think that God has a body (a male body, some will attest), or is subject to time and space (who can only be in only one place at one time), and needs to have something in order to create (that he needs a preexisting "substance"), just like we need physical matter to fashion things, then we have inadvertently reduced God to an "image made to look like mortal man."

God is not created. He does not have a body. Bodies are put together or composed, and God is neither put together nor composed of anything. He is the Creator, not the created. Until God created, there was nothing. Only God is eternal. Only God is uncreated. There is no eternal matter or "spiritual substance" that co-existed with God. That would mean that God did not create everything, and such a God is not the God of the Bible. Such a God is a limited God, a less-than-supreme God, a God who needs something beside himself to act as God.

One other important point. God is personal — and he relates to us in a personal way. We should never think of God as so transcendent, so unlike us, that we cannot relate to him in a personal way. That is precisely why he reveals himself to us in the Bible in human terms, in terms we can understand. That is why the Son of God became human to reconcile us to God. God wants a close and personal relationship with us. He wants fellowship with us. That is the reason he made us, and he has made it possible (despite our sin) through our mediator, the God-made-human Jesus Christ.

Ralph Orr and Paul Kroll

WHAT DOES DEUTERONOMY 6:4 MEAN?

"Hear, O Israel: The Lord our God,
the Lord is one" (Deuteronomy 6:4, NIV).

The problem in translating this verse is not the meaning of the Hebrew term for "one," but the division of the sentence "*Yahweh Elohim Yahweh echad*." Since the Hebrew text has no punctuation, various renderings are possible, all requiring the addition of the verb "is." The four most important possibilities can be found in the New Revised Standard Version and its footnote on this verse:

Yahweh (is) our God, Yahweh alone.

Yahweh our God (is) one Yahweh.

Yahweh our God, Yahweh (is) one.

Yahweh (is) our God, Yahweh (is) one.

These versions have major differences in emphasis. The question here is not about the psychological effect created by each possibility, but the meaning of the passage for its theological import.

The King James Version of 1611 and the Revised Version took option 2, probably because the repetition of the subject of the sentence ("Yahweh") in 3 and 4 seems forced, unnatural. Option 1 has the disadvantage of using "*echad*" (one) in a sense that is unusual and unexpected. In other passages, a different word is used for "alone."

Theological importance

The theological possibilities behind Deuteronomy 6:4 are two. The first is that this verse stresses God's unity, and the second is that it stresses God's uniqueness. "Unity" means oneness (a state of being single). In a theological context, it does not mean harmony among people (unity of mind, etc.) – it means that there is only one God. "Uniqueness" means a state in which there is no equal. Although many gods may exist, only one is to be Israel's God.

This passage, then, is announcing either that there is only one single being in the Godhead, or that Israel is not to worship any of the other (existing) gods. A possibility of the combination of the two need not concern us, because it does not alter anything significant, as will become clear below.

In determining which of these meanings is correct, it is necessary to give some thought to the second possibility, the notion that the Israelites are to accept Yahweh as their national God (rather than any other existing deity). This can be held by those who take Deuteronomy to be an anthropological account (one that explains the ideas current in a polytheistic Israel) rather than an actual revelation from the true God. Or it can be held by those who believe that God limited his self-revelation to accommodate the polytheistic ideas of the day. Both of these approaches clash with Deut. 4:35 and 39, which assert that only the Lord is God, and there is none other besides him. Deut. 6:4 should not be interpreted to imply that the people thought that other gods might exist, but that only Yahweh should be worshiped.

Although God is unique, Deut. 6:4 is not about his uniqueness. It is about God's unity. This is not to assert that the Israelites totally understood the true God, or that they abstained from the worship of other (false, non-existing) gods — far from it; the record indicates the opposite. It would be equally wrong to assume that Deuteronomy 6:4 says that God is pure spirit. This concept is the result of abstract reasoning concerning God, which was foreign to the society that received and read the Torah.

Irrespective of what Israel thought about God (or about Deuteronomy), Deut. 6:4 is a divine revelation. It proceeds from the true God. The meaning is that there is no other divine being in existence, and that Yahweh is that being, a single being, whom we should worship.

IS GOD A FAMILY?

I'm sometimes asked why we do not refer to God as a "family." Isn't that term appropriate, given that there is a Father and a Son who are bringing "many sons to glory"? My answer is that whereas the analogy of God as a family works at some levels, we must be very careful because it can lead in directions that distort the biblical revelation of the one God who is Father, Son and Holy Spirit.

The analogy of God as a family can be used in a limited way to indicate that just as there are relationships between family members, there are relationships in the triune God. However this analogy is easily misunderstood as indicating that just as in a family there are separate persons who each have their own being, so God is made up of persons with separate beings.

But that is not the case. What is true of human relationships in families is not necessarily true of God, who is not a creature. While there is a triune relationship within God's one being, that relationship is not between separate beings. The three "persons" of the Trinity, through their absolutely unique relationships, constitute the one being of God in a way that is quite unlike a human family.

The uncreated God cannot be explained in terms of a created human family. Trying to do so amounts to mythology and even idolatry.

Most of us probably are familiar with the Hebrew word *Elohim*. It is one of several names used for God in the Old Testament. Some people claim that *Elohim* is a "uniplural" noun—like the noun "family." Following this line of reasoning, they erroneously conclude that there are two separate Gods (Father and Son), comprising a "God family."

From the Akkadians and Egyptians to the Greeks and Romans, pagan religions have taught a plurality (pantheon or family) of gods. The Greeks even constructed a family tree for their pantheon.[1] This pagan conception is known as polytheism (many gods, like the pantheon of Egyptian gods pictured below), or bitheism or ditheism in the case of two gods.

In contrast to the polytheistic misconceptions of paganism, God revealed himself to Israel as one (single, exclusive) God. He commanded his people: "You shall have no other gods before me" (Exodus 20:3). "Before me" is literally, "before my face"—a Hebrew idiom meaning "beside me" or "in addition to me."[2] Though *Elohim* is a plural noun, it was never understood as a reference to many gods, and certainly not a reference to a family of gods.

The pantheon of gods in pagan religions ruled the realm of the gods, the supernatural and, ultimately, the human world. Typically one of these gods was designated head of the pantheon and, like the other gods, would have at least one consort (female partner). But God forbade Israel to think of him in these polytheistic and sexual terms. Yahweh definitely is not the head of a pantheon. He has no consort. There are no other gods in his presence.[3] Therefore, Moses proclaimed: "Hear, O Israel, the LORD [*Yahweh*] our God [*Elohim*], the LORD [*Yahweh*] is one" (Deuteronomy 6:4).

Old Testament Hebrew does not support the idea of a "God family." The nouns used for God's names and titles are coupled with singular verbs. For example, it is said in Genesis 2:7 that "the Lord [*Yahweh*—a singular noun] God [*Elohim*—a plural noun] formed [a singular verb] a man from the dust of the ground." Though *Elohim* is a plural noun, the Bible almost always couples it with a singular verb.

Note, however, that while emphasizing the unity and uniqueness of one God, *Elohim* does allow for the idea of a plurality of persons in the one Godhead. We see this hinted at in Genesis 1:2, 26: "Now the earth was formless and empty, darkness was over the surface of the deep, and the Spirit of God was hovering over the waters…. Then God said, 'Let us make mankind in our image, in our likeness…'" This rich linguistic character of *Elohim* is found only in Hebrew and in no other Semitic languages—not even in Biblical Aramaic.[4]

Note also that, as is true in the English language, Hebrew has both singular and plural nouns. However, quite unlike English, Hebrew is able to specify singular, dual and plural meanings for nouns. [5] For example, in the Old Testament, God is named *Eloah* (a singular noun) 57 times; he is named *Elohim* (a plural noun referring to three or more) 2570 times; and he is named *Elohiam* (a plural noun referring to two) exactly zero times.

The nature and usage of the plural noun *Elohim* in biblical Hebrew, taken together with the singular verbs that are coupled with it, while allowing for the possibility of some kind of plurality in God, does not allow for separate beings who make up a pantheon (family) of gods. When we add to this the Old Testament's emphatic teaching that there is only one God, it becomes clear that our former teaching that God is a family of two separate Gods is not biblical. Even though the Hebrew Scriptures hint at a plurality of persons in the Godhead, the notion of there being two separate "god beings" is ditheism (a form of polytheism)—a belief expressly prohibited by God himself.

God is one being with a plurality of what we refer to as divine "persons." This is why I say we should be very careful in saying that "God is a family." The truth about the nature of God, which is only hinted at in the Old

Testament, is revealed to us fully by Jesus Christ. Given that revelation, we can say with confidence that the Father, Son and Holy Spirit live in a loving, eternal relationship as one Triune God—a relationship in which, by grace, we have been included.

1 See http://en.wikipedia.org/wiki/Family_tree_of_the_Greek_gods.

2 H.D. Spence. *The Pulpit Commentary: Exodus Vol. II.* Logos Research Systems, S. 131.

3 Victor Harold Matthews; Mark W. Chavalas; John H. Walton. *The IVP Bible Background Commentary: Old Testament.* Electronic ed., sv. Ex. 20:3.

4 Gustav Oehler, *Theology of the Old Testament,* p. 88.

5 E. Kautzch, ed., *Gesenius' Hebrew Grammar*, p. 244.

Joseph Tkach

DOES THE HEBREW WORD *ELOHIM* REFER TO A FAMILY OF DIVINE BEINGS?

The word *elohim* can refer to the true God, to a false god, to angels, and to human beings. In its wide application, this name is unusual and difficult to translate into English. The ability of this word to refer correctly to God, angels, humans, and false gods can be understood only if the root of the word is kept in mind. The root means somewhat like the "powers that be," whether they are human or divine, singular or plural. In this light, it becomes clear that the Hebrews applied the name *elohim* to the true God because it conveyed one of his attributes – that of power.

When *elohim* refers to a singular being (the true God or a false god), it takes a singular verb. When it refers to more than one being, as in the heavenly powers (the angels or God and the angels) or in the human powers (the judges), it takes a plural verb. The one form can be either singular or plural, and its meaning is indicated by whether the verb is in a singular or a plural form. In no case does the word *elohim* refer to a family of beings, whether they are human or divine. The following passages are sufficient to make the use of this word clear.

God (*elohim*) created

In Genesis 1:1 *elohim* takes the singular verb *bara,* which means "he created." The verb tells us what was done by the one God. Even with this point in mind, the objection can be raised that collective nouns in English (church, nation, etc.) take singular verbs. That answer will not do, in this case, because one needs to ascertain first that *elohim* is such a word. It cannot simply be assumed to be so. It is not obvious in Hebrew, and no authority on the Hebrew language has ever said such a thing. The voice of scholarship has been united on this point, that *elohim,* when speaking of the Creator, refers to a single deity. The use of the word in the Old Testament is ample testimony of this truth, as the following examples show.

Greater than all the gods (*elohim*)

Exodus 18:11 compares the true God with all the false gods (*elohim*) and says that none of them is like him. This is clearly a plural reference, yet it does not refer to a family of beings. The false gods to which Exodus refers were not considered to be members of one family.

Ashtoreth the goddess (*elohim*)

1 Kings 11:5 is one of the clearest examples of the singular use of *elohim*

in which it cannot possibly be construed to refer to a family of divine beings. "Ashtoreth the goddess (*elohim*) of the Sidonians" was but only one deity, not a family of such beings.

Lower than the angels (*elohim*)

Psalm 8:5 says that God made humans a little lower than the angels (*elohim*). Since all the angels were created beings, there are no father angels, mother angels, or offspring angels. Angels do not marry. This use of *elohim* is not in the context of a family.

Bring him to the judges (*elohim*)

Exodus 21:6 is a law regarding Hebrew slaves. If freed slaves expressed a desire to continue to serve their masters, they were to be brought before "the judges [*elohim*)]," who would make it official. The judges were an institution of Israel and did not constitute a family.

The above passages may be enough to indicate that the word *elohim* – in its reference to God, angels, judges, and false gods – is not a collective noun; it is not like "church," "nation," etc. The concept of a divine family of beings is not applicable to the true God, and did not arise out of the Holy Scriptures. It may be helpful to note some reasons why this concept is inappropriate.

The names "Father" and "Son" indicate a family relationship. (We can omit reference to the Holy Spirit, in this light, because the name "Holy Spirit" does not immediately suggest a family relationship.) This is acceptable – and biblically sound. The error creeps into the concept when the relationship is understood in terms of separate beings. The following explanation will make this easier to understand.

In a human family, a father and a son are two beings. One is the father because he existed while the son was not yet born. The father provides for the son, because the son needs his help. Human beings are limited beings. They have a beginning, they have needs, and the father-son relationship is meaningful in light of these limitations.

It is a gross misunderstanding to think of God in such terms. God is spirit. He has no limitations in space or time. The Son did not have a beginning, and at no time did the Father exist while the Son did not. Neither is it true that the Father looked after a young Son during some childhood, or provided for the Son's "needs." We should not form our concepts of God based on what human fathers and sons are.

The book of Hebrews speaks of the Son in various ways. He is referred to as a Son, as the "brightness of his glory," and as the "express image of his person." These are three ways of expressing the same idea. As the Son is God, he has no needs, and he is not in the same relationship to the Father that a human son is to his parent.

The names "Father" and "Son" are applied to God by analogy, without the limitations that hold true in a human family. This is another way of saying that God is not a family (for that word has meaning only in the context of limited human beings). God is infinite, eternal, and in all ways unlimited. The attempt to make *elohim* refer to a family of divine beings is not only impossible historically, linguistically and culturally; it is theologically wrong and inappropriate in the discussion of the true God.

IS *ELOHIM* A PLURAL WORD?

People will occasionally read statements to the effect that the Hebrew word *elohim* is plural, as can be seen from the ending *-im.* The thought behind this claim is that this plural form indicates that there is plurality in the Godhead. Some conclude that the biblical references to a Father and a Son are a biblical way of supporting the idea that God is a family of divine beings headed by the Father.

Is the form *elohim* plural? So long as the question is about the *form,* the answer is yes. That, however, does not mark the end of the relevant questions that should be asked. There is a second important question to be answered, about the meaning of the word. Is the *sense* of the word *elohim* plural? The answer is that it is not.

All languages make a distinction between the form and the sense of a word. In English, the word "put" has one form. This form is made up of three specific letters laid out in a particular order, but the senses or meanings of that form are many. "Put" may mean the act of placing something in a particular location (in the present tense). It may mean the act of having already placed something in a particular location (in the past tense). It may mean an entirely different kind of act, such as a ship's sailing into a port or harbor. Moreover, "put" can take a singular construction or a plural one (he put, or they put). The person who knows English is not confused when the same form is used with different senses. Neither is the Hebrew speaker confused by the one form and the different senses of *elohim.*

Those who argue the nature of God from the fact that *elohim* is a plural form make a fundamental mistake. They are under the impression that it is the form of this word that determines its sense! No English speaker would insist that the form of "put" be the guideline in determining its sense. Neither is that possible in Hebrew. That would generate confusion. In Genesis 1:1, for example, to take *elohim* as plural in sense would distort the Hebrew text for the following reason:

The English verb "created" has the same form in the singular and in the plural. The sense, however, is clearly seen when a pronoun is attached (he created, or they created). In Hebrew, the singular and plural of this verb are two different forms. Genesis 1:1 uses the singular form (*bara,* "he created"). This verb, then, prevents the interpreter from considering only the form of Hebrew noun. The noun is plural in form, but the verb is singular in form, telling the reader that both the noun and the verb are singular in meaning.

One must look at the sense, or else a wrong interpretation will be attached to the verse. In the Hebrew text of Genesis 1:1, both the form and the sense of the verb "created" are singular. There is no possibility of a different understanding of that verb. By itself, it means "he created."

Those who propose the idea of a family of divine beings acknowledge that the verb is in the singular number and that its form and sense are singular. But they dismiss this detail by saying that there are instances (in English, for example) in which a singular verb accompanies a collective noun (a family is, a nation is, etc.). This move is in error, because it presupposes (it starts with the premise) that the name "God" stands for a group of beings. Thus a new, third, relevant question must be asked: Does the word "God" refer to a group of divine beings? The Jews say, "Of course not. That is preposterous." The Muslims say the same, and the Christians traditionally have held the same view as the Jews and Muslims.

The advocates of "family of divine beings" acknowledge that such a concept is preposterous to Jews, Muslims, and Christians, but they see that as an indication of the error in which these religions are steeped. For traditional Christianity, the attack is leveled at the church councils. The claim is made that such councils were the devil's playground, because the only thing that seemed to matter was what people thought, not what God's word teaches.

This approach to the subject invites a fourth relevant question regarding the family of God. How do the advocates of a family of God beings proceed to establish that God's word, the Bible, means a group of divine beings when it uses the word *elohim*? Their answer is that this is a plural form. But, as explained above, a plural form does not necessarily suggest a plural sense. This is where the fundamental mistake lies.

There is one more question: How did a reference to the true God end up as a plural form? Since the question is about the form, it is a question about the Hebrew language. It is not about the nature of God. Even so, the answer is not difficult to understand. Hebrew has its own characteristics as a language. Among these is the way in which it expresses might, authority, and reverence. An example from the Old Testament may make the point clear.

In Exodus 4:16, Moses is told that Aaron would be to him for a mouth, while he would be for a god (*elohim*) to Aaron. The form of *elohim* is plural, yet Moses was clearly one person — not a group or family of beings. This is sufficient to indicate that a distinction that must be drawn between the form and the sense of a word. Second, Moses was to be like *elohim* to Aaron only in the sense that he would be in a position of more authority and respect. The same expression is used in 7:1, where Moses is told that he would be like *elohim* to Pharaoh.

These examples show that *elohim* has a singular sense, despite its form. In order to understand how the form arose, one needs to examine the development of linguistic forms that the Israelites inherited from those who spoke Semitic languages before them. In polytheistic societies such as those of the Canaanites, Amorites, Egyptians, etc., a plural reference to the gods would be standard, and hardly out of place. As the language undergoes changes in a monotheistic society such as Israel, it is natural that older forms would be used with new senses.

For example, in English, the form of the word "conversation" has remained unchanged since the days of the King James Bible, but the sense of this word has changed to suggest speaking, rather than conduct. The reasons for the semantic shift are to be found in a detailed study of the way the language developed under certain internal and external influences. This is a linguistic project, whether the focus is on an English word like "conversation," or a Hebrew word like *elohim*. Just as the form of the word "conversation" does not bring to mind a person's conduct, so with *elohim;* it does not bring to mind any concept of polytheism, and there is no discrepancy with the consistent rejection of polytheism throughout the Scriptures.

YOU CAN PROVE WHAT *ELOHIM* MEANS

In Genesis 1:26, God says, "Let us make man in our image." "Let us...." Does this mean that there is more than one God? Some say yes. They say that the Hebrew word *elohim* is a plural noun, showing that there is more than one God. Yet the Hebrew Bible plainly quotes God as saying that there is only one God. "I am God," he says, "and there is no other" (Isaiah 45:22). God does not say, "we are God."

So what does the Hebrew word *elohim* mean? Is it plural? Does it prove there is one God or many? If we can't read Hebrew, how can we find out?

You can prove it yourself

You may already have some Bible-study tools that can help you learn what *elohim* means. We do not have to be Hebrew scholars, but will will need to do some study.

We should begin with prayer, to ask God to give us understanding. Tell him of our willingness to give up old cherished ideas if he shows us that they are wrong. Confess any pride, vanity or anger that might inhibit our understanding. Express faith in Christ's leadership. Admit to him that our humanity sometimes limits our vision and distorts our thinking. Pray in faith that God will teach us and that he will grant us ears that hear and a heart that responds.

Having done that, we'll be ready to study. We'll be like the Bereans, who "received the message with great eagerness and examined the Scriptures every day to see if what Paul said was true" (Acts 17:11).

To help us know the truth about the word *elohim,* we should be aware of one important concept: To know what any word means, we need to observe how it is used. We need to note whether the word is used as a noun, verb, pronoun, adverb or another part of speech. If the word is used as a noun, we should see if it is a singular, plural or proper noun. We should analyze how the word is used.

We should note the words that are used with it, too. For example, if we are uncertain if the noun is plural or singular, are there any pronouns associated with it that could help us find out? The more examples that we have of its use in context, the more certain we can be of its definition. We might even discover that a word has different meanings in different contexts. Some words are verbs in one context but nouns in another. The English word "saw" is an example of this.

A study in Strong's concordance

Our study can begin with Strong's *Exhaustive Concordance.* Those who own other concordances or computer Bible programs can apply the same principles with slight modifications for their situation. Some resources will make the job easier than Strong's does.

Look up the English word "God" in Strong's concordance. Under that heading we'll find a list of all the verses where we can find the word *God* in the King James Version. The verse list begins with Genesis 1:1, "God made the heaven and the earth." To the right of that verse is the number 430. If we turn to the Hebrew and Chaldee dictionary in the back of the concordance and look up word number 430, we'll find that this word is *elohim.* Genesis 1:1 is the first place in the Bible where the word *elohim* occurs.

You can now read elohim in Genesis 1:1 by reading the text like this. "In the beginning *elohim* made the heaven and the earth." If we read Strong's definition of *elohim,* we will notice that it has several definitions and that it is a plural noun. By this, Strong means that *elohim* is plural in form. However, we should not assume in advance that it is always plural in meaning. The context tells us the meaning.

Returning to the verse list for God, notice that for the vast majority of times that we read "God" in the Old Testament, it corresponds to the Hebrew word *elohim.* The *NIV Exhaustive Concordance* claims that one can find *elohim* 2,602 times in the Old Testament. The New International Version translates it 2,242 times as "God." It's the most common word in the Old Testament translated as "God." We have more than 2,200 verses that can help us understand what *elohim* means. If we want to be convinced what *elohim* means, then we can start reading those verses.

It may help to take Strong's verse list of "God" and to read each verse aloud, substituting *elohim* for "God" at the appropriate places. Substituting *elohim* into the text is probably the closest we will ever come to reading the Hebrew Bible. Yet it's a simple way of cementing the true meaning of *elohim* in our minds. But don't just read the verse by itself — read it in its broader context.

Substituting *elohim* for God in Genesis 1:1 can change our perspective of that verse and it can begin to help us understand this subject. Let's notice that applying this principle affects the reading of other verses in that same chapter. Genesis 1:2-5 will read:

> Now the earth was formless and empty, darkness was over the surface of the deep, and the Spirit of *elohim* was hovering over the waters. And *elohim* said, "Let there be light," and there was light.

Elohim saw that the light was good, and he separated the light from the darkness. Elohim called the light "day," and the darkness he called "night." And there was evening, and there was morning — the first day.

Notice that shortly after *elohim* is used, singular pronouns are used to refer to it: "he separated…he called." These reflect the fact that in Hebrew, these verbs are in the singular form.

Genesis 1:26 reads, "Then God [*elohim*] said, 'Let us make man in our image, in our likeness.'" I don't know Hebrew, so I can't tell if the verb "said" is singular or plural. But I do read English, and the pronouns here are plural. But does it automatically follow that *elohim* is plural? Before answering the question, I will ask another. Should we base our theology on one unusual verse or on more than 2,000 clear verses? What would lead to sound doctrine — 2,000 sure witnesses or one aberrant witness?

Genesis 1:26 is an enigmatic witness. It does not tell us why *or to whom* God is speaking. It does not say, "The Father said to the Son" or "God said to God" or "God said to the angels" or any other combination. Because the Bible remains silent as to whom and why God said this, any conclusions about these points would be conjectures, and therefore not a solid basis for doctrine. Note that there are several possibilities that do not require the existence of more than one God for them. Many commentaries will give us those explanations. You might think of some yourself.

Second, this is not the only verse that quotes God. Many of the later verses are God's revelation of himself to us in which he unambiguously says that there is but one God. Those other verses are the verses that should decide our doctrine — the verses that address the question directly and clearly.

Singular pronouns for *elohim*

Third, the context of the verse proves the plurality theory wrong. Genesis 1:27, the very next verse, reads: "So *elohim* created man in his own image, in the image of God [*elohim*] he created him; male and female he created them." Just as they are in the rest of the chapter, the pronouns here are singular. When *elohim* creates humanity, God reveals himself to be but one God.

As we continue our study, we'll notice several other interesting facts about *elohim*. For example, it was *elohim* who said "I give you every seed-bearing plant" (verse 29). It was *elohim* who said, "I will make a helper suitable for him" (Genesis 2:18). Later *elohim* told Noah, "I am going to put an end to all people" and "This is the sign of the covenant I am establishing between me and you" (Genesis 6:13; 9:12). God refers to himself with singular pronouns.

A beautiful trait of *elohim* is that he never lies. He thundered to Israel, "I am the Lord your *elohim*…. You shall have no other gods before me" (Exodus 20:2-3). Moses, the prophet of The God Who Does Not Lie, encouraged the Israelites to "acknowledge and take to heart this day that the Lord is *elohim* in heaven above and on the earth below. There is no other" (Deuteronomy 4:39).

In the Bible, it was *elohim* who walked in the Garden, made a covenant with Abraham, wrestled with Jacob and spoke out of the burning bush. There was only one. It was *elohim* who thundered from Sinai, gave victory to Joshua, sanctified the Temple and spoke to the prophets. This God, The God Who Does Not Lie, reveals himself to be the only God there is. "Turn to me and be saved, all you ends of the earth; for I am *elohim,* and there is no other" (Isaiah 45:22). The God of truth says, "See now that I myself am he! There is no *elohim* besides me" (Deuteronomy 32:39).

Elohim is not the only word plural in form but singular in meaning

Elohim is not the only Hebrew noun that can be plural in form but singular in meaning. Such Hebrew noun forms are sometimes used for abstract nouns and as intensifiers. Gesenius' *Hebrew Grammar* devotes several pages to this subject. The following list is not exhaustive, but it illustrates the point. The masculine plural ending is *-im;* *-oth* is the feminine plural ending.

zequnim — old age (Gen. 21:2, 7; 37:3; 44:20).

ne'urim — youth. David was only a boy (*na'ar*), but Goliath "has been a fighting man from his youth [*ne'urim*]" (1 Sam. 17:33).

chayyim — life. (This is used in the song "To life, to life, *lechayyim*" in Fiddler on the Roof.)

gebhuroth — strength. The singular form *gebhurah* is the usual word for strength, but the plural form is used in Job 41:12.

tsedaqoth — righteousness. The singular form *tsedaqah* is the usual word, but *tsedaqoth* is used in Isaiah 33:15 — "he who walks righteously [or "in righteousness"]."

chokmoth — wisdom. *Chokmah* is the usual form, but *chokmoth* is used in Prov. 1:20.

'adonim — lord. *'adon* means "lord," and *'adonim* normally means "lords," but Isaiah 19:4 says, "I will hand the Egyptians over to the power of a cruel master ['adonim]."

behemoth. This word normally means beasts, but in Job 40:15 it refers to one animal.

Specifically discussing *elohim,* Gesenius observes: "The language has entirely rejected the idea of numerical plurality in *'elohim* (whenever it denotes one God).... [This] is proved especially by its being almost invariably joined with a singular attribute" (such as a singular adjective or verb). For more information on the subject, consult Gesenius' *Hebrew Grammar,* pages 396-401, 1909 edition.

DOES THE DOCTRINE OF THE TRINITY TEACH THREE GODS?

Some people take issue with the use of the word "Person" in the doctrine of the Trinity when the word is applied to the Father, Son and Holy Spirit. They wrongly assume that the doctrine of the Trinity inadvertently teaches that three Gods exist. Their reasoning goes something like this: If God the Father is a "Person," then he is a God in his own right (having the characteristics of being divine). He would count as "one" God. The same could be said about the Son and Holy Spirit. Thus, there would be three separate Gods.

The Trinity doctrine has the opposite intent – to preserve the biblical witness to the oneness of God's Being, yet at the same time accounting for the divinity of the Father, Son and the Spirit. When we speak of God's divine nature, we must not confuse tritheism with the Trinity or think of "persons" as we do in the human sphere. What the Trinity says is that God is one with respect to his essence but is three with respect to the internal distinctions within his Triunity.

Here is how Christian scholar Emery Bancroft described it in his book *Christian Theology,* pages 87-88:

> The Father is not God as such; for God is not only Father, but also Son and Holy Spirit. The term Father designates that personal distinction in the divine nature in virtue of which God is related to the Son and, through the Son and the Spirit, to the church.
>
> The Son is not God as such; for God is not only Son, but also Father and Holy Spirit. The Son designates that distinction in virtue of which God is related to the Father, and is sent by the Father to redeem the world, and with the Father sends the Holy Spirit.
>
> The Holy Spirit is not God as such; for God is not only Holy Spirit, but also Father and Son. The Holy Spirit designates that distinction in virtue of which God is related to the Father and the Son, and is sent by them to accomplish the work of renewing the ungodly and sanctifying the church.

When we are seeking to understand the Trinity doctrine, we need to be careful how we use and understand the word "God." For example, whatever the New Testament says about the oneness of God, it also draws a distinction between Jesus Christ and God the Father. This is where the above formula from Bancroft is helpful. To be precise, we should speak of "God the Father," "God the Son" and "God the Holy Spirit" when we are referring to each hypostasis or "Person" of the one God.

There are limitations of using the word "person" when explaining the nature of God. Do we really understand how God can be one in Being and three in Person? We have no experiential knowledge of God as he is. Not only is our experience limited, but so is our language. Using the word "Persons" for each of the three hypostases of God is in some ways a compromise. But, when speaking of God's nature, we need a word that emphasizes his personalness in relationship to us human creatures and within himself, and yet carries with it the concept of distinctiveness. "Person" is the most appropriate word we have in the English language to do this.

Unfortunately, the word "person" also contains the notion of separateness when used of human persons. How can we deal with this? We understand that God does not consist of the kind of persons that a group of human beings do. Human persons are separate from each other and have separate wills because they only have external relations with each other, while the Persons of God have internal relations and share the same essence.

The Trinity doctrine uses the word "Person" for each hypostasis of God because it is a personal word, and God is a personal being in his dealings with us. Only a personal being can love, and love is the defining essence of God, according to the biblical witness (1 John 4:8; John 3:16; 15:9-10)

The word "persons" distinguishes between the three Persons of God and the one Being of God in the sense that the three Persons constitute his one Being. Thus, the doctrine preserves both the biblical revelation that there is but one God and no other, as well as its testimony that the Father, the Son and the Spirit are all equally divine and true God of true God.

Those who reject the Trinitarian explanation of God's nature are in a quandary. If they reject the theology of the Trinity, they have no explanation that preserves two biblical truths about God's Being: God is One Being and also he is plural in his Being. If they accept the biblical fact that Jesus is divine, they need some way of explaining that God is one, yet has more than one Person.

That is why Christians formulated the doctrine in precise technical language — so that we could rightly speak of God, according to the witness he has left us of himself through Christ and in the Spirit, as attested to by the New Testament. The church confesses the biblical testimony that God is one divine Being. But Christians also confess that Jesus Christ and the Holy Spirit are divine, true God of true God, according to the New Testament.

The Trinity doctrine was developed with the intent of explaining, as well as human words and thought would allow, the reality that God has existed from eternity both as One Being and yet as three Persons. The Trinity doctrine says that God is one and that in his oneness he is Triune.

Explanations of the nature of God other than the Trinity have been put forth throughout the history of the Church. Arianism is one example. This theory claimed that the Son was a created being. The Arians thought they had preserved the oneness of God in their explanation, but created a heresy that did not rightly speak of God's nature. The Arian conclusion was fundamentally flawed in that if the Son was a created being, he would not be divine, of the same essence of God, and therefore, could not be our Savior and could not be worshipped. Only God can save us and make us new creations. All other theories advanced to explain God's nature in terms of the revelation of the Son and Holy Spirit have proved equally unfaithful to the gospel and the nature of God.

On the other hand, the Trinitarian explanation takes into consideration the divinity of the Father, the Son and Holy Spirit – and the biblical truth that there is only one God. That's why the doctrine of the Trinity has survived for centuries as the explanation of God's nature that preserves the truth of the biblical witness of who God is – and that he has saved us in himself through the Son and in the Spirit.

Paul Kroll

THE TRINITY: 1 + 1 + 1 = 1 ?

It Just Doesn't Add Up

The Father is God, and the Son is God, and the Holy Spirit is God, but there is only one God. "Wait a minute," some people say. "One plus one plus one equals one? This can't be right. It just doesn't add up."

True, it doesn't add up—and it's not supposed to. God isn't a thing that can be added. There can be only one all-powerful, all-wise, everywhere-present being, so there can be only one God. In the world of spirit, the Father, Son, and Holy Spirit are God, unified in a way that material objects cannot be. Our math is based on material things; it does not always work in the infinite, spiritual realm.

The Father is God and the Son is God, but there is only one God being. This is not a family or committee of divine beings—a group cannot say, "There is none like me" (Isaiah 43:10; 44:6; 45:5). God is only one divine being—more than one Person, but only one God. The early Christians did not get this idea from paganism or philosophy—they were led to it by statements in Scripture.

Just as Scripture teaches that Jesus Christ is divine, it also teaches that the Holy Spirit is divine and personal. Whatever the Holy Spirit does, God does. The Holy Spirit, like the Son and the Father, is God—three Persons perfectly united in one God: the Trinity.

Michael Morrison

IS JESUS REALLY GOD?
A LOOK AT THE ARIAN CONTROVERSY

Few Christians are aware that two of the most fundamental doctrines of the Christian faith — the divinity of Jesus Christ and the Trinity — were not finally decided until some 350 years after the death of Jesus.

Both doctrines were forged in the fourth century out of the religious and political firestorm sparked by Arius, a popular presbyter of the church in Alexandria, Egypt. Arius had a simple formula for explaining how Jesus Christ could be divine — and therefore worthy of worship along with God the Father — even though there is only one God.

The simple formula taught by Arius was well received by the common believers in Alexandria, but not by Arius' supervisor, bishop Alexander. Each man lined up supporters and the battle lines were drawn for what history would call the Arian Controversy. This bitter ordeal for the Christian churches of the eastern and western Roman Empire began in A.D. 318, led to the Creed of Nicea in 325 and finally ended with the Nicene Creed established at the Council of Constantinople in 381.

Monarchianism

Church Fathers from as early as the late 100s had been writing that the Word of God, the *Logos* of John 1:1-2, was co-eternal with the Father — and therefore uncreated and without beginning. The presbyter Arius was not the first to dispute this. Similar challenges had already arisen by the late second and early third centuries in the form of Monarchianism.

Monarchians fell into two broad categories. The Adoptionist or Dynamic Monarchians held that Jesus was only a man in whom dwelled the power of the supreme God.[1] The Modalist Monarchians taught that God revealed himself in three modes — as Father, Son and Spirit — but never at the same time. This preserved the idea of the full divinity of the Son, but at the expense of any real distinction between the Son and the Father. Some Modalists believed that Jesus Christ was actually the Father in the flesh. All forms of Monarchianism were eventually branded as heresy and rejected by the Christian churches across the empire.

Arius

In one sense, Arius was simply the latest thinker to try to reconcile monotheism (belief in one God) with the Christian belief that Jesus Christ was divine. But there was a great difference between Arius' attempt and all previous efforts. No longer was Christianity an officially unsanctioned, often underground and persecuted religion. Now the Roman emperor Constantine had granted Christianity unprecedented legitimate status in the Empire, so that the question of who Jesus is could finally come before the whole Church to be settled.

Arius was a popular senior presbyter in charge of Baucalis, one of the twelve "parishes" of Alexandria in the early fourth century.[2] By A.D. 318, Arius had begun teaching his followers that the Son of God (who is also the *Logos* or Word of John 1:1-2) did not exist until the Father brought him into existence. To Arius, the Father first created the Word, and then the Word, as the Father's unique and supreme agent, created everything else.

Arius' idea seemed to preserve monotheism as well as uphold the divinity of the Son, even if it was a bestowed divinity as distinct from the inherent and eternal divinity of the Father. With the help of catchy rhymes and tunes, Arius' ideas quickly caught on among the common converts of Alexandria.

Alexander

Alexander, the bishop of Alexandria, and his assistant, a presbyter named Athanasius, saw great danger in Arius' teaching and took action to arrest it. Contrary to Arius' teaching that God was once without the Word, Alexander asserted that God *cannot* be without the Word, and that the Word is therefore without beginning and eternally generated by the Father.

Alexander sent letters to neighboring bishops requesting support and convened a council at Alexandria that excommunicated Arius and a dozen other clergy.[3] Arius also sought backing, however, and obtained the support of several leaders, including Eusebius, the bishop of Nicomedia. Eusebius enjoyed a close relationship with Emperor Constantine, which would play a major role in the unfolding of the controversy. Another supporter of Arius was the historian, Eusebius of Caesarea, whose history of the early Christian church is still available today.

Constantine steps in

The Emperor Constantine became aware of the developing problem, and saw a need to resolve it. As Emperor, Constantine's concern was not so much for the unity of the Church as for the unity of the empire itself. Theologically, he viewed it as a "trifle."[4] Constantine's first move was to send his religious advisor, Bishop Hosius of Cordova, Spain, to sort out the differences. Hosius was unsuccessful in bringing Arius and Alexander to peace, but he presided over a council in Antioch in early 325 that condemned Arianism and censured Eusebius of Caesarea.[5] But the division continued, so Constantine called a universal council of the Church to settle the dispute.

Ancyra had been the original choice of venue, but Constantine changed the location to Nicaea, a city closer to his Nicomedia headquarters. The emperor personally opened the council in June of 325 with about 300 bishops present (most from the east). Constantine was looking for mutual tolerance and compromise. Many of the bishops present were also apparently prepared to find compromise.

As the proceedings unfolded, however, thoughts of compromise quickly eroded. Once the tenets of the Arian position became clear, it did not take long for them to be rejected and condemned. The ideas that the Son of God is God only as a "courtesy title" and that the Son is of created status were vehemently denounced. Those who held such views were anathematized. The divinity of the Logos was upheld, and the Son was declared to be "true God" and co-eternal with the Father. The key phrase from the Creed established at Nicaea in 325 was "of the essence of the Father, God of God and Light of Light, very God of very God, begotten, not made, being of one substance with the Father."

Homoousios (of the same essence) was the key Greek word. It was intended to convey, against the Arians, that the Son is equally divine with the Father. This it did, but it also left unanswered the question of how the Son and the Father, if they are of the same essence, are in fact distinct. Consequently, though Arianism was condemned and Arius banished, the Council of Nicaea did not see an end to the controversy.

A little letter makes a big difference

Athanasius and most other eastern bishops said that the Son was *homoousios* with the Father, meaning "of the same essence." The Arian theologians disagreed, but suggested a compromise: they could accept the word with the addition of only one letter, the smallest Greek letter, the iota. They said that the Son was *homoiousios* with the Father — a Greek word meaning "similar essence."

But similarity is in the "i" of the beholder, and the Arians actually meant that Jesus was not the same kind of being as the Father. It would be like saying that he was "almost" divine. The orthodox theologians could not accept that, and would not accept a word that allowed such an unorthodox interpretation.

Imperial reversals

Eusebius of Nicomedia, who presented the Arian cause to the Council and was deposed and banished for it, enjoyed a close personal relationship with Emperor Constantine. In time, he was able to convince Constantine to ease the punishment on the Arians, and to order Arius himself recalled from exile. Eventually, after a council at Jerusalem formally acquitted him of the charge of heresy in 335, Arius was to have been received back into the fellowship of the church in Constantinople. Philip Schaff wrote:

> But on the evening before the intended procession from the imperial palace to the church of the Apostles, he suddenly died (A.D. 336), at the age of over eighty years, of an attack like cholera, while attending to a call of nature. This death was regarded by many as a divine judgment; by others, it was attributed to poisoning by enemies; by others, to the excessive joy of Arius in his triumph.[6]

Athanasius, meanwhile, had succeeded Alexander as bishop of Alexandria in 328 only to be condemned and deposed by two Arian councils, one at Tyre under the presidency of Eusebius of Caesarea, and the other at Constantinople in about 335. He was then banished by Constantine to Treves in Gaul in 336 as a disturber of the peace of the church.[7]

This turn of events was followed by the death of Constantine in 337 (who received the sacrament of baptism on his deathbed from the Arian Eusebius of Nicomedia). Constantine's three sons, Constantine II, Constans, and Constantius succeeded him. Constantine II, who ruled Gaul, Great Britain, Spain, and Morocco, recalled Athanasius from banishment in 338. In the east, however, matters were quite different. Constantius, who ruled the east, was firmly Arian. Eusebius of Nicomedia, the leader of the Arian party, was appointed Bishop of Constantinople in 338. Before long, war in the west between Constantine II and Constans gave Constantius a free hand to again exile Athanasius in 340.

When Constantine II died, however, and the western empire was united under Constans, Constantius had to follow a more moderate line with the Nicene party. The two emperors called a general council in Sardica in 343, presided over by Hosius, at which the Nicene doctrine was confirmed. Constans also compelled Constantius to restore Athanasius to his office in 346.[8]

Semi-Arianism

When Constans died in 350, the pendulum swung again. Constantius, now the sole emperor and still Arian, held councils supporting Arianism and banished bishops who opposed their edicts, including Hosius and Athanasius. By now, Arianism had itself become divided into two factions. One party had slightly modified its position to affirm *homoiousios*, or similarity of essence, rather than the original *heteroousios*, or difference of essence, still held by the strictest Arians.

This "compromise," sometimes called "semi-Arianism," still represented an unbridgeable chasm from the orthodox *homoousios*, or same essence. It only served to pit the Arians against one another. For Nicenes who still had difficulty with the apparent lack of distinction between the Father and the Son represented by *homoousios*, though, the semi-Arian *homoiousios* did, for a time, afford a compromise. In any case, by the time of the death of Constantius, the Church had become Arian, at least on the surface.

Imperial reversals

It was the death of Constantius in 361 that set the stage for the permanent triumph of Nicene faith. Julian the Apostate became emperor and implemented a policy of toleration for all the Christian parties. Though Julian's policy, at first glance, seems positive toward Christianity, his real hope was that the opposing factions would destroy one another. He recalled the exiled bishops, including Athanasius (though Athanasius was soon banished again as an "enemy of the gods" but was again recalled by Julian's successor Jovian).[9]

It was through the efforts of Athanasius that the concerns of the Nicenes and the semi-Arians about blurring the distinction between the Father and the Son were assuaged. Athanasius argued that *homoousios* could be interpreted in such a way as to affirm the same essence as long as the distinction between the Father and Son were not destroyed. In other words, he made it plain that "same essence" must retain the unity but never be allowed to destroy the distinctions in the Godhead. With this understanding, along with the compelling work of the Cappadocian bishops, Basil, Gregory of Nazianzus, and Gregory of Nyssa, the Nicene faith again began to gain ascendancy.

Julian died in 363, and was followed by Jovian, who was favorable toward Athanasius and the Nicene faith. His reign was short, though, ending in 364. He was succeeded by Valens, a fanatical Arian, whose intensity against both semi-Arians and Nicenes tended to bring those two parties together. In 375, he was followed by Gratian, who was of Nicene faith, and who recalled all the exiled orthodox bishops.

By the end of Gratian's reign, Arianism was greatly waning in intellectual defense and in morale. At last, it was the long reign of Theodosius I, who was educated in the Nicene faith, that finally ended the long controversy. He required all his subjects to confess the orthodox faith. He appointed a champion of Nicene faith, Gregory of Nazianzus, as patriarch of

Constantinople in 380. In 381, Gregory presided over the Council of Constantinople.

The Council of Constantinople

The Council of Constantinople affirmed the Creed of Nicaea, altering it only slightly and in non-essential ways. It is the form of the Creed adopted at Constantinople that today bears the name Nicene Creed. The controversy was at last ended in the empire. However, Arianism would continue to impact the Church for the next two centuries in the form of the various peoples outside the empire who had become Christians according to the Arian faith (most of whom scarcely even knew the difference).

Athanasius, who had so diligently and unswervingly opposed the Arian heresy, did not live to see the conflict ended. He died in 373 in his native Alexandria. In the end, the unyielding Athanasius is a fair representation of the unyielding truth of the orthodox Christian faith. Fundamental to the validity of Christianity is the reality of redemption, made possible only by the work of no being less than true God, the Lord Jesus Christ.

Arius believed that a Christ designated as divine by virtue of his special creation could serve as true Redeemer and true Mediator between God and humanity. It took the dogged, relentless, unwavering faith of an Athanasius to hold fast to the truth that no being less than true God could in fact reconcile humanity to God.

The apostle Paul wrote to the church in Corinth: "No doubt there have to be differences among you to show which of you have God's approval" (1 Corinthians 11:19). Likewise, the Arian controversy became an essential waypoint on the journey of the church, for despite the trial and pain of controversy, the truth of the nature of the divine One who had come to redeem humanity had to be made plain.

Who was who?

- Arius (c. 250-336): Theologian in Alexandria, Egypt, a presbyter (an elder) of the church. He taught his followers that the Son of God did not exist until he was brought into existence by the Father.
- Alexander of Alexandria (d. 326): Bishop of Alexandria and Arius' supervisor. He strongly opposed Arianism.
- Athanasius (293-373): A presbyter of the church in Alexandria and assistant to Bishop Alexander. He later succeeded Alexander as Bishop of Alexandria and spearheaded the effort to oppose Arianism and establish the Nicene faith.
- Eusebius of Caesarea (c. 263-339): Bishop of Caesarea and author of

several works chronicling the history of early Christianity, including *Ecclesiastical History*. He hoped for a compromise in the Arian controversy, and as a historian he recorded the proceedings at the Council of Nicea.

- Eusebius of Nicomedia (d. 341): Bishop of Nicomedia. He supported Arius' ideas and presented the Arian side of the controversy at the Council of Nicea.

- Constantine the Great (272-337): Emperor of the Roman Empire who legalized Christianity in the Empire. He called the Council of Nicea in an effort to bring an end to the dispute among the churches that was threatening the security of the Empire.

- Hosius of Cordova (c. 256-358): Bishop of Cordova, Spain. He was sent to Alexandria by Constantine to mediate the Arian controversy.

Endnotes

1 Clyde Manschreck, "Monarchianism," in *Dictionary of Bible and Religion* (Nashville: Abingdon, 1986), 704.

2 David Wright, "Councils and Creeds," *The History of Christianity* (Herts, England: Lion Publishing, 1977), 156.

3 Wright, 157.

4 Wright, 159.

5 William Rusch, *The Trinitarian Controversy* (Philadelphia: Fortress, 1980), 19.

6 Philip Schaff, *History of the Christian Church* (Charles Scribner's Sons, 1910; reprinted by Eerdmans, 1987), vol. III, 663.

7 Schaff, 663.

8 Schaff, 635.

9 Schaff, 638.

J. Michael Feazell

DON'T JUST ACCEPT THE TRINITY

About 15 years ago, when my denomination was correcting certain longstanding doctrinal errors, I was asked to supervise our churches in Britain. Since we had decided to once again publish the denominational magazine, we applied to take a display stand at the Christian Resources Exhibition. The prestigious CRE is open to all legitimate churches, charities and manufacturers and distributors of religious products. On the first morning of the conference, a tall, thin, rather severe-looking clergyman made a beeline for us.

"I must say," he said pompously, "that I am surprised to see you people here."

"I don't see why you should be," I answered, "This is the Christian Resources Exhibition and our magazine is a Christian resource. Why shouldn't we be here?"

"Because you're not orthodox," he said imperiously.

"Yes we are," I replied, and reached for a copy of our *Statement of Beliefs*. I had some on hand, suspecting this objection might come up.

"No you are not," he insisted. "You do not accept the Trinity."

"Yes we do — read this." Reluctantly he read the relevant paragraph. It seemed to take the wind out of his sails. But only temporarily.

He handed the document back to me, and said, "That is all very well. But do your people *understand* the Trinity?"

"Do yours?" I asked.

"My people" he said, with a rather smug smile, "don't need to understand it, because we never rejected it." Then he stalked off. I think my comments upset him, but his comments made me think.

Most Christians do not give the Trinity a second thought. It is one of the "givens" of their faith. If you have believed something all your life, you probably take it for granted. But when you come to a belief later, you have to think it through carefully. I had spent many years rejecting the doctrine of the Trinity as an explanation of God's being. It was difficult to abandon my suspicion about it, even though I had to accept that my reasons for rejecting it had no basis in Scripture. I had been taught that it was an idea that had been injected into Christianity by pagans who wanted to distort a true understanding of God. It was humbling to see that, far from trying to hide the truth, the doctrine was formulated in technically precise theological language by devoted Christian scholars who were striving to combat and eliminate some corrosive ideas that could undermine the role of Jesus as

Savior.

Okay, so I could see why Trinitarian theology was a litmus test for being accepted as a "legitimate." But it was a fearfully difficult doctrine to use. I am a practical person, and I find analogies helpful. But I could not come up with the perfect analogy that would clarify things sufficiently to put the Trinity to practical use in preaching and teaching.

As the combatant vicar pointed out, most Christians, including many learned and scholarly theologians, haven't needed to do this. They have just accepted the Trinity as part of the historical backdrop of their faith. In doing so, they may have short-changed themselves. Through the ages, however, some prominent theologians have gone beyond just an acceptance of the doctrine, and asked searching questions about what the tri-unity of God *means*. They realized that the doctrine is more than just a useful barrier erected to keep the faith safe from dangerous heresies. They have seen that it highlights foundational biblical concepts that are very exciting and, indeed, quite important for our Christian faith. These are not new ideas, but they have been somewhat neglected, and as such, they are sometimes looked on with suspicion.

They needn't be, for they pose no threat. What they can do is confront you with the real Jesus of the Bible, who is the perfect revelation of his Father, and show you how knowing the Father, the Son and Spirit can blow fresh air through your faith, removing the stale smell of guilt and fear, and transform your everyday life. We have been exploring these ideas. We hope you will share our enthusiasm — and see how the good news of the gospel is even more exciting than you may have thought.

John Halford

PERICHORESIS – WHAT'S THAT?

A discussion with C. Baxter Kruger, founder of Perichoresis, Inc.

Question: Most of us can't even pronounce *perichoresis,* much less spell it. What does it mean?

Baxter Kruger: Some years ago a woman walked into my office around Christmastime with a stack of newsletters in her hand. She was crying, and she slammed the newsletters down on my desk and said, "I just feel like a pile of junk!"

I said, "What is wrong?"

She said, "I've been reading these newsletters from these people from all over the world, and they and their children are all doing all these great things for God, and it just hit me what a worthless life I have. For Pete's sake, I'm married and I've got three kids. When I'm not grocery shopping, I'm cooking the groceries, and when I'm not cooking the groceries I'm cleaning up, and when I'm not doing that I'm trying to find clothes for my children and keep this mess of a house presentable. And sometime in there I'm trying to find time for my husband. I don't even have time to read my Bible. What do I have that I can do for God?"

I stopped her, and I said, "Wait a minute, hang on here a minute. Yesterday you spent two hours driving around Jackson searching for a coat for your daughter. A winter coat, and not just any winter coat but one she would like, one that would be large enough to put away for next year but not look like it was bought this year. And one that was on sale. And you did it, you found it, and she's thrilled."

The woman said, "What's that got to do with this?"

I said, "Where did that concern for your daughter come from? Did you wake up yesterday morning and decide you were going to be a good momma?"

She said she had been thinking about the coat for a week.

"The Triune God meets us not in the sky or in our self-generated religions, but in our 'ordinary' human existence."

I said, "Isn't Jesus the good Shepherd who cares about all his sheep? He put his concern for this sheep (your daughter) in your heart. You are participating in nothing less than Jesus' life and burden. He was tending to his sheep through you. What is greater than that?"

In the light of the fact that Jesus Christ has laid hold of the whole human race, cleansed us in his death, lifted us up in his resurrection and has given us a place in his relationship with his Father and Spirit in his Ascension, we've got to rethink everything we thought we knew about ourselves and others and our ordinary human life.

The simple truth is there is nothing at all ordinary about us and the life we live. Caring for others, from orphans to our friends and the poor, our love for our husbands and wives and children, our passion for music and beauty, for coaching, gardening and fishing; these things do not have their origin in us.

They are not something that we invented. It is all coming from the Father, Son and Spirit. When this dreadful secular/sacred divide is exploded, we can see and honor life as it truly is—the gift of participating in the life and relationship of the Father, Son and Spirit.

So we're really talking about God meeting us in our day-to-day lives?

BK: Exactly. Through the work of Jesus, we have been adopted into the Trinitarian life. The concept of perichoresis helps us understand what our adoption means for us. We could define perichoresis as "mutual indwelling without loss of personal identity." In other words, we exist in union with the Triune God, but we do not lose our distinct personhood in the process. We matter. We are real to the Triune God.

Only the Trinity could have union without loss of personal distinction. If you have union without distinction, you tumble into pantheism, and we would be united to God in such a way as to be completely absorbed into him. There would no longer be a distinct "us" to feel and taste and experience the Trinitarian life.

If you have distinction without union, you end up with deism, where God is just up there watching us from a distance, and we never see our humanity as included in the Trinitarian life. Motherhood and fatherhood, work and play and music then appear to be merely secular, non-divine aspects of our human experience. Deism leaves us with a Christ-less humanity, and forces us to search beyond our humanity for connection with God.

In Trinitarian theology we say "no" to both pantheism and deism. We have union but no loss of personal distinction, which means that we matter and that our humanity, our motherhood and fatherhood, our work and play and music form the arena for our participation in the Trinitarian life of God. The Triune God meets us not in the sky or in our self-generated religions, but in our "ordinary" human existence.

So the gospel is about God knowing us and us knowing God.

BK: Exactly. Let me give you a quick story. I like stories better than long and convoluted theological explanations. Many years ago when my son was six (he's 18 now), I was sitting on the couch in the den sorting through junk mail on a Saturday afternoon. He and his buddy came in and they were decked out in their camouflage, face paint, plastic guns and knives, the whole nine yards. My son peers around the corner of the door and looks at me, and the next thing I know, he comes flying through the air and jumps on me. We start wrestling and horsing around and we end up on the floor. Then his buddy flies into us and all three of us are just like a wad of laughter.

Right in the middle of that event the Lord spoke to me and said to pay attention. I'm thinking, it's Saturday afternoon, your son comes in and you're horsing around on the floor, it happens every day all over the world, so what's the big deal? Then it started to dawn on me that I didn't know who this other kid was. I had never met him. He had never met me. So I re-wound the story and thought about what would have happened if this little boy would have walked into my den alone. Remember, he didn't know me and I didn't know him, and he didn't know my name and I didn't know his name. So he looks over and sees me, a complete stranger, sitting on the couch. Would he fly through the air and engage me in play? Would we end up in a pile of laughter on the floor? Of course not. That is the last thing that would have happened.

Within himself, that little boy had no freedom to have a relationship with me. We were strangers. He had no right to that kind of familiarity and fellowship. But my son knows me. My son knows that I love him and that I accept him and that he's the apple of my eye. So in the knowledge of my love and affection, he did the most natural thing in the world. He dove into my lap. The miracle that happened was that my son's knowledge of my acceptance and delight, and my son's freedom for fellowship with me, rubbed off onto that other little boy. He got to experience it. That other little boy got to taste and feel and know my son's relationship with me. He participated in my son's life and communion with me.

Then it dawned on me that that's what perichoresis and our adoption in Christ mean. Jesus is the one who knows the Father. He knows the Father's love and acceptance. He sees the Father's face. Jesus has freedom for fellowship with his Father. And Jesus shares his heart with us. He puts his own freedom for relationship with his Father in us through the Spirit, and like that little boy we get to taste and feel and experience the relationship Jesus has with his Father. He shares it all with us. He unites himself with us, and we get to experience his divine life with him. He shares with us his own knowledge of his Father's heart, his own knowledge of the Father's acceptance, his own assurance of his Father's love, his own freedom in knowing the Father's passionate heart. He reaches into his own soul, as it were, and pulls out his own emotions, and then puts them inside of the whole human race. We're all included in the Son's relationship with the Father in the fellowship of the Holy Spirit.

Then we never have to worry about whether God accepts us and loves us?

BK: Never. What does the understanding that we are accepted into the mutual indwelling and communion with God remove from our hearts? Fear and hiding. So because of Jesus' knowledge of the Father's acceptance, which he shares with us, we now are free to let go of our racial and personal prejudices, and to love and accept one another, which leads to the freedom to know and be known, which leads to fellowship and mutual indwelling.

This is what the kingdom of the Triune God is all about. The kingdom is simply the life and love, the communion, the fellowship, the camaraderie and joy of the Father, Son and Spirit, being shared with us and coming to full and abiding and personal expression in us, in our relationships with one another and in our relationships with the whole creation, so that the whole earth is full of the Son's knowledge of his Father in the Spirit. As to why we don't experience our life in Christ more fully, that is a question for another day.

C. Baxter Kruger is Director of Perichoresis, Inc.— A Trinitarian Ministry. Dr. Kruger's resources can be accessed at www.perichoresis.org.

OUR TRIUNE GOD: LIVING LOVE

If asked to identify the oldest living thing, some might point to Tasmania's 10,000-year-old pine trees or its 40,000-year-old shrub. Others might point to the 200,000-year-old seagrass on the coast of Spain's Balearic Islands. As ancient as these plants may be, the oldest living thing is far older—it's the eternal God, who is revealed in Scripture to be *living love*. Love is God's nature, and the intra-personal love of the Trinity has existed from before creation. There never has been a time when true love did not exist because our eternal, Triune God is the Source of authentic love.

Augustine, Bishop of Hippo (d. 430), emphasized this truth by referring to the Father as "Lover," the Son as "Beloved," and the Spirit as the love existing between them. Out of his infinite abundance of love, the Triune God created all that exists, including you and me. In *The Triune Creator*, theologian Colin Gunton argues for this Trinitarian explanation of creation, noting that we must consider the whole biblical witness and not just the Genesis creation accounts. Gunton notes that this approach is not new—it's how the early church understood creation. For example, Irenaeus noted that a Trinitarian perspective requires viewing creation in the light of what happened in Jesus. The God who created everything out of nothing (*ex nihilo*) did so with great purpose—out of love, in love, and for love.

As T.F. Torrance and his brother J.B. liked to say, creation was the result of the overflow of God's love. This is seen clearly when God said, "Let us make mankind in our image, in our likeness…" (Genesis 1:26). In the phrase "Let us…" we find a hint of God's triune nature. Some interpreters disagree, saying that viewing this as a reference to the Trinity is to impose New Testament understanding on the Old Testament. They typically explain either that "Let us" is a literary device (the "majestic we"), or that God is talking with the angels as his co-creators. But Scripture never attributes creative powers to angels. Further, we should interpret all Scripture through the lens of Jesus' person and teaching. The God who said "Let us," was the Triune God whether or not ancient humans knew it.

As we read the Bible through the lens of Jesus, we come to understand that God's creation of humankind in his image is a profound expression of God's nature, which is love. In Colossians 1:15 and 2 Corinthians 4:4, we learn that Jesus, himself, is the Image of God. Jesus images the Father to us because he and the Father are one in being in a relationship of perfect love. Scripture tells us that Jesus is connected to creation (including humankind), referring to him as the "firstborn" of creation. Paul calls Adam (the first man), the copy ("type") of Jesus "the one who was to come" (Romans 5:14, NRSV). Jesus is thus the prototype of all humanity. Paul also calls Jesus the "last Adam," who as the "life-giving spirit" renews fallen Adam (1 Corinthians 15:45), thus transforming humankind into his own image.

As Scripture tells us, we have "put on the new self, which is being renewed in knowledge in the image of its Creator" (Colossians 3:10), and "we all, who with unveiled faces, contemplate the Lord's glory, are being transformed into his image with ever-increasing glory, which comes from the Lord, who is the Spirit" (2 Corinthians 3:18). The author of Hebrews tells us that Jesus is "the radiance of God's glory and the exact representation of his being" (Hebrews 1:3). He is the true Image of God, who in taking on our human nature, "tasted death for everyone." By uniting himself to us, Jesus sanctified us and made us his brothers and sisters (Hebrews 2:9-15). We have been created and now are being re-created according to the image of the Son of God who, himself, images for us the holy loving relationships in the Trinity. We are to live and move and have our being in Christ, who has his very being in the tri-personal communion of love of the Father, Son and Spirit.

In Christ and with Christ, we are God's beloved children. But sadly, those lacking understanding of God's Triune nature of love easily miss this important truth, embracing instead various misunderstandings:

- *Tritheism,* which denies God's unity, claiming there are three separate and distinct gods, thus making any relationships between them external and not essential to God's nature.

- *Modalism,* which teaches that God is a single being who appears at various times in one of three different modes. This teaching also denies any relationships internal and eternal to God.

- *Subordinationism,* which teaches that Jesus is a creature (or a divine being who is less than the Father) and thus not eternally the divine Son of God. This teaching also denies that God in his being is a triune relationship of holy love for all eternity.

- Other teachings, though affirming the doctrine of the Trinity, fail to grasp its deepest glory: that the Triune God is loving in his very being before there ever was a creation.

Understanding that the Triune God is, in his very nature, love, helps us see that love is the foundation of all things. At the center of that understanding is that all things come from and revolve around Jesus, who reveals the Father and sends the Holy Spirit. Thus, the place to start in understanding both God and his creation (including humankind), is in asking this question: Who is Jesus?

It is inescapably Trinitarian that the Father has created all things and established his kingdom by placing his Son at the center of his plan, purpose and revelation. The Son glorifies the Father and the Father glorifies the Son. The Holy Spirit, who doesn't speak of himself, constantly points to the Son, thus glorifying the Son and the Father. The Father, Son and Spirit delight in this triune interaction of love. And when we, God's children, confess Jesus as Lord, we do so by the Holy Spirit to the glory of the Father. As Jesus predicted, true worship is "in spirit and in truth." When we worship the Father, Son and Spirit, we are worshiping the oldest living thing who, in love, created us to love him and dwell with him forever!

Joseph Tkach

INTRODUCTION TO THE HOLY SPIRIT

The Holy Spirit is God at work—creating, speaking, transforming us, living within us, working in us. Although the Holy Spirit can do this work without our knowledge, it is helpful for us to know more.

The Holy Spirit is God

The Holy Spirit has the attributes of God, is equated with God and does work that only God does. Like God, the Spirit is holy—so holy that insulting the Spirit is just as sinful as trampling the Son of God under foot (Hebrews 10:29). Blasphemy against the Holy Spirit is an unforgivable sin (Matthew 12:32).[1] This indicates that the Spirit is holy by nature rather than having an assigned holiness such as the temple had.

Like God, the Holy Spirit is eternal (Hebrews 9:14). Like God, the Holy Spirit is everywhere present (Psalm 139:7-9). Like God, the Holy Spirit knows everything (1 Corinthians 2:10-11; John 14:26). The Holy Spirit creates (Job 33:4; Psalm 104:30) and empowers miracles (Matthew 12:28; Romans 15:18-19), doing the work or ministry of God.

Several passages discuss the Father, Son, and Holy Spirit as equally divine. In a discussion of spiritual gifts, Paul puts the Spirit, the Lord, and God in parallel constructions (1 Corinthians 12:4-6). He closes a letter with a three-part prayer (2 Corinthians 13:14). Peter begins a letter with a different three-part formula (1 Peter 1:2). These are not proof of unity, but they support it.

The baptismal formula has a stronger indication of unity—"in the name [singular] of the Father and of the Son and of the Holy Spirit" (Matthew 28:19). The three have one name, suggesting one essence and being.

When the Holy Spirit does something, God is doing it. When the Holy Spirit speaks, God is speaking. When Ananias lied to the Holy Spirit, he lied to God (Acts 5:3-4). As Peter said, Ananias did not lie to God's representative, but to God himself. People do not "lie" to an impersonal power.

In one passage, Paul says that Christians are God's temple (1 Corinthians 3:16); in another he says that we are a temple of the Holy Spirit (1 Corinthians 6:19). A temple is for the worship of a divine being, not an impersonal power. When Paul writes "temple of the Holy Spirit," he implies that the Holy Spirit is God.

The Holy Spirit and God are also equated in Acts 13:2: "The Holy Spirit said, 'Set apart for *me* Barnabas and Saul for the work to which *I* have called them.'" Here, the Holy Spirit speaks with personal pronouns, speaking as

God. Similarly, the Holy Spirit says that the Israelites "tested and tried *me*"; the Holy Spirit says that "*I* was angry.... They shall never enter my rest" (Hebrews 3:7-11).

But the Holy Spirit is not just another name for God. The Holy Spirit is distinct from the Father and the Son, as shown in Jesus' baptism (Matthew 3:16-17). The three are distinct, but one.

The Holy Spirit does the work of God in our lives. We are born of God (John 1:12), which is the same as being born of the Spirit (John 3:5). The Holy Spirit is the means by which God lives in us (Ephesians 2:22; 1 John 3:24; 4:13). The Holy Spirit lives in us (Romans 8:11; 1 Corinthians 3:16)— and because the Spirit lives in us, we can say that *God* lives in us.

The Spirit is personal

Scripture describes the Holy Spirit as having personal characteristics.

- The Spirit lives (Romans 8:11; 1 Corinthians 3:16).
- The Spirit speaks (Acts 8:29; 10:19; 11:12; 21:11; 1 Timothy 4:1; Hebrews 3:7; etc.).
- The Spirit sometimes uses the personal pronoun "I" (Acts 10:20; 13:2).
- The Spirit may be spoken to, tested, grieved, insulted or blasphemed (Acts 5:3, 9; Ephesians 4:30; Hebrews 10:29; Matthew 12:31).
- The Spirit guides, intercedes, calls and commissions (Romans 8:14, 26; Acts 13:2; 20:28).

Romans 8:27 refers to the "mind" of the Spirit. The Spirit makes judgments—a decision "seemed good" to the Holy Spirit (Acts 15:28). The Spirit "knows" and "determines" (1 Corinthians 2:11; 12:11). This is not an impersonal power.

Jesus called the Holy Spirit the *parakletos*—translated as the Comforter, the Advocate or the Counselor. "I will ask the Father, and he will give you *another Counselor* to be with you forever—the Spirit of truth" (John 14:16-17). The disciples' first Counselor was Jesus. Like him, the Holy Spirit teaches, testifies, convicts, guides and reveals truth (John 14:26; 15:26; 16:8, 13-14). These are personal roles.

John uses the masculine form of the Greek word *parakletos;* it was not necessary to use a neuter word. In John 16:14, masculine pronouns (he) are used even after the neuter word "Spirit" is mentioned. It would have been easy to switch to neuter pronouns (it), but John does not. The Spirit may be called *he.* However, grammar is relatively unimportant; what is important is that the Holy Spirit has personal characteristics. He is not an impersonal power, but the intelligent and divine Helper who lives within us.

The Spirit in the Old Testament

The Bible does not have a section titled "The Holy Spirit." We learn about the Spirit a little here and a little there, as Scripture happens to mention what the Spirit does. The Old Testament gives us only a few glimpses.

The Spirit was involved in creating and sustaining all life (Genesis 1:2; Job 33:4; 34:14). The Spirit of God filled Bezelel with skill to build the tabernacle (Exodus 31:3-5). He filled Moses and came upon the 70 elders (Numbers 11:25). He filled Joshua with wisdom and filled leaders such as Samson with strength or ability to fight (Deuteronomy 34:9; Judges 6:34; 14:6).

God's Spirit was given to Saul and later taken away (1 Samuel 10:6; 16:14). The Spirit gave David plans for the temple (1 Chronicles 28:12). The Spirit inspired prophets to speak (Numbers 24:2; 2 Samuel 23:2; 1 Chronicles 12:18; 2 Chronicles 15:1; 20:14; Ezekiel 11:5; Zechariah 7:12; 2 Peter 1:21).

In the New Testament, too, the Spirit caused people to speak, including Elizabeth, Zechariah and Simeon (Luke 1:41, 67; 2:25-32). John the Baptist was filled with the Spirit from birth (Luke 1:15). His most important work was announcing the arrival of Jesus, who would baptize people not only with water, but with "the Holy Spirit and with fire" (Luke 3:16).

The Spirit and Jesus

The Holy Spirit was involved throughout Jesus' life. The Spirit caused his conception (Matthew 1:20), descended on him at his baptism (Matthew 3:16), led him into the desert (Luke 4:1) and anointed him to preach the gospel (Luke 4:18). Jesus drove out demons by the Spirit of God (Matthew 12:28). It was through the Spirit that he offered himself as a sacrifice for sin (Hebrews 9:14) and by that same Spirit was raised from the dead (Romans 8:11).

Jesus taught that the Spirit would speak through his disciples in times of persecution (Matthew 10:19-20). He told them to baptize followers in the name of the Father, Son, and Holy Spirit (Matthew 28:19). He said that God was certain to give the Holy Spirit to those who ask (Luke 11:13).

Some of Jesus' most important teachings about the Holy Spirit come in the Gospel of John. First, people must be "born of water and the Spirit" (John 3:5). People need a spiritual renewal, and this does not come from inside themselves: it is a gift of God. Although spirit can't be seen, the Holy Spirit does make a difference in our lives (verse 8).

Jesus also taught, "If anyone is thirsty, let him come to me and drink.

Whoever believes in me, as the Scripture has said, streams of living water will flow from within him" (John 7:37-38). John adds this explanation: "By this he meant the Spirit, whom those who believed in him were later to receive" (verse 39). The Holy Spirit satisfies an internal thirst. He gives us the relationship with God that we were created for. We receive the Spirit by coming to Jesus, and the Spirit can fill our lives.

John also tells us, "Up to that time the Spirit had not been given, since Jesus had not yet been glorified" (verse 39). The Spirit had filled various men and women before Jesus, but the Spirit would soon come in a new and more powerful way—on Pentecost. The Spirit is now given on a far larger scale: to all who call on the name of the Lord (Acts 2:38-39).

Jesus promised that his disciples would be given the Spirit of truth, who would live in them (John 14:16-18). This is equivalent to Jesus himself coming to his disciples (verse 18), because he is the Spirit of Christ as well as the Spirit of the Father—sent by Jesus as well as by the Father (John 15:26). The Spirit makes Jesus available to everyone and continues his work.

Jesus promised that the Spirit would teach the disciples and remind them of what Jesus had taught (John 14:26). The Spirit taught them things that they could not understand before Jesus' resurrection (John 16:12-13).

The Spirit testifies about Jesus (John 15:26; 16:14). He does not promote himself, but leads people to Jesus Christ and the Father. He does not speak on his own, but only as the Father wants (John 16:13). Since the Spirit can live in millions of people, it is for our good that Jesus left and sent the Spirit to us (John 16:7).

The Spirit works in evangelism, convicting the world of their sin, their guilt, their need for righteousness, and the certainty of judgment (verses 8-10). The Holy Spirit points people to Jesus as the solution to guilt and the source of righteousness.

The Spirit and the church

John the Baptist said that Jesus would baptize people in the Holy Spirit (Mark 1:8). This happened on the day of Pentecost after his resurrection, when the Spirit dramatically gave new power to the disciples (Acts 2). This included speaking that was understood by people from other nations (verse 6). Similar miracles happened on a few other occasions as the church grew (Acts 10:44-46; 19:1-6), but there is no indication that these miracles happened to all new believers.

Paul says that all believers are baptized in the Holy Spirit into one body— the church (1 Corinthians 12:13). Everyone who has faith is given the Holy

Spirit (Galatians 3:14). Whether miracles happen to them or not, all believers have been baptized with the Holy Spirit. It is not necessary to seek any particular miracle as proof of this.

The Bible does not command any believer to seek the baptism of the Holy Spirit. Instead, every believer is encouraged to be continually filled with the Holy Spirit (Ephesians 5:18)—to be fully responsive to the Spirit's lead. This is a continuing relationship, not a one-time event.

Rather than seeking a miracle, we are to seek God, and leave it to God's decision as to whether miracles happen. Paul often describes the power of God not in terms of physical miracles, but in the transformation that comes in a person's life—hope, love, patience, serving, understanding, suffering and preaching boldly (Romans 15:13; 2 Corinthians 12:9; Ephesians 3:7, 16-18; Colossians 1:11, 28-29; 2 Timothy 1:7-8). We might call these psychological miracles—the power of God at work in human lives.

The book of Acts shows that the Spirit empowered the church's growth. The Spirit gave the disciples power to testify about Jesus (Acts 1:8). He gave the disciples great boldness in preaching Christ (Acts 4:8, 31; 6:10). He gave instructions to Philip and later transported him (Acts 8:29, 39).

The Spirit encouraged the church and set leaders in it (Acts 9:31; 20:28). He spoke to Peter and to the church at Antioch (10:19; 11:12; 13:2). He inspired Agabus to predict a famine and Paul to pronounce a curse (11:28; 13:9-10). He led Paul and Barnabas on their journeys (13:4; 16:6-7) and helped the Jerusalem council come to a decision (15:28). He sent Paul to Jerusalem and warned him what would happen (20:22-23; 21:11). The church existed and grew only through the Spirit working in the believers.

The Spirit and believers today

God the Holy Spirit is intimately involved in the life of believers today.

- He leads us to repentance and gives us new life (John 16:8; 3:5-6).
- He lives in us, teaches us and leads us (1 Corinthians 2:10-13; John 14:16-17, 26; Romans 8:14). He leads us through Scripture, prayer and other Christians.
- He is the Spirit of wisdom, helping us look at choices with confidence, love and self-control (Ephesians 1:17; 2 Timothy 1:7).
- The Spirit circumcises our hearts, seals us and sanctifies us, setting us apart for God's purpose (Romans 2:29; Ephesians 1:14).
- He produces in us love and the fruit of righteousness (Romans 5:5; Ephesians 5:9; Galatians 5:22-23).
- He puts us into the church and helps us know that we are God's

children (1 Corinthians 12:13; Romans 8:14-16).

We are to worship God "by the Spirit," with our minds set on what the Spirit wants (Philippians 3:3; 2 Corinthians 3:6; Romans 7:6; 8:4-5). We strive to please him (Galatians 6:8). If we are controlled by the Spirit, he gives us life and peace (Romans 8:6). He gives us access to the Father (Ephesians 2:18). He helps us in our weakness, interceding for us (Romans 8:26-27).

The Holy Spirit also gives spiritual gifts, including leaders for the church (Ephesians 4:11), basic functions within the church (Romans 12:6-8), and some abilities for extraordinary purposes (1 Corinthians 12:4-11). No one has every gift, nor is any gift given to everyone (verses 28-30). All gifts, whether spiritual or "natural," are to be used for the common good, to help the entire church (1 Corinthians 12:7; 14:12). Every gift is important (12:22-26).

In this age, we have only the firstfruits of the Spirit, only a deposit that guarantees much more in our future (Romans 8:23; 2 Corinthians 1:22; 5:5; Ephesians 1:13-14).

In summary, the Holy Spirit is God at work in our lives. Everything God does is done through his Spirit. Paul therefore encourages us: "Let us keep in step with the Spirit.... Do not grieve the Holy Spirit of God.... Do not put out the Spirit's fire" (Galatians 5:25; Ephesians 4:30; 1 Thessalonians 5:19). Be attentive to what the Spirit says. When he speaks, God is speaking.

[1] Blasphemy against the Holy Spirit is a deliberate rejection of the agent God uses to help people understand the gospel—the people reject the message even though they know it is from God. Anyone who is worried about this unpardonable sin shows, by their worry, that they have not committed it. The fact that they *want* to do the right thing shows that they have not deliberately rejected the Holy Spirit.

For further reading

Max Anders, *What You Need to Know About the Holy Spirit.* Nelson, 1995.

Michael Green, *I Believe in the Holy Spirit.* Eerdmans, 1975.

Craig S. Keener, *Gift and Giver.* Baker, 2001.

J.I. Packer, *Keep in Step With the Spirit.* Revell, 1984.

Clark Pinnock, *Flame of Love.* InterVarsity, 1999.

Anthony Thiselton, *The Holy Spirit.* Eerdmans, 2013.

Michael Morrison

THE DEITY OF THE HOLY SPIRIT

Christianity has traditionally taught that the Holy Spirit is the third Person or Hypostasis of the Godhead. Some, however, have taught that the Holy Spirit is an impersonal force used by God. Is the Holy Spirit God, or simply a power of God? Let's examine the biblical teachings.

I. The deity of the Holy Spirit

Summary: Scripture speaks repeatedly of the Holy Spirit, known also as the Spirit of God and the Spirit of Jesus Christ. Scripture indicates that the Holy Spirit is of the same essence as the Father and the Son. The Holy Spirit is ascribed with the attributes of God, is equated with God and does work that only God does.

A. Attributes of God

1. Holiness: In more than 90 places, the Bible calls the Spirit of God "the Holy Spirit." Holiness is a basic characteristic of the Spirit. The Spirit is so holy that blasphemy against the Spirit cannot be forgiven, although blasphemy against Jesus could be (Matthew 12:32). Insulting the Spirit is just as sinful as trampling the Son of God under foot (Hebrews 10:29). This indicates that the Spirit is inherently holy, holy in essence, rather than having an assigned or secondary holiness such as the temple had. The Spirit also has the infinite attributes of God: unlimited in time, space, power and knowledge.

2. Eternality: The Holy Spirit, the Counselor, will be with us "forever" (John 14:16). The Spirit is "eternal" (Hebrews 9:14).

3. Omnipresence: David, praising God's greatness, asked, "Where can I go from your Spirit? Where can I flee from your presence? If I go up to the heavens, you are there; if I make my bed in the depths, you are there" (Psalm 139:7-8). God's Spirit, which David uses as a synonym for the presence of God himself, is in heaven and in *sheol* (verse 8), in the east and in the west (verse 9). God's Spirit can be said to be poured out on someone, to fill a person, or to descend — yet without implying that the Spirit has moved away from or vacated some other place. Thomas Oden observes that "such statements are grounded in the premises of omnipresence and eternality — attributes ascribed properly only to God" (*Life in the Spirit,* p. 18).

4. Omnipotence: The works that God does, such as creation, are also ascribed to the Holy Spirit (Job 33:4; Psalm 104:30). Miracles of Jesus Christ were done "by the Spirit" (Matthew 12:28). In Paul's ministry, the work that "Christ has accomplished" was done "through the power of the Spirit" (Romans 15:18-19).

5. Omniscience: "The Spirit searches all things, even the deep things of God," Paul said (1 Corinthians 2:10). The Spirit of God "knows the thoughts of God" (verse 11). The Spirit therefore knows all things, and is able to teach all things (John 14:26).

Holiness, eternality, omnipresence, omnipotence and omniscience are attributes of God's essence, that is, characteristic of the nature of divine existence. The Holy Spirit has the basic attributes of God.

B. Equated with God

1. Triadic formulas: Several passages discuss the Father, Son, and Holy Spirit as equals. In a discussion of spiritual gifts, Paul puts the Spirit, the Lord, and God in grammatically parallel constructions (1 Corinthians 12:4-6). Paul closes a letter with a three-part prayer: "May the grace of the Lord Jesus Christ, and the love of God, and the fellowship of the Holy Spirit be with you all" (2 Corinthians 13:14). Peter begins a letter with this three-part formula: "who have been chosen according to the foreknowledge of God the Father, through the sanctifying work of the Spirit, for obedience to Jesus Christ and sprinkling by his blood" (1 Peter 1:2).

The triadic formulas used in these and other scriptures do not prove equality (for example, Ephesians 4:5 puts unequal elements in parallel construction), but they do support it. The baptismal formula has a stronger implication of unity — "in the name [singular] of the Father and of the Son and of the Holy Spirit" (Matthew 28:19). The Father, Son, and Spirit share a common name, indicating common essence and equality. This verse indicates both plurality and unity. Three names are given, but all three share one name.

2. Word interchanges. Acts 5:3 says that Ananias lied to the Holy Spirit; verse 4 says that Ananias lied to God. This indicates that "the Holy Spirit" and "God" are interchangeable and thus that the Holy Spirit is God. Some people try to explain this by saying that Ananias lied to God only indirectly, simply because the Holy Spirit represented God. This interpretation might be grammatically possible, but it would still imply that the Holy Spirit is personal, for one does not "lie" to an impersonal power. Moreover, Peter told Ananias that he lied not to humans, but to God. The force of the passage is that Ananias has lied not merely to God's representatives, but to God himself, and the Holy Spirit is God to whom Ananias lied.

Another word interchange can be seen in 1 Corinthians 3:16 and 6:19. Christians are not only temples of God, they are also temples of the Holy Spirit; the two expressions mean the same thing. A temple is a habitation for a deity, not a habitation for an impersonal power. When Paul writes "temple of the Holy Spirit," he implies that the Holy Spirit is God.

Another type of verbal equation between God and the Holy Spirit is seen in Acts 13:2: "The Holy Spirit said, 'Set apart for me Barnabas and Saul for the work to which I have called them." Here, the Holy Spirit speaks on behalf of God, as God. In the same way, Hebrews 3:7-11 tells us that the Holy Spirit says the Israelites "tested and tried me"; the Holy Spirit says that "I was angry.... They shall never enter my rest." The Holy Spirit is equated with the God of the Israelites. Hebrews 10:15-17 also equates the Spirit and the Lord who makes the new covenant. The Spirit who inspired the prophets is God. This is the work of God the Holy Spirit.

C. Divine work

1. Creating: The Holy Spirit does work that only God can do, such as creating (Genesis 1:2; Job 33:4; Psalm 104:30) and expelling demons (Matthew 12:28).

2. Begetting: The Spirit begot the Son of God (Matthew 1:20; Luke 1:35), and the full divinity of the Son (Colossians 1:19) implies the full divinity of the Begetter. The Spirit begets believers, too — they are born of God (John 1:12) and equally born of the Spirit (John 3:5). "The Spirit gives [eternal] life" (John 6:63).

3. Indwelling: The Holy Spirit is the way God lives in his children (Ephesians 2:22; 1 John 3:24; 4:13). The Holy Spirit "lives" in us (Romans 8:11; 1 Corinthians 3:16) — and because the Spirit lives in us, we are able to say that God lives in us. We can say that God lives in us only because the Holy Spirit is in some way God. The Spirit is not a representative or a power that lives in us — God himself lives in us. Geoffrey Bromiley gives a concise conclusion: "to have dealings with the Spirit, no less than with the Father and the Son, is to have dealings with God" ("The New Holy Spirit," in *The New Life,* edited by Millard Erickson, p. 23).

4. Sanctifying: The Holy Spirit makes people holy (Romans 15:16; 1 Peter 1:2). The Spirit enables people to enter the kingdom of God (John 3:5). We are saved "through the sanctifying work of the Spirit" (2 Thessalonians 2:13).

In all these things, the works of the Spirit are the works of God. Whatever the Spirit says or does, God is saying or doing; the Spirit is fully representative of God.

II. Personality of the Holy Spirit

Summary: Scripture describes the Holy Spirit as having personal characteristics: The Spirit has mind and will, speaks and can be spoken to, and acts and intercedes for us. All these indicate personality in the theological sense: The Holy Spirit is a Person or Hypostasis in the same sense that the Father and Son are. Our relationship with God, which is accomplished by the Holy Spirit, is a personal relationship.

A. Life and intelligence

1. Life: The Holy Spirit "lives" (Romans 8:11; 1 Corinthians 3:16).

2. Intelligence: The Spirit "knows" (1 Corinthians 2:11). Romans 8:27 refers to "the mind of the Spirit." This mind is able to make judgments — a decision "seemed good" to the Holy Spirit (Acts 15:28). These verses imply a distinct intelligence.

3. Will: 1 Corinthians 12:11 says that the Spirit "determines" decisions, showing that the Spirit has a will. The Greek word means "he or it determines." Although the Greek word does not specify the subject of the verb, the most likely subject in the context is the Spirit. To find a different subject, one would have to backtrack through five verses and six mentions of the Spirit. But this grammatical leapfrogging is not necessary. Since we know from other verses that the Spirit has mind and knowledge and judgment, there is no reason to reject the conclusion in 1 Corinthians 12:11 that the Spirit also has will.

B. Communication

1. Speaking: Numerous verses say that the Holy Spirit spoke (Acts 8:29; 10:19; 11:12; 21:11; 1 Timothy 4:1; Hebrews 3:7; etc.). Oden observes that "the Spirit speaks in the first person as 'I'; 'It was I who sent them' (Acts 10:20).... 'I have called them' (Acts 13:2). None but a person can say 'I'" (*The Living God,* p. 200).

2. Interaction: The Spirit may be lied to (Acts 5:3), which indicates that the Spirit may be spoken to. The Spirit may be tested (Acts 5:9), insulted (Hebrews 10:29) or blasphemed (Matthew 12:31), which implies personal status. Oden gathers additional evidence: "The apostolic testimony applied intensely personal analogies: guiding (Romans 8:14), convicting (John 16:8), interceding (Romans 8:26), calling (Acts 13:2), commissioning (Acts 20:28).... Only a person can be vexed (Isaiah 63:10) or grieved (Ephesians 4:30)" (*Life in the Spirit,* p. 19).

3. Paraclete: Jesus called the Holy Spirit the *parakletos* — the Comforter, Advocate or Counselor. The Paraclete is active, teaching (John 14:26), testifying (15:26), convicting (16:8), guiding (16:13) and making truth known (16:14).

Jesus used the masculine form of *parakletos;* he did not consider it necessary to make the word neuter or to use neuter pronouns. In John 16:14, masculine pronouns are used even after the neuter *pneuma* is mentioned. It would have been easy to switch to neuter pronouns, but John did not. In other places, neuter pronouns are used for the Spirit, in accordance with grammatical convention. Scripture is not finicky about the grammatical gender of the Spirit, and we need not be either. We use personal pronouns for the Spirit to acknowledge that he is personal, not to imply that he is male.

C. Action

1. New life: The Holy Spirit regenerates us, giving us new life (John 3:5). The Spirit sanctifies us (1 Peter 1:2) and leads us in that new life (Romans 8:14). The Spirit gives various gifts to build the Church up (1 Corinthians 12:7-11), and throughout the book of Acts, we see that the Spirit guides the church.

2. Intercession: The most "personal" activity of the Holy Spirit is intercession: "We do not know what we ought to pray for, but the Spirit himself intercedes for us…. The Spirit intercedes for the saints in accordance with God's will" (Romans 8:26-27). Intercession implies not only receiving communication, but also communicating further on. It implies an intelligence, a concern, and a formal role. The Holy Spirit is not an impersonal power, but an intelligent and divine Helper who lives within us. God lives within us, and the Holy Spirit is God.

III. Worship

There are no scriptural examples of worshipping the Holy Spirit. Scripture talks about praying *in* the Spirit (Ephesians 6:18), the fellowship *of* the Spirit (2 Corinthians 13:14), and baptism in the name of the Spirit (Matthew 28:19). Although baptism, prayer and fellowship are involved in worship, none of these verses shows worship of the Spirit.

As an opposite of worship, however, we note that the Spirit can be blasphemed (Matthew 12:31).

There are no scriptural examples of praying to the Holy Spirit. However, Scripture indicates that a human can talk to the Spirit (Acts 5:3). If this is done in reverence or request, it is, in effect, praying to the Spirit. If Christians are unable to articulate their desires and they want the Spirit to intercede for them (Romans 8:26-27), they are praying, directly or indirectly, to the Holy Spirit. When we understand that the Holy Spirit has intelligence and fully represents God, we may ask the Spirit for help — never thinking that the Spirit is a separate being from God, but recognizing that the Spirit is the Hypostasis of God interceding for us.

Why does Scripture say nothing about praying to the Spirit? Michael Green explains: "The Holy Spirit does not draw attention to himself. He is sent by the Father to glorify Jesus, to show Jesus' attractiveness, and not to take the centre of the stage" (*I Believe in the Holy Spirit,* p. 60). Or, as Geoffrey Bromiley puts it, "The Spirit is self-effacing" (p. 21).

Prayer or worship directed specifically to the Holy Spirit is not the scriptural norm, but we nonetheless worship the Spirit. When we worship God, we worship all aspects of God, including the Father, the Son, and the Holy Spirit. A fourth-century theologian explained it this way: "The Spirit is jointly worshipped in God, when God is worshipped in the Spirit" (Ambrose, *Of the Holy Spirit* III.X.82, quoted in Oden, *Life in the Spirit,* p. 16). Whatever we say to the Spirit we are saying to God, and whatever we say to God we are saying to the Spirit.

IV. Summary

Scripture indicates that the Holy Spirit has divine attributes and works, and is spoken of in the same way that the Father and Son are. The Holy Spirit is intelligent, and speaks and acts like a divine Person. This is part of the scriptural evidence that led early Christians to formulate the doctrine of the Trinity. Bromiley gives a summary:

> Three points that emerge from this survey of the New Testament data are: (1) The Holy Spirit is everywhere regarded as God; (2) He is God in distinction from the Father and the Son; (3) His deity does not infringe upon the divine unity. In other words, the Holy Spirit is the third person of the triune Godhead....
>
> The divine unity cannot be subjected to mathematical ideas of unity. The fourth century learned to speak of three hypostases or persons within the deity, not in the tritheistic sense of three centers of consciousness, but also not in the weaker sense of three economic manifestations. From Nicaea and Constantinople on, the creeds sought to do justice to the essential biblical data along these lines. (pp. 24-25)

Although Scripture does not directly say that "the Holy Spirit is God," or that God is triune, these conclusions are based on scriptural evidence. Based on biblical evidence, we teach that the Holy Spirit is God in the same way that the Father is God and the Son is God.

Michael Morrison

WHAT THE FOUR GOSPELS TEACH US ABOUT THE HOLY SPIRIT

The Holy Spirit was an essential part of Jesus' ministry. Not only was Jesus enlivened by the Spirit, Jesus also taught his disciples that the Holy Spirit would be an essential part of their ministry.

1. When and how did the Holy Spirit begin the life of Jesus? Matthew 1:18, 20; Luke 1:35. What did the Holy Spirit do to Jesus at the beginning of his ministry? Luke 3:22; John 1:32-33.

Christ "made himself nothing" (Philippians 2:7), and the Holy Spirit caused Jesus to begin growing in Mary's womb. Although the Spirit remained in Jesus from conception onward, a visible sign was given at his baptism that the Holy Spirit was empowering him.

However, Jesus was not the first person to be given God's Spirit. The Old Testament describes a variety of people who were given power, wisdom and understanding by the Spirit. Jesus said that David — and presumably all other writers of Scripture — spoke by the Holy Spirit in the Psalms (Matthew 22:43).

But in the first century, the Jews had gone a long time without a Spirit-filled prophet. They were waiting for someone to come in the spirit and power of Elijah.

2. Before Jesus was born, was John the Baptist filled with the Holy Spirit? Luke 1:15. Even while Jesus was in Mary's womb, who was filled with the Spirit? Verse 41. What was Elizabeth inspired to say? Verses 42-45. Several months later, what was her husband, Zechariah, inspired by the Spirit to prophesy? Verse 67. And shortly after Jesus was born, did the Holy Spirit move upon yet another person? Luke 2:25-27.

3. After Jesus was baptized and filled with the Holy Spirit, what did the Spirit lead him to do? Luke 4:1. After his victory over the satanic temptations, was he drained of power? Verse 14. What did he tell the people that the Spirit was leading him to do? Verse 18. What emotion filled him because of the Holy Spirit? Luke 10:21.

4. John tells us that God gave Jesus the Holy Spirit without limit (John 3:34). Jesus was filled and led by the Spirit in all his work. One work in particular showed that he was empowered by the Spirit. What did that miracle prove? Matthew 12:28. In his ministry, how did Jesus fulfill a prophecy about God's Spirit? Verses 15-18.

Jesus' comment about "blasphemy against the Spirit" (verse 31) refers to people who become enemies of God (Isaiah 63:10). The Pharisees became worse than unbelievers — they were actively resisting the power of God. By calling Jesus' power satanic, they were fighting against God, making themselves enemies of the only agent able to lead them to salvation and forgiveness.

5. What did John the Baptist predict that Jesus would do with the Spirit? John 1:33. When was this done? John 7:39. Is it Jesus who sends the Spirit, or is it the Father? Luke 11:13; John 4:10; 7:37; 14:16, 26; 15:26; 16:7.

Jesus sent the disciples out to preach, heal and cast out demons, and they presumably did this with the same power Jesus had, the Holy Spirit. The Spirit was living with them, but was not yet in them (John 14:17). They would be filled with the Holy Spirit after Jesus had been glorified. Both the Father and the Son would send the Holy Spirit to live within the believers.

6. What does the Holy Spirit do in a person's life? John 3:5; 6:63. What does the Spirit bring to our minds? John 14:26; 15:26. What is the focus of this spiritual work? John 15:26; 16:13-14.

The Spirit of God does not teach us truths about math, but about the Truth, Jesus himself, the way of salvation (John 14:6). The Spirit enabled the disciples to understand what Jesus had taught, and to understand what was "yet to come" — his death and resurrection. By causing the disciples to understand, the Spirit enabled them to preach the good news of life through Jesus Christ.

Jesus sent his disciples with a message, told them to receive the Holy Spirit (John 15:27; 20:21-23) and to wait until they received the "power from on high" that they needed (Luke 24:49). The gospel work of the church is done in the power of the Holy Spirit.

Through the Spirit-led disciples, the world hears the message of truth, the message of Jesus — but many people do not accept that message (John 14:17). In this way, the Holy Spirit convicts the world of guilt in regard to unbelief and judgment (John 16:8-11). The world may be hostile, but even in times of persecution, the Holy Spirit speaks through the disciples (Luke 12:11-12).

Disciples are baptized into the name of the Father, Son, and Holy Spirit (Matthew 28:19). The Spirit is as much a part of our identity as the Father and the Son are.

Jesus said that he would go away, and yet live in his disciples (John 14:18; Matthew 28:20). He lives in us by means of the Holy Spirit, the Counselor who continues the teaching work of Jesus.

Michael Morrison

THE HOLY SPIRIT IS
THE PERSONAL PRESENCE OF GOD

Christians believe in one God whose being is the Father, the Son and the Holy Spirit. We do not worship an undifferentiated, monad God, and we do not worship three Gods or Beings. Rather, we worship the one God who is eternally triune within himself in three eternal and co-equal Persons.[1] Each of the three Persons is distinct from the other two persons of the Godhead, and each is God of God, but there are not three Gods, but only one Being called God whom Christians worship.

In respect to the Person called the Holy Spirit in the New Testament, some people believe that the Spirit is not personal in the same sense that the Father and Son are personal. In the extreme, the claim is made by a few that the Holy Spirit is no more than a power used by God that is outside of and detached from himself or his Being.

Sometimes not mentioned

One of the arguments against the Spirit's personal nature is based on some verses in the New Testament in which God and Christ are discussed together, but they contain no reference to the Spirit. It is asked, "If the Holy Spirit is divine in the same way as the Son and the Father, and is co-eternal and co-equal with them, why is the Spirit not mentioned in such cases?"

A second argument used in an attempt to deny the equal divinity of the Holy Spirit is based on the observation that the New Testament does not present a personal "face" for the Spirit in the same way that it does for the Father and Son. The conclusion is the Holy Spirit is a power outside of the being of God, a power that God uses to carry out his will.

The first argument assumes that all three Persons of the Trinity *must* be mentioned together if they are equally divine. No scriptural rationale is given for such a claim. Perhaps some people think it *ought* to be so. But let's ask, Why should the Spirit always be mentioned along with the Father and Son? The Father is often mentioned without the Son, and the Son is often mentioned without any mention of the Father or the Holy Spirit. The book of Acts often mentions the work of the Holy Spirit without reference to the Father or the Son.

In short, it is an unsubstantiated assumption and a quibbling over irrelevant details to claim that the Holy Spirit must always be mentioned wherever the Father and Son are discussed. We cannot assume that the absence of the Holy Spirit in some biblical passages tells us anything definitive about the relationship of the Spirit to the other Persons of the Godhead.

For example, in his introduction to 1 Corinthians, the apostle Paul brings the congregation grace and peace from "God our Father and the Lord Jesus Christ" (1:3), but mentions Christ four times and "God" only twice. Are we to conclude that Jesus is twice as important as the Father? In his short conclusion to the same letter, Paul refers to "Christ Jesus" and the "Lord Jesus," but makes no mention of the Father or the Holy Spirit (16:23-24). Must we then conclude that only Jesus is divine?

In the opening to 2 Corinthians, Paul mentions variants of "Jesus Christ" twice and God twice, but doesn't refer to the Holy Spirit (1:1-2). However, in his conclusion, Paul says, "May the grace of the Lord Jesus Christ, and the love of God, and the fellowship of the Holy Spirit be with you all" (13:14). Here all three divine Persons – God, Jesus and the Spirit – are mentioned together.[2] We would be hard pressed regarding what conclusion to draw about the nature of God in general and the Holy Spirit in particular from Paul's various references to God, to Jesus, to the Father and the Holy Spirit in the openings and closings of these two letters.

There are many passages in the New Testament where all three Persons of the Godhead – the Father, Son and Holy Spirit – are mentioned together. Here are the most prominent places: Matthew 28:19; 2 Corinthians 13:14; 1 Peter 1:1-2; Romans 14:17-18; 15:16; 1 Corinthians 2:2-5; 6:11; 12:4-6; 2 Corinthians 1:21-22; Galatians 4:6; Ephesians 2:18-22; 3:14-19; Ephesians 4:4-6; Colossians 1:6-8; 1 Thessalonians 1:3-5; 2 Thessalonians 2:13-14; Titus 3:4-6. We should see these Scriptures as the controlling ones in any conclusion they may imply about the nature of God, since they mention all the relevant parties.

We will now move from these superficial arguments based on formulas and isolated references to essential considerations about the work of the Holy Spirit as true God of true God. As we do so, we will occasionally refer to the important work of Thomas Torrance in understanding the doctrine of the Trinity as he discusses it in his book *The Christian Doctrine of God – One Being Three Persons*.[3]

Not prominently featured

The second objection to accepting the Holy Spirit as a divine Person and God of God is based on the observation that the Holy Spirit is not as prominently featured as the Father and Son are in the New Testament. (For example, there are no occasions in the New Testament where we are told to worship the Holy Spirit.)

This kind of distinction vis-à-vis the Spirit is explained by the fact that the three Persons of the Godhead are distinct and they have distinct roles in the plan of salvation. We conclude from the New Testament that the Holy Spirit is not sent to draw attention to himself, that is, to take center stage or to glorify himself.

When Jesus introduces the Holy Spirit – the Spirit of Truth – in John 14-16, he says of him: "When the Counselor comes, whom I will send to you from the Father, the Spirit of Truth who goes out from the Father, he will *testify about me*" (15:26, italics ours throughout).

Later, Jesus says: "But when he, the Spirit of Truth, comes, he will guide you into all truth. He will *not speak on his own;* he will speak only what he hears... He will bring *glory to me* by taking from what is mine and making it known to you" (16:13-14).

We see here that the Spirit is another Counselor, Paraclete or Helper who is sent by Christ to be with the church. The Spirit performs his own distinctive work in redemption: he enlightens, transforms, guides and sanctifies the followers of Christ. "It is not the function of the Spirit, then, to bear witness to himself in his distinctive personal Being, but to bear witness to Christ and glorify him as Lord and Savior," writes Torrance.[4]

Torrance explains why the Holy Spirit is not presented with a personal "face," as are the Son and the Father:

> The Holy Spirit is God himself speaking although he is not himself the Word of God. It was not of course the Spirit but the Word who became incarnate, and so the Spirit does not bring us any revelation other than or independent of the Word who became incarnate in Jesus Christ. The Holy Spirit has no "Face", but it is through the Spirit that we see the Face of Christ and in the Face of Christ we see the Face of the Father. The Holy Spirit does not manifest himself or focus attention upon himself, for it is his mission from the Father to declare the Son and focus attention upon him. It is through the speaking of the Spirit that the Word of God incarnate in Christ is communicated to us in words that are Spirit and Life and not flesh.[5]

And again, Torrance writes about the presence of the Holy Spirit as true God of true God:

> While God the Father and God the Son are revealed to us in their distinctive personal subsistences...God the Holy Spirit is not directly known in his own Person...for he remains hidden behind the very revelation of the Father and the Son which he mediates *through* himself.

He is the invisible Spirit of Truth who is sent from the Father in the name of the Son, but not in his personal name as the Holy Spirit, and thus does not speak of himself, but declares of the Father and the Son what he receives from them, while effacing himself before them.... He is the invisible Light in whose shining we see the uncreated Light of God manifest in Jesus Christ, but he is known himself only in that he lights up for us the Face of God in the Face of Jesus Christ.[6]

The Paraclete

It has not been given for us to know directly the "face" of the Holy Spirit in a personal sense. Yet, in one place Jesus does give us something of a personal "face" for the Holy Spirit. When Jesus introduced the Holy Spirit to the disciples on the night he was betrayed, he used the Greek word *parakletos* to refer to him (John 14:16, 26; 15:26; 16:7). As a title for the Holy Spirit, *parakletos* is found exclusively in the above four passages, in the so-called "Paraclete sayings" of Jesus' farewell discourse. *Parakletos* has been translated by such words as "Comforter," "Advocate," "Helper" and "Counselor." Some versions simply transliterate the Greek word into "Paraclete."

In Greek and Roman society, a paraclete could refer to a person called on for assistance as a legal advisor, advocate or helper in a court of law. But the technical meaning "attorney" or "lawyer" is rare. A Greek lexicon explains: "In the few places where the word is found in pre-Christian and extra-Christian literature as well it has for the most part a more general sense: one who appears in another's behalf, *mediator, intercessor, helper.*"[7]

Thus, Jesus is telling his disciples that his physical presence will be replaced by "another Helper," the Holy Spirit. Since the Spirit is "another" helper, we understand that Jesus himself was a helper for the disciples. In that the Holy Spirit can "replace" Jesus, we can only take this to mean that the Spirit is to be thought of as equal to Christ. Otherwise, how could the Spirit be able to come in the place of Jesus and perform saving work?

For those who insist on having a personal "face" for the Holy Spirit, Jesus has given it to us in his choice of metaphor in his reference to the Spirit as "Paraclete." He doesn't say, "I'm going to send a non-personal abstract power to you in my place."

On the other hand, we have been given in the New Testament the anthropomorphic analogy of "Father" and "Son" for the other two Persons of the Godhead, through which their personal "faces" are given. But even here we should avoid any gender-like thinking in our visioning. We "must think of 'Father' and 'Son' when used of God as *imageless relations*" and "we may not read the creaturely content of our human expressions of 'father' and 'son' analogically into what God discloses of his own inner divine relations," cautions Torrance.[8]

We must use human language when we speak of the Persons of the triune God, because we have no other language to use. But we should never lose sight of the fact that our language is inadequate and can only approximate in an approximate way the reality of God to which our words point.

Only a force?

Finally, let us take up the question of whether the Holy Spirit could be simply a force detached from the Being of God. An analogy would be that of electricity. Human beings use the power of electricity to achieve their will and work in countless ways. Electricity is not internal to our human selves, but is an external power we use.

Let's begin with an obvious point: There is no place in either the Old or New Testaments where the Holy Spirit is said to be or is regarded as an "appendage" to God rather than the presence of God himself. On that basis alone, we have no evidence to back up the assertion that the Spirit is not the presence of God, and therefore, not God of God.

To help us understand that the Holy Spirit *is* true God of true God, we begin by looking at the salvific work of Jesus, something that Thomas Torrance has explained. That is, Jesus as the Son must be God of God for his work to be effective in our salvation. Only God himself is our Savior. "This is to say, unless God himself were directly involved in the saving work of Christ in the depths of our human existence and in the heights of his eternal Being, what took place on the Cross would have been in vain," says Torrance.[9]

Jesus could not have been simply a special human being to whom God gave a mission, in the way he did to the Old Testament prophets such as Moses or David. Our Savior had to be very God with us, though as a human being, in order to perform his saving work.

Salvation is the gift of eternal life given to creatures who do not possess such spirit life within themselves. As creatures, we are spiritually fallen and mortal beings who ultimately die. How can mortal creatures be given eternal life – something that mortal creatures by definition do not have and cannot obtain on their own? They must somehow be taken up into God so that the eternal life that only God has may be something that adheres to them as well.

John 14:5-27 explains how the life of God can adhere to us, if we are careful to see the implications of what Jesus says in the passage. His explanation demands that the Holy Spirit be true God of true God. Jesus, having finished the redemptive work through which we are reconciled to God, will send the Holy Spirit. The Spirit will be "in" the believers, and through him, the Father and Jesus will make their "home" with them (verses 17, 23). Through the Spirit, the disciples can be in Jesus and he in them (verse 21). The passage shows the unity and salvific work of the Father, of the Son as Jesus Christ, and of the Holy Spirit. All three Persons bring about the salvation of believers, and all must be true God of true God in order to do so – including the Holy Spirit.

As 1 Peter 1:3 states, we have a "new birth into a living hope" through the Holy Spirit. We are joined to God through the Spirit, and the eternal life of God becomes ours in that union. Those who are God's "have been born again, not of perishable seed, but of imperishable, through the living and enduring word of God" (1 Peter 1:23).

The apostle Paul explains that the completion of our salvation results in the "putting on" of immortality (1 Corinthians 15:50-54). In another place, he says: "If the Spirit of him who raised Jesus is living in you, he who raised Christ from the dead will also give life to your mortal bodies *through his Spirit, who lives in you*" (Romans 8:11).

It is not some "power" separate from God that accomplishes this miracle, but the presence of God himself in the Person of the Holy Spirit. When the Holy Spirit lives in us, God lives in us. When the Holy Spirit gives us new birth, we are children of God. We are joined by the Holy Spirit to God, and through the Holy Spirit we become God's children as this work of transformation and life-giving is accomplished (verses 15-16).

We do not become God. We are creatures, and will always remain creatures. But God in his freedom can unite himself to our creaturely state so that his eternal life can be ours in that union. God himself must be present for this union to occur, and he is present in the Person of the indwelling Holy Spirit.

In saving us, the Holy Spirit cannot be "something" outside of God himself. The Spirit must be divinity himself – God of God – working in the church and transforming human creaturely beings into the image of Christ, who is Life himself. Torrance explains this point in this way:

> If the Act which God directs towards us is other than or detached from his Being, then he does not give *himself* to us in his activity and cannot therefore be known by us as he is in himself; but if his Act and his Being instead of being separate from one another inhere in each other, then in giving us his Spirit God actively makes himself open to

us and known by us.[10]

In order for us to participate in the eternal life that alone belongs to God, it is necessary that the Holy Spirit – who transforms our minds and hearts from within – must be Divinity, and true God of true God. "To *be* 'in the Spirit' is to *be* in God, for the Spirit is not external but internal to the Godhead," says Torrance.[11]

Thanks be to God, who in the Person of the Father sent Jesus Christ to reconcile us to himself by the forgiveness of sin and sinfulness. Jesus as Son of Man and Son of God overcame every enemy of God – including sin and death – on our behalf. In the Person of the Holy Spirit, whom Jesus sent, we are transformed and united to God, and we partake of the eternal life that is God's alone.

Endnotes

[1] "Person" is the English word we use in place of the Greek *hypostasis*. The word "Person" shows that God in his Triune Being is personal and that we are dealing with the personal presence of God in the Father, Son and Holy Spirit. The word "Person" has its drawback in that people may wrongly apply to God, in an anthropomorphic way, our experience of persons as individual human beings.

[2] We are assuming in this verse that Paul's reference to "God" is not absolute, but that he uses the term relatively of the Person of the Father, something we cannot know for certain here.

[3] Most footnoted references in this article are to Thomas Torrance's book *The Christian Doctrine of God.*

[4] Ibid., page 66.

[5] Ibid., page 63.

[6] Ibid., page 151.

[7] *A Greek-English Lexicon of the New Testament and other Early Christian Literature,* 4th edition, revised and edited by Frederick William Danker, page 766.

[8] Torrance, pages 157-158.

[9] Ibid., page 146.

[10] Ibid., page 152.

[11] Ibid., page 153.

Paul Kroll

THE HOLY SPIRIT AT WORK

"The Lord [Jesus] is the Spirit" (2 Corinthians 3:17) and "God [the Father] is Spirit" (John 4:24). Biblically speaking, the Holy Spirit is God. It is evident from Scripture that the Father, Son and Holy Spirit are distinct, and yet one.

But what does the Holy Spirit do? Many good books, and some questionable ones, have been written about this question.

From the Bible, we know a lot about what the Holy Spirit does in and with Christians. For example, the Spirit dwells in those who belong to Christ (Romans 8:9). The Spirit regenerates us (John 3:5-6). The Spirit testifies that we are God's children (Romans 8:16), guarantees our inheritance (Ephesians 1:14, 2 Corinthians 1:22), produces godly fruit in us (Galatians 5:22), sanctifies us (2 Thessalonians 2:13), and unifies us with other believers (Philippians 2:1, Ephesians 4:3-4), etc. Scripture describes the Holy Spirit as the Spirit of truth (John 14:17), of life (Romans 8:2), and of grace (Hebrews 10:29).

After Jesus had washed the feet of his disciples and explained that one of them would betray him, he prepared them for his death by telling them what would happen once he had accomplished his sacrificial work on the cross. Jesus' discourse is recorded in John 14 through 17. Jesus told the disciples that the Father would send the Holy Spirit, and that the Holy Spirit would do certain things. Let's use John 14:26 as a summary framework for understanding what the Holy Spirit does today.

John 14:26 reads, "The Helper, the Holy Spirit, whom the Father will send in my name, he will teach you all things, and bring to your remembrance all things that I have said to you."

The Helper, whom the Father will send in my name

The Spirit helps us in our Christian walk. The Greek word used here is usually transliterated *Parakletos,* meaning Advocate or Comforter—someone who beseeches on behalf of another. This term does not appear often in the New Testament. An additional usage is in 1 John 2:1, where Jesus is described as an Advocate for us with the Father. Jesus, who knows our frame and our weaknesses, having shared humanity with us as God in the flesh, comforts us by pleading our cause through his sacrifice and resurrection for us.

Jesus uses the term *Parakletos* to refer to himself and the Holy Spirit – "I will send you *another* helper" (John 14:16). Jesus is our helper in heaven, whereas the Holy Spirit is our helper on earth, now that Christ has ascended to the Father.

The Spirit also pleads the cause of Christ in our hearts and in our minds. He educates and prompts our consciences, helping us resist the temptations of the devil. He reminds us of Christ's will for us so we can be led by Christ, and helps us in our prayer life when words and thoughts fail us (Romans 8:14, 26-27), thus making intercession for us.

This is not an independent work of the Spirit. Whatever the Spirit does is according to the will of the Father. The Spirit continues, in Jesus' name, the work of the Father and the Son in the world and in the church (Ephesians 1:17).

Some churches speculate that this is the "Age of the Spirit" referred to in Acts 2:18 – "I will pour out my Spirit in those days." The context of this passage reveals that the prophecy, originally from Joel 2:29, had its fulfillment on the day of Pentecost (see Acts 2:14-16). There is no indication that there was to be a special "end-time" repeated application of this verse.

"The Age of the Spirit" is an appealing concept, especially to people who have been influenced by New Age thinking. However, there is no biblical evidence to support it. The idea is reminiscent of a third-century heresy called Sabellianism. Sabellius taught that in the history of salvation God is revealed in three stages – first as the Father (the Creator), then as the Son (the Redeemer) and finally (now) as the Holy Spirit. Sabellius did not believe that God could be Father, Son, and Holy Spirit all at the same time.

Perhaps Sabellius was trying to counter Tritheism, the idea, in contrast to monotheism (the teaching that there is only one God), that God is three different gods! Today, tritheistic thought occurs when people imply that the Holy Spirit has a separate will from the Father and the Son, or when they claim that the work of the Spirit is independent of or in addition to the work of the Father and the Son.

The work of the Holy Spirit *is* the work of the Father and the Son, not the Spirit's own agenda. The Father does nothing apart from the Son and the Spirit; the Son does nothing apart from the Father and the Spirit; and the Spirit does nothing apart from the Father and the Son.

We are "elect according the foreknowledge of God the Father, in sanctification of the Spirit, for obedience and sprinkling of the blood of Jesus Christ" (1 Peter 1:2). The "age of the Spirit" is not an age in which the Spirit calls attention to himself or sets up shop independently or in addition to the Father and the Son; rather, it is the age in which the Spirit carries out the Father's will by making known to the world that the Father sent the Son for the redemption and salvation of humanity. In that sense, we *are* in the age of the Spirit.

He will teach you all things

In John 16:13 Jesus says, "The Spirit will guide you into all truth." This is not an independent action of the Spirit. John 16:13 stresses, "He [the Spirit] will not speak of his own *authority*, but whatever he hears he will speak." Just as the words that Jesus spoke were the words of the Father (John 17:8), so it is with the Holy Spirit – the Spirit does not speak his own thoughts, but the thoughts he hears from the Father. The Father, the Son, and the Holy Spirit are one. The Spirit and the Son do only the will of the Father.

How does the Spirit lead and teach us? Sometimes we forget the most obvious way, or we feel (mistakenly) that it is not enough. "Moved by the Holy Spirit" (2 Peter 1:21), people of God wrote the Old and New Testaments. The Gospels, the Acts of the Apostles, the epistles of Paul, Peter, James, John and Jude, the books of Hebrews and Revelation were given to the church through the Spirit's inspiration since the day of Pentecost. They are instructive for us, showing what God's will is for us, teaching us more fully in the way of Christ. "The sword of the Spirit…is the word of God" (Ephesians 6:17).

The Spirit also guides believers to take opportunities to spread the gospel. This can be observed in the book of Acts. When opportunities presented themselves, such as the gathering on the day of Pentecost and the crowds at the market place near Mars Hill in Athens, the Holy Spirit inspired Christians to take advantage of those opportunities.

Within the church context, the Holy Spirit provides gifts and strengths to individuals for the furtherance of the gospel and for the edification of the believers. This "demonstration of the Spirit" is part of teaching and guiding (1 Corinthians 2:4, 12:11).

And bring to your remembrance
all things that I have said to you

The Holy Spirit helped the apostles remember the life and teachings of Christ and to write about them for future generations, including us. The Spirit also helps us remember the example and words of Jesus so we can become more like the Son.

The Spirit points us to Jesus. Always. The Spirit does not draw attention to himself, but he glorifies Jesus, and declares him to us (John 16:14). Confessing that Jesus Christ, God incarnate, came and died and rose for us is a work of the Spirit of God in us (1 John 4:2). The Holy Spirit never minimizes Christ by taking center stage for himself. Never. The Gospel is about the atoning work of Jesus Christ, enabled by the Father and proclaimed through the Spirit.

God the Father sent Jesus Christ to us and pointed to him, saying that Jesus is his beloved Son in whom he is well pleased (Luke 3:22). The Son affirmed that he did the works of the Father who sent him (John 5:36) – so the Son pointed us to the Father. The Son also pointed to the promise of the Father – the Holy Spirit, who always points us to Jesus. These three are one – God the Father, God the Son, God the Holy Spirit.

"By this we know that we abide in him, and he in us, because he has given us of his Spirit" (1 John 4:13).

James R. Henderson

CAN YOU HEAR THE HOLY SPIRIT?

When the church in Antioch gathered for worship, the Holy Spirit spoke to them: "Set apart for me Barnabas and Saul for the work to which I have called them." Does the Holy Spirit speak to us today? Can we hear what he says to us today?

Paul tells us that those who are led by the Holy Spirit are the children of God (Romans 8:14). We should expect the Holy Spirit to lead us, and we want to know how he does it.

In different ways

God works in different ways with different people. He spoke in different ways to Adam, Abraham, Moses, Deborah, Samuel, Elijah, Mary and Paul. He can speak in different ways to us today. The messages given to Philip (Acts 8:29) and Peter are so specific (Acts 10:19) that distinct words may have been involved. But he spoke in a different way at the Jerusalem council (Acts 15). It is only after all the discussion had taken place that the apostles concluded that the Holy Spirit had made the decision for them (verse 28).

Just as the Holy Spirit decides to give different abilities to different people (1 Corinthians 12:11), he works with us in different ways. A person with the gift of miraculous words is likely to hear the Spirit in a different way than a person with the gift of compassion. The Spirit will lead a teacher in a different way than a server, because he has different jobs for each person.

The Spirit shapes us in different ways, and as a result, we value different goals. Someone with the gift of administration will value order and organization; someone with the gift of serving will ask whether people are being helped; someone with the gift of encouragement will focus on peoples' attitudes; people with the gift of generosity will look for needs that they can fill. The Spirit works with us in the way that he has caused us to be, according to our interests and values.

For some people, he speaks subtly, in general principles; for others, he must speak with unmistakable details. Each of us must listen in the way that God has made us, in the way that he chooses to deal with us. The important thing is that we listen—that we are ready and willing to hear what he says. We should be looking for his leadership rather than ignoring it.

Dangers

There are several dangers to take into account. First, all sorts of people have claimed to hear the Holy Spirit when he didn't really speak to them. They have made false prophecies, given foolish advice, led people into cults and made Christianity look bad. If God spoke to them, they badly misunderstood what he was saying. There is a danger of "hearing" things that God never said. We should be careful, for we do not want to use his name in vain.

A second danger is that some people, afraid of hearing incorrectly, refuse to hear anything at all. But as Dallas Willard has pointed out, we should not "shun the genuine simply because it resembled the counterfeit" (*Hearing God*, p. 88). Our Father in heaven does speak to us, and the Holy Spirit does lead us, and we will shortchange ourselves if we close our ears.

Hebrews 3:7 says that the Spirit speaks in the words of Scripture, and we should not refuse to follow what he says. He does communicate to us today, convicting us of what we should do, guiding us in how we serve God.

A third danger is that some people seek the Holy Spirit for selfish reasons. They want the Spirit to make their decisions for them, to tell them what job to take, which person to marry, when to move and how to live. They want the Holy Spirit to be like a Ouija board or a horoscope, to save them the trouble of thinking and making decisions.

But God wants us to grow in maturity, to learn through experience what is right and wrong (Hebrews 5:12-14). Many of the decisions we face are not matters of sin and righteousness—they are simply choices. God can work with us no matter which we choose, so he leaves the choice up to us—the Holy Spirit doesn't speak on everything we want him to.

Some people would like to have the Holy Spirit as a conversational companion to keep them company. They want to chat, but the Holy Spirit isn't involved in idle words. He does not call attention to himself (John 15:26), and is often silent because he has already given us enough information and guidance. He wants us to use what he has already given; he has been training our conscience to respond rightly to what faces us. That does not mean that we rely on ourselves, but that we rely on what God has already done in our lives and what he has already taught us.

Scripture

The Holy Spirit speaks to us primarily through the Scriptures that he inspired to be written and canonized. This is our foundation of faith and life. It is the word that everyone has access to, the word that can be studied and discussed most objectively. Often the word that we need to hear has already been written, and the Spirit simply needs to bring it to mind. When Jesus was tempted by the devil, his responses were quoted from Scripture. He had studied and memorized those words, and in each situation the Spirit led him to the appropriate response.

The Spirit does not bypass our need to think, or our need to read and meditate on his words. If we are not seeking the words he has already given in Scripture, then we should not expect him to suddenly give us new words for new situations. Nor can we expect the random-access method of Scripture skimming to provide good answers for difficult questions. We cannot force, coerce or goad the Spirit to speak when he does not choose to speak.

With Scripture, we have the potential for nearly constant communication with God, as we read and pray and live consciously in God's presence. As we pray, we should also listen, for God may use our meditations about Scripture to help us understand how we should live. We have the responsibility to read and study, for the Spirit usually works with words that are already in our minds. He works with our vocabulary, with our ways of reasoning, with the desires and values he has given us.

The devil can use Scripture, too, and the Bible is often misunderstood and misused. But the Bible is still an important means of being led by and hearing the Holy Spirit. Scripture is the standard of comparison for all other words from God. If we think that the Spirit is leading us to do something, our first question needs to be, "Is this in agreement with Scripture?" The Spirit does not contradict himself. He does not lead us to lie, steal, gossip or be greedy, for he has already told us that those things are not godly.

So if we think the Spirit is leading us in one direction, we need to check it with Scripture—and the only way we can do that is to know what Scripture says. We need to study it, and since we will never know it all, we need to keep studying it. Memorization can be helpful, but what we need most of all is understanding. We need to see the principles of salvation, of Christian living, of divine love, of the way that God has worked and is working with his people; that will help us understand how he is working with us.

Experience

We can also hear the Holy Spirit through experience. God sometimes changes his methods with us, but most often he works with us in a similar way from one year to another. Through experience, we see how he has answered our prayers and led us in past situations. This will help us recognize his "voice" when he speaks to us in the present. Experience comes through time, submission and meditation. The Spirit helps the humble, not the self-exalting.

We can gain even more wisdom by drawing on the experience of other Christians. The Spirit does not isolate us, but puts us into a church, into a community of other believers. He distributes his gifts so that we stay together, work together and benefit from one another's strengths (1 Corinthians 12:7). In the same way, we can help one another hear the Holy Spirit because we each have different experiences of how God works in our lives.

When a message from God comes to one person, other people are to consider it carefully (1 Corinthians 14:29). They are to consider, for one thing, whether it is really a word from the Lord. The Spirit can speak through the community as well as through certain individuals—the Jerusalem conference is a good example of that. The people learned from their experiences with the Gentiles, saw that those experiences agreed with the Scriptures (Acts 15:15), and through the discussion heard the decision of the Spirit (verse 28).

The Holy Spirit often speaks to people through other people: in worship songs, in small group discussions, in a whispered word of encouragement, in a silent smile, a picture or a magazine article. There are many ways we can learn from others, to receive godly guidance from others. But this is for each person to discern. Rarely does the Spirit tell one person to give orders to another.

Sermons are a common means of spiritual speech. Those who speak should strive to speak the words of God (1 Peter 4:11), so those who speak in church should strive to listen to God as they prepare the sermons, and those who hear the sermons should likewise listen for the words of the Lord. We need to let our worship services be times of listening, of thinking, of communing with God so that we are letting him change us to be more like Christ. Let us draw near to him, and he will change us.

Circumstances are another experiential means of "testing the spirits." We may have an open door, or all the doors may be closed. Obstacles may test our convictions, or they may be indications that we need to think about whether we have correctly understood the directions. They force us to think again, to seek God again, to check with Scripture, and to check with others who have spiritual maturity.

Responding to the Holy Spirit

If we want to hear, we need to listen. But if we want to hear in the biblical sense, we also need to respond. If we hear his voice, if we believe that God is telling us to do something, then we need to do it. We need to do what he has gifted us to do. We are to submit to God, for everything he says is for our own good. We bring him honor, and we bring ourselves blessings, by doing his will. It begins with listening. Can you hear the Holy Spirit?

Joseph Tkach

CAN YOU TRUST THE HOLY SPIRIT
TO SAVE YOU?

I was in a conversation with a friend who had been a Christian for many years. The topic of his baptism came up.

"Why did you want to be baptized?" I asked him.

"Because I wanted to receive the power of the Holy Spirit so that I could overcome all my sins."

"Did it work?"

He laughed. "No."

His intentions were good, but his understanding was flawed. (No one understands perfectly, and we are saved by God's mercy despite our misunderstandings.)

The Holy Spirit is not something we can "switch on" to achieve our overcoming goals, like some kind of supercharger for our willpower. We do not call the shots. The Spirit serves us, but he is not our servant.

The Holy Spirit is God, present with us and in us, giving us the love, assurance and fellowship that the Father has for us in Christ. Through Christ, the Father has made us his own children, and the Holy Spirit gives us the spiritual sense of knowing his love for us (Romans 8:16).

The Holy Spirit gives us fellowship with God through Christ, but he does not remove our ability to sin. We still have wrong desires, still have wrong motives, still have wrong thoughts, words and actions. Even though we may want to stop a particular habit, we find that we are still unable to do it. We know that it is God's will for us to be freed from this problem, but for some reason we still seem to be powerless to shake its influence over us.

Can we believe that the Holy Spirit is at work in our lives—especially when it seems like nothing is really happening, because we are not being very "good" Christians? When we struggle with sin again and again, when it seems like we are not changing much at all, do we conclude that we are so messed up that not even God can fix the problem?

Babies and adolescents

When we come to faith in Christ, we are born again, regenerated, by the Holy Spirit. We are new creatures, new persons, babes in Christ. Babies are not powerful, not skilled, not self-cleaning. As they grow, they acquire some skills, and they also begin to realize that there is a lot they cannot do, and this sometimes leads to frustration. They fidget with the crayons and scissors and fret that they cannot do as well as an adult can. But the fits of frustration do not help— only time and practice will help.

This is true in our spiritual lives, too. Sometimes new Christians are given dramatic power to break a drug habit or a bad temper. Sometimes new Christians are instant "assets" to the church. But more often than not, new Christians struggle with the same sins they had before, have the same personalities they had before, have the same fears and frustrations. They are not spiritual giants.

Jesus conquered sin, but it seems like sin still has a grip on us. The sin nature within us has been defeated, but it still treats us like we are its prisoners. O wretched people that we are! Who will save us from the law of sin and death? Jesus, of course (Romans 7:24-25). He has already won the victory—and he has made that victory ours.

Alas! We do not yet see the complete victory. We do not yet see his power over death, nor the complete end of sin in our lives. As Hebrews 2:8 says, we do not yet see all things under our feet. What we do is trust Jesus. We trust his word that he has won the victory, and we trust his word that in him we are also victorious, and we trust his word that the Holy Spirit will finish the work that Jesus began in our lives.

Still, even though we know we are clean and pure in Christ, we would also like to see progress in overcoming our sins. Such progress may seem excruciatingly slow at times, but we can trust God to do what he has promised—in us as well as in others. After all, it is his work, not ours. It is his power, not ours. It is his agenda, not ours. When we submit ourselves to God, we have to be willing to wait on him. We have to be willing to trust him to do his work in us in the way and at the speed he knows is right.

Adolescents often think they know more than Dad knows. They think they know what life is all about and that they can handle it all pretty well on their own. (Not all adolescents are like that, but the stereotype is based on some evidence.) We Christians can sometimes think in a way similar to adolescents. We may begin to think that "growing up" spiritually is based on right behavior, which leads us to start thinking of our standing with God in terms of how well we are behaving. When we are behaving well, we might tend to look down on people who don't appear to have their act together so well. When we aren't behaving so well, we might fall into despair and depression, believing God has left us.

But God does not ask us to make ourselves right with him; he asks us to trust him, the one who justifies the wicked (Romans 4:5), who loves us and saves us for the sake of Christ. As we mature in Christ, we rest more firmly in God's love demonstrated supremely for us in Christ (1 John 4:9). As we rest in him, we look forward to the day described in Revelation 21:4: "He will wipe every tear from their eyes. There will be no more death or mourning or crying or pain, for the old order of things has passed away."

Perfection!

When that day comes, we will be changed in the twinkling of an eye. We will be made immortal, imperishable, incorruptible (1 Corinthians 15:52-53). And God redeems the inner person, not just the outer. He changes our innermost being, from weak and corruptible, to glorious and (most important of all) sinless.

Instantly, at the last trump, we will be changed. Our bodies will be redeemed (Romans 8:23), but more than that, we will finally see ourselves as God has made us to be in Christ (1 John 3:2). We will then see plainly the as-yet-invisible reality that God has made true in Christ.

Through Christ, our old sin nature has been defeated and demolished. It is dead. "You have died," Paul puts it, "and your life is hidden with Christ in God" (Colossians 3:3). The sin that "so easily entangles us" and which we strive to "throw off" (Hebrews 12:1) is not part of the new person God has made us to be in Christ. In Christ, we have new life.

At Christ's appearing, we will at last see ourselves as our Father has made us in Christ. We will see ourselves as we really are, as perfect in Christ, who is our true life (Colossians 3:3-4). It is for this reason, because we have already died and been raised with Christ, that we work to "put to death" whatever in us is earthly (verse 5).

We overcome Satan (and sin and death) in only one way—by the blood of the Lamb (Revelation 12:11). It is through the victory of Jesus Christ, won on the cross, that we have victory over sin and death, not through our struggles against sin. Our struggles against sin are expressions of the fact that we are in Christ, that we are no longer enemies of God, but his friends, in fellowship with him through the Holy Spirit, who works in us both to will and to do God's good pleasure (Philippians 2:13).

Our struggle against sin is not the cause of our righteousness in Christ. It does not produce holiness. God's own love and grace toward us in Christ is the cause, the only cause, of our righteousness. We are made righteous, redeemed from all sin and ungodliness, by God through Christ because God is full of love and grace, and for no other reason. Our struggle against sin is the product of the new and righteous self we have been given in Christ, not the cause of it. Christ died for us while we were still sinners (Romans 5:8).

We hate sin, we struggle against sin, we want to avoid the pain and sorrow for ourselves and others that sin produces, because God has made us alive in

Christ and the Holy Spirit is at work in us. It is because we are in Christ that we fight the sin which "so easily entangles us" (Hebrews 12:1). But we gain the victory not through our own efforts, not even our own efforts as empowered by the Holy Spirit. We gain the victory through the blood of Christ, through his death and resurrection as the incarnate Son of God, God in the flesh.

God has already done in Christ everything that needed doing for our salvation, and he has already given us everything we need for life and godliness simply by calling us to know him in Christ. And he did this simply because he is so almighty good (2 Peter 1:2-3).

The book of Revelation tells us that there will come a time when there will be no more crying and no more tears, no more hurt and no more pain, and that means no more sin, for it is sin that causes pain. Suddenly, in the twinkling of an eye, the darkness will end and sin will no longer be able to deceive us into thinking we are still its prisoners. Our true freedom, our new life in Christ, will shine forever with him in all its glorious splendor. In the meantime, we trust the word of his promise.

Joseph Tkach

DO YOU HAVE THE HOLY SPIRIT?

Christians sometimes wonder whether they have been given God's Holy Spirit. What are some guidelines we can use in trying to understand our own spiritual state? Since the Holy Spirit is spirit, we cannot feel, touch or sense the Spirit in the way that we might discern a physical object. So we can't talk about having the Spirit in those terms.

Our emotions and feelings are part of our spiritual life. But we can sometimes "feel" as though we are charged with the Holy Spirit and at other times "feel" as though we aren't. Both feelings can't be right, because the Holy Spirit does not enter and leave us on a repeated basis. When we are born of God's Spirit, we are a new creation and always have the Spirit within to guide us.

How can we know we have the Holy Spirit? Let's answer a few questions.

- Do we believe in Jesus Christ as our Savior and Lord (Romans 10:9)?
- Are we moved in prayer to God in ways that sometimes surprise us (Romans 8:26-27)?
- Do we have a desire to obey God in love and bear the fruit of the Spirit (Galatians 5:6-18, 22-25)?
- Do we love others and show them acts of kindness as we have opportunity (James 1:27)?
- Conversely, do we see the need to avoid things that are contrary to God's way (James 1:27; 1 John 2:15-17)?

If we can answer "yes" to these questions, we can have assurance that God's Spirit is leading us. Gradually, as we live in Christ, we will find clear marks of his presence in our thoughts, action and life.

One individual explained the signs of the presence of the Holy Spirit in the following ways, with references to the first letter of John. As Spirit-filled Christians we will have a new:

- Desire to please God (2:5).
- Assurance of pardon (2:1-2).
- Willingness to face opposition (3:13).
- Delight in the company of fellow Christians (3:14).
- Generosity of spirit (3:17).
- Experience of victory over temptations (4:4; 5:4).

- Discovery of answers to prayer (3:22).
- Understanding of life and set of priorities (5:20-21).

If we see that these factors have been at work in our lives, we should be confident that the Holy Spirit is working in us. We should be careful not to deny these manifestations, as though we are not worthy of them. It is not pride to know we have been born again of God. We should be humbly thankful for God's mercy in bestowing his grace upon us.

As human beings, even with God's Holy Spirit we will sin (1 John 1:8-2:5). We will never be perfect in this human life. This may cause us to *feel* as though God is not with us. But the things mentioned above will be working in our lives because we do have the Spirit. When we sin, we will go to God in prayer acknowledging our sinfulness and our need for his mercy (Luke 18:9-14). *That in itself is a demonstration that we have the Holy Spirit.*

We can always have confidence in the fact that once God begins to work with us and gives us his Holy Spirit, he will never leave us. Despite the ups and downs of life, despite the problems we may have, we can be assured of God's faithfulness. In the words of the apostle Paul: "Being confident of this, that he who began a good work *in you* will carry it on to completion until the day of Christ Jesus" (Philippians 1:6).

Joseph Tkach

GOD TOLD ME...

"God told me to move my family to Saudi Arabia."

Alex stared at his friend, wondering if he was just joking or had gone mad. Alex had known Tom for more than 10 years. He'd been best man at Tom's wedding, and godfather to Tom's and Alicia's twin girls. Alex knew that Tom and Alicia were as suited for missionary life in Saudi Arabia as toads are for an omelet.

"That's, well, a pretty big decision, Tom. How do you know it's really God's will for you?"

"Well, just a lot of things." Tom stared deep into his coffee cup. "Pastor Mel's sermon a few weeks ago really got me thinking." He glanced up at Alex. "We're pretty selfish enjoying the good life here in America while people all around the world need help. I gave it a lot of prayer, and God seemed to answer that we should go."

Alex nodded thoughtfully, weighing how to respond. "How did God give you that answer?"

"Well, for one thing, I was talking to the Hogarths, you know, the missionaries in Saudi Arabia. They said they could use some help."

"What kind of help?"

"Well, you know, I'm pretty good at carpentry, and they said that's just what they'd been praying for—somebody good at carpentry. It was like God was just saying to me, 'This is what I want you to do, Tom.'"

"What does Alicia think about it?"

"Oh, she's not as excited as I am, but I'm praying she'll come around."

"Not as excited?" Alex said.

"Well, actually she's dead set against it. She can get pretty hardheaded sometimes. But I think the Lord will show her it's the right thing for us to do."

"Hmm, I see," Alex dumped a pack of sweetener into his coffee. "What if he doesn't?"

"He will, Alex. I trust the Lord. I have a really good feeling about this decision."

Tom is not unique. Every day, Christians somewhere are convincing themselves that God is telling them to marry a certain person, take a certain job, go to a certain college, or "get out there" and do something really big and meaningful for him.

But is he—really?

How can we know whether God is leading us into some major life decision, or whether, just maybe, we are simply bored and frustrated with our current situation and looking for a change or a way out? A way out with

God's name stamped on it?

A few thoughts

Here are a few thoughts God told me to pass along about decision-making. Or maybe he didn't. In any case, here are my two cents' worth. I believe they are a biblically rooted two cents' worth.

When God spoke to people in the Bible, there was no question that it was a message from God. It usually was delivered by an angel, and it usually scared the people.

When God had to tell people what he wanted them to do, it was usually something they did not want to do.

Sometimes, our prayers for God's blessing are really our prayers to get our own way despite what God thinks. Take King Ahab, when he wanted to attack the King of Aram, who had captured some of Ahab's cities. Ahab asked Micaiah the prophet if he'd be victorious. Micaiah told Ahab the truth, even though all the other "prophets" had said Ahab would surely win the battle. Ahab wasn't looking for God's will; he was looking for affirmation of his own will. He was doing a bullheaded thing, but he also wanted God's blessing to cover his backside. But God is apparently not into covering the backsides of bull-headed people. Ahab attacked the king of Aram and was killed. God doesn't stop us from making stupid decisions when we are determined to make them.

God is pretty clear about what he tells us to do: "The entire law is summed up in a single command: 'Love your neighbor as yourself.'" For what it's worth, we don't have to go half way around the world to find our neighbors.

One of the reasons we crave to do something "great" for God is that we are unsure of how we stand with him, and we hope that if we do something "great," like move to a faraway corner of the earth and be a missionary, God will like us more and we can feel better about our relationship with him. That's not gospel thinking—that's superstitious thinking. God loves us where we are, and there is a "great" Christian work in us being ourselves in Christ and showing his love to the people we run into every day.

Changing our location does not change us. We can't run away from our problems. If I'm a lazy curmudgeon in Peoria, I'll be a lazy curmudgeon in Bangladesh. If I'm a short-tempered mule with my first spouse, I'll likely be a short-tempered mule with my second, or third, too. If we need to change, we might need to change our *selves* first, not merely our circumstances. We might need to pray for a clean and godly heart of love, and then take that clean heart wherever life leads us, not where we think there might be more spiritual glory.

Spiritual glory is invisible, and it's present in every act of kindness and self-sacrificial love. Geography or possessions have nothing to do with it. If I want to do "more" for God, I might do well to start by being a better husband and father, or wife and mother.

Some ordained people give poor advice. When a pastor or missionary says, "I think God is calling you to such-and-such," don't think that they necessarily know what they are talking about. "In a multitude of counselors, there is safety," says the proverb. We shouldn't take one hyped-up person's opinion as though it were God's sacred word just because it's what we wanted to hear.

Concluding thoughts

"God told me to… " is often a euphemism for "I want to and have decided to…"

It isn't wrong to want to do something and decide to do it. But why not be honest? Why not say: "I have decided to go to Africa and work in a health clinic. Please pray for me." That would be honest.

God can and does bless us in our decisions without making them for us. God gives us the ability to weigh the factors in our lives, get advice, do some research, study the issues involved and make informed, well-considered decisions. And we should ask him to lead us.

Wouldn't it be nice to enjoy the godly freedom to say: "Lord, I've got several paths before me, and based on all the facts as I understand them, here's what I think I should probably do. If there's something I'm missing here, would you show me before it's too late? And if I miss the cue, then please have mercy on me, a sinner and a frequent dumbbell. And if this is a trap door instead of an open door, would you mind not letting go of my hand until I get back to where I ought to be? Thanks. Amen."

J. Michael Feazell

HOLY SPIRIT: PERSON OR POWER?

Some claim that the Holy Spirit is an impersonal power. But viewing him in that way falls far short of what the New Testament teaches, undermining a full understanding of one of the most exciting and encouraging dimensions of our relationship with God.

In teaching about the Holy Spirit, the New Testament uses analogies related to both power and personhood. But why the mixture? If the doctrine of the Trinity is so important, why didn't the New Testament authors spell it out more clearly?

It's important to remember that the Bible was written within a particular cultural setting where some things were understood without detailed explanation. It's the same today. If I mention "Monday morning quarterbacking" to Americans, most know what I mean without elaboration. But people unfamiliar with American football culture would not understand.

As we read what the Bible says about the Holy Spirit, we need to ask, are we expecting it to answer questions that were not questions in its original cultural setting? Would the original audience have assumed without further explanation that the Holy Spirit was personal and acted as a powerful agent? Scripture shows us that the answer is yes.

There are many places in Scripture where the Holy Spirit is referred to in personal terms. In John 16:14, Jesus refers to the Spirit using a personal (rather than a neuter) pronoun, saying "He will glorify me." In Acts 15:28, the apostles spoke of the Spirit in personal terms when they said "It seemed good to the Holy Spirit and to us." The characteristics of a person are assumed by the biblical authors when they spoke of the Holy Spirit acting as do human persons: teaching, comforting, guiding, giving, calling and sending. They spoke of the Spirit as being resisted (Acts 7:51), argued with and personally replied to (10:14-20), grieved (Ephesians 4:30) and lied to (Acts 5:3-9). They also spoke of the Spirit distributing gifts according to his own will (1 Corinthians 12:11).

The early church recognized that "Holy Spirit" was used throughout Scripture as a proper name, just as are "Father" and "Son." Jesus indicates that all three are personal names when he directs his disciples to baptize in "the name of the Father and of the Son and of the Holy Spirit" (Matthew 28:19). This command hearkens back to Jesus' own baptism where the Father, the Son and the Spirit were each personally present (Matthew 3:13-17).

Jesus distinguished the Spirit from himself in a personal sense when he said, "I tell you the truth; it is expedient for you that I go away for if I go not away, the Comforter [Paraclete] will not come unto you; but if I depart, I will send him unto you" (John 16:7 *KJV*). Jesus regarded the Holy Spirit not as an effect (comfort) but as a person who brings comfort (the Comforter).

In saying that he would send the Holy Spirit, Jesus distinguished the Spirit from himself and the Father in a personal sense: "But the Counselor [Paraclete], the Holy Spirit, whom the Father will send in my name, he will teach you all things and will bring to your remembrance all that I have said to you" (John 14:26 *RSV*). "When the Counselor [Paraclete] comes, whom I shall send to you from the Father, the Spirit of truth who proceeds from the Father, he will bear witness to me" (John 15:26 *RSV*).

Because the name *Paraclete* is unfamiliar to us (my spell-check keeps asking if I mean "parakeet"!), English Bibles translate it as Counselor, Helper, Advocate or Comforter. But these translations fall short in conveying the name's full meaning. Those who spoke *Koine* Greek understood Jesus' meaning—they recognized that Jesus was speaking in personal terms when referring to "the Paraclete," just as he was speaking in personal terms when referring to "the Son" and to "the Father." Though these personal names were revolutionary, they were not ambiguous.

In the ancient world, *paracletos* often was used in a legal sense—like our words advocate, attorney or lawyer (though likening the Spirit to a lawyer might not go down so well today!). *Paracletos* also was used in a military sense. Greek soldiers went into battle in pairs, standing together as they fought off the enemy. The Greeks called this trusted soldier and friend a *paraclete*. So when the first disciples heard Jesus refer to the Spirit as the Paraclete and speak of him otherwise in personal terms (as in Acts 1:5, 8), Jesus' meaning would have been apparent to them without further explanation.

From the beginning, the early church was functionally and implicitly trinitarian. Like Jesus, it spoke of the Father, the Son and the Spirit using personal terms. However, as Christianity spread, other teachings arose. Church leaders had to counter heretical teachings concerning the nature of Jesus Christ and the Holy Spirit and the relationships between the divine persons. Out of these debates came the doctrine of the Trinity, which was formalized in the Nicene Creed (shown below) where the Father, Son and Spirit are presented as unique divine persons who are inter-personally related. Note this comment from Thomas Torrance:

> A definite doctrine of the Trinity was found to arise out of a faithful exegetical interpretation of the New Testament and out of the evangelical experience and liturgical life of the Church from the very

beginning. *It made explicit what was already implicit in the fundamental deposit of faith.* It was with the formulation of the *homoousion* [meaning "of one being"---the term used in the Nicene Creed] clarifying and expressing the essential connection of the Son to the Father upon which the very Gospel rested, and with the application of the *homoousion* to the Holy Spirit to express his oneness in being with the Godhead of the Father, that the theological structure of the Trinitarian understanding of the Godhead unfolded and established itself firmly within the mind of the Church (*The Trinitarian Faith,* p. 199, emphasis added).

Though the Nicene Creed made explicit the personhood of the Father, the Son and the Spirit, some Western thinkers (particularly since the Enlightenment) have explained God's nature in impersonal, mechanistic and creaturely ways, including saying that the Holy Spirit is not God, but an impersonal power that emanates from God. But impersonal explanations of God's nature always fall short. Why? Because God is not a creature, nor is he a mechanism. His true nature as a tri-personal, relational God is known only by revelation, from Jesus, recorded in Scripture. There the Holy Spirit is revealed as the Paraclete—a divine Person who is personal just as are the Father and the Son.

Grounded in this stunning revelation, we may think, speak, worship and act with assurance, knowing that the Holy Spirit is God just as the Father is God and the Son is God. One God; three persons: blessed Trinity!

Joseph Tkach

A THEOLOGY OF THE HOLY SPIRIT

By Gary W. Deddo

Introduction

Seeking to understand and know the Holy Spirit is a wonderful, rewarding endeavor that ties in with every aspect of the Christian faith and life. But if ever there was a topic we are likely never to get to the bottom of, the doctrine of the Holy Spirit would qualify. The very name of this Divine Person, the Holy Spirit, already tells us that we're in pretty deep. But we do have a good amount of insight given us in Scripture that can inform our understanding and help us stay away from pure speculation. God has seen fit to reveal himself to us as Father, Son and Holy Spirit and has provided and preserved teaching about the Holy Spirit. Because he wants us to know, trust and worship him, we by faith can dare to pursue understanding on that basis. But we proceed only by God's grace.

In this essay we will touch on a few key points that address questions that are, first, foundational to our faith in the Holy Spirit and are, second, of more immediate importance given current discussions and debates. Hopefully, this essay will also help keep further explorations and other discussions in perspective. We will not be able to offer anything near a comprehensive view, so regard this as more of a beginning than an ending.

Jesus on the nature and work of the Spirit

I'd like to start by recalling the passage in the Gospel of John where Jesus, trying to explain to Nicodemus something foundational regarding the nature and work of the Spirit, says this: "Truly, I say to you, unless you are born of water and the Spirit, you cannot enter the Kingdom of God." Jesus continues, "That which is born of flesh is flesh, that which is born of Spirit is Spirit. Do not marvel that I said to you, you must be born anew [from above]. The wind blows where it wills, and you hear the sound of it, but you do not know whence it comes or whither it goes. So it is with everyone who is born of the Spirit" (John 3:5-8).

Nicodemus wants to understand how God works. Jesus tells him that how God works with us is by the Holy Spirit. But Nicodemus is not exactly satisfied with that answer. He wants to know, if he can, how then the Spirit works. Jesus' answer to that *how* question amounts to him saying: How the Spirit works is like trying to talk about how the wind works. We see the effects, but we know very little about it, not even where it was a few moments ago, or where it will end up going a few moments later. The Spirit is not predictable or controllable by us. We don't and can't have an answer as to how the Spirit works, the mechanics of it. Apparently the *how* question is the wrong one to ask. And, given Jesus' reply to Nicodemus, we can assume that it's not necessary for us to know either, even to receive the benefits of the working of the Spirit.

Jesus' "no-explanation" answer does makes sense. How can we possibly put in words, concepts and ideas something about the Spirit given that it is like the wind? You can't actually predict its movement or say much about it except that "it blows where it wills." The Spirit has a mind of his own! I think that's part of our experience. The wind of the Spirit blows where it wills. We did not necessarily see it coming and don't necessarily see exactly where it's going to go. So it is with the Spirit.

So why not just stop right there? Well, in some cases I think that might be the right thing to do. There is a lot of speculation taking place, especially about how the Spirit works. However, we are given other words and descriptions in biblical revelation that refer to the Holy Spirit. But not surprisingly, they don't tell us how the Spirit works nor especially how to bring the Spirit under our control or how we can influence or predict the working of the Spirit. Rather, most of what we are given relates to the nature and purpose and character of the Spirit, not the mechanics of his working. All sorts of problems can be avoided if we simply pay attention to what biblical revelation actually tells us and resist using what we discover in ways that actually disregard Jesus' own teaching on the limits of our knowledge of the Holy Spirit's wind-like working.

Sometimes, people think the Holy Spirit gets less attention than deserved — the short end of the stick, as we say, or short-shrift. The complaint that the Spirit is under-represented can be heard both at the levels of theological discussion as well as at the daily and practical level of church life. That's a perfectly good concern to raise. We should be aware and take to heart all we are told regarding the Spirit. Neglecting any part of biblical witness is not a good idea. Faith seeks whatever understanding of the Spirit we are given, as in any other part of the Christian faith. But we can ask the counter question as well: Is it true that in practice and preaching we don't properly emphasize the Holy Spirit? If so, in what ways do we fail to give the Spirit sufficient attention? And, what measure or criteria can we use to evaluate whether or not we have under (or over) emphasized the Holy Spirit?

Whether or not we give full attention is best gauged by the norm of biblical teaching. We can look to Scripture to weigh its own emphasis on the Spirit relative to other matters. We can also consider the full range of insights it actually presents us. Then we can compare our own current emphasis and range of teaching to the pattern and proportion found there. While we will not be able to conclude with something like a numerical measurement, I think there will be many indicators in biblical teaching that can greatly assist us in our process of discernment. And of course, we can also borrow understanding on this matter from teachers of the church down through the ages, including our present time as their teaching seems in alignment with biblical revelation considered as a whole.

Now, if there is some kind of deficit, then we'll also need to explore how best to correct for that lack. We'll need to discern this issue as well, because there are various ways to correct for it. But some correctives aren't as useful or faithful as others. And some promoted in recent times have seemed not only speculative but harmful to the health of the Body of Christ. But again, biblical teaching can help us in discerning how best to make any kind of corrective called for.

The basics of revelation concerning the Spirit

Any theology built on biblical revelation must seek first and foremost to answer the question of *who* the God of the Bible is, for that is its central concern and controlling topic. Biblical revelation is not geared nearly as much to answer the questions of how or why, where or when. So our understanding must also begin by seeking to know first who the Holy Spirit is.

Let's begin with a review of the most basic truths we have been given about the Holy Spirit. Most fundamentally we are told about the Spirit's relationship with the Father and the Son. And those relationships identify who the Spirit of God is. Who is the Spirit? The Spirit is the Spirit of the Father and the Son. The Spirit is one with the Father and one with the Son. Jesus is conceived by the Spirit, he has the Spirit for us ,and he ministers in and by the Spirit even in his atoning work on the Cross. Jesus and the Father send the Spirit to us. The Spirit takes us to the Father through the Son. By the Spirit we are united to Christ so that we share in his life, life in fellowship and communion with the Father. And we share, by the Spirit, in Jesus' ongoing ministry in the church and in the world.

Notice that what Jesus teaches Nicodemus (and us) fits the overall pattern of revelation about the Spirit throughout Scripture. Nicodemus wanted to know how one can be "born again" or "born from above." But Jesus' response indicates that such *how* questions can't really be answered in connection with the Spirit! Nicodemus is not told how the Spirit blows to bring us new life. Rather, Jesus' answer to his *how* question identifies *who* is behind the how. But Jesus does describe in a comprehensive way the effect of the working of the Spirit, namely, bringing us a new kind of life.

The Gospel of John goes on to shed even more light on the relationship of the Spirit to Jesus and to the Father which includes the inter-relationship of their missions and ministries. These relationships are especially prominent in chapters 13-17. The central concern throughout this Gospel remains their conjoint relationships. They are inseparable, always being together and always working together.

One in being, united in act

Borrowing now from the more developed doctrine of the Trinity, we can say that the three Divine Persons of the Trinity are "one in being." This technical phrase helps us to remember there are not three Gods, but only one. So, the Spirit isn't a separate God that has his own independent mind, his own action, his own plan, and his own purpose. The Spirit is joined in one being and so joined in one mind, action, plan, and purpose with the Father and the Son. Even the name, Holy Spirit, indicates to us the unity of the Spirit with Father and Son, since only God has the name Holy.

The point here is not to let our minds think about the Holy Spirit as an independent operator. That's one of the biggest mistakes that we can make. Always remember, whatever the Spirit does, wherever the Spirit is at work, that Spirit is the Spirit of the Father, and of the Son, because they are one in being. They do not act separately, apart from one another. They act out of one shared mind, heart, purpose in unity with each other. St. Augustine famously summarized this in the fourth century: "All the works of God are inseparable."

A number of special phrases have been used down through the ages to convey the oneness or unity of the divine Persons besides saying that they are "one in being." They are said to "co-exist." They "co-inhere" in one another. They "in-exist" one another, or they "mutually in-dwell" one another. They "co-envelop" one another, or "mutually interpenetrate" each other. Their oneness of being has been expressed by saying that the whole God is present in each of the Divine Persons. The whole God is present in the Father. The whole God is present in the Son. The whole God is present in the Spirit. That's all to say: they're one in being even though they're distinguishable, we say, in person. An early creed sums it up this way: the Triune God is a Unity in Trinity and a Trinity in Unity.

Sharing all the divine attributes

This means that the Holy Spirit is fully and completely divine and has from all eternity all the attributes that the Father and the Son have. The Spirit is not subordinate or less than the others. All that you can say of the Father, such as being omniscient, holy, omnipotent, eternal, and even being a Creator, can all be said of the Spirit (and can all be said of the Son). Dividing up among the Persons the attributes of God and the actions of God towards creation is ruled out because they are one in being.

That's a hard rule for us to follow because we have developed poor habits of thinking and speaking in the church, and likely were never taught otherwise. We also like to divide things up and align certain attributes or actions with the Father and others with the Son or the Spirit. A typical way we do this is by saying the Father creates, the Son redeems and the Spirit perfects or sanctifies. We might think the Father is just and holy in comparison to the Son who is merciful and gracious. However, if we take such a division of labor in a strict way, we would be embracing a very inaccurate, even misleading way of speaking about God. The distinct Persons of the Trinity do not have separate jobs or wear different hats or play different roles they accomplish by themselves. God acts as the one being that God is. His being does not fragment in mind, will, purpose or action.

So, to repeat, everything you can say about the eternal nature and character of the Father, you can say about the Son and you can say about the Spirit. They are each all powerful, omniscient, omnipresent, eternal, good, merciful, righteous, holy. They are all to be worshiped together because they're one in being. So we can say of our worship, we worship the Father through the Son and in the Spirit. Or, we pray to the Father, through the Son and in the Spirit. And we proclaim that the Father has redeemed us through the Son and in the Spirit. The whole God is our Savior.

The unity of the being and so of action, character and attributes of God is one of the most fundamental things to hold on to and to watch out for when we go on to say other things about the Spirit. We want to avoid talking as if the Divine Persons are separate, wear different hats, have divergent purposes, or as if they are operating independently of one another. Simply remembering they're one in being will prevent a lot of problems down the theological road.

PART 2

One in being, distinct in Person

In part 1, we noted that every act of God, whether in creation, redemption or bringing about the perfection of creation itself, is done *together as one God*. But how then are we to understand those places in Scripture that ascribe certain acts of God to one of the divine Persons? Take, for example, the Incarnation. The Father and the Spirit are never said to be incarnate, as is the Son. Note also that the Spirit seems to descend on Pentecost and indwell the believing church in a way distinct from the Son and the Father. The explanation in these two and similar examples is that all three of the divine Persons are involved together in all the acts of God, but often in different (distinct, unique) ways.

How are the divine Persons distinct?

Scripture leads us to understand that each of the divine Persons contributes to the unified act of God from their own, particular "angle." We could say that one "takes the lead" in certain actions: the Father in Creation, the Son in atonement, the Spirit in perfecting creation. But we can only say that if we aren't thinking of the three Persons as acting separately, or as being out of phase with the others. The three Persons always act in a conjoint way. Theologians call this the *doctrine of appropriation*. An act can be appropriated to the Person of the Trinity who takes the lead, as long as the other two are not regarded as having nothing to do with it, but are co-involved, each in their own way.

We should not think that the contribution to an act of God by one of the Persons is what constitutes their being as a distinct Person in the Trinity. For example, it is an error to think that being the Creator is what makes the Father different in Person from the Son, or that being Incarnate is what makes the Son different in Person from the Father. The Father is the Father, the Son is the Son, and the Spirit is the Spirit, whether or not they perform any actions external to their own triune being. The three Persons are distinguished by their *internal relationships*, not by their *external actions*. The being of God is not dependent upon God's relationship to that which is external to God.

So, as long as we don't leave the Son and the Spirit behind, we can say the Father leads in creation. We can also say the Son leads in our redemption. But if we think the Father is absent or has a different view, attitude, purpose or intention for the Cross than does the Son, then we've split the Trinity apart, placed them at odds with one another! Even in Jesus' earthly life, we need to remember that he only does what he sees the Father doing. He only says what the Father is saying. They're saying things together. They're doing things together. They're never separate because they're *one in being.*

The work of the Son

It is proper to say the Son takes the lead and that only the Son is incarnate. So, we can affirm that the Son physically suffers on the cross and not the Father or Spirit. Not being incarnate in our humanity, they cannot physically suffer and die. But, if we think the Father is absent or the Spirit has gone on vacation and isn't around when Jesus is on the Cross, then we've strayed way off the theological path. The Spirit and the Father are present with Jesus, each in their own non-incarnate way. So, Jesus says, "Father into your hands, I commend my Spirit." In the book of Hebrews we read, "how much more shall the blood of Christ, who through the eternal Spirit offered himself without blemish to God, purify your conscience from dead works to worship the living God (Heb. 9:14). They're all acting together in Christ's redeeming work. Yes, we can say one leads. But don't let them fall apart just because one is leading.

The work of the Spirit

We can say that the Spirit perfects. However, we must also say that he perfects human beings with the perfection accomplished by Christ. The Spirit shares with us the holiness and the sanctification of Jesus, himself, in our humanity. He doesn't give us a spiritualized or divine perfection, a non-bodily, inhuman existence. But rather the Spirit joins us to Christ's glorified human body, mind and soul. The Spirit makes us to share in Jesus' self-sanctification. The work of the Spirit is not separate from the work of the Son, but the Spirit does lead in dwelling in us now.

Beware the error of *tritheism*

Though we can talk about the Spirit leading, we must not think of the Spirit branching off, saying, "Father and Son, you've done a good job over there, but now I've got to go do something over here that you don't have anything to do with. It's my turn to do my own thing." That's a mistake. That could only happen if God wasn't one in being and was three beings—*tritheism!* We don't want to go there. We can distinguish between the various contributions the Father, the Son and the Spirit make by the way they take their lead, but we don't want to separate them or place them in any kind of opposition or in tension with each other. And we don't want to say that their differing contributions to what they accomplish together are what make them distinct in Person from all eternity.

As so we distinguish but we don't separate. The divine Persons are *one in being and distinct in Person*, both in their internal and eternal being and in terms of what they do in creation, redemption, and consummation.

Beware projecting on God

Why do we get tripped up in this? I think there are a number of reasons, but one is that we tend to think of God in ways we think of ourselves. We start with ourselves, then try to get to our understanding of God. Think of how we usually distinguish ourselves from each other. How do I know I'm not you and you're not me? I note that you have a different body. You're over there, and I'm over here. You do this, but I do that. You live there, but I live here. You think that's funny, but I don't. I want X, but you want Y. We're different in all these ways, and that's how we know we are distinct persons.

So we can project this perspective on God, and think that's how the Father, Son and Spirit are distinguished. The Father is over here, the Spirit's over there. The Father wants A, and the Son wants B. They each have different jobs to do. We try to distinguished them from each other in the same way we distinguish ourselves. The problem is, *God is not a creature like we are*. So, you can't just take the idea of how we distinguish ourselves and apply that reasoning to God. Thinking that way would only work if God was a creature. But he is not.

Names and relations

The essential way we have been given to distinguish between the divine Persons is by means of their different names: the Father, the Son, and he Holy Spirit. These names reveal a difference of their Persons. That is also why we believe there are three, not four or two Persons in the Godhead. The names we are given in Scripture are revelatory of real differences in God. They are not just arbitrary words, concepts, ideas, or conventional labels. So we address God in worship, in prayer, by means of these three names. And in doing so, we follow Jesus' example and instruction. He uses these names in his relationship to the Father and the Spirit, and directs us to do so as well. So he instructs us: "Pray like this: Our Father in heaven…"

Notice that divine names represent *unique relationships*. The Father has a different relationship with the Son than the Son has with the Father. And the Spirit has a different relationship to the Father than does the Son. The names identify and reveal to us unique relationships. Following biblical teaching, we can also find distinct designations for the different relationships.

Corresponding to the Father is the relationship of begetting to the Son. *Begetting* is the special term used to describe more particularly how the Son comes from the Father. The Father begets the Son. Begetting indicates a certain kind of relationship. For instance, in the early church they recognized that begetting is different from making. What is made is of a different kind of thing than the maker. But what is begotten is of the identical kind of being. So we say that the Son is begotten, indicating a unique kind of relationship to the Father. The Son doesn't beget the Father and the Father isn't begotten by the Son. They each have a different relationship with each other and that difference of relationship, which is internal and eternal to God, is what makes them personally distinct from one another. The Father *begets* (is not begotten of the Son). The Son is *begotten* (does not beget the Father).

The unique names and relationships identify who the divine Persons are. They are who they are in relationship with each other. Without the relationships with each other, they would not be who they are. And they are not interchangeable. The Father is not the Son, the Son is not the Father. Being the begetter and being the begotten one are different and not reversible. There is a direction to the relationships that can't be reversed. You can't say the Son begets the Father. The Son has always been the begotten Son. The Father has always begotten the Son. The Son is eternally the Son, and the Father, eternally Father. That's why we can say they are the divine Persons of Father and Son.

But the words/names don't themselves explain everything. They represent what we have to go on and explain, namely, what they do and don't mean as far as we can tell. In the case of the Father and Son, we have to rule out, or "think away" as Athanasius said, some aspects of the meaning of the words begotten or begetting as used of human creatures. Among creatures these words include the idea of a time sequence. But when it comes to God, the aspect of time does not apply. God is eternal and so, then, are the divine Persons. So the Father generates the Son from all eternity.

Time sequence doesn't apply to God. There never was a time when the Son was not. The Son was always the begotten Son of the Father, which is simply to say the Son is eternally the Son and the Father is eternally the Father, begetting the Son. The discipline of theology is to discern where and how words used to refer to God must be used differently from how they are used of creatures. This would be impossible if we did not have biblical revelation to lead us.

The Holy Spirit proceeds (*spirates*)

Now what about the Holy Spirit? There has always been the Spirit who has eternal relationships with the Father and the Son. We use a special word to talk about those relationships, a word given in the New Testament; we say the Holy Spirit *proceeds* from the Father and, or through, the Son (John 15:26). Another word has also been used down through the ages to indicate that unique relationship, "spirates." These words indicate unique and non-interchangeable relationship. The name and relationship indicate who the Spirit is. The Spirit would not be the Spirit without spirating from the Father and the Son. And the Father and Son wouldn't be Father and Son without the Spirit proceeding. The relationship of the Spirit is essential to who the Spirit is and so to who the Triune God is.

We likely want to ask, "So how does that work? How does a *procession* work in God?" We don't actually know. We can't say exactly how it is different from begetting or being begotten. Along with the name, Holy Spirit, the word procession indicates that there is a unique kind of relationship of the Spirit with the Father and the Son, one that is different from the relationship of the Son to the Father. It indicates that the Spirit is from the Father and/through, the Son in such a way that the Son and Father do not proceed from the Spirit and are not the Spirit. With this unique relationship, the Spirit is not interchangeable with the other Persons. And it means that the Holy Spirit has always been the Holy Spirit. We affirm in this way that God has always been a Trinity. *There never was a time when God was not Triune.*

Conclusion: triune relations

The three divine Persons eternally exist in absolutely unique relationships and that is what is essential to their being distinct Persons. That's it. They have unique relations. Each has a different relationship with the other two. We don't know how to explain all that, what that means, but we use unique words because there are unique relations. And that's also why we address them according to their unique names that correspond with the relations. The Father is the Father, not the Son. The Son is the Son, not the Father. The Holy Spirit is the Holy Spirit of the Father and the Son. We have unique names to indicate the unique persons and they have unique relationships and they're not interchangeable.

When God through Jesus says, to address him as Father, Son and Holy Spirit, we're being told something. The triune name identifies who God is, which God we're speaking of, and even what kind of god that God is. God is the Triune God. That's the only God that is or has ever been. God is Father, Son and Spirit. The Father is the Father. The Son is the Son. The Holy Spirit is the Holy Spirit. Don't separate them — they are one in being. But don't collapse them into one Person with no relationships — they are distinct in Person.

PART 3

The Triune God: one in *being*, three distinct *Divine Persons*

You have probably heard the triune God referred to as *one in three and three in one*. Though not incorrect, this statement is easily misunderstood. Why? Because it can sound as if we're saying that God is both three and one of the exact same thing. But that makes no sense. God is not one being and three beings; nor is God one person and three persons. To avoid misunderstandings, it's better to say that the triune God is *one in being and three in divine Persons*. Let's explore what this means as we continue this series on the doctrine of the Holy Spirit.

Fundamental to the discipline of theology is making sure we don't talk about God as if God was a creature. This way of disciplining our thinking takes some time and effort to catch on to, and that is why Grace Communion International and Grace Communion Seminary both take great care in teaching people to think about God *according to God's nature*. That means, for example, not thinking about God as a big human being in the sky.

God is *three divine Persons*

The doctrine of the Trinity asserts that God is *three divine Persons*. What does that mean? We begin by noting that God is not a "person" the way we are. As humans, we are images of God, but God is not an image of us. Because divine Persons are not exactly the same as human persons, we have to distinguish them. Were God three persons exactly like we are persons, then God would be three beings, since human persons are separate beings. When speaking about God, we're not using the word "person" in exactly the same way we do about ourselves.

In speaking of the Father, Son and Holy Spirit as divine (not human) Persons, we affirm that these personal names and personal relationships between the three Persons reveal the reality of who God is. God knows himself as Father, Son and Spirit. There are real and eternal relationships in God which Scripture characterizes in several ways including mutual knowing, loving, glorifying, and oneness.

What we think about human persons in living, loving and holy relationship with each other does, to a degree, reflect the truth about God in the sense that God is more like a community of three human persons than like any other created thing. We could switch this around and say that the

Father, Son and Holy Spirit are the original and real Persons, and since we are somewhat like them, we can borrow the term "person" to speak of ourselves as individual human creatures. That said, we must be careful to note that God is not like a single, lonely, isolated individual.

God is *one in being*

As individual human persons, we do not, and we cannot have the same kind of unity (oneness) with other persons that the three divine Persons have. Their unity is their being — *the three divine Persons are one in being.* The sense of unity we experience as human persons cannot match that.

The kind of unity of God revealed in Christ was so unique that the church teachers eventually came up with a unique word to represent that one-of-a-kind unity. That word is *perichoresis*. It is Greek and often is not translated because it has a unique meaning that can't exactly be translated. It means most literally to *envelope* one another or to *make space* for one another. It has also been translated as *mutually indwelling* each other, or having a *coinherence* in each other, or *in-existing* in one another. This language represents Jesus' teaching that he is "in the Father and the Father is in [him]" (John 14:11). It is also just what we see lived out in the Gospels as we watch and hear Jesus in his dynamic relationship with the Father and the Spirit. This unique unity has also been explained by saying that *the whole of God, all three Persons, are present in each of the Persons.* So, each in being is fully God even though distinct in Person so that there is a real relationship and exchange going on from all eternity between the three divine Persons. As the Athanasian Creed summed it up: the unity of God is a Trinity and the Trinity of God is a Unity. We can try to put this into a single word: God's unity is a *tri-unity.*

Given this tri-unity, everything we can say about the Spirit, we can say about the Father (or the Son), except that the Spirit is not the Father (or the Son). Why? Because the divine Persons mutually indwell one another, and so are equally God — equally and together God. They have an absolutely unique kind of unity so that they are distinct in divine Person but united in being. Unlike creatures, the unity of being doesn't undo the difference of Person and the distinction of Person doesn't undo the unity of being. Remembering this will help us get our language squared away so that we don't grossly misrepresent who God is.

What kind of God is the triune God?

The doctrine of the Trinity, so far as it goes, faithfully identifies who God is. However, its purpose is to protect the mystery of God's nature, not explain it away. That said, when we add up what the doctrine asserts, we are given significant, biblically accurate understanding about the kind of God that God is. It declares that God has his being by being a fellowship, a communion of divine Persons. The biblical witness then shows us that all the relationships that flow from God's being are forms of love. Begetting, being begotten and proceeding are all relationships of loving exchange. This is why we can say with John that *God is love*. We also can see what Jesus means,   and why he says he loves the Father and the Father has loved him from all eternity. It makes sense that Jesus tells us that as the Father has loved him, so he loves us; and that as he has loved us, so we ought to love one another. No wonder then that the ways of the people of God can be comprehensively summed up in the two commands to love God and love neighbor.

The relationships internal and external to God are filled with holy loving. God is a fellowship kind of God — a communion kind of God. God is not a lonely being floating out there from all eternity "looking for someone to love." God is the fullness of holy love, the fullness of fellowship and communion. Bringing it all together, we can say that the Father and Son have their fellowship and communion in the Holy Spirit.

The triune God who in his being is love, is very different than an isolated individual God who can't love until there is something else outside of God to love. The God that is fullness of fellowship is very different from one who exists with no internal and external relationships, one in whom there is no giving and receiving, in whom there is no exchange of knowing, loving, glorifying of one another. Such a god would be very different from the God we come to know through Jesus Christ, according to Scripture.

To summarize: the Christian God is a fellowship, a communion. This triune God has his being by being in relationships of holy loving. Those relationships are, in particular, eternally begetting, being begotten, and proceeding — each a unique form of holy, loving exchange. Those are the key words we have in allowing us to point to the amazing reality of who God is. And these are the essentials to remember if we are going to go on and talk about the Holy Spirit.

Who is the Holy Spirit?

If the Holy Spirit first exists in relationship with the Father and the Son, then that is the first thing we need to know, not the Spirit's relationship to us or our relationship to the Spirit. Those come afterwards. There was a time when nothing other than God existed and the Holy Spirit was perfectly happy being the Spirit of the Father and the Son. The Spirit doesn't need us to be the Spirit. There was a time when there was no creation. At that time God was the fullness of fellowship in Father, Son and Holy Spirit.

In answer to the question, *who is the Holy Spirit?* the simplest answer is that *the Spirit is the Spirit of the Father and the Son.* That means that whenever we speak of the Father and Son, or hear about them in Scripture, since God is one in being, the Spirit is also involved in some way, whether or not it is explicitly stated. The Spirit *always* has something to do with the Father and Son. It's true that we don't always remember this connection. And we probably should make it more explicit more often.

So, when speaking of the Father or the Son we do not exclude the Spirit, because the Spirit is the Spirit of the Father and the Son. Reference to the Son involves the Spirit, and the other way around. We can't talk about the Holy Spirit apart from the Son, because the Holy Spirit is the Spirit of the Son. If we assume we can think of one without the other, we're misrepresenting who the Spirit is, because the Spirit has his being, is the Person he is, by being in an essential relationship. We don't always spell this all out, and it would be better if we did see and make all these connections. A full understanding will always seek to grasp *all* the Persons in their relationships.

The *who,* not *how,* of the Spirit

When seeking further understanding about God, we tend to look for answers to *how?* questions, such as, *how does God operate his providence over all of history and nature and everything else?* It's understandable that we would ask such questions. We want to know the mechanisms, the machinery. We want to know the chain of cause and effect as it pertains to God's acts. The problem is that the *how?* questions tend to take us in a wrong direction. Instead we need to as the *who?* questions. We need first to identify the agent responsible for what takes place. And when it comes to *who?* questions concerning God, the answer often is the Holy Spirit, who is the agent of God's actions. In short, our *how?* questions are frequently answered this way: *By the Holy Spirit!* And the reality is this: we can know the *who,* without knowing the *how!*

Consider this: does Jesus tell Nicodemus the mechanism of *how* one becomes born from above? Does Jesus offer Nicodemus a technique? Does he list a bunch of rules that if you do this and that and the other, then bingo, the new birth happens? No. Jesus explained to Nicodemus that, because the

Spirit works more like the wind, no such *how?* explanation can be given. The working of the Spirit can't be controlled or predicted by us. That's the nature of *who* the Spirit is, and so *how* the Spirit works!

It's understandable that we have many questions — especially about the Christian life. But such questions are actually answered simply by identifying the agency of the Holy Spirit. And that's it. But we often want more — we want an explanation about some mechanism, technique or about steps to take. We feel that there needs to be a combination of conditions that we fill in order to get the Spirit to work. There is quite a bit of teaching in Christian circles that speculates about and even invents techniques and methods that can be used to fill in the gaps between what Scripture tells us, and what we, like Nicodemus, often want to know — answers to our *how?* questions that would tell us exactly what conditions we need to fill in order to get the Spirit to work, or to work more effectively. However, shouldn't we stop where Scripture stops, rather than succumb to speculation or invention?

Many of the current controversies and differences of emphasis between various teachings and ministries actually have to do with their lining up behind a favorite technique or mechanism, or a particular list of conditions needed to get what we're looking for from the Holy Spirit. The arguments and controversies are most often over which teaching offers the best *how to.* But when we go down that road, we've already forgotten most of who the Spirit is. On that road we easily are tempted to mistakenly assume that God can be divided up, asking such questions as "can you have the Spirit without having the Son?" or "can you have the Son without having the Spirit? Another mistake is to assume that the presence and blessing of the Spirit comes not by grace but by technique or by us fulfilling certain preconditions, leading us to ask "what steps do we need to take before we can effectively have and use the gifts of the Spirit?"

By the Spirit of the Father and Son answers the *how?* question

When we take into account the full testimony of Scripture, the questions and controversies that arise concerning the Spirit can be addressed. This involves accounting for the very nature and character of the Spirit. That means, for example, understanding that the Father, Son and Holy Spirit are one in being, and thus you cannot have one without the other. The unity of the Persons in being and in action is indicated in biblical revelation. For example, we are told that no one truly proclaims Jesus is Lord except by the Spirit (1 Cor. 12:3). God doesn't split up, having the Son heading off saying, "Goodbye, Spirit. I hope you catch up later." God is one in being but also one in action. The three divine Persons act and work together.

Many if not most current controversies have forgotten some of the most fundamental things about who God the Spirit is. But, of course, if forgotten, this is what can happen. Our thoughts can head in all directions and we can end up speculating in order to answer misguided questions. We can just grab random Bible verses and try to throw them together to come up with an answer. When that happens, we end up with different groups gravitating around what they regard as key verses to prove their point, but they have left behind the more fundamental teaching and reality of who the Spirit is. The fundamental thing, the answer to the Who? question regarding the Spirit is often forgotten and so the answers promoted are inconsistent with the deeper more central truth of the Spirit who is one in being and one in working with the Father and the Son.

Biblical revelation about the ministry of the Spirit is often presented in connection with mention of at least one other divine Person. So for example, only the Holy Spirit can break into a person's pride and enable them to recognize that Jesus really is their Lord and Savior, come in the flesh, as one of us (1 John 4:2). We only have the Spirit because he is sent by the Son from the Father (John 15:26). If anyone is convicted by the message of the gospel it is because the Spirit is at work (1 Thess. 1:3-5). Jesus sends the Spirit to bring persons to an acknowledgment of sin and the need for judgment and righteousness (John 16:8).

As Paul tells us, when the "Spirit of sonship" comes upon us, we cry out "Abba Father" (Romans 8:15; Galatians 4:60). Why do we cry out "Abba Father"? If you know who the Spirit is, the answer is obvious. Because God is one in being and one in action. Isn't that amazing? The whole Trinity is involved in that one simple and profound cry of our hearts. When the Spirit acts, he acts in unity with the Father and the Son, bringing our worship all together in the fellowship of the Trinity.

When Jesus says, "Go out and baptize them in the name" (singular) and then gives them the one name: "Father, Son and Holy Spirit," we should not be surprised. The name we're given matches the reality: Father, Son and Holy Spirit is the one name of God. A simple way to say this is that God is the Father-Son-Holy-Spirit-God, as if it is one name instead of three names. It really isn't three separate names, but a threefold name. It is three divine Persons, but we're baptized into one name. Jesus' instruction makes sense if that is who God is, and so how God acts and has his being.

Conclusion

All our thinking about the Holy Spirit needs to be contained within these Trinitarian boundaries. That will help us interpret Scripture properly, and see more deeply into Scripture so that we come to know the reality ever more profoundly. Rather than taking us away from Scripture, good theology helps us see more clearly how Scripture comes together. Though theology doesn't answer every question we might have, it does answer the questions God most wants us to grasp and proclaim. Thus, our goal is to help one another read and interpret Scripture in a way that brings all the pieces of Scripture together. Good theology helps us attain this important goal.

PART 4

The importance of the Spirit

Why say anything about the Holy Spirit beyond simply acknowledging him? One reason is to overcome the tendency to disconnect the three divine Persons. We see this in churches where one Person is emphasized to the near exclusion of the other two. But this fragmented approach trips us up in our faith and in our lived relationship to the Triune God. So, our goal is to have an understanding of the Trinity that is faithful to and coherent with the reality of who God actually is in the fullness of all three divine Persons. Our understanding of the Holy Spirit, and our ability to join more fully in what he is doing, will grow as we view him *theologically*—in relationship to the Father and the Son.

What a theological understanding of the Spirit offers

Theological work aims to fix things on our side, not fix things on God's side. So, we can grow in understanding even if the reality is not changed by our better grasp. And if we have misunderstandings, it will be good to clear them up. As the Spirit is working it is far better to be aware of that work compared to being unaware. But our better understanding does not make something real or change the nature of the Spirit's working. God does not all of a sudden become the Holy Spirit when we recognize the Spirit. The Holy Spirit is not tied up, unable to do anything until we figure the Holy Spirit out. That would be like saying the wind is tied up until we can figure out the wind. No, the Spirit still works, but we may not recognize it. And by recognizing it we may more fully participate, we become more involved, become more in tune with the truth and reality of who God is. So, we're trying to make sure our understanding matches the truth about who God is such as the Spirit has been revealed to us.

So we need to remember that our understanding may be fragmented but God is not fragmented. Our understanding of the working in the ministry of the Spirit may be fragmented but that doesn't mean the actual working of the Spirit is fragmented. We're not controlling God by our understanding. If that were the case then God would be dependent upon us. But we want to sort this all out and let our understanding be as full and faithful as can be.

How do we fix a lack of awareness and understanding of the Spirit?

How do we then bring our understanding of the ministry of the Spirit up to speed in a way that recognizes the Spirit is one of the three divine Persons of the Trinity? Some are concerned about the need to speak proportionately about the Holy Spirit. We might say, giving the Holy Spirit equal time or equal emphasis. What's behind that concern?

There are situations where our faith and understanding of the Spirit is indeed lacking and so lags behind the Father and Son. It might be that this is often the case, the rule, rather than the exception. Wherever we find this situation it ought to be rectified. We should become familiar with all that's been revealed to us about the Spirit and then pass that on to others. So in those cases additional teaching and focus on the Spirit is called for. (Although this should never be the exclusive focus.) In that way our faith and knowledge of the Spirit will become better aligned with the other divine Persons.

Objections to pursuing the Spirit

In pursuing this kind of correction we may run into some obstacles that contributed to the unbalanced situation in the first place. For, example, some persons might not be interested in the Spirit and so have neglected the topic. Hopefully those in this condition who worship the Triune God will come around and see that the Holy Spirit is no less important than the Father and Son.

Others may not want to know or have much to do with the Holy Spirit because the Spirit seems kind of, well, spooky. We usually don't want to be around ghosts, especially one you can't control or that you can't identify or you can't nail down, can't make a part of your program and who's, well, like the wind, (or maybe even a typhoon!). Who wants that? So, some people, may be avoiding the Spirit because they have certain worries. That's not the best reason not to have an interest in the Holy Spirit. Their fears may be based in part (or perhaps in whole) on ignorance or misinformation about the nature of the power and working of the Holy Spirit. Those who have misgivings may not have a good grasp on who the Holy Spirit is. The Spirit isn't like a ghost or something to be fearful of in the sense that it might do us harm. So helping people know that the Spirit is Holy, is good, is crucial.

The best way to do this is to emphasize regularly that the Spirit and has the exact same character and purpose as Jesus. There is no slippage in mind, attitude, or aim between the two. The best way to identify the working of the Spirit is to compare it directly to what we know about Jesus. It is his Spirit. If it doesn't, feel, sound, taste, and work like Jesus, then it is not his Spirit. Knowing Jesus is how we best discern the spirits, that is, which is the Holy Spirit.

Some could think the Spirit is now irrelevant to our current situation or no long available to us, at least as in the days of the early church. That was back in those days, some may think. That would be another poor reason, however, to have little or no interest in the Spirit. While it's perfectly acceptable to raise questions about the working of the Spirit today, there is no biblical teaching designed to inform us that the Spirit cannot or will not continue to work as in the days of the early church. Of course this does not mean that the Spirit cannot adjust the mode of his ministry as, in his wisdom, he sees fit from time to time and place to place. He can in his sovereign grace make adjustments.

However, there is no absolute reason that the Spirit could not continue to work today as in the days of the New Testament. But that is up to the Spirit. Those who have dogmatically concluded that the Spirit does not work and cannot work in the same manner have argued from their own experience and on that basis selected and interpreted Scripture to explain their lack of experiencing the working of the Spirit. But such arguments do not have binding authority in the church—and especially upon the Spirit! It might simply be that the Spirit at some times and places chooses to work behind the scenes, mostly undetected even perhaps by Christians—and that's why the church's experience of the Spirit is not evenly distributed all the time.

Especially thinking that the ministry and manifestation of the Spirit depends upon us, what we do, what condition we're in, what we want, or on our level of understanding, is to put the cart way before the horse. If the Spirit is dependent upon us in these ways, then the Spirit does not (cannot?) minister by grace. The ministry of the Spirit then is being regarded as a reward for works. Whatever the Spirit does and however he works, *it is all of grace*. We do not condition the Spirit to act — he is faithful whether or not we are.

Now some are concerned about abuses and misrepresentations of the Spirit. Indeed, there are legitimate reason for folks to be cautious or concerned. There have been, since the days of the New Testament, abuses, misuses and misleading teaching about the Spirit. There are many cases where an emphasis on the Holy Spirit has contributed to conflict and even church splits. There have been deceitful things said and done in the name of the Holy Spirit. And some things have occurred in connection with an emphasis on the Spirit that are bizarre and in some cases even abusive. But are these good reasons to entirely neglect the Spirit? No. Any good thing can be misused. As an ancient maxim states: abuse does not rule out proper use. So if these things can guarded against, all the while coming to understand and welcome the ministry of the Spirit, I think the way can be clear to address any imbalance. But checks and balances, spiritual discipline and discernment need to be in place provided by wise pastors and elders ministering under the authority of the whole teaching of Scripture. That is a legitimate requirement to guard against spiritual pride and abuse, disunity and division. There are real dangers.

Equal proportions?

Given all that, however, setting up a goal of equality of emphasis or parity of focus on the three divine Persons is really not the best way to go about making a healthy correction if there is an imbalance or ignorance about the Spirit. There are valid reasons why there necessarily always will be a certain kind of faithful disproportion or inequality of emphasis or focus on the Spirit compared to the other two Persons of the Trinity. The reason has to do with the nature and character of the Spirit himself as indicated by fact that in Scripture there is less biblical information about the Holy Spirit than is provided concerning the Father and the Son.

Though in the Old Testament we find multiple references to the Spirit (e.g. Joel 2:28; Ezek. 11:19) far more consideration is given to God the creator, covenant maker and deliverer of Israel. However, this disproportion does not indicate that the Spirit is less important. In the Gospels there is much more said about Jesus and the Father, though Jesus speaks frequently and definitely about the Spirit, who has an essential part in Jesus' life and message. The same goes for the Epistles where there is plenty of important teaching about the Spirit, with more detail than found in the Gospels concerning our living in relationship with the Spirit. However, the Epistles give more information about the Son and his relationship with the Father, than they give about the Spirit. Note, however, that this disproportionate treatment does not signal an inequality of importance since it is clear that faith in the Spirit and his ministry is not only important, it is vitally connected to the ministry of Jesus.

In the New Testament, rather than being addressed separately, the Spirit is mentioned as being in relationship with the Son (primarily) and Father (secondarily). When Jesus acts he does so in or by the Spirit. Jesus' sacrifice on the cross involves offering himself up in the Spirit (Heb. 9:14). The Spirit "proceeds" from the Father, and is "sent" from the Father (in the Son's name). However, this way of addressing the Spirit is no reason to overlook what Scripture tells us concerning the person and work of the Spirit. In fact, that there is less information about the Spirit than about the Father and the Son, suggests that we should given even more attention to what we are told, though caution is in order related to seeking "equal time" for the Spirit.

Misguided attempts at correction

Given that we have less information about the Spirit, we might be tempted to give him "equal time" by extending what we say through the fabrication of long logical chains of argumentation leading to various inferred conclusions. But such speculation about the Spirit, even if it starts with a bit of Scripture, can offer nothing secure, since simple logical inferences even from some true starting point are never necessarily true. In fact, that's where a lot of heresy and bad teaching about the Spirit comes from. Some preachers and teachers have taken a few biblical verses and then attempted to make strings of logical arguments from them, oftentimes not paying attention to other biblical teaching regarding the Spirit. But the conclusions reached are *speculative*. And in reaching them, a lot had to be added in, such as making someone's experience (and their understanding of it!) normative for all Christians, in order to establish a purportedly doctrinal statement. But all that additional information and the logical chains developed from them do not amount to reliable Christian doctrine. So, giving the Spirit more attention by generating more information than we actually have been given in Scripture concerning the Spirit, is not a recommended or reliable procedure.

Why is less revealed about the Spirit?

Is there some reason there is less information given about the Holy Spirit in Scripture than is given about the Father and the Son? It seems to me the disproportion ought to be expected because of what we do find out about the Spirit. Given the very nature of the Spirit and the nature of his work, it makes sense that there is less to say concretely and authoritatively about the Spirit than the Father or the Son. Why is that? First, because the Spirit, unlike the Son, is not incarnate. We don't have an embodied revelation of the Holy Spirit. The Spirit remains undetectable himself, but is identified indirectly by the effects of his working (like the wind).

The purpose of Jesus' coming in human form was to be the self-revelation of God. Jesus is the Word of God to us. The Spirit doesn't have his own incarnation. The Spirit, as a matter of fact, doesn't have his own independent word. Jesus is the *Logos*, the intelligibility, the communication, the living interpretation of God to us. In fact, without the incarnate life and teaching of Jesus we would know far less about the Spirit, for the Son reveals to us not only himself, but the Father and the Spirit. The Incarnate Son takes us to the Father and sends us the Spirit. So we approach the Spirit through the mediation of the Son.

Even when the Spirit is present and active within creation, he doesn't establish his own revelation and doesn't convey his own self-explanation. The Spirit remains the Spirit. That is, remains unincarnate while present to and within creation. The Spirit's remaining unincarnate actually serves a positive purpose. It prevents us from reducing God simply to a creature or thinking that we can understand God entirely in terms of creaturely realities. It preserves the transcendence, the spirituality of God. God is not a creature and so we cannot explain God as if God were a creature subject to its ways and limitations. We cannot simply read back onto God the creaturely nature of Jesus.

Now, some people mistakenly think that when the Son of God took on human form, the Father (or God) turned into a man, a creature. Two mistakes here. First, it was the Son of God who became incarnate, not the Father (nor the Spirit). Second, the Son of God did not cease being the eternal, divine, Son of God when he took on human being. He remained what he was, but added to himself a fully human nature and lived a human life. He didn't stop being something he was and turn in into something else, a man. Early church teachers put it this way: The eternal Son of God, remaining what he was, assumed also a human nature to himself. You can recognize this kind of confusion when, considering the possibility of the incarnation, people ask, "Then, who is running the universe?"

Now how the eternal Son of God can be incarnate in human form is indeed a mystery. We can't imagine how such a change of that order could be true for human beings. But, remember God is not a creature. Admittedly, it is easier to think of Jesus' incarnation as his turning into what he was not and ceasing to be what he was. If A becomes B, then it ceases to be A. It's now B. That's easy to think because that's how most if not all creaturely things work. However, such thinking just doesn't apply to the truth about who the Son of God is. He remains what he was, the eternal Son of God, assuming a human nature as well.

The Spirit then never did take on a human nature himself. If you ask, "How was Jesus conceived in the womb of Mary?" What's the answer? By the Spirit. The agency of the Spirit is the answer to the "how" question. But this answer doesn't tell us the mechanisms involved. No mention of DNA. Or what happened with the chromosomes. We don't get that type of explanation. Rather we get an explanation of who, the agent involved who knows how! I suppose if we asked the Spirit and he thought it was important for us to know, the Spirit could explain it to us if we were educated and intelligent enough to grasp it. But apparently, it's far more important to know by whom it occurred rather than how.

But we definitely learn something about the Spirit in this event. The Spirit can interact in time and space, with flesh and blood without being incarnate himself. The Spirit is able to be present and active at the deepest levels of creaturely existence, down to the DNA and chromosomes if need be. The Spirit is not absent but able to be very present to creation. That's one way God can work directly within creation—by the Spirit. Recognizing that God is the Spirit and the Spirit is God and he remains the Holy Spirit prevents us from thinking of God as merely being a creature but that the Spirit doesn't have to be incarnate to have a direct ministry to us. As Jesus said, he is sending another Comforter who was with us, but will be in us (John 14:17).

There is another reason we find that makes sense as to why there is a disproportion in the amount of information we have about the Spirit in the biblical portrayal. Again this distinction is not one of importance but of the extent of the revelation. And if what we say and teach about the Spirit depends upon that revelation, then this will make a difference in how much we can say and how much we can understand about the Spirit.

This second reason has to do with the very character of the Spirit and of his ministry. It seems that the whole purpose and character of the ministry of the Holy Spirit is actually to always direct attention away from, not bring it to himself. The ministry of the Spirit, Jesus tells us, is to direct us to Jesus (John 15:26) So he doesn't come with his own independent message but bears witness to the truth He has heard spoken by the Son. The Spirit does not glorify himself but Jesus by taking his words and declaring them to us (John 16:13-14). And that is the glory of the Spirit!

So, the Holy Spirit isn't saying, "Hey, Jesus, you've had the microphone now for plenty of time. Now, it's my turn to tell people about myself." No. When the Holy Spirit "gets the microphone," what does he announce? He helps us recall all that Jesus taught, the truth that he taught. he, perhaps annoyingly, passes up his opportunity to shed light on himself.

The Holy Spirit doesn't really draw attention to himself. Rather he points away from himself. Why? Because that's his ministry, so that we see who Jesus is, who reveals to us the Father. The early church put it this way. The Holy Spirit is like light and the light shines. And the Holy Spirit shines light on the face of Jesus who has an actual, flesh and blood human face. And when the Holy Spirit's light shines on the face of Jesus, what do we see mirrored in the face of Jesus? The invisible face of the Father. Isn't that a beautiful thing?

So, the Holy Spirit doesn't say, "Hey, look at me. Look at me. I'm the light. I'm shining. I'm shining, can't you see how bright I am?" Not at all. The whole reason for the Spirit's shining is so that when we look at the face of Jesus, we see the face of the Father. That's the whole point of the light. The light doesn't draw attention to itself.

That doesn't mean the Spirit's not important, but the contrary! If the light didn't shine, what would result? We wouldn't see the face of the Father in the face of the Son. In fact, there wouldn't even be a face of the Son incarnate if the Spirit hadn't been involved in the conception of the Son in the womb of Mary. The Spirit has a coordinated but different mission and ministry than the Son. But that ministry would be somewhat compromised and not demonstrate the true nature and character of the Spirit if it drew attention to itself.

One theologian has said, if you add the biblical picture up, the Spirit is the "shy one" of the Trinity, the "retiring one." We could also say that the Spirit displays the humility of God because he serves the Father and the Son. Theologian Thomas Torrance brings out this same point regarding the character of the Spirit. Relatively speaking he stays in the background. We conclude from this understanding that the Spirit serves the Father and Son rather than himself. We'd be somewhat impoverished if we didn't know this. We are learning something about the Spirit when we see that he doesn't draw attention to himself! As a result, whenever we find revelation concerning the Spirit, what we discover is more about the Father and the Son. The Spirit actually promotes the disproportion of detailed understanding concerning the Triune Persons. Why? Because that's the Spirit's ministry. He says, "Yes, excellent. You saw the face of the Father and the face of the Son. Wonderful. That's what I do. That's why I'm here."

PART 5

In this part, we'll explore the Holy Spirit's ministry viewed *corporately* (in the church) and *personally* (in individual lives). Let's start with a question: Why does any group or individual repent instead of hanging on to their self-justifying pride? The answer is that the Holy Spirit is at work in them, though that work is often unseen. Let me explain.

The Spirit's often unseen work

We typically do not see the Holy Spirit working in a direct way — most of his ministry among us is deep and internal, working directly with our human spirits (1 Cor. 2: 9-11). Thus, we don't see the Holy Spirit acting. However, we do see the results. When we're repenting, when we're hearing God speak his Word, when we're seeing the face of the Father in the face of the Son, when we're grasping the Word of God, when we're interpreting Scripture as God intends — in all these instances, we're experiencing the effects (results, outcome) of the Spirit's work. But we're not seeing the gears turning — we don't watch the machine running. It seems the Holy Spirit does not draw attention to himself. You might say he is the shy one, the humble one, the retiring one. TF Torrance calls the Spirit the "self-effacing" one. He does not show us his own face — The Spirit is not worried about that.

Has the Spirit been short-changed?

When we compare the names of the three divine Persons, we find a certain asymmetry. Father and Son are more concrete terms, and are obviously mutually referential. Thus, the Father-Son relationship is easier to think about using creaturely terms. The name of Holy Spirit is different — it does not lend itself as easily to being described using creaturely terms. Father and Son sound much more familiar to us than Spirit. So, has the Holy Spirit been short-changed? Maybe not, though perhaps that's how it's supposed to be. Maybe being given that identifying name is not a mistake.

Maybe the name Holy Spirit is given to prevent us from trying to nail down the Spirit's identity in the same way we might the identity of the Father and the Son. Perhaps this "inequality" is meant to lead us to identify with and pay primary attention to the Father and Son. Perhaps by being named Holy Spirit, we are kept from merely reducing the Father and Son to creaturely definitions, thinking God is Father and Son in the way human beings are. After all, Scripture can refer to the whole Triune God as Spirit. Thus we understand that the name Holy Spirit reminds us of the transcendence and sovereignty of God and the fact that God cannot be reduced to an idol —

one made by human hands or minds.

Given the pattern and content of what is said in the Bible concerning the Holy Spirit, we should not expect to be able to have as much to say, or be able to say it in as much detail as we can say about the Father and the Son. Though we expect some disproportion, we understand it does not indicate any inequality of importance among the divine Persons. But why not correct this disproportion by giving greater individual emphasis to the Spirit? The answer is that giving the Spirit individual, independent emphasis would tend to place his ministry in isolation from the ministry of the Father and the Son. Why would that be a problem? Because, as we will see, the Holy Spirit does not have an independent ministry.

The Spirit's ministry — a summary

In summary, we can say that the Holy Spirit's ministry is to deliver to us all the benefits of the work of Christ — the benefits Christ accomplished as the Son of the Father the one sent who was sent from the Father and returned to the Father so that we might know the Father. The work of the Spirit can't be grasped apart from this work of the Father and the Son. Of course, if we are to understand and fully appreciate the work of the Father and the Son, we must understand the "behind the scenes" work of the Spirit. Thus to fully understand the Spirit's ministry, we must understand the coordinated ministry of all three divine Persons.

How does the Spirit work? Well, speaking a bit facetiously, it's not as though the Spirit says, "Jesus, you did that awesome work on the cross. You took your turn and accomplished that great task. I know everyone will praise you for all you've done. But now it's my time to get to work — I'm going to go off and take my turn to accomplish my own mission, and so make my own addition to what you've done." That misguided thinking regards the triune God as dividing up his work and will into a division of labor, each relatively separate from the others. But that is not the case — the will and working of God can't be sliced up that way. Doing so splits God into parts and roles as creatures would. That misguided approach obscures the oneness of God in being and in action. A simple way to point to the unity of the working of God — while allowing for distinction of contribution to the one whole work — is to say this: *what Christ has done for us, the Holy Spirit does in us.*

Now when we say that the Spirit takes all of what Christ has done for us in his humanity and delivers it to us, does that amount to little or nothing? No! From the Spirit's point of view, that is *everything!* The Holy Spirit cannot accomplish his deepest work except on the basis of what Jesus accomplished for us in the name of the Father. They (Father, Son, Spirit) are one God —

they are all together Savior. The Father sends the Son. The Son sends the Spirit. And this was all done so we might have the life of the whole God over us, with us and in us.

As T.F. Torrance has expressed it, it seems that rebellious human beings can share in God's kind of life, eternal life, only after it's been worked out in such a way that it can fit us fallen creatures. That means that we first need to be reconciled to God and have our human nature regenerated, sanctified, made new. That's what God accomplished in the incarnate Son who assumed our human nature. Jesus reconciled and transformed that nature, perfecting it so that the Holy Spirit could indwell us and make us share in Jesus' sanctified humanity. The Spirit could not come and take up residence in us ("indwell" is the New Testament word) until the Son has completed his incarnate work in our fallen humanity.

No, the Holy Spirit is not being left out or diminished when we say that he takes what the Son has done and delivers and builds it into us. It would be senseless for the Spirit to say, "I need my own ministry apart from the Son." They are one in being. They are one in act. They are one in mind, one in heart — perfectly coordinated in their ministry to give us a share in God's own eternal life. Each contributes in their own way.

Understand this: the whole God (Father, Son and Spirit) is Savior. The Spirit's part is to lead in working out in us what Christ has accomplished for us in his humanity. That's a marvel. The Spirit does work in us in unique ways. This is why Jesus says it is an advantage that another Comforter come to us, to deliver to us and within us his life by the indwelling of the Spirit — the Spirit who is the Spirit of Jesus, the One who has accomplished everything for us in his human nature.

Perhaps now we can see the problem if, wanting to give the Spirit equal time, we were to say, "Yes, Jesus did this, but the Spirit does that" and focus on "that," as if it was independent. But there is no independent mission. The three divine Persons work entirely together in an ordered and coordinated way. That insight ought to guide our thinking, our explanations, our preaching and teaching about the Holy Spirit. Describing the joint mission of the three Persons requires mutually referring to one another because the Spirit is the Spirit of the Son and the Spirit of the Father. That's who Holy Spirit is, and his ministry is to work out in us what the Son has done for us. That's an amazing, vital ministry!

Particular manifestations of the Spirit's work

There are particular manifestations of the working of the Spirit — times and ways in which he is active, as it were at the leading edge of what the triune

God is doing. The Spirit's relationship to creation, after Christ's incarnate ministry, is very dynamic and variable, not static or fixed or mechanical, but personal and relational. We see this at Pentecost. When the Spirit came down that day, no human agency initiated, conditioned or controlled it. Rather, Jesus had promised it in the name of the Father. That's all that preconditioned that mighty event. And Jesus indicated that this even would be at the Father's initiative, in accordance with the Father's timing. The church was simply to wait. That's it.

But why at that particular time? Because Christ in his earthly form had finished his dimension of the saving work that God was accomplishing. So, of course, the Spirit is aware of Jesus' promise. The Spirit is the one promised by the Son. So, yes, perfectly coordinated, the Spirit showed up on time. But notice what happened when the Spirit descended. The people started talking about the great and mighty things that God had done to accomplish their salvation in Jesus. They don't just focus on the immediate amazing event they had just experienced! And they were now able to relate to each other in new amazing ways as the Spirit was now working in them in new ways. But notice they didn't just focus on the Spirit, or their experience of the Spirit. Their view was much larger, much more comprehensive of all that God had done, was doing and would yet do.

Pentecost is a primary example of a manifestation of the working of the Spirit that is dynamic, variable, not static, not fixed, not mechanical, but personal and relational. In Paul's admonitions to not quench or grieve the Spirit, and to be continually filled with the Spirit, we see anticipation of a dynamic interaction with the Holy Spirit. Paul is not thinking of a situation in which the switch to the Holy Spirit is simply now in the "on" position, and then in the "off" position. Paul understands that the Holy Spirit is never a billion miles away — never completely absent, having nothing to do with anything, but then is immediately near, causing everything to happen in an almost magical way. Paul knew it doesn't work like that. Instead, there is dynamic interaction between God's people and the Spirit. The Spirit can apparently be present in a wide range of ways, or at least in a range of ways that have a wide variety of effects that we can notice.

Paul's admonition to be "continually filled with the Spirit" is a good way for us to understand those places where Paul talks about our relationship with the Spirit. The Spirit should not be approached as if he is a vending machine: put in the right coins, push the right buttons and get your soda or your candy bar or something else. No our relationship with the Spirit is not contractual or automatic; not simply a matter of being "on" or "off." It's not a mechanical relationship. It is dynamic; like the wind blowing (John 3:8).

The gifts of the Spirit and the dynamic working of the Spirit

Let's look at another aspect of the manifestation of the working of the Spirit in the church — *the gifts of the Spirit*. These too involve dynamic interactions. So, Paul encourages churches to use these gifts in particular ways. They should let those with the gift of giving give with liberality; those who give aid, with zeal; those who do acts of mercy, with cheerfulness (Rom. 12:6-8). These gifts of the Spirit can be used well or misused. They are received and then to be used well, rightly, faithfully. That is a dynamic process, not a magical chain of effects impersonally sparked. But it's easier to think of the working of the Spirit in mechanical terms, isn't it? Especially if we think of the Spirit as an impersonal power, energy, like electricity. Just on or off; here but not there; near or far. But God is not like that. I supposed we could say especially that the Spirit is not like that!

There is a dynamic to living in the Spirit. The Spirit is living and moving, acting as an intelligent agent; interacting with us in a deep and personal way. And it seems even acting in many ways of which we aren't even aware. Often, by the time we've become aware of it, the Spirit's probably already moved on to another thing. Yes, we're going recognize the activity and say, "Yes! the Spirit was working, we were blessed" and rejoice in that. However, the Spirit may have already moved on to another "project" by the time we acknowledge it. The Spirit is active and moving!

Avoid wrong understandings of the Spirit's working

Because there is a variability, a dynamic ebb and flow to the activity and manifestation and interaction of the Spirit with humanity (both the Church and the world) we must avoid thinking of the Spirit as an impersonal force. We must also not think of him as a genie where we approach the Spirit thinking, "If I'm going to be blessed by the Spirit, I'll have to do things just right. I'm going to have to rub the lamp exactly three times and say just the right words and then the power of the spirit-genie will work for me or those I love." But note that his is a very impersonal, mechanical approach to the Spirit. One that is just as misguided is the idea that we must take the initiative or fulfill certain preconditions to please, or to obligate or cajole the Holy Spirit to act. We can think the working of the Spirit is unlocked (or not) by us. Unfortunately, it is not difficult to find teaching like this, suggesting we act towards the Holy Spirit as if "it" was a magical power much like a genie. And what we have to do to get the Spirit to work is fulfill certain conditions just exactly right — then (like magic!) the Spirit is somehow set free (or is obligated!) to accomplish his ministry!

Of course those special techniques promoted by some for activating the Spirit don't usually involve rubbing a lamp just the right number of times. However, other conditions are laid out, some sequence of events under our control are specified in order to "prime the pump" or "release" the Spirit to work in particular ways. And if the Spirit doesn't show up, the explanation will be: "You didn't get things quite right. You weren't sincere enough. You didn't have enough faith. You weren't humble enough. You were stuck in your head and thinking too much. You didn't "let go" enough to "let God.""

In essence, such explanations say the spirit-genie is not going to come out because you said "abricadabro," not "abracadabra." Or you said it with the wrong accent! Or …, or …, or …. Any number of conditions can be specified. And each particular ministry will likely specialize on describing and prescribing exactly which set of conditions are called for as compared to how another ministry is mistaken in the set of conditions it thinks are required. And on the basis of their understanding each ministry will prescribe the real, true, and proper set of conditions that must be met, and spell out how we can then meet those certain conditions called for.

Notice how these approaches put us in charge and make the Holy Spirit dependent upon us, with the Spirit having little say himself when put under just the right circumstances. Such approaches make our relationship with the Spirit legal, contractual, mechanical, conditional — like a genie or mechanical power, the Spirit has no more choice in the situation than electricity does when you plug your iPhone in or turn on the lights. It is a cause-effect relationship from us to the Spirit. Only when the conditions are just right can the Holy Spirit do its work. And when they are set right, apparently "It" (the Spirit viewed impersonally) can't decide "No, I'm not going to charge your iPhone!"

Let's avoid thinking about and approaching the Holy Spirit in ways that are impersonal, mechanistic, superstitious and magical. Rather let us see and relate to the Spirit for who he truly is — one of the three divine Persons whose work is fully coordinated with that of the Father and the Son.

PART 6

In thinking about the Holy Spirit and how he works in our lives, it's important to understand that he is a *personal agent* — as personal as the Father and the Son. The Holy Spirit works in *sovereign grace* according to his nature. Perhaps we're clear as to his grace, but what about his sovereignty?

Don't overlook the Spirit's sovereignty

When we overlook the Spirit's sovereignty, it's easy to think of him as under our control, as though he is a vending machine, electricity, or genie in a bottle. Such misguided thinking places us in a position of sovereignty over an impersonal power, seeking to control it — focused on what steps to take, what techniques to use, what conditions to fulfill in order to get the Holy Spirit to work as we want. When we begin to think that way we are headed toward the *error of Simony*. Let me explain.

The error of Simony

You'll recall the story of Simon Magus (Simon the Magician) in the book of Acts. He became a convert, but then what did he want to do? As soon as he found out about the awesome power of the Holy Spirit, he wanted to purchase it from Peter. Buy it! Now why did he approach the Spirit in that way? You see, he was formerly a magician (sorcerer). Apparently, his magician's mind hadn't been sanctified yet. He didn't know the nature and character of this Holy Spirit. He thought like a magician: "Wow, what power! Power for good. If only I could get hold of it like the power I had as a magician. Then, I could do miracles for the glory of God!"

You see, Simon was still thinking like a magician, looking to possess and control the power of the Spirit. He had switched in his desire for a different power, but he hadn't yet changed his approach to power. He switched loyalty to the Holy Spirit, but he approached the Holy Spirit in the same way he did evil power. His mind had not yet been converted. Notice he received some very strong words of correction. He was repudiated by Peter with very sharp words, "May your silver perish with you, because you thought you could obtain God's gift with money!" and was told to repent immediately about this because God's power cannot be used or controlled by us. (Acts 8:14-24).

This is one of the first heresies actually recorded in the New Testament besides denying the divinity of Jesus and his being raised from the dead. This heresy actually has a name, called "Simony." Simony is the desire to control the Holy Spirit as if it were an impersonal power and not sovereign Holy God. Such a view does not regard the Spirit as free to blow where it wills, as one who works according to Sovereign Grace.

When the specific character and mind of the Holy Spirit is not taken into account, the door is left somewhat open for us to think we can shape the Spirit into our own image and use him/it for our own purposes. However, when known in relationship to the Son and the Father, that door is closed. Simon needed to see, "Oh, this is the Spirit of the Father and the Son" not just an impersonal power. The Spirit shares God's sovereign and freely given grace. There is nothing impersonal about the power of the Spirit. In fact, we could say the Spirit is the most personal and the most sovereign working of God, not only around us but in us!

The problem with Simon Magus was he wanted to use the Spirit. It wasn't that he wanted to use it for evil things. He saw the apostles healing people. He said, "I want to have that power." What was wrong was his entire approach to the Spirit, his whole understanding of who the Spirit is. He wanted to use the power to serve like the apostles, but his desire was to possess and control, to manipulate or to think that the Spirit needed to be conditioned or appeased to bless. That was to think of the Holy Spirit as if it were really an evil spirit.

Thinking he needed to or even could buy the Spirit misrepresents the nature and the character of the Holy Spirit who is at work with the apostles. The apostles received the Spirit as a gift of sovereign grace. You could not buy the Spirit any more than you could purchase God's grace. They had a whole different kind of relationship with the Holy Spirit than Simon was imagining. They must have been shocked when he came up to them and asked, "Hey, can I buy some of that power too?"

They grasped that he was thinking like he used to, of the Spirit in the same way he had about his former magical powers. They recognized immediately that that was entirely wrong. The Holy Spirit is not just another magical power. This is a huge lesson the church needed to learn at the very beginning. And it still is!

For us to take to heart that lesson is really important as well, since the temptation to Simony never completely disappears. The story reminds us of who the Holy Spirit is in relationship to the Father and the Son. The Holy Spirit is sovereign and not under our control . The Holy Spirit is also gracious because the Holy Spirit doesn't need to be cajoled or conditioned or manipulated into working. He doesn't need to be persuaded. He's not locked up in some kind of transcendent bottle, waiting for us to get him out. The grace of the Spirit is moving before we even ask or think of it. His ministry is one of sovereign grace, as are those of the Son and the Father. One in being, one in action.

If we have to condition or persuade or somehow exert some influence on the Spirit to work, then actually, the Spirit no longer is operating out of sovereign grace. And we are not thinking of the Holy Spirit, really, but of false spirits not of God.

Ironically, it's possible to be just as legalistic and contractual towards the Spirit as towards the Father or the Sabbath or salvation. Somehow, it's possible to claim that the blessings of the Spirit are conditioned by us, are dependent upon us. A magical view or an impersonal view of the Spirit is a form of legal relationship. But the gracious work of the Holy Spirit is a continuation of the gracious working of the Father and the Son. So, the Spirit always works graciously.

How should we approach the Spirit?

That naturally brings up the question as to whether it makes any difference as to how we approach the Spirit. The answer is of course, yes. But whatever difference is made cannot amount to changing the sovereign grace of the Spirit into its opposite! The difference is in our reception, awareness and participation in what the Spirit is graciously and sovereignly doing. Yes, we can resist the Spirit. We can participate or not. We can be more or less ready to recognize and receive the full benefits of the Spirit. But the Spirit is not dependent upon us to initiate and make the first move. In fact the Spirit ministers to enable us to do just those things, even overcoming our resistance as he shares with us Christ's own responses to the Father in our place and on our behalf. The Spirit moves us, frees us, guides us. And we then can respond.

So, yes, we can describe ways we can participate and ways to grow in our understanding and in our recognition of the ministry of the Spirit. When we do that we'll respond: "Wow. That was the work of the Holy Spirit. That is incredible. Praise God, Father, Son and the Holy Spirit. Yes, indeed, that was a marvel of sovereign grace we just saw manifested among us."

We can participate more fully and be filled with His glory or we can resist it or avoid it. But if we resist, we are resisting his gracious work just like the gracious work of Christ. It's no less gracious so we shouldn't think about participating in the life of the Spirit in any other way as if it's not sovereign grace and the grace that comes from God's sovereignty. It's freely given.

But by participating more fully and seeking through prayer to be filled with the Spirit, we are not conditioning the working of the Spirit. We're not earning his blessing and presence. We're especially not "channeling it." We're not manipulating, controlling or determining the working or manifestation of the Spirit. Rather, we're simply receiving a freely given gift.

These are important things to remember since we ought always to affirm the gracious sovereignty of the Spirit. This clear understanding will prevent us from committing Simony, from flipping over into that false view, since there will always be temptations to go in that direction. We like techniques and we like to make God predictable. A lot of times when we're in big trouble, we feel a need to bring some kind of pressure on God to act in this situation. Perhaps we're desperate. Or maybe we're curious to discover some technique or some formula or to identify some pattern or secret where essentially, we hold the key.

Especially in times of desperation we want God to be more like a magical and impersonal power. We don't like the sovereignty of God sometimes because it doesn't match my will or my speed or my immediate need. I've been there. We've all been there. We're sorely tempted to be like Simon Magus at certain moments in our lives where, "I just want to know the formula, God, because something needs to happen here and you're not doing it."

At that point evil temptation can enter our minds and suggest: "Right, God didn't show up. And you know why? It's because it's up to you and you're missing it. If you only knew the formula. If only you were holy enough. If only you were sincere enough. If only your expectations were high enough. If only your church was more united. If only you read the Bible more. If only, if only, if only x, y and z had been done, then maybe God would show up." But every "if only" mentioned that makes us the key says grace isn't grace. They throw us back on ourselves and undermine our trust, our faith in God. They represent a means to purchase blessings, not participation in and humble reception of the sovereign grace of God.

The working in the Spirit is of the exact same character as the saving work of Christ. And we receive it in the same way, by trusting God to freely give it to us. Yes, there are ways to participate with what the Spirit is doing, but the Spirit will never relinquish his sovereignty nor cease to be gracious and somehow become conditional and set up a legal relationship with us. But we can be tempted, and certain teachings tend to push us in just that direction.

What's it like to participate with the Spirit?

Who the Spirit is carries a number of implications we can draw out with the help of other insights from the biblical revelation. Let's explore our participation in this gracious ministry of the Holy Spirit.

Sanctification. The first thing is that the primary ministry of the Holy Spirit is transforming us, sanctifying us and enabling us to share in that new nature Christ shares with us. This is primarily a work in us. Transformation into Christ-likeness then is key. Christian maturity is of central concern in NT teaching. The Christian life is presented there as one of continual growth in faith, in hope and in love for God and that life lived out towards others. And there are many obstacles to be overcome or avoided in taking that journey of spiritual maturity and health. These obstacles are not just internal temptations but also external pressures, ways of living, habits, even mindsets that are not engendered by the Spirit but by "the world, the flesh and the devil." So, it's an uphill battle. It is a fight of faith. It is not easy, but it can be joyful and peaceful. It involves dying to the old self over and over again and being raised up in newness of life, being restored. Calvin described the Christian life as mortification and vivification. It involves repentance and renewed faith, hope and love. It involves forgiving and asking forgiveness. The Spirit enables us to share more and more in the new life we have in Christ, so that we live in daily union and communion with him, dying and being raised up every day. He, our crucified and risen Lord, is the center of our life.

Fruit and gifts. There is a good amount of information on the Holy Spirit involving both the gifts of the Spirit and the fruit of the Spirit. These indicate something of the shape of the Spirit's ministry. The Spirit is a "Giving Gift" as one theologian has put it. When we hear of gifts, we often think of abilities or capacities to do something; to serve in certain ways. But notice that the fruit of the Spirit are also gifts from the Spirit! The fruit point to the qualities of the life of Jesus that the Holy Spirit is building into us. While I won't review each of them here, remember, their ultimate definition is demonstrated for us in life of Jesus lived out in the power of the Spirit.

I also want to note that one of these fruit-gifts is "self-control." Self discipline is essential to sharing in the life of Christ by the Spirit. So often it is heard that the Spirit is all spontaneity and "letting go" and "going with the flow" or is aligned with our feelings or with love and these characteristics are then put in direct contrast with our thoughts, mind or truth or with any kind of intentional process or, well, discipline. But this particular fruit of self-control serves as a clear reminder that Christian freedom is on the far side of self-discipline not on the near side. The Spirit can never be used as an excuse for irresponsibility. The Spirit always joins truth with love, freedom with self-discipline, feelings with order or structure, especially with the moral order of right and good relationships. The Holy Spirit brings wholeness to life, not compartmentalization.

The gifts of the Spirit mentioned by Paul refer to the variety of ways members of the body of Christ are enabled to serve one another. We will not take time to explore the individual gifts. But let me point out a problem that often arises when there is a strong focus on these serving gifts of the Spirit. The problem arises when the serving-gifts of the Spirit are separated from the fruit of the Spirit or simply not seen to be in vital connection with them. That dis-junction is a huge mistake. It really amounts to dividing up the ministry of the Spirit into separate parts and pieces. What often happens in that case is that the gifts of the Spirit are exercised in ways that don't exhibit the fruit of the Spirit. Serving-gifts used without love, joy, peace, patience, self-control, etc. are being misused! It seems that it has often been assumed that if the gifts come from the Spirit, they can't be misused. But that is plain wrong. Even gifts of the Spirit can be misused. And they often are when not joined with an equal emphasis on the fruit-gifts of the Spirit.

Jesus, fruit and gifts. The primary work of the Spirit is to deliver all the benefits of Christ to us and in us. That includes both the fruit and the gifts. The Spirit doesn't give us the option of choosing one kind over the other, placing an emphasis on one and neglecting the other. If we look to the life of Jesus, we can see in him there is no disconnect between the fruit of his character and the quality of his ministry of service to others. These are perfectly joined in his humanity lived out in perfect communion with the Holy Spirit. So, when we talk about Christ's likeness, we're talking about the fruit of the Spirit which then shapes all his ministry service. Jesus lived by the Spirit. He's one of us. In his life, we find him using the gifts of the Spirit through the fruit of the Spirit.

Fruit, primary — gifts, secondary. The fruit is primary, is foundational, to the gifts of service. Paul indicates this when he teaches that love is the primary thing when he's talking about the gifts. What went wrong in Corinth is they went ahead with the gifts but exercised them without love. And the result was damage to the body. We cannot separate the fruit from the gifts. Fruit is essential who we are. The gifts are the manifestations of who we are and who we're becoming in Christ, filled with his likeness or his sanctification, that is, with his fruits.

Perhaps unexpectedly, the Holy Spirit doesn't directly give us his own sanctification. He gives us Christ's sanctification which was worked out in his human nature. The holiness of the Spirit apart from what Christ accomplished for us in his incarnate life wouldn't fit us directly as human beings. We'd just explode. But the sanctification that Christ has worked out for us in his humanity by the Spirit has become in him suited to us. And that is what the Holy Spirit shares with us!

Love. That's why, as the Holy Spirit works, we become like Christ, exhibiting the spiritual fruits of his perfected humanity. The primary center of that fruit, as Paul describes it, is best identified as love. In his letter to the Corinthians he makes it clear that such love will work itself out through a desire for unity, peace, harmony and up-building. The working of the Spirit generates no sense of superiority or competition, possessiveness or even self-sufficiency. Paul's image of being differing members of a united body holds these elements together well.

Paul surrounds his discussion of the gifts of the Spirit with the fruits of the Spirit even though he doesn't use that term but names the central fruit, love. They cannot be disconnected. Any working of the gifts should be a form of loving and serving others. If the gifts do not serve the unity, peace harmony and up-building of one another, then they're not gifts of the Spirit. Love like Christ's is a proper test of the working of the Spirit.

Since the Spirit both works distinctly through individuals but also promotes unity and harmony, we would not expect the movement of the Spirit to set up some kind of hierarchy of super-spiritual over less spiritual persons. The Spirit wouldn't foster envy and jealousy, moving some to think or saying that "They're less spiritual than we are" or "Their fellowship is more spiritual than ours." Nor would anyone be moved to say "I'm less spiritual than they are" or "my gift is more important than yours" or "My gift is less important than yours." That's simply not where the Spirit is going to take us.

That's not what the Spirit's about. For in that case the fruit and the gifts would be falling apart rather being brought together by the Spirit. But they can never come apart because the Spirit is one in its ministry and its Person. The Spirit will not foster competitiveness of one trying to be more spiritual than another. Unfortunately that's what was going on in the church in Corinth.

Freedom *for* others, not *from* others. Another expression of the separation of the fruit from the exercise of the gifts arises when individuals insist on using the gift in their own way. Such a person may think, "I've got my freedom in Christ and that justifies my using this gift however I see fit!" This is what was going on in Corinth. Certain persons were attempting to use a gift of the Spirit without regard for others. And they did so by claiming freedom in Christ. They took freedom to mean they didn't have to consider how the exercise of their gifts would affect others. But such an orientation is not going to come from the Spirit. The Spirit does not move persons to insist on their own way, even when it comes to serving others. Why not? Because, as Paul tells us (1 Cor. 13) insisting on your own way does not demonstrate Christ's love. Because the gifts are never to be used apart from the fruit. Paul tells us even he, the apostle, does not exercise all the freedoms he may have. Why not? For the sake of the body, he tells us (1 Cor 9:12).

Not seeking my own "spiritual" experience. There is another way in which we can take up an interest in the Spirit without much regard for others. I realize that this next point could be more controversial than the previous ones. But it needs to be addressed. Some turn to the Spirit primarily to have a strong, moving or powerful personal experience. The assumption seems to be that the ministry of the Spirit is primarily to give us an experience of the Spirit itself. The main result sought is being able to say, "I had an extraordinary experience of the Spirit." Some, by this means, are perhaps seeking security or greater assurance of their salvation, or perhaps of their spiritual maturity. But a survey of the New Testament does not support that approach. The ministry of the Holy Spirit is not to give us special individual experiences. Rather, it is to enable us to serve and to build up each other — to help and to assist each other, and to deepen the quality of relationships within the Church's in-reach and its ministry and outreach in service to others.

Yes, we'll have experiences of the manifestation of the working of the Spirit. But the resulting benefit will not be our saying, "Wow, I had an experience of the Spirit. Now if I could just have another one of those." We all will have experiences of the Spirit, but they're going to be experiences of love and service and fellowship and joy and worship that look away from the experience itself. The experience is a *byproduct* of something else the Spirit is doing in us and for us.

It seems Jesus wanted his disciples to learn just this lesson when they returned from a short mission trip and had worked miracles. They came back elated that in Jesus' name they were given authority over demons. Jesus cautions them: "Nevertheless, do not rejoice at this, that the spirits submit to you, but rejoice that your names are written in heaven" (Luke 10:20).

Who we are worshiping and serving is more important than having some kind of experience. A Spirit that is not preoccupied with itself is not likely to want to make us preoccupied with him or even ourselves! A focus on our seeking or having individual experiences of the Spirit can actually disrupt the ministry of the Holy Spirit in the Body of Christ. The Spirit will not want to take us in the direction where everyone is saying: "I had an experience and then I had another experience! Let me tell you about them." Sharing in this way usually brings out responses such as, "Oh, you had an experience. I wish I had that experience. I want that experience. How could you get that experience and I didn't have that experience? Wow, God must not like me," or, "God must like me (because…well, I can't say this out loud, but I must be somehow more favored than others) since I was given such an awesome experience that others, too, really should have." Spiritual pride of this sort can slip in when there is a focus on individual experiences of the Spirit.

How then shall we proceed?

Given these concerns, should we simply avoid talking about the Spirit and his fruits and gifts? No, not at all; though let us do so in ways like this: "Wow! Someone noticed some fruit of the Spirit in my life. How did that happen? It must be the work of the Spirit!" Or, "Wow. I actually tried to serve somebody even though I wasn't sure how, and they benefited in amazing ways that led them to love God more. How did that happen? It must have been by the

Spirit! I sure hope by the grace of God I can live in the middle of that more often."

This appropriate responses are quite different from ones that are based on seeking some sort of spiritual experience — a response I saw quite often in the Charismatic movement in the 1970s. Many who became Christians then were primarily seeking to "get high" on the Spirit (or Jesus) rather than something else. "I just want to get high on Jesus," I heard some say. And there were plenty of ministries ready to feed that desire. Certainly, that was a definite move in the right direction. But all too often those whose Christian lives were not much more than going from one "spiritual" experience to another did not experience much of the fruit of the Spirit. The rest of their lives remained pretty much a wreck. There was little fruit and no service. They were having or seeking experiences with the Spirit but there was little sign of life transformation. Some did move on, grow and mature. But others didn't. They seemed stuck, getting "high on Jesus." Then, sometimes, they'd go back to getting high on other things, too. Why not? One high is just as good as another, isn't it? Unfortunately, they were often simply looking for ways to escape their problems or gain some affirmation or attention for themselves. Admittedly, these are complicated situations. The point being, however, that looking to the Spirit for personal experiences really doesn't acknowledge the real, full ministry of the Holy Spirit who enables us to respond more fully and freely to the truth and reality of God and the Gospel.

In the next part of this series, I'll make a few more comments about the shape of the ministry of the Holy Spirit that might help us have a healthy approach.

PART 7

Last time we noted various aspects of the Spirit's ministry to us both corporately and individually. As we now bring this series to a close, let's look at a primary aspect of the Spirit's ongoing ministry which involves enabling us to make a full and proper *response* to the truth and reality of who God is, and what he has done, is doing and will yet do in our world, church and individual lives.

The nature of our response to God

The Holy Spirit works actively in our lives, both individually and corporately, to unbind our wills, unscramble our minds, and refashion our affections so that we can more fully respond with all that we are to all that God is. The Spirit frees us to be receptive at *every level* of who we are. However, it sometimes seems that we think the Spirit enables us to respond to God only emotionally. While the Spirit certainly does enable our emotional response (in thanksgiving, praise, adoration, joy, sorrow and repentance), the Spirit (who is called *the Spirit of truth* in John 14:17; 15:26) also enables us to respond with our minds — with our understanding or intelligence (1 Cor. 14:15). The Spirit also sets our minds free to be obedient to the truth (Romans 2:8). Throughout the New Testament, the heart (emotions, human spirit) and the mind, when healthy, are not split apart. Instead, they are coordinated. Thus the Spirit enables us to respond with all of what we are.

There is no reason to think that the working of God in and among us is divided, as if Jesus addresses our minds, and the Spirit addresses our emotions. We're not compartmentalized like that. The whole of God (Father, Son, Spirit) interacts with the whole of who we are (body, mind, heart). Note as well that the Son of God, via the Incarnation, assumed our fully humanity — a whole human nature, with all its aspects. We thus understand that Jesus is a full human being with body, mind and heart. In the Gospels we see Jesus responding fully with all that he is to the truth and reality of his heavenly Father and his relationship to him and the Spirit. Jesus obeys in the Spirit and rejoices in the Spirit. He overcomes temptation by the Spirit. He overcomes evil by the Spirit and sets people free. He offers himself on the cross to the Father through the Spirit (Heb. 9:14). Jesus lives his fully human life in and by the Spirit.

Thus, we understand that when the Spirit of Jesus comes upon us, he enables us to respond fully to the truth and reality of who God is and who we are in relationship to God with all we are and have. If there is part of us that is not yet responding, whether it be body, mind or heart, the Holy Spirit works to bring us to the point that we respond in all that we are. The Spirit does not divide us. Rather, he heals and makes us whole, giving us human integrity before our Lord and God.

The objective work of the Spirit in us

So, we should not align the Holy Spirit exclusively with what is subjective (internal or affective) in human experience. Yes, the Spirit works in us, works *in* our subjectivity, but not *as* our subjectivity. The Holy Spirit cannot be identified with our subjective states (feelings, emotions, consciences) as if they are identical. There is no denying that the Spirit works in our subjectivity. If not, we would remain in bondage to our fallen, rebellious wills and hard hearts, and our self-justifying and rationalizing minds. However, the Spirit works in us, in our subjectivity, but does so objectively, so that we can respond with our whole being to the truth and reality of who God is and who we are in relationship to him.

The Holy Spirit objects to our false, resistant, self-justifying subjective orientations. He is not the subjective aspect of human beings that can be shaped and formed any way we like, made to say what we want, made to reflect our preferences, prejudices, biases and desires. The Spirit has a *particular* character, mind, will, purpose, desire and heart, which is identical to that of Jesus. We have no power over the Spirit to recreate him in our image. The Spirit has his own objective reality that works within our subjectivity to open our eyes, minds and hearts to God.

The Holy Spirit, then, is a healer that brings the whole of human being together from the inside out. He does not split us up. He does not say to us, "I'm just in charge of your emotions, your imagination and your desires. What you think and believe and come to know, the rational part, well, Jesus takes care of that. I don't know anything about that." No, the Spirit does not divide up human being into compartments. Instead, he harmonizes the internal with the external, sharing with us the reestablished integrity of Jesus' humanity (which is true humanity).

The Spirit humanizes us

Thus we understand that a key aspect of the Holy Spirit's ministry is to *make us more fully human,* like Jesus, the one in whose image we were created and are being renewed or transformed (Col. 3:10; 2 Cor. 3:18). The Spirit shares with us the sanctified humanity of Jesus, which makes us fully human, more completely human, more personal, more full of the fruit of the Spirit. *True spirituality is mature humanity in full and right relationship with God.*

So, we can say that the Holy Spirit humanizes by making us share in the glorified humanity of Jesus Christ. Now in the process of this transformation, the Spirit brings us to have a humility before God in which we confess that God is God and that we are not; that we are entirely dependent upon God; that we need the grace of God and that we must hand over to him all our sin in repentance, and our whole selves in faith. But in leading us to confess these things, the Spirit will not submit us to humiliation. He will not make us feel less than human, or regret that we were ever human, or think that God despises humanity and creaturely limits.

There is a huge difference between humility and humiliation. Putting it this way may be surprising, since there are some who teach that humility in the Spirit comes by way of our humiliation. It is sometimes taught that the ministry of the Spirit not only focuses exclusively on the subjective side of human being, but requires that we set aside our rationality or intelligence, and act in less than human ways, perhaps like an animal or a person who has lost self-control (like a drunk person). It would be strange indeed for the Spirit to lead persons to lose self-control and act in ways beneath human being, since one of the gifts of the Spirit is precisely self-control, and the Spirit is the Spirit of Jesus who came to bring us into conformity with him. Though Jesus was humble before the Father and the Spirit, the Father never treated Jesus in a way that denigrated his humanity. Nor did Jesus respond to God in ways that denied a healthy and whole humanity. In Jesus, humanity was glorified, not denigrated. Jesus showed what it really means to be a human being.

Given who the Holy Spirit is, and what we know of his ministry, we can affirm that the Spirit does not dehumanize or depersonalize us. So when he leads us into humility before God, he does so in a way that is deeply personal — a way that is not alien to our humanity. This humility, which is the fruit of human maturity in relationship to God, is *not* about being humiliated, being treated as less than a person, as less than fully human — a form of humility that involves a relationship the opposite of the kind of ministry Jesus performed in the power of the Spirit. Abject humiliation does *not* represent the kind of relationship Jesus had with his heavenly Father.

Even though Jesus' enemies, especially in the end, attempted to humiliate him to the fullest extent they could, the end result was not Jesus' humiliation in the sense of him collapsing into a dehumanized heap of regret and shame for taking on humanity. Rather, Jesus reacted in such a way that we are encouraged to look to him as "the pioneer and perfecter of our faith, who for the sake of the joy that was set before him endured the cross, disregarding its shame, and has taken his seat at the right hand of the throne of God"

(Heb. 12:2). Jesus, who is exalted in his bodily resurrection and ascension, and who calls us his brothers and sisters, is not ashamed of us (Heb. 2:11). Jesus, by the Spirit, shares with us his glorified and perfected humanity.

Rather than denigrating us, the Holy Spirit works to humanize us. He does so by enabling us to share in Jesus' own glorified humanity. To be fully spiritual does not mean becoming non-human, nor does it mean becoming some kind of super-spiritual disembodied ghost, vapor or ethereal gas that is distributed throughout the cosmos. We come to a biblical understanding of true spirituality by observing the life of Jesus lived out in the Spirit. True spirituality is a human being fully responding to the truth of who God is — firing, as it were, on every cylinder, responding totally to who God is and who we are in relationship to him. It means responding to god in praise and prayer, and in every other way of service and love. The Holy Spirit, who is the humanizing Spirit, leads us in this, helping us share in the perfect humanity of Jesus. The presence and working of the Holy Spirit will always demonstrate just that kind of spirituality and not some other. Evil spirits dehumanize and destroy.

What about the Spirit's ministry to those not yet repenting and believing?

So far, we've been addressing primarily the Holy Spirit's ministry in connection with persons who are responsive to the gospel and receptive to Spirit's working. Let's now address the Spirit's ministry to those not yet responding, not yet believing, not yet receptive to the Spirit's work. We can start by asking whether or not the Spirit acts upon those who are resistant, or not yet believing, that is, those who are not Christians. The answer must be *yes.* No one becomes a believing person except in response to the ministry the Spirit. If no one comes to the Father except by the Son who sends the Spirit, and it is the Spirit who opens eyes, convicts of the need for forgiveness and life in Christ, then no one could become a conscious member of the body of Christ unless the Spirit drew them. The Spirit must work on those not yet believing and responding, or no one would ever become Christian, no one could enter into their salvation. The Spirit goes out after people to bring them to Christ and so to the Father. That is essential to the Spirit's mission in the world. We can see this in a dramatic way in the conversion of Saul/Paul.

A related question is whether we can say that the Spirit is "in" everyone. While there is not a lot to go on conveyed in biblical revelation, there is sufficient teaching that can enable us to answer this question. If by "in" everyone we mean in the deepest most personal and intensive way that the Spirit ministers, I think we have to say *no*. Jesus indicates to those who are following him that the Spirit was "with" them, but will be "in" them (John 14:17). Jesus at one point breathes on the twelve the Holy Spirit in the Upper Room. As a result, they have the Spirit now in a way they didn't previously. But Jesus also tells them to wait for the coming of the Spirit in Jerusalem, indicating that there is more yet to come involving the Spirit. And then the Spirit becomes present at Pentecost in a new and different way. But also notice that there were some who rejected the Spirit and mocked those who received the Spirit. Not all received the Spirit even though He was now present in a new way. So the Spirit can be present in a variety of ways, a range of intensities, and we could say at a number of different levels of depth.

The Spirit inhabiting (dwelling in)

One of the ways of speaking of the Spirit's presence in the New Testament is through use of the word which can be translated "dwelling in" or "inhabiting." This coming and indwelling of the Spirit in persons is viewed as the fulfillment of the promise God made through the prophet Joel (Joel 2:28) and Ezekiel (Ezek. 18:31; 36:26), as Peter tells us in Acts 2:17. The biblical notion of the Spirit's "dwelling in" or "inhabiting" is exclusively applied to those who are believing, receptive and responsive to the leading and working of the Spirit (see Rom. 8:9, 11; 1 Cor. 3:16). This word designates the most intense, personal and abiding presence of the Holy Spirit in persons and in the community of believers.

But this special presence of the Spirit does not mean that the Spirit is absent from everyone else. Clearly, the Holy Spirit was with those in ancient Israel, and sometimes in special ways upon the prophets and even some of the skilled tabernacle workmen. But that kind of presence did not represent what God had ultimately promised. That only occurred on Pentecost to those who received the preached word and were receptive of the presence and working of the Spirit. Further, we can see that the dynamic nature of relationship to the Spirit continues even at the deepest level of indwelling. This becomes clear when we consider the teaching that those who are part of the believing body are not to "quench" or "grieve" the Spirit (1 Thess. 5:19; Eph. 4:30) but rather are to "be continually filled" with the Spirit (Eph. 5:18).

We thus understand that the Holy Spirit can be present to anyone and everyone. The Spirit is God's presence throughout the creation. But we can also say that the Spirit can work in anyone and everyone. The Spirit's ministry is to open people's minds, soften their hearts, open their eyes to truth, unbind their resistant wills and convict them of the need for forgiveness and the life of salvation that comes only from God by grace. The Spirit delivers to unbelieving people the gift of repentance and faith, hope and love. Doing that requires working within them, within their persons, in their subjectivity. So, we can say that the Spirit works in them and is present to them in that way. However, that kind of inner working does not represent the promised indwelling that comes only with receiving Christ by being responsive to the promptings of the Spirit. For the Spirit does not work causally, mechanically, impersonally or coercively so that all necessarily are forced to receive the benefits of the Spirit's ministry. Those who in response to the Spirit's ministry receive the Spirit, who are receptive and submissive, then participate (have *koinonia*, fellowship) in a much deeper way and experience a unique quality of relationship with the Holy Spirit that is manifested in a conversion of heart and mind, a turning to face in a new directions toward God. Such submission and turning is exhibited in repentance and faith in God through Jesus Christ.

In Christ, united to Christ by the Spirit

This seems to explain why in the New Testament only those who are receptive to the Spirit, not resistant, and those who respond with repentance, faith, hope and love to the Gospel of Jesus Christ are said to be "in" Christ, or dwell "in the Lord." They alone are said explicitly to be united to Christ (1 Cor. 6:17). The relationship of Christ with his people is compared to the marital unity (Eph. 5:23; Rev. 19:7; 21:9; 22:17). The most intensive, intimate, deep and personal unity described in the New Testament is reserved for those who are believing, for those who are members of the body of Christ, united to him as the head is to the body of a living being.

So, by means of the use of certain words and images there is in the New Testament a distinction made between the Spirit's relationship with those who are receptive and open to the ministry of the Spirit, and those who are not yet responsive. How the Spirit is present, that is whether or not indwelling or inhabiting, will involve whether or not persons are receptive to the gospel and the ministry of the Spirit to receive it, welcome it. How one responds to the ministry of the Holy Spirit does make a difference in the kind of relationship one has with the Spirit.

But such a distinction should not be construed as meaning that the Spirit is not for all persons, is not capable of ministering in and to all persons at the deepest level, speaking to their individual human spirits. The Holy Spirit is "for all" in just the same way that Jesus Christ is for all those created through him. The Father sends the Spirit for the same purpose as he sent the Son.

But the Spirit is able to be present in a range of ways. And this fact is represented in biblical understanding and so we have to account for it in our understanding as well.

What about the Spirit in other religions?

What we can say about the ministry of the Holy Spirit in other religions is an extension of what we have just covered. No religion itself can keep the Holy Spirit out or away. The Holy Spirit is God's sovereign grace at work. The Spirit can be present to anyone and anywhere without becoming polluted, just as we see take place with Jesus' being present among sinners. And the Spirit is present to bring to bear all the fruits of reconciliation accomplished for all humanity in Christ. So in those situations where the official religion being practiced is resistant (even hostile) to the gospel, the Spirit will be present and working within, but against those points of resistance/hostility.

The religion itself will not be responsible or earn any credit for the presence and working of the Spirit. If hostile, the religion is actually an impediment to the working of the Spirit, an obstacle to receptivity to the ministry of the Spirit of Jesus. However, that does not stop the Holy Spirit from working. The Spirit will work to bring individuals and groups out of bondage to false ideas about God, and false ideas about their relationship to God. The Spirit will minister to open people's minds and hearts to be receptive to God's grace, love, faith and hope. The Spirit will draw people to a humble repentance and a dependence upon some kind of grace.

Individuals and groups can be drawn by the Spirit even while remaining outwardly a part of their non- or anti-Christian religious community. In that case, the Spirit will be making heretics within that religion—individuals or sub-groups who in their own minds and hearts take exception to at least some of what they have been told and are taught by the formal religion—as the Spirit leads. These persons may not know that they have become willing to follow the Spirit of Jesus. The Spirit may be anonymous to them, especially at first. But they, in their spirits, will have become responsive and receptive to the promptings of the Holy Spirit of Jesus.

People in this state can be said to have *implicit faith*, not *explicit faith*. There can be made an analogy between these people and those of faith in the Old Testament, whose faith in Jesus was not explicit. Although they did not know Jesus by name, nor of the nature of his future work, they nevertheless lived by faith and repentance and trusted in the covenant love and free grace of God to renew it when they broke it. They didn't know exactly how God's covenant was going to be fulfilled, but they knew and trusted and hoped it would somehow it would be.

That's how the New Testament depicts these Old Testament persons of faith. On the other side of their death, they will see how the promises they had hoped in were explicitly fulfilled. These persons, of course, are not excluded from God's salvation. So too, if through no fault of their own, persons responsive to the even anonymous ministry of the Holy Spirit do not come to have explicit faith, there is no reason to believe that they will not be included in God's ultimate salvation. Such persons have not committed the absolute and complete repudiation (blasphemy) of the Spirit but have been welcoming and receptive. Their implicit faith will become explicit as soon as it is made possible.

Of course, it is normally God's will for all who have implicit faith to come to have explicit faith in this life. And after all, is it not true that everyone who comes to have explicit faith, first had, at least for a moment, implicit faith? But faith can become explicit, it seems, only if and when there is a conscious and explicit proclamation of the gospel so that in the hearing of it, it is welcomed and received. And where there is such implicit faith it is always welcomed and received since there has already been a responsiveness to the Spirit that is working even as they hear the explicit Word announced. There are numerous missionary stories that corroborate just this kind of scenario. People have somehow become ready to receive the proclamation of the gospel before any missionary had ever arrived. So when the explicit gospel is proclaimed by the evangelist or missionary, it is recognized as fulfilling what they have been waiting for. Well, we know how this comes about—by the Spirit, that's how they were prepared.

But it may be the case that in not every instance where there is implicit faith engendered by the Holy Spirit that God brings about an opportunity for that faith to become explicit in this life. Yes, it could be that God sees to it that this never comes about. It could be that in every case where there is genuine implicit faith, God may send dreams or angels or miraculously appearing evangelists (as in Philip's encounter with the Ethiopian Eunuch, shown in the picture below), so that their implicit faith can become explicit through a conscious testimony to Christ. But we cannot know about these situations. And knowing how God works in every case does not practically concern us.

The point here is that we do not need a final theory as to how things will necessarily play out in situations in which we have no part. Rather, our ministry is to serve in ways that count on the working of the Holy Spirit within people so that implicit faith can become joyfully explicit. And in that way, our and their joy and thanksgiving will be increased. They will become members of the body of Christ (Christians) and be able to join in explicit worship and in consciously bearing witness to God so that others can also come to have explicit faith as well. But in any and every case, we can rest assured that God will, one way or another, take care of all those situations where faith is implicit because he is merciful and faithful. God always acts on the basis of his grace operating through the faithful working of the Holy Spirit, who is the Spirit of the Son and of the Father, sent by both in accordance with their sovereign grace.

Conclusion

With that comment we now end this series on the doctrine of the Holy Spirit with a focus on the Spirit's Person and work. Though the series has not answered all questions on the topic, and the answers given are not exhaustive, hopefully understanding has been gained concerning fundamental questions we have regarding the Holy Spirit.

SPEAKING IN TONGUES
PART ONE: JESUS' PROMISE

"What you are seeing is real," a church member told the visitor. "These people are filled with the Holy Spirit." The visitor was seeing a hundred men and women speaking in tongues, raising their hands in the air and singing praises. It was real, not imaginary — but were these people really filled with the Holy Spirit?, he wondered.

Speaking in tongues was a dramatic miracle that helped the Christian church begin (Acts 2). The book of Acts records two other occasions on which the Holy Spirit caused people to speak in tongues, and in his letter to the church at Corinth, the apostle Paul gave instructions about speaking in tongues.

Some churches emphasize the practice of speaking in tongues. They teach that every Christian should speak in tongues as evidence of receiving the baptism of the Holy Spirit. Some of these churches are among the fastest-growing segments of Christianity.

Other churches allow the practice of speaking in tongues, but do not encourage it. In these churches, tongue-speakers may form charismatic fellowship groups within the larger congregation. (*Charismatic* is defined in the glossary at the end of chapter 3.)

Still other churches forbid their members from speaking in tongues.

Speaking in tongues has been vigorously debated during the past century. The major questions are these:

- Does every Christian who receives the Holy Spirit speak in tongues?
- Does speaking in tongues prove that the Holy Spirit has come to a person?
- Are those who speak in tongues more spiritual or closer to God than those who do not?
- What role should tongue-speaking have in church meetings?

To answer these questions, we need to consult the Bible.

Acts 2:1-4

Shortly after Christ had risen into heaven, his disciples were observing the annual festival of Pentecost (Acts 2:1). "Suddenly a sound like the blowing of a violent wind came from heaven and filled the whole house where they were sitting. They saw what seemed to be tongues of fire that separated and came to rest on each of them. All of them were filled with the Holy Spirit and began to speak in other tongues as the Spirit enabled them" (verses 2-4).

What kind of tongues were these? They were foreign languages. "There were staying in Jerusalem God-fearing Jews from every nation under heaven. When they heard this sound, a crowd came together in bewilderment, because each one heard them speaking in his own language. Utterly amazed, they asked: `Are not all these men who are speaking Galileans? Then how is it that each of us hears them in his own native language?... We hear them declaring the wonders of God in our own tongues!'" (verses 5-8, 11).

The people, amazed and perplexed, asked one another, "What does this mean?" (verse 12). Peter first explained that they were seeing a fulfillment of a prophecy about God's Spirit (verses 14-21). He then preached a message about Jesus as the Messiah or Christ, and the need for repentance and baptism (verses 22-40). The miraculous languages got the attention of the crowd and allowed Peter, even though he was not a rabbi, to speak with authority to the people.

This experience on the Day of Pentecost is the most dramatic "tongues" incident described in the Bible. This is the most complete description. Let's note a few details about it:

- There were three miracles: a miraculous sound, an appearance like fire and speaking in other tongues.

- The "other tongues" were languages currently understandable by Jews from other nations. No interpreters were needed.

- The crowd may have thought the miracle was in the hearing (verses 6, 8, 11), but the biblical writers call it a miracle of speaking (verses 4, 18).

- Some people ridiculed the apostles and accused them of being drunk (verse 13).

- There is no indication that Peter's sermon, beginning in verse 14, was given in a miraculous "tongue."

- Peter proclaimed to those who accepted his message that they should repent and be baptized and thereby "receive the gift of the Holy Spirit" (verse 38). This promise applies to Christians of every century, but the verse does not make clear whether the "gift of the Holy Spirit" means that the Holy Spirit is the gift, or whether Peter meant that, in addition to receiving the Holy Spirit, they would receive speaking in tongues or some other manifestation of the

Spirit as the gift.

- Peter spoke of repentance and baptism, but he did not describe any other action needed for the gift of the Holy Spirit.
- Thousands were baptized, and many miracles were done (verses 41-43), but there is no further mention of miraculous tongues on that occasion.

The way the story is told in Acts, the apostles' miraculous ability to speak in foreign languages was only one of many kinds of miracles experienced by the early church. Acts describes many other miracles as God guided the new church into growth through the Holy Spirit. None of those miracles is presented as a requirement for every Christian.

The book of Acts describes two other occurrences of speaking in tongues — one in Caesarea and one in Ephesus. We'll examine those passages next. (Some scholars say that Acts 8:14-18 reports a tongue-speaking incident in Samaria. The Holy Spirit came upon people in some noticeable way, but there is no mention of tongues, so we do not learn anything about tongues in that passage.)

Acts 10:44-46

The second description of speaking in tongues comes when non-Israelites were first added to the church — perhaps 10 years after Christ's death and resurrection. Up until that time, the church had been primarily Jewish. The apostle Peter had been invited to the house of Cornelius, a gentile (non-Jewish) army officer in Caesarea who worshiped the true God (Acts 10:24-25). Many people were in the house, and Peter told them about Jesus Christ, faith and forgiveness (verses 27, 34-43).

"While Peter was still speaking these words, the Holy Spirit came on all who heard the message" (verse 44). The Jews with Peter "were astonished that the gift of the Holy Spirit had been poured out even on the Gentiles. For they heard them speaking in tongues and praising God" (verses 45-46).

It is difficult to discern from this brief mention what these "tongues" sounded like. It says nothing about interpreters, for example, or foreign languages. Nor does it say that the gentiles were seeking the gift of tongues; they simply listened to the gospel and believed. The "tongues" were regarded as miraculous, and Acts 11:15 indicates they were similar to the tongues mentioned in Acts 2.

The miraculous tongues of Acts 10, combined with the miracle of Acts 2, helped Jewish Christians realize that God was adding non-Jewish people to the church. Since religious Jews had traditionally separated themselves from gentiles, God used a special sign to demonstrate to the Jewish Christians that he had also accepted gentiles as his children (Acts 15:7-8).

Acts 19:1-6

Christianity continued to expand to new geographic regions and include more people. The third and final example of tongues from the book of Acts occurred in the city of Ephesus. Paul found some disciples who followed the teachings of John the Baptist. They didn't know about the Holy Spirit, so Paul informed them more fully, and taught them that John told people to believe in Jesus (Acts 19:1-4).

Tongues-speaking in the book of Acts - conclusion

Let us go back to our first question: Does every Christian who receives the Holy Spirit speak in tongues? The book of Acts records many healings and other miracles, but only three incidents of tongues. This suggests that tongue-speaking was not a common occurrence, but rather a miraculous sign for special occasions as the apostles preached the gospel and established the church.

It seems that most New Testament Christians did not speak in tongues. Several verses tell us that people were "filled with the Holy Spirit," but without any mention of tongues. Let's notice the following verses:

Not long after Pentecost, the apostles were praying for God's help. After they finished praying, "the place where they were meeting was shaken. And they were all filled with the Holy Spirit and spoke the word of God boldly" (Acts 4:31). The apostles had already been filled with the Spirit on the Day of Pentecost. Here they are filled again. Miraculous shaking is mentioned, but speaking in tongues is not.

There is no mention of tongues when the Holy Spirit came on converts in Samaria (Acts 8:14-17), when the Ethiopian eunuch was converted (Acts 8:38), when Saul, who became Paul, was converted (Acts 9:17-18), when he confronted a sorcerer (Acts 13:8-11) or when Paul first preached in Asia (verses 44-52). This doesn't prove that tongue-speaking did not occur, but it does indicate that it was not important to mention it. Last, we note that the Gospels do not describe Jesus himself as speaking in tongues.

The evidence, so far, is limited. Acts is primarily a story of what happened; the book doesn't contain many commands or promises. Like many histories, it focuses on unusual or ground-breaking events. There is little attempt to describe ordinary practices. The book of Acts gives us only a limited picture of speaking in tongues. However, Paul wrote a great deal about tongues in a letter to the Corinthian Christians. His instructions help us understand whether tongue-speaking is evidence of God's Spirit, of deeper conversion, or of being closer to God.

Seeking the Gift of Tongues

Pentecostal churches teach that Christians receive the Holy Spirit when they are first converted, but that they are not filled with the Spirit until they are baptized with the Spirit. This second blessing, this baptism of the Spirit, is not considered necessary for salvation, but people are encouraged to seek it in order to receive additional power to witness.

Spirit-baptism, Pentecostals believe, always includes speaking in tongues. Therefore, those who desire Spirit-baptism will seek to speak in tongues. However, any attempts to imitate the tongues of Pentecost are attempts to imitate only one of the miracles of that day. There were other miracles that day, too. God will give what he wants to give.

The real lesson of Pentecost is not in the miracles, but in Peter's message: "Repent and be baptized...in the name of Jesus Christ for the forgiveness of your sins. And you will receive the gift of the Holy Spirit" (Acts 2:38).

Loosening the tongue does not necessarily require a miracle, but loosening the heart in real repentance does. Whoever believes, repents and is baptized will receive the gift of the Holy Spirit. No further steps or tarry meetings are needed.

"On hearing this, they were baptized into the name of the Lord Jesus. When Paul placed his hands on them, the Holy Spirit came on them, and they spoke in tongues and prophesied" (verses 5-6).

Again, it is impossible to tell what these tongues sounded like. All we know is that these disciples were rebaptized so they could receive the Holy Spirit. Whether they were expecting the gifts of tongues and prophecy isn't stated.

The tongues in Acts 2 and 10 came with significant developments in the expansion of the church. But in Acts 19, we are not told why this group of John's disciples was significant enough for special mention. We do know that it emphasized the need for all Jews, even those who already lived repentant, obedient lives, to accept Christian baptism. It also showed that Paul was an apostle of Christ and that his mission to the gentiles was approved by God.

Michael Morrison

PART TWO:
TONGUE-SPEAKING IN CORINTH

On Paul's second major journey to preach the gospel to gentiles, he went into Europe, preaching briefly in Philippi, Thessalonica, Berea and Athens (Acts 16:12-17:15).

In Corinth, however, Paul spent a year and a half (Acts 18:1, 9-11) — a long stay for an apostle who was "constantly on the move" (2 Corinthians 11:26). Corinth was a seaport city with a reputation for immorality. There Paul found Jews and gentiles who wanted to be taught the Word of God.

After the congregation had been established in Corinth, Paul eventually moved on — to Ephesus in Asia Minor, Caesarea in Judea, Antioch in Syria, and, after a few years, to Ephesus again (Acts 18:18-23; 19:1).

Bad news from Corinth

While Paul was back in Ephesus, he heard about the Corinthian church. The news was not good — the new Christians were arguing among themselves about several aspects of Christian behavior. Their example made Christianity look bad, even to the immoral pagans!

The Corinthian Christians sent Paul a letter asking him for advice about a number of topics, including the topic of tongues. They had been speaking in tongues frequently, and they asked him about this spiritual gift. Their letter gave him an opportunity to give them the guidance they needed.

In his letter Paul criticized them because their arguments were ruining the unity that Christians ought to have. "Some from Chloe's household have informed me that there are quarrels among you" (1 Corinthians 1:11). "I hear that when you come together as a church, there are divisions among you, and to some extent I believe it" (1 Corinthians 11:18). "Your meetings do more harm than good" (verse 17).

In their disagreements, some of the people claimed to follow one Christian leader, and some claimed to follow another (1 Corinthians 1:12). The behavior of the Corinthian Christians was wrong, and Paul had to correct them.

"I appeal to you, brothers, in the name of our Lord Jesus Christ, that all of you agree with one another so that there may be no divisions among you and that you may be perfectly united in mind and thought" (verse 10).

Paul writes about their problems

In chapters 1-4, Paul tried to help the Corinthians see the problems of disunity. They were acting like unbelievers, not like Christians (1 Corinthians 3:3).

He told them what to do about sexual immorality within the Church (1 Corinthians 5:1-13; 6:12-20) and lawsuits between Christians (verses 1-8). These subjects illustrate the problems the congregation was having. Paul had to set them straight with strong words.

Then Paul began to answer their questions. "Now for the matters you wrote about..." (1 Corinthians 7:1). First, he dealt with the topic of marriage in chapter 7.

Chapter 8 begins to address their next subject: "Now about food sacrificed to idols: We know that we all possess knowledge. Knowledge puffs up, but love builds up" (verse 1).

From the way Paul writes his letter, we can tell that the Corinthian Christians were proud of their "knowledge." Paul points out that their knowledge, at least the way they were using it, was harmful to their spiritual growth. Their knowledge was causing arguments and divisions in the congregation. Love, he writes, is more valuable, and it is a better indicator of Christian living.

Chapter 9 explains Paul's right as an apostle, and chapter 10 continues the subject of food sacrificed to idols. In chapter 11, Paul comments on some problems the Corinthians had in their worship meetings.

Various spiritual gifts

In chapter 12, Paul begins a new section, which contains comments on tongues. "Now about spiritual gifts, brothers, I do not want you to be ignorant" (verse 1). They needed instruction to help them use their spiritual gifts in a helpful way.

There are different kinds of spiritual gifts, Paul tells us, even though they are all inspired by the same Spirit (verse 4). God gives these special abilities "for the common good" — so Christians can help one another (verse 7). Paul lists various gifts, including "speaking in different kinds of tongues, and...the interpretation of tongues" (verse 10).

What are these tongues? Are they foreign languages, like the miraculous tongues spoken on the Day of Pentecost (Acts 2:1-11)? Or does this gift of tongues produce other kinds of sounds? The fact that a supernatural gift was needed for interpreting the sounds (1 Corinthians 12:10; 14:13) indicates that the speaking may not have been a human language. But we cannot know whether modern tongue-speaking is anything like the Corinthian practice.

Paul lists similar spiritual gifts in his letter to the Roman Christians (Romans 12:6-8), but that list doesn't mention tongues or interpretation. Corinth seems to have been the only church congregation where tongues were spoken regularly.

Not everyone has the same spiritual gift or ability, Paul notes. God distributes them: one power to one person, another gift to the next person, a third ability to another, just as God determines (1 Corinthians 12:8-11). By dividing the gifts in this way, God encourages members to work with and help one another.

The analogy of a human body illustrates this. Feet, hands, eyes and other parts serve different functions. By contributing to the body as a whole, the various parts serve one another. So it is in the Church, the Body of Christ (verses 12-27). God appoints people with various spiritual functions: apostles, prophets, teachers, miracle-workers, healers, helpers, administrators and speaking in different kinds of tongues (verse 28).

"Are all apostles?" asks Paul. Of course not. Neither are all Christians prophets, teachers, miracle-workers, healers, tongue-speakers or interpreters (verses 29-30).

From the way Paul presents his argument, it seems that some Corinthians expected every Christian to have the same gift when it came to tongues. They doubted the spirituality of anyone who did not have that gift. That isn't a reasonable way to judge Christianity, Paul tells them. None of these spiritual gifts can be singled out as the one and only test of the Holy Spirit.

The best spiritual quality

It is good to desire the greater spiritual gifts, says Paul, perhaps agreeing with something the Corinthians had written in their letter (verse 31). It seems that the Corinthian Christians eagerly desired to be spiritual and to appear spiritual.

In chapter 13, Paul describes the best evidence of spirituality — love. If love is not present, it does not matter what kind of miracle-working gifts a person might have (verses 1-3).

Paul mentioned "tongues of men and of angels" (verse 1). "Tongues of men" means human languages, but what are the "tongues of...angels"? There is no indication in the Bible that angels speak to humans in mysterious languages. Every time they spoke to humans, they were understood.

So why did Paul mention angelic languages? It may be that some of the Corinthian tongue-speakers claimed that their sounds were angelic. Or perhaps Paul used the term as the most exalted tongue-speaking he could imagine. And, of course, in the realm of spirits there certainly is a different vocabulary. In any case, Paul tells us that tongue-speaking without love would be nothing, no matter how "spiritual" it might appear.

God's way of life is based on love. Love perseveres and endures forever; it will never fail or become unnecessary (verses 7-8). In contrast, spiritual gifts will eventually no longer be needed. Knowledge, at least the kind that the Corinthians were proud of, will pass away (verse 8). Even prophecy, a gift that Paul praises, will cease.

"For we know in part and we prophesy in part, but when perfection comes [at the return of Christ], the imperfect disappears.... Now I know in part; then I shall know fully" (verses 9-12).

When God's people are resurrected and become completely perfect, special spiritual knowledge will no longer be important, because everyone will know fully. Divine messages and predictions will no longer be important, for the same reason. Tongues will likewise cease. Certain spiritual gifts have value in this temporal age, but they are not of eternal significance in the way that love is.

A better form of speaking

Spiritual gifts do have value, so we should want to have them (1 Corinthians 12:31). But what kind of gifts should we desire? We follow the way of love. We should eagerly desire a gift that helps others. "Since you are eager to have spiritual gifts, try to excel in gifts that build up the church" (1 Corinthians 14:12).

Paul recommends "the gift of prophecy" (verse 1). He does not necessarily refer to predicting the future. The Greek word Paul used here means "an utterance inspired by God...the capacity or ability to utter inspired messages." The verb translated "prophesy" means "to speak under the influence of divine inspiration, with or without reference to future events" (Louw and Nida — see the bibliography).

In other words, the gift of prophecy is, as Edgar Goodspeed translates it, "inspired preaching." Today's English Version calls it "the gift of proclaiming God's message." Speaking in prophecy, Paul says, is better than speaking in tongues. "He who prophesies is greater than one who speaks in tongues" (verse 5). Why? Because inspired preaching can be understood, and tongues cannot (without an interpreter).

"Anyone who speaks in a tongue does not speak to men.... No one understands him.... But everyone who prophesies speaks to men for their strengthening, encouragement and comfort" (verses 2-3). Inspired preaching can be understood; its purpose is building or edifying the Church (verses 4, 31) — helping Christians live better lives.

Paul says it is good to speak in tongues, but it is much better to prophesy (verse 5). "I would rather speak five intelligible words to instruct others than ten thousand words in a tongue" (verse 19). "Unless you speak intelligible words with your tongue, how will anyone know what you are saying?" (verse 9).

"If I pray in a tongue, my spirit prays, but my mind is unfruitful" (verse 14). If the mind is unfruitful, it implies that even the tongue-speaker didn't understand the sounds. The speaker wouldn't be able to explain it without supernatural help (verse 13).

This is also shown in Paul's comments about musical instruments: The tune isn't identifiable "unless there is a distinction in the notes" (verse 7). Similarly, messages cannot be understood if there is no distinction in sounds. In the tongues spoken by the Corinthians, it seems, words couldn't be distinguished from one another. The message could not be understood.

Were the Corinthians speaking foreign languages that no one in Corinth understood?

Or were the sounds simply not part of any human language?

Paul doesn't clearly tell us. His comments cover both possibilities — sounds that had no meaning, or a foreign language that no one knew. In either case, the result was the same: In Corinth, the tongues could not be understood. They may have had some value to the speaker (verse 4), but they were of no value to the congregation.

Interpretation and order

Paul used part of his letter to tell the Corinthian Christians how to use the gift of tongues. It seems that it was their regular custom to speak in tongues. But tongues had become a problem — enough of a problem for the Corinthians to ask Paul's advice about the situation.

For the specific circumstances at Corinth, Paul advised tongue-speakers to pray for the gift of interpretation (verse 13); it is only through interpretation that others could learn something from the sounds (verse 5).

"If there is no interpreter, the speaker should keep quiet in the church" (verse 28). This implies that the speakers were able to control themselves. They had to be silent unless someone known to have the gift of interpretation was also there. They should speak in an orderly way. They should not disrupt services but contribute to them. Paul explained, "For God is not a God of disorder but of peace" (verse 33). When spiritual gifts are being used, there is no excuse for confusion. If there is chaos, the people are not allowing God to work in them in the way he wants.

Paul stressed that worship services "should be done in a fitting and orderly way" (verse 40). Apparently the Corinthian meetings had been disorderly, with many people speaking at the same time. "If the whole church comes together and everyone speaks in tongues, and some who do not understand or some unbelievers come in, will they not say that you are out of your mind?" (verse 23).

In contrast, Paul says, if some outsiders hear inspired speaking and teaching, they may worship God (verses 24-25).

So Paul gave the Corinthians some simple rules for improving the organization of their worship meetings. People could come prepared to participate in various ways, according to their gifts or abilities. The primary rule, based on the way of love, was that "all of these must be done for the strengthening of the church" (verse 26).

Only one person should speak at a time, and there should be only two or three speaking in tongues in any one meeting (verse 27). (This rule applied to prophets, too.) If anyone speaks in a tongue, someone must interpret. If no one could explain the message, the tongue-speaker had to be quiet (verse 28).

Paul forcefully corrected the Corinthians on some of their problems, but on the topic of tongues he was gentle. He did not want the correction to cause more division than the problem had caused. "Do not forbid speaking in tongues. But everything should be done in a fitting and orderly way" (verses 39-40).

Michael Morrison

EVALUATING SPIRITUAL GIFTS

"My friends, you asked me about spiritual gifts," Paul wrote the Corinthian Christians (1 Corinthians 12:1; quotes are from the Contemporary English Version, copyright 1991, American Bible Society). "I want you to desire the best gifts" (verse 31).

The Corinthians desired spiritual gifts. Paul took this opportunity to emphasize the spiritual gifts that would best serve the entire community of believers. "If you really want spiritual gifts, choose the ones that will be most helpful to the church" (1 Corinthians 14:12).

"Love should be your guide. Be eager to have the gifts that come from the Holy Spirit, especially the gift of prophecy.... When you prophesy [speak an inspired message — see *prophecy* in the glossary], you will be understood, and others will be helped" (verses 1, 3).

Purpose of speaking: to be understood

Paul was giving the Christians in Corinth some guidance that they had asked for. He corrected a mistake they were making. They had been seeking the gift of tongues, but they were misusing the gift.

These tongues weren't helping the congregation. "If you speak languages that others don't know, God will understand what you are saying, though no one else will know what you mean.... By speaking languages that others don't know, you help only yourself" (verses 2, 4).

Paul said they didn't have to stop speaking in tongues (verse 39), but he did want them to turn their enthusiasm into more helpful channels, either by interpreting the unknown sounds, or simply by speaking words that could be understood.

"I am glad for you to speak unknown languages, although I had rather for you to prophesy. In fact, prophesying does much more good that speaking unknown languages, unless someone can help the church by explaining what you mean" (verse 5). "When we speak languages that others don't know, we should pray for the power to explain what we mean" (verse 13).

The most helpful gift is the gift of inspired speaking (verse 1). It can encourage, comfort and teach (verses 3, 31).

Meetings should be orderly

Paul also gave the Corinthians advice about a related concern: order in worship meetings. "My friends, when you meet to worship, you must do everything for the good of everyone there" (verse 26).

First, he gave instructions for people who spoke in tongues: "No more than two or three of you should speak.... You must take turns, and someone should always be there to explain what you mean. If no one can explain, you must keep silent in church" (verses 27-28).

Similar instructions were given for people who prophesied in language that could be understood: "Let only one person speak at a time, then all of you will learn something and be encouraged" (verse 31).

The Corinthians needed some advice about this; apparently their meetings had been full of confusion. "Suppose everyone in your worship service started speaking unknown languages, and some outsiders or some unbelievers come in. Won't they think you are crazy?" (verse 23).

Paul was disappointed with how the Corinthian church meetings had been conducted. Earlier, Paul had scolded them because they had been arguing: "Your worship services do you more harm than good. I am certainly not going to praise you for this. I am told that you can't get along with each other when you worship.... You are bound to argue with each other" (1 Corinthians 11:17-19).

So Paul stressed order. "God wants everything to be done peacefully and in order.... Do everything properly and in order" (1 Corinthians 14:33, 40).

Was it really the Holy Spirit?

The Holy Spirit can inspire tongue-speaking, as Paul wrote in 1 Corinthians 12:7-11 and as we see in the book of Acts. But tongue-speaking can happen in other ways, too. Non-Christians, both ancient and modern, have spoken in tongues. Several ancient religions included tongue-speaking, usually (as far as we can tell) not a real language, but simply strings of syllables, also called ecstatic speech:

> There are records of ecstatic speech and the like in Egypt in the eleventh century B.C. In the hellenistic [Greek] world the prophetess of Delphi and the Sibylline priestess spoke in unknown or unintelligible speech. Moreover, the Dionysian rites contained a trancelike state as well as glossolalia. Many of the magicians and sorcerers of the first century world exhibit similar phenomena. (G.R. Osborne, in the *Evangelical Dictionary of Theology*, 1984, page 1100.)

> Descriptions of ecstatic speech are common in the study of comparative religions.... The Delphic and Pythian religions of Greece understood ecstatic behavior and speech to be evidence of divine inspiration by Apollos. [C.M. Robeck, Jr., in *The International Standard*

Bible Encyclopedia, Vol. 4, 1988, page 872.)

How did these ancient pagans speak in tongues? Perhaps they were given supernatural abilities by demons, but perhaps they did it simply from human ability. Modern investigations have found that tongues — or at least something that sounds like tongues — can come from a natural source, the human brain:

> The tongues phenomena can be explained on psychological, sociological, physiological and linguistic ground alone.... The consensus of most social scientists is that glossolalia (tongue-speaking) takes place when a person is functioning in some type of altered mental state.... Psychologists consider them [tongues] to be explainable in terms not necessarily supernatural or spiritual.... The psychological state of the glossalalist is altered in some way. (Klemet Preus, *Concordia Theological Quarterly,* Vol. 46, 1982, pages 280-281.)

> Glossolalia is not language in the ordinary sense.... It is, rather, a willed and welcomed vocal event in which, in a context of attention to religious realities, the tongue operates within one's mood but apart from one's mind in a way comparable to the fantasy-languages of children.... Glossolalia is regularly both taught...and learned, and is in fact easy to do if one wants to. (J.I. Packer, Churchman, Vol. 94, 1980, pages 108-109)

> Glossolalia is a learned skill, however unconscious its mechanism. The occasions on which it is manifest are to a high degree dependent upon expectations of a specific group, expressed in part through ritualized procedures. Even the characteristic bodily motions accompanying dissociation and some aspects of modulations in the utterances are specific to a particular group and even to the leader who has "taught" the glossolalist. And the interpretation given to glossolalia depends upon the belief system of the group. (Wayne A. Meeks, *The First Urban Christians: The Social World of the Apostle Paul,* 1983, page 120.)

Ecstatic speech, although unusual, is a natural ability that can be taught. Tongue-speaking is not necessarily a miracle, so it cannot be proof of the Holy Spirit. The Corinthian Christians, however, had been assuming that tongue-speaking was proof of supernatural inspiration.

From the way that Paul writes, we conclude that some of the Corinthians had a real spiritual gift for speaking in tongues. However, others — the ones causing confusion — were imitating the gift. Perhaps influenced by the importance given to ecstatic sounds in pagan religions, some of the Corinthians emphasized tongue-speaking as a visible evidence of being spiritual. In doing so, they were neglecting the more important parts of Christianity, such as love.

Paul redirected their thoughts to help them see a better way. He started by reminding the Corinthians of their pagan past (1 Corinthians 12:2), and he gave an extreme example to show that not every saying is inspired by God (verse 3). Messages need to be examined before they can be accepted (1 Corinthians 14:29, 1 Thessalonians 5:20-21). God will not inspire a message that contradicts the Bible or the way of love.

Since the message needs to be evaluated, it has to be understood. That is why Paul says the gift of tongues, if there is no interpreter, is for private use (1 Corinthians 14:28), and that is why he emphasizes prophecy.

Understandable speaking is better than ecstatic sounds in several ways: It can be controlled and orderly, it can teach and edify both believers and unbelievers; and it is not noisy chaos. No one would confuse it with the ecstasy that occurred in groups who, for example, worshipped the wine god while drinking and making noise with musical instruments.

"Brothers, stop thinking like children" (verse 20). Paul did not mean that tongue-speaking was childish, but rather that the Corinthian overemphasis on tongues was childish. Paul quoted a passage from Isaiah 28:11-12 to point out that speaking in strange tongues is not always an effective way to bring people to God.

Tongues are a sign "for unbelievers." People who don't yet believe in God look for miraculous proofs (1 Corinthians 14:22). But even if they see tongues, they may scoff, perhaps saying the people are drunk, crazy or even demon-inspired (verse 23, Acts 2:13).

Tongues, as a sign, do not lead people to the obedience and faith in Jesus our Lord. Christians, who already believe, need to look for the less spectacular but more important change in the human heart, a change Paul describes as the way of love.

Did Paul speak in tongues?

But didn't Paul himself speak in tongues? He says he did in 1 Corinthians 14:18, but we do not know what kind of tongues he spoke. He knew several languages, but this is probably not what he meant. He did not say he spoke in more languages; rather, he said he spoke in tongues more often than the Corinthians did. He could pray in a tongue, but he preferred to pray with understanding (verses 14-15).

Paul described many of his supernatural and natural experiences (2 Corinthians 12:1-5, 11:21-30), but he doesn't say anything more about tongues. Apparently it wasn't important for Christians then or now. From the instructions he gave the Corinthians, it is clear that Paul would not have spoken in a church meeting in a language that others could not understand (1 Corinthians 14:19).

Paul said that tongues could edify the speaker (verse 4), but the importance of self-edification is limited. After all, the Corinthians had been overestimating themselves in wisdom and knowledge and spirituality; they were puffed up with self-importance. They did not need more attention on self — for spiritual maturity, they needed to exercise love for others, and build up the church, not themselves (verses 3-4).

What did Paul mean when he wrote, "I would like every one of you to speak in tongues" (verse 5)? Perhaps he wished that all the Corinthians were really speaking messages from God. Whatever he meant, he immediately clarified that his greater desire was that the Christians speak in a way that could be understood: "I would rather have you prophesy. He who prophesies is greater than one who speaks in tongues, unless he interprets, so that the church may be edified."

The Corinthian experience with tongue-speaking seems to have been an isolated case, and Paul dealt with it in a tactful, instructive way. He allowed a limited amount of tongue-speaking, but he did not allow it in church meetings if there was no interpretation. He did not allow several people to speak at once (verses 27-28). He clearly said that orderly, understandable messages were better.

But if a person wanted to speak in an unknown tongue at home, in private, the Church should allow it (verse 39). The unusual speech might encourage people to continue building their relationship with God. At least it would be a reminder that we are not always able to clearly describe our needs (Romans 8:26).

Summary

Does speaking in tongues prove that the Holy Spirit has come to a person? No. Gifts or abilities, no matter how miraculous they appear, should not automatically be accepted as divine. They should be tested to see whether they are in harmony with God's Word and the Christian way of life.

Are those who speak in tongues more spiritual or closer to God than those who do not? Not necessarily. If those who speak in tongues don't have love, Paul says, they are useless noisemakers — no matter what language they speak (1 Corinthians 13:1).

What role should tongue-speaking have in the Church? Paul does not forbid tongue-speaking, but he strictly limits its role in the meetings of the Church. He tells the Corinthians not to do it during their meetings unless someone could interpret. Even if interpreters are there, only one person should speak at a time.

The gift of tongues, or any other gift, is not a special mark of spirituality. All the gifts of the Spirit are given as God decides (1 Corinthians 12:11). As we follow the example given in the book of Acts, we do not need to make special effort to experience this particular gift. (See "Seeking the Gift of Tongues," page 6.) No one, no matter what gifts one has, has any reason to be proud or to look down on others (verses 21-25). And Christians with "small" gifts need not feel bad. Each should simply use his or her abilities to best serve others (Romans 12:6-13).

Mark 16:15-18

We have no biblical evidence that Jesus ever spoke in tongues. And as far as we know, he didn't say anything about it. It is mentioned in Mark 16:15-18, but there are two problems with this passage.

First, the oldest, most reliable manuscripts of the New Testament do not have this passage. Most scholars conclude that it was added to the text by a scribe who wanted to give Mark a more complete ending. Almost all modern translations indicate that these verses were most likely not in the original version of Mark.

Second, even if these verses are authentic, they tell us almost nothing about tongues. They say: "These signs will accompany those who believe: In my name they will drive out demons; they will speak in new tongues; they will pick up snakes with their hands; and when they drink deadly poison, it will not hurt them at all; they will place their hands on sick people, and they will get well" (verses 17-18).

These verses do not predict how often these signs would occur, or whether every believer would be involved in each of these signs, or whether believers should make special efforts to display these miracles. To answer such questions, we need to look at other scriptures.

The book of Acts describes incidents of casting out demons, healings and supernatural protection against deadly things. However, believers did not go out of their way to find demons or to be exposed to deadly things. In the case of healing, we know that there were times when it did not happen (2 Corinthians 12:7-10, for example).

Mark 16:17-18 simply lists a few of the many types of miracles that God's church would experience. This list is neither a command nor a promise for every Christian. To answer our questions about speaking in tongues, we must examine other scriptures.

Glossary

Caesarea. A city about 80 miles northwest of Jerusalem, where the Holy Spirit came upon the gentile Cornelius and his household.

Charismatics. Those of various denominations who emphasize spiritual gifts such as tongue-speaking, healing or prophecy. They usually do not teach that everyone should have the same gift. The Greek word *charismata* means "gifts."

Ecstatic speech. Non-language syllables produced when the brain sends signals to the organs of speech (throat, tongue and lips) but the language center of the brain does not organize the signals. The person can be conscious or in a trancelike state.

Ephesus. A city in western Asia Minor, near modern Izmir in western Turkey. The miraculous tongue-speaking at Ephesus showed that disciples of John the Baptist were accepted into Christian churches after faith, baptism and the laying on of hands.

Glossolalia. Speaking in tongues. The Greek word *glossa* means "tongue," and *laleo* means "speak."

John the Baptist. A Jewish prophet who prepared the way for Jesus. He had many disciples even 20 years after his death.

Pentecost. One of the annual religious festivals God told the Israelites to observe. It comes about seven weeks after Passover. It was on Pentecost that the Holy Spirit filled the disciples, causing them to speak in tongues, and the New Testament Church was founded.

Pentecostalism. A movement that stresses the importance of tongue-speaking as a "second blessing." People are taught that they receive the Holy Spirit upon conversion, but are not filled with or baptized with the Holy Spirit until they speak in tongues. Some Pentecostal churches stick to this definition more closely than others do.

Prophecy. A God-inspired saying or a message from God. The verb translated "prophesy" means to speak under divine inspiration, with or without referring to future events.

Samaria. A region about 40 miles north of Jerusalem. The Samaritan people were of mixed ancestry, both Israelite and gentile. When the gospel was preached in Samaria, the Holy Spirit came upon converts in some noticeable way, but tongues are not specifically mentioned (Acts 8:14-18).

Bibliography

- Fee, Gordon D. *The First Epistle to the Corinthians.* The New International Commentary on the New Testament. Grand Rapids: Eerdmans, 1987, pages 569-712.

- Gaffin, Richard B., Jr. *Perspectives on Pentecost: New Testament Teaching on the Gifts of the Holy Spirit.* Phillipsburg, N.J.: Presbyterian & Reformed, 1979.

- Green, Michael. *I Believe in the Holy Spirit.* Grand Rapids: Eerdmans, 1975.

- Hoekema, Anthony A. *Tongues and Spirit-Baptism: A Biblical and Theological Evaluation.* Grand Rapids: Baker, 1981.

- Holdcroft, L. Thomas. *The Holy Spirit: A Pentecostal Interpretation.* Springfield, Missouri: Gospel Publishing House, 1979.

- Johnson, Luke Timothy. "Tongues, Gift of." *The Anchor Bible Dictionary,* Vol. 6, edited by David Noel Freedman. New York: Doubleday, 1992, pages 596-600.

- Louw, Johannes P., and Eugene A. Nida. *Greek-English Lexicon of the New Testament Based on Semantic Domains.* Vol. 1. New York: United Bible Societies, 1988, pages 389-390, 440-441.

- Meeks, Wayne A. *The First Urban Christians: The Social World of the Apostle Paul.* New Haven: Yale University Press, 1983, page 120.

- Osborne, G.R. "Tongues, Speaking in." *Evangelical Dictionary of Theology,* edited by Walter A. Elwell. Grand Rapids: Baker, 1984, pages 1100-1103.

- Packer, J.I. "Theological Reflections on the Charismatic Movement." *Churchman,* Vol. 94, 1980, pages 7-25, 103-125.

- Preus, Klemet. "Tongues: An Evaluation From a Scientific Perspective." *Concordia Theological Quarterly,* Vol. 46, 1982, pages 277-293.

- Robeck, C.M., Jr. "Tongues, Gift of." *The International Standard Bible Encyclopedia,* Vol. 4, edited by Geoffrey W. Bromiley. Grand Rapids: Eerdmans, 1988, pages 871-874.

- Roberts, Phil. *The Gift of Tongues: An Evaluation.* Hatfield, Pennsylvania: Interdisciplinary Biblical Research Institute, 1991.

Michael Morrison

FRUIT, GIFTS, AND BAPTISM OF THE SPIRIT

Fruit of the Holy Spirit

"Live by the Spirit," Paul tells us in Galatians 5:16, not by the "desires of the sinful nature." These phrases represent opposite approaches to life (verse 17). In verses 19-21, Paul describes some of the acts of the sinful nature, and in verses 22-23 he describes some of the fruit or results of the Holy Spirit: "love, joy, peace, patience, kindness, goodness, faithfulness, gentleness and self-control."

In Ephesians 5:9, Paul describes more "fruit" of the Christian life: "goodness, righteousness and truth." The Holy Spirit also produces life and peace (Romans 8:6), hope (Romans 15:13) and spiritual wisdom (1 Corinthians 2:6-15). All Christians should have all these qualities.

As we yield to God's Spirit (Romans 8:13-14), and as we are led by the Spirit of Christ (verse 9), we will have Jesus Christ's mercy and compassion for others and his love for God's way of life.

"By their fruit you will recognize them," said Jesus (Matthew 7:20). Many people will call Jesus "Lord," and they will prophesy and perform miracles in his name (verses 21-22), but unless they do the will of the Father, they are false prophets (verses 21, 15). "By their fruit [by the way they live] you will recognize them" (verse 16). All Christians should have the fruit of God's Spirit.

Gifts of the Holy Spirit

The "gifts" of the Spirit are God-given abilities distributed as God knows is best for different aspects of Christian service. But not every Christian has the same gift, just as not every part of the human body performs the function of seeing, hearing or walking (1 Corinthians 12:14-26). Through a division of labor, God encourages us to work with one another to be more efficient. As we work together, Christ gives his Church growth (Ephesians 4:15-16).

What are the various gifts? Paul lists some in 1 Corinthians 12:28-30: Church leadership positions such as apostle, prophet and teacher, or gifts of miracles and healings, or less spectacular but equally necessary abilities such as helping others and administration.

Another list is in verses 7-10: messages of wisdom or knowledge, faith and healing and miracles, inspired messages of prophecy, tongues or interpretations, or a special gift for distinguishing between spirits. (The Greek word for "distinguishing" is also used in 14:29. This gift was probably used to tell which prophecies or tongue-interpretations were genuine and which were false.)

The precise difference between wisdom and knowledge, or faith and healing and miracles may not be important in this list; Paul is simply making the point that spiritual gifts come in many varieties, although they are all "for the common good."

Romans 12:6-8 gives yet another list of gifts (none of the lists is exhaustive): prophesying, serving, teaching, encouraging, giving to others, leading others or showing mercy. Some of these service gifts should be found in all Christians, but some people are distinctly better at certain activities than other people are.

As God gives us these abilities, we should apply them as best we can for the common good of the Body of Christ.

The gifts in these lists come in three major categories: Church leadership, speaking, and serving others. Peter summarizes "gifts" under the categories of speaking and serving (1 Peter 4:11). "Each one should use whatever gift he has received to serve others, faithfully administering God's grace in its various forms" (verse 10).

Paul said that God had given (the Greek verb is similar to the noun used for "gift") the Philippian Christians the ability to believe in Christ and also the opportunity to suffer for him (Philippians 1:29-30).

Suffering patiently and faithfully can also be a useful spiritual gift. Paul described a "thorn in my flesh" (2 Corinthians 12:7), which served by emphasizing Paul's weaknesses, therefore showing that the power of his message came not from himself but from God (verses 8-10).

Paul referred to marital status, whether married or not, as a gift (1 Corinthians 7:7). Any of life's circumstances can be considered a gift of God if we are able to use it to glorify Christ and serve others. It does not matter how spectacular or seemingly ordinary the gift is — what matters is how it is used (1 Corinthians 13:1-4). Love, a fruit of the Spirit that all Christians must have, is the test of whether an ability or gift is good.

All gifts should be used to glorify Christ and to benefit others.

Baptism of the Holy Spirit

John the Baptist predicted that Jesus would baptize people with the Holy Spirit (Mark 1:6-8). In Acts 1:5, Jesus told his disciples that they would receive this baptism in a few days. On the Festival of Pentecost, the Holy Spirit filled the disciples (Acts 2:4), fulfilling the predictions of John and Jesus. Peter said the Spirit had been poured out on them (verses 17, 33).

Years later, the Holy Spirit came on Cornelius and other gentiles (Acts 10:44-45). This was the same as the Holy Spirit being "poured out," or having "received" the Holy Spirit (verses 45, 47), or being "baptized" with the Holy Spirit (Acts 11:15-17).

All these terms refer to the same thing: The Holy Spirit is given to God's people. The promised baptism is available to all who believe (Acts 2:38-39). Paul indicated that people usually received the Holy Spirit when they believed (Acts 19:2). The book of Acts records several instances when people were filled with the Holy Spirit (see page 8).

Paul and the other New Testament writers do not use the phrase "baptism of the Spirit," but they do write about the Holy Spirit being given to God's people. The Spirit is available to all believers as "a deposit guaranteeing our inheritance" (Ephesians 1:13-14).

In 1 Corinthians 12:13, Paul writes that all believers are baptized by the Spirit into the Body of Christ, the Church. In Ephesians 5:18 he tells us to "be filled with the Spirit." In Greek, a writer could use a different form of a word to indicate whether a command was for a onetime event or for a continual activity. Paul used the continual form, indicating that Christians should always live according to the Spirit. He was not writing about an unusual experience that initiates people into a new status.

Nothing in Paul's epistles suggests that the gift of the Spirit comes in two steps or blessings. He does not suggest that the gift of tongues, for example, is evidence of having more spiritual power. Romans 12 doesn't even mention tongues as a gift of importance. Church leaders were not required to have the gift of tongues. Instead, they should be able to teach in language that could be understood (1 Timothy 3:1-2, Titus 1:5-9).

What is the evidence of God's Spirit? What can prove that God is in us? His love. If we love others, if we love even our enemies, it is evidence that God's Spirit is guiding us.

If we are inspired to live God's way, if our lives show the fruit of the Holy Spirit (Galatians 5:22-23), we are giving evidence that God's Spirit is filling our minds and hearts. A good Christian example is a powerful witness to faith in Jesus Christ.

Seeking after signs

Jesus said in Mark 16:17-18: "These signs will accompany those who believe: In my name they will drive out demons; they will speak in new tongues; they will pick up snakes with their hands; and when they drink deadly poison, it will not hurt them at all; they will place their hands on sick people, and they will get well."

Some people have taken these verses as a requirement, as if it were a commission that Christians ought to try to fulfill to prove their authenticity. Some groups attempt to pick up poisonous snakes without being harmed. The handlers usually avoid being bitten, but sometimes they are bitten and die. The success rate does not matter. What is important is whether God wants his people to be doing this.

Should God's people do dangerous things so God will rescue them with a miracle for all to see that God approves of them? Are miracles necessary to prove that Christianity is right?

Faith does not come from seeing miracles. The Israelites who crossed the Red Sea saw numerous miracles, but they did not have the faith to obey God. And many Christians have believed without seeing anything dramatic. Faith comes when God allows someone to believe the gospel (Romans 10:13-14; John 6:44). The primary miracle is in the heart and mind, not necessarily anything that can be seen.

Moreover, God does not want us to do dangerous things in order to prompt his intervention. Satan tempted Jesus with such a challenge, and Jesus answered, "Do not put the Lord your God to the test" (Matthew 4:5-7). We should not try to force God to do anything. Such conduct shows a lack of faith.

The scripture in Mark 16 is a prediction, not a command. It simply says that some Christians would experience these miracles; it is not a promise to protect all Christians, or to heal all, or that all would speak in tongues, or that all would cast out demons. It indicates that various miracles would happen; it does not say how often they would happen.

Miracles still occur today — healing, for example. Demons have been cast out. Christians have been miraculously spared from accidents. But others have died in faith.

The real proof of Christianity is not miracles. It is the love of God, the fruit of the Spirit of Christ in us, motivating us to love one another and to love and obey God (Romans 5:5; Galatians 5:22; John 13:34-35; Romans 8:14; Acts 5:32).

Michael Morrison

Editor's note: For studies of 1 Corinthians 12–14, see *Exploring the Word of God: The Letters of Paul.* Or go to https://archive.gci.org/articles/1-2-corinthians/.

THE USE AND MISUSE
OF SPIRITUAL GIFTS

We have come to a greater awareness of the spiritual gifts God gives his people. We understand from Scripture some basic points:

- Every member has at least one spiritual gift, usually two or three.
- Every member should be using his or her gifts to serve others in the church.
- No member has all the gifts, so we need each other.
- No gift is given to all members.
- God decides who receives which gift.

Every member ought to be involved in some ministry, some area of service ("ministry" refers to all types of service, not just pastoral work). Every Christian should be using his or her gifts to serve others "for the common good" (1 Cor. 12:7; 1 Pet. 4:10).

This awareness of spiritual gifts has been a great blessing for members and congregations. However, even good things can be misused, and a few problems have developed in connection with spiritual gifts. These problems are not unique to us, of course, and it is sometimes helpful to see how other Christian leaders have dealt with them.

For example, some people use the concept of spiritual gifts as an excuse to refuse to serve others. For example, they say that their gift is administration and they refuse to do anything except try to meddle in how the church is administered. Or they may claim to be a teacher and refuse to serve in any other way. I believe that this is the opposite of what Paul intended — he explained that God gifts people for service, not for refusal.

Sometimes work needs to be done whether anybody is especially gifted for it or not. Meeting halls need to be set up and cleaned up. Compassion needs to be given when tragedies strike, whether or not you happen to have the gift of compassion. All members need to be able to teach (Col. 3:16) whether or not they have the gift of teaching. All members need to be able to explain the gospel (1 Pet. 3:15) whether or not they have the gift of evangelism.

It is unrealistic to think that every member will do only those forms of service for which he or she is specially gifted. Not only do other forms of service need to be done, each member needs to experience other forms of service. Service often requires that we get out of our comfort zones, out of the area in which we feel gifted. After all, God may be wanting to develop in us a gift we did not know we had!

Each person has one to three major gifts, and it is best if the person's primary area of service uses one or more of those primary gifts. But each person should also be willing to serve in other ways, as the church has needs. One large church uses the principle that, "you choose your primary ministry based on your own gifts, and be willing to serve in a secondary ministry based on the needs of others." Such a policy helps members grow — and the secondary ministries are assigned only for limited periods of time. Those less-desirable service roles are then rotated to other members. Some experienced pastors estimate that members can expect only about 60 percent of their service to be within their primary spiritual gifts.

The most important thing is that each member serve in some way. Service is a responsibility, not a matter of "I will accept it only if I like it."

Finding your gifts

Now a few thoughts about how we determine what spiritual gifts we have. There are several approaches to this: 1) written tests, surveys and inventories, 2) self-analysis based on interests and experiences, and 3) confirmation from people who know you well. All three approaches can be helpful, and it is especially helpful if all three lead to the same answer. But none of the three is infallible.

Some of the written inventories are simply a method of analyzing yourself and others' opinions about you. The questions might go like this: What do you like to do? What have you done well? What do other people say that you do well? What kinds of needs do you see in the church? (This last question is based on the observation that people are usually most aware of the needs that they are able to help with. For example, a person with the gift of compassion will think that the church needs more compassion.)

Often, we do not know our gifts until we have put them to use and seen whether we do well in that type of activity. Not only do gifts grow through experience, they can also be discovered through experience. That is why it is helpful for members to occasionally try different areas of service. They may learn something about themselves, as well as helping others.

Those are a few comments about gifts in general. But for the rest of this article, I want to focus on a particular gift that raises the most questions.

The gift of tongues

Historically, the most controversial gift has been tongues. It was controversial on the day of Pentecost in Jerusalem; it was controversial a few years later in Caesarea; it was controversial later on in Corinth. Throughout the centuries, small groups of Christians have occasionally spoken in tongues, almost always generating controversy.

Today, millions of Christians speak in tongues. Some are found in Roman Catholic churches, some in liberal mainstream groups, some in conservative evangelical churches, and many in Pentecostal denominations. Even though tongues-speaking has such diverse participants, it is still controversial. So now, I hope to give some perspective on this practice, both to help people who are afraid of it, and those who think too highly of this gift.

The modern resurgence of tongue-speaking is generally traced to the turn of the century. In 1900, Charles Parham and a small group in Kansas began to speak in tongues after studying about this gift in the Bible. In 1906, Parham went to Los Angeles and spoke at the Azusa Street Mission Revival (no connection with Azusa Pacific University), and the movement quickly spread from there.

In the early years, most denominations rejected tongues-speaking as lunacy or demonic, and as one might expect, tongues-speakers left such hostile churches and formed churches in which they were allowed and encouraged to speak in tongues. Thus Pentecostal denominations such as the Assemblies of God were formed.

There is no question that many of these Pentecostal churches had numerous theological errors. They made many mistakes in their zeal to follow God. As time went on, they learned more and corrected many of their errors. This is a dynamic that we should well understand.

In the 1960s, another wave of tongues-speaking occurred in more traditional churches. This time, many churches did not ridicule or drive these people away; they were accepted as charismatic sub-groups within the churches. Nevertheless, tongues-speaking is still controversial. Some Christians teach that God simply does not give miraculous gifts to anyone in the church today; yet others still claim that all Christians ought to seek and practice the gift of tongues.

As recounted in his Autobiography, Herbert Armstrong encountered some Pentecostal people in his early ministry, and he found them to be divisive. And after such experiences, he was strongly opposed to tongues-speaking, even though he was strongly in favor of other miraculous gifts, such as healing. We remained opposed to tongues for decades, and if anybody ever spoke in tongues, they kept pretty quiet about it.

But more recently, we have recognized that some Christians do indeed speak in tongues. We have been slower to criticize and more willing to consider the possibility that tongues-speaking may be an authentic gift of the

Holy Spirit. Meanwhile, our members have visited tongues-speaking churches, and some of our members and ministers have begun to speak in tongues, usually in private.

Knowing how controversial tongues have been in other churches, and knowing our previous dogmatic rejection of tongues, it is no surprise that questions arise when some of our members and ministers begin to speak in tongues, even privately. Due to our lack of experience in this area, it is also no surprise that some excesses have occurred. New-found zeal sometimes carries people further than it should.

Information about tongues

Since Scripture is our ultimate authority for doctrine and Christian living, it is essential that we understand what the Bible says about tongues. Here I will refer you to chapters 1-3 of this e-book. For those who want further study on this subject, there is a bibliography of helpful resources, written from several perspectives. I also refer you to the book *Are Miraculous Gifts For Today? Four Views,* edited by Wayne Grudem (Zondervan, 1996). I will not enter the detailed arguments addressed in the book, but I will simply affirm that I believe that God still performs miracles today. I see no biblical reason to think that he no longer gives anyone the ability to speak in tongues.

However, simply because someone "speaks in tongues" does not mean that he or she has this spiritual gift. As chapters 1-3 point out, various non-Christians, from ancient pagans to modern Buddhists, have spoken in tongues. Tongues-speaking, in itself, is no proof of anything. (Similarly, non-Christians may also have leadership, service, compassion, teaching and other abilities that are similar to spiritual gifts.)

Some tongues-speaking is also called ecstatic speech, which is a psychomotor function of the brain. In normal speech, two parts of the brain work together. In ecstatic speech, one part of the brain tells the mouth and tongue to speak, but the conscious portion of the brain does not supply any particular guidance for what words to speak, so unintelligible syllables come out. This can happen if a person is startled, for example, or if consciousness is altered in some way.

Also, some tongues-speaking may be done in imitation (perhaps subconsciously) of a respected leader. People who are seeking a particular experience are (like hypnotized people) psychologically very susceptible to suggestions like that.

However, I do not think that all tongues-speaking can be explained in these ways, and I believe that some tongues-speaking is genuinely a gift of God. I also recognize that God sometimes works through observable phenomena, and just because some tongues-speaking has a psychomotor explanation does not mean it isn't a gift.

As I have written before, the psychological state in which tongues-speaking occurs is usually pleasant. It is liberating to get rid of some of their inhibitions. It is encouraging to put oneself in a very responsive state, ready to respond to God working in their lives. Tongues-speaking is not the only way to do this, but it is one way, and it encourages people in their walk with the Lord.

One pastor observed the irony that most Christians can talk about almost any spiritual gift with nothing but praise, but as soon as tongues is mentioned, it has to be accompanied by all sorts of cautionary statements. I agree that this is an irony. All sorts of spiritual gifts can be misused, and cautions can be given for them all. But historically, and in our present experience, tongues causes the most problems and needs the most caution. But still, I affirm that it is one of God's spiritual gifts, and it is therefore good.

I respect and honor Christians who speak in tongues; I respect and honor those who do not. I do not want to quench the Spirit; I do not want to "forbid speaking in tongues" (1 Cor. 14:39).

But I also want to follow what Paul said in the very next verse: "Everything should be done in a fitting and orderly way" (verse 40). So let me address how tongues, if used, should be done in an orderly way. Again, since Scripture is our ultimate guide for doctrine and Christian living, let us examine what Scripture says about how tongues should be used.

Biblical data

First, Paul reminds the Corinthians that God divides his gifts among his people (1 Cor. 12:8-11; 29-30). It is not realistic to expect everyone to speak in tongues — and yet that is what some Pentecostals unfortunately do. This is divisive today, just as it was in ancient Corinth.

When a Christian says, my gift is better than your gift, it is an insult to other Christians, and an insult to God. No one should feel superior about a spiritual gift, since no one deserves any of the gifts. The gifts are given to serve others, not to feel superior to others.

We do not need to seek the gift of tongues. We need to seek God, and let him decide which gift is best for us. Paul says we should seek the "more excellent way"— love (1 Cor. 12:31 and chapter 13)— or the gift of prophecy, which is speaking words of encouragement, comfort and edification (1 Cor. 14:1-4).

Without love, we are spiritually worthless, no matter what tongues we speak. It reminds me of the story of one person who attended a Pentecostal church for several years and became a lay leader in one of the ministries. Eventually it was learned that this leader had never spoken in tongues, and people were shocked that the leader was "deficient" in the Christian experience! Yet the person drew a different conclusion from the situation: speaking in tongues made no discernible difference in the way a person lives. Even after years of being around a person, others simply could not know whether the person had ever spoken in tongues.

My friend Jack Hayford says he speaks in tongues in his prayers every day. That does not impress me, nor does he expect it to. That is not its purpose. Tongues is not a show of spirituality. It is to edify the self, not to impress others (verse 4). If it edifies the self, that's wonderful. If it is done to impress others, it's being used in a wrong way, a carnal way. Paul said he spoke in tongues a lot (verse 18). He knew what it meant to pray in words he did not understand (verse 14). But he also knew that this was not proof of spiritual greatness.

I don't care how often Jack speaks in tongues. What I care about is the way he lives the rest of his time. Does he live and function in love? Does he use his other gifts to edify the body of Christ? Does he walk humbly and give all glory to God? I think he sets a good example in all these areas. His tongues-speaking neither adds to nor takes away from his character as a Christian.

To use another example, I don't care whether you eat cereal or eggs for breakfast. Neither one makes you a better person. But I do care if you exalt your particular preference into a badge of betterness. "Everybody ought to be like me because I like the way I am." Such approaches are divisive and un-Christian. They also miss Paul's point, that God has distributed his gifts among his people and he wants them to work together in their diversity.

The Corinthian Christians had a lot of problems, and apparently the way they spoke in tongues was a problem in the church. Paul told them to stop being proud and arrogant. He told them to stop being self-centered. He told them to grow up and be more sensible (verse 20). But he did not tell them to stop speaking in tongues.

However, he did lay down some regulations, and they were quite limiting. For example: Only one person should speak at a time (verse 27). Church services should not be a competition to see who can talk the most. The Holy Spirit does not inspire more than one person to speak at a time.

Second, people should speak in tongues only if an interpreter is present (verse 28). Incidentally, it is interesting that many people want to speak in tongues, but not many "seek" the gift of interpretation, even though interpretation is of greater value to the church. I think this shows that tongues have been overvalued. Unfortunately, in some churches, tongues are often spoken without an interpreter present. The person simply speaks whether or not an interpreter is there, contrary to the instructions Paul gave.

And what if the speaker doesn't know whether an interpreter is present? Then the speaker ought to remain silent. After all, if the gift is genuine, the speaker should be able to control it (verse 32). God does not bypass a person's willpower. Indeed, part of the fruit of God's Spirit is self-control (Gal. 5:23; 2 Tim. 1:7).

Balanced approach

One Pasadena church that I know of has an interesting approach to tongues-speaking. People who want to practice this gift may do so — not during the regular church service, but in their own small group meetings. And then there must be two or more interpreters present. The interpreters write down the interpretation, and then they see whether the interpretations match. Sometimes they do, but often they do not, which means that at least one of the three speakers is mistaken. This cautions us not to be too quick to believe any uncorroborated interpretation — and certainly not if it contradicts Scripture!

It would just be a lot easier if people sought the gift of prophecy — speaking edifying and intelligible words — rather than tongues, which might not help anybody else (verse 5). Tongues and interpretations are often misunderstood. Even prophesy can be misunderstood, which is why Paul advises us, "the others should weigh carefully what is said" (verse 29).

However, even if an interpreter is present, it is simply best not to speak in tongues in the church service. The gift of tongues is for self-edification, not for edifying anyone else (verse 4). It just doesn't make sense for one member to interrupt everyone else and say, "Hold everything. Just wait a few minutes please while I edify myself. Watch me and listen to me, even though it won't do you any good." Tongues, since they help only the speaker, are appropriate for private prayers, but not for public assemblies.

Tongues are also a distraction. Public tongues-speaking almost always focuses attention on the speaker, not on God. Non-Christians are usually put off by tongues-speaking. Some find it quite fascinating, of course, and some even consider it to be proof of divine blessing, but most do not. It is confusing, and if the person realizes that various non-Christians also speak in tongues, it is also inconclusive. People need to be impressed by the gospel, not by unusual phenomena. If the person is convinced by emotional impressions rather than truth, the person has an unstable foundation for belief. Emotions are important, of course, but they should be a response to the gospel, not a substitute for it.

Our practice

Paul warned the Corinthians not to allow tongues to get out of control in their worship services, since it could confuse unbelievers: "If the whole church comes together and everyone speaks in tongues, and some who do not understand or some unbelievers come in, will they not say that you are out of your mind?" (verse 23). It is not surprising, then, that some Christians also consider it inappropriate.

However, Paul had nothing against tongues-speaking. After all, he spoke in tongues himself (verse 18). But he did have a lot to say against tongues-speaking in church assemblies. "In the church I would rather speak five intelligible words to instruct others than ten thousand words in a tongue" (verse 19).

That is what we prefer. We want intelligible words; we do not want unintelligible words in our meetings. That is why I say that we are not a tongues-speaking fellowship. Some people in our fellowship speak in tongues, and I defend their privilege to do so in private or in small groups where everyone agrees to accept it. Even then, it needs to be controlled according to the scriptural guidelines.

As a fellowship, when we are gathered as a congregation, we do not want tongues-speaking. This is based not on some irrational fear of things we don't understand — it is based on the guidance Paul has given us, guidance we accept as authoritative, as inspired by the Holy Spirit.

If somebody wants to speak in tongues in a worship service, there are other denominations that allow that sort of thing. If they find it to be self-edifying, that's good, but I encourage them to seek and to use some other spiritual gift that will be helpful to others.

I might also add that even some Pentecostal churches do not allow tongues-speaking in church services. Many of them also recognize that it is unscriptural to allow everybody to speak at once, to speak without an interpreter present, etc. If the pastor were giving a sermon, for example, and a person in the audience began to speak in tongues, then the pastor would tell the person, "Lady (or Sir), control your gift. The spirits of the prophets are subject to the control of prophets. If you cannot control your gift, the ushers will escort you out." Interrupting the sermon would be just as inappropriate as a person trying to sing a hymn in the middle of the sermon. It is good to sing hymns, but only at the right time and place. Similarly, we do not allow tongues-speaking in our regular worship services.

Expressing joy in Christ

I love our Pentecostal brothers and sisters a great deal. Many of you interact with them in ministerial associations, and you have also come to love them. Many of them have warmly embraced us as fellow-members in the family of God. The Four Square denomination in particular has been helpful to us. I praise their love for the Lord and their love for neighbor. Many of them set an excellent example.

Pentecostal churches are now the fastest-growing segment of Christianity, especially in Latin America, but also in North America, Europe and Asia. I suspect that one reason it is growing is that Pentecostal churches encourage people to express their emotions rather than suppress them. This can be bad, of course, if people's faith is built on emotions, but it is good if those emotions are a genuine response to the good news of Jesus Christ.

If people really understand the depths of their sinful state, of how utterly disgusting it is, and of the greatness of Jesus' sacrifice for us, of how astonishing his grace toward us is, then it is natural to respond with joy and exuberance — and this emotion does not need to be suppressed, though how it is expressed may vary widely from person to person. We have something worth singing about, something to be happy about. Although we may still be in poverty, we have experienced something wonderful in the love of Jesus Christ, and we share it.

Pentecostal churches are generally freer in how they express this joy. Visitors who attend a Pentecostal church are likely to see people expressing joy and happiness because of their faith in Jesus Christ. This example is an effective aid in evangelism and church growth.

Of course, Pentecostal churches are not the only ones who effectively express their joy in worshiping their Savior, and they are not the only churches that are growing, but as a group, they seem to do it more actively than most. Although I do not agree with all their theology, and certainly not the emphasis on the public practice of tongues-speaking, I do applaud them for the things they are doing well.

Scripture is the ultimate authority for what we do. If growth alone were evidence of truth, then we might all become Muslims or Mormons. Experience may be helpful, but it is not authoritative. Experience may even be very impressive, but that alone does not make it authoritative. Even so, it is still very impressive.

Seeking experience

Consider a not-so-unusual example, a person who attends a Protestant church every week, but rarely (if ever) experiences the presence of God in his or her own church services. He has doubts as to his own walk with the Lord. He wants to have greater assurance that he is making progress. He wants to have tangible, observable evidence that the Lord is with him. Then he attends a church in which the preacher confidently, boldly, dogmatically says that "yes, you can have confidence if you have a certain experience. That will give you the assurance of the presence of God in your life."

The person wants this experience. It doesn't matter whether it is really proof — it is desirable. And once it comes, it is extremely self-authenticating and reinforcing. The person wanted reassurance, was told in a persuasive way that the particular experience would give him that assurance, and then he had the experience, and true enough, he gained assurance! The person becomes sold on the experience and sometimes even becomes an "evangelist" for the experience.

This has happened within our fellowship, just as it has happened in other denominations. People who were spiritually yearning, and not completely grounded doctrinally, were overwhelmed by a particular experience. I do not doubt that the experience was powerful and spiritual. It may have been an enormous spiritual boost, or the highlight of one's life. But that does not mean that it is true, or that everyone should have the same experience, or that Christians should be looked down on if they do not have the same experience. The shock treatment that helped one patient is not the right medicine for the next patient.

More unusual manifestations

For many years, speaking in tongues was the primary experience promoted in some Pentecostal circles. But in more recent years, more exotic experiences have been promoted — such things as being slain in the Spirit (fainting and remaining motionless for several hours), laughing in the Spirit (uncontrollable waves of laughter), weeping in the Spirit, barking like a dog, or other para-normal activities. These may be called the Toronto Blessing or the Pensacola Blessing or some other blessing. Several prominent speakers, including Benny Hinn, have promoted some of these exciting phenomena.

These phenomena have been controversial, even in Pentecostal churches. The Toronto Blessing, for example, began in the Vineyard church. Some Vineyard churches promoted the blessing; others resisted it, and now they have split into two denominations. But the blessing makes ripples in many other denominations, too, and has affected some members. The Pensacola Blessing has circulated primarily in the Assemblies of God, but it has also affected other denominations, including our own.

I do not doubt that these experiences are extremely powerful. They feel authentic. But they have unfortunately led some astray, away from biblical authority and into an authority that is based on personal experience. As an extreme example, a pastor who has become enamored with a particular blessing may exhort everyone in the congregation to seek this particular blessing (the blessing, it sometimes seems, gets more focus than Jesus does). He may publicly berate those who do not accept the experience. He may call out names or tell people to leave if they don't like it.

This is, to put it bluntly, legalism. (Sometimes it is easy to call things we don't like an insulting term, like "legalism," but I am confident that in this case I am using the term legalism correctly. It is teaching as a requirement something that is not in Scripture.) We've had experience with old covenant legalism. These people are experiencing a completely nonbiblical legalism. Legalism is unfortunately found in many segments of Christianity, and some of these "blessing" people have fallen into a form of legalism, in which they insist that everybody ought to be like them.

Now suppose the whole congregation got touched and remained unconscious for three hours. Would that make them better Christians, better followers of Jesus Christ? Jesus never did anything of the sort. People who are slain in the spirit do not come out any better than they went in. The experience may encourage them, reassure them, but it does not edify the body of Christ and it should not be promoted as normal or preferable. Would these people eventually yearn for something yet more exotic? At least for some, that has been the pattern. Since the experience is not grounded in any objective truth, it does not give people the solid assurance that they seek. Some eventually seek even more unusual "signs."

One of our pastors observed the results of the Pensacola revival at a nearby Pentecostal church. After an initial flurry of excitement, attendance gradually dropped in half. The same manifestations week after week simply did not build the people up. The focus was on what happened to people during church, and not on what they did the rest of the time. The "revival" has driven away half the church!

Many of the "blessing" people are Christians who love Jesus. But as we know from our own experience, it is quite possible to be Christian while also seriously wrong on major doctrinal questions. I do not want to bash and condemn. I do not attack the people, or call them agents of Satan, but I do have the responsibility, as an under-shepherd of Jesus Christ, to warn our members about false, destructive and divisive doctrines. I want to help people avoid the pain and suffering that comes from following religious errors. The truth sets people free, but errors lead people into bondage.

We do not speak in tongues in our worship services, and we do not promote the more exotic "Pentecostal" manifestations.

To use an analogy, what you eat for breakfast is your own business — but no matter how good it tastes to you, do not act like your choice is spiritually better than other people's. Do not try to get everyone to act like you do. If you have a particular gift, be thankful and rejoice, but do not be divisive. Whatever gift you have, use it to serve others, keeping Scripture as your ultimate authority for faith and practice.

Joseph Tkach

SPIRITUAL GIFTS AND CHURCH GROWTH

Christ gives each of us grace, in the form of spiritual gifts, as he determines to apportion it (Eph. 4:7). These gracious gifts include various roles within the church — apostles, prophets, evangelists, pastors and teachers (verse 11). And what are these leaders supposed to do? They are to "prepare God's people for works of service" (verse 12). A more literal translation is "a work of ministry." In other words, the leaders of the church are to prepare the members for action in the work of the ministry of the gospel.

But not everyone has been given the gift of preaching, any more than all parts of a body are mouths. Acts 6:2-4 describes two overall types of ministry in the work of the gospel: the ministry of tables, and the ministry of the Word — giving physical nourishment through service and giving spiritual nourishment by preaching and teaching the gospel. Both kinds of ministry are essential to the church.

Gifts to work together

Christ gives different gifts to different members of the Body. Our job is not to compare our gifts and abilities, nor to feel superior or inferior to other members of the Body, but to make use of our respective gifts to serve others. Our works of service are to be used for building up the body of Christ (Ephesians 4:12).

As we work together, each of us serving according to the gifts and opportunities Christ gives us, we will grow into "unity in the faith" (verse 13). Although there is only one faith (verse 5), God's people reach unity of the faith through works of service, ministering to one another's needs in Christ.

Further, it is only through mutual service that we all reach unity "in the faith and in the knowledge of the Son of God" (verse 13). Our faith is in the Son of God, Jesus Christ. Part of knowing him is doing what he said. Two of his most frequent commands are, first, that we believe on him and, second, that we love one another. Belief in Christ makes us Christian, and love for one another demonstrates the validity of our faith. Belief and love are hallmarks of our Christian identity. Indeed, mutual love is the primary means by which the public can know that we are his disciples (John 13:35). Love, of course, is not just a feeling — it is action. It results in works of service.

By living the way of love in Christ, by implementing mutual service in him, the church comes to maturity, "attaining to the whole measure of the fullness of Christ" (Eph. 4:13). Through mutual love and service, we become mature in the faith, closer to what Christ wants us to be, closer to the example of service he set for us. With that maturity, Paul says, we will not be easily misled by erroneous teachings (verse 14).

But by speaking the truth (in this context, true doctrines) in love, we will grow up — become mature — into Jesus Christ (verse 15). Jesus himself is the goal.

From Christ, the church grows up "as each part does its work" (Eph. 4:16). Jesus has given a variety of gifts to the members of the Body as it pleases him, so that each of us can use our respective gifts as a vital part of the Body — in service, in the work of the ministry, to help each other. It is in this way that the church "builds itself up in love" (same verse). In the Body of Christ, as in any healthy body, each part contributes in its appropriate way to the overall growth, development, maintenance, and work of the Body as a whole.

For the common good

We find a similar emphasis on mutual service in 1 Corinthians 12, where Paul also discusses spiritual gifts. There is only one Spirit, Paul says, but there are different kinds of gifts (verse 4). There is only one Lord, but there are different kinds of service (verse 5). As members of the Body of Christ, we serve in different ways, each according to the gifts Christ has given us through the Spirit. There is only one God, but he leads and equips each of us to do the kinds of work that please him (verse 6). These spiritual gifts are distributed "for the common good" (verse 7), in other words, for the overall healthy functioning of the Body.

If he had wanted to, God could have given each of us ability to do everything, but he did not. He distributes his gifts differently to each of us, and this means we have to work *together*. Working together is, in a way, just as important as getting the job done — because working together in Christ is an expression of God's love, which itself is part of the work of God. God is love, and he wants us to grow in love for one another.

Some spiritual gifts are spectacular; others are not. That fact can lead to pride, or to feelings either of superiority or inferiority. But Paul's point in this passage is that all gifts are *from God,* and he is the one who distributes them *as it pleases him, as he desires and determines best.* Therefore, none of us has any reason to boast or to think our particular gift is more important than another, or to think our gift shows that *we* are more important than others. And, on the other side of the coin, no one has any reason to feel inferior, or to feel that his or her gift is not so important.

The truth is, Paul explains, each person has at least one gift or ability given by God, and each person has the responsibility to use it for the common good of the Body of Christ. I hope we can begin to see why mutual service, cooperation and love are vital to the health and growth of the church.

Just as a human body has to have a variety of parts, the church of God must have a variety of members, each doing a variety of functions for the common good. Every member can have faith, but some have an unusual gift of faith (verse 9). Every member can be a personal witness to the life-transforming power of the gospel, but some have the gift of evangelizing unbelievers. Every member can teach others, but some have the gift of being an unusually effective teacher (verse 28). Every member can help others (same verse), but some have an unusual ability to help others.

Paul does not list every possible gift here. He could not, because they are too numerous to mention. There could be as many gifts as there are people in the church! God distributes them according to his own purpose and plan.

Use gifts in love

Seek the best gifts, Paul encourages us (verse 31), and then he shows us in the love chapter "the most excellent way." Each member, no matter what gift he or she may have, should seek to express love for others — that is how *every* gift should be used — in loving service to others. Whatever God gives us, whether it is physical or spiritual, should be used for others' benefit.

We are called to serve. We exist to serve. That is Christian maturity. And our works of service should point to Christ. They should give evidence that we are his disciples. They are done for his honor and glory, and in his name. We do not deserve any of the credit ourselves. It is *his* work in us. It is Christ in us that identifies us as his own disciples. We are his slaves, with all being done in service to him in the work of his gospel.

We need to train and mobilize our congregations for the work of the gospel — evangelism. We need to develop positive godly relationships with others through Christian love and service, as individual Christians and as local congregations. This means pure, holy living in Jesus Christ as his ambassadors. It means being ready, when asked, to give an answer about the hope that lies within us, and about living in such a way that we are more likely to be asked. We should remember the first part of 1 Peter 3:15: "In your hearts set apart Christ as Lord."

Evangelism means the whole Body of Christ working together in unity, each one doing his or her part according to the gifts God has given, whether in ministries of physical service or of teaching the Word, supervised and led by the local pastor and supported by headquarters, all to the glory of God in the work of the gospel. It means diligent, prayerful, focused effort, by one and all, in unified cooperation and mutual encouragement and strengthening in love, so that the light of Christ might shine in the darkness through us, as his faithful servants.

Paul, speaking to the elders from Ephesus, said, "However, I consider my life worth nothing to me, if only I may finish the race and complete the task the Lord Jesus has given me — the task of testifying to the gospel of God's grace" (Acts 20:24). The same is true of God's elect today. *The Body of Christ lives to do the work of Christ, to proclaim and exemplify the gospel of the grace of God.*

Spiritual gifts for the gospel

Look around — not only are the fields white and ready for harvest, there are already many laborers in the fields. The main problem is, they aren't all laboring! The work of harvesting is not reserved for the ordained ministers alone — all members are encouraged to participate in the harvest. Many already are, but we need to expand the role of the members.

Jesus commands us to make disciples. He commands us to teach and to help each Christian mature in the faith. Therefore, we want to help our members grow in grace and knowledge, and to recognize and use the gifts that the Holy Spirit is giving them. God places members in the body as it pleases him, and he gives them gifts for the common good (1 Corinthians 12:4-27). Therefore, for the maximum growth and health of the church, we want each member to use his or her gifts, working together, being led by Jesus Christ to build the church up (Ephesians 4:11-16).

There is much that we could say about spiritual gifts. Right now we can highlight a few simple facts:

- The Holy Spirit gives spiritual gifts to each member (1 Cor. 12:11).
- These gifts are for the common good (verse 7).
- There are many types of gifts (verses 8-11).
- All gifts help the body of Christ function (verses 12-18).
- No one should envy another member's gifts (verses 15-17).
- No one should despise another member's gifts (verses 21-23).
- Therefore, the members should have concern for one another (verse 25).
- Gifts should be used, not hidden under a basket (Matthew 5:15-16).
- Ministers should prepare members for works of service (Eph. 4:11-12).
- Works of service build up the body of Christ (verse 12).
- Our goal is unity in the faith and knowledge of Christ (verse 13).

- Christ is the full measure of Christian maturity (verse 13).
- Only in that maturity will we have doctrinal stability (verse 14).
- Our goal is to grow up into our Head, Jesus Christ (verse 15).
- From Christ, we build ourselves up in love (verse 16).
- We grow as each member does his or her work (verse 16).

Therefore, we encourage members to do the work God has called them to do. We want them to use the gifts God has given. This mutual service is what builds the church internally, helps it function in its mission and helps it grow by attracting and incorporating new members. Every member has a role in ministering to others. But each member must perform that role in such a way that it builds up the whole body, not tears down the body. We do not all serve in the same way, evangelize in the same way, show compassion in the same way, etc. Everyone cannot be forced into the same pattern or mold, but we are to work together in our diverse approaches.

This is part of the great commission. Jesus told his disciples to make disciples and teach them to obey everything he commanded them (Matthew 28:19-20). It is to be an endless cycle: The disciples become disciplers. Those who are taught become teachers. We all do this in different ways, of course, according to the gifts God supplies, but we all have a part to play in the work of the body of Christ.

Each member should serve. Each member should minister (which simply means "to give aid or service") to others. Each member has a ministry, that is, a way in which God has gifted him or her to serve in the kingdom work of the church. Each member is a minister of Jesus Christ. The church is a royal priesthood, Peter wrote (1 Peter 2:9), and each member has a priestly role, interceding in prayer for others, serving one another's needs, bearing one another's burdens and sharing in the work of the gospel.

We want all members to grow and participate in the work. We do not have the money to hire every worker, of course, nor should we want to. The Bible presents a picture of every member doing some work. Church pastors serve in the role of administrative leadership, facilitating the work of Christ's loved ones — casting the joyous vision of their calling to Christ's kingdom, praying for them, training them, developing them, empowering them, encouraging them, advising them, supporting them — and, of course, preaching the word — all supervised by Jesus Christ through the Holy Spirit and the Holy Scriptures.

We have much to do — so much that it usually seems overwhelming. That's because we often only see with physical eyes. But when we look with the eyes of faith, we are assured of Jesus' promise: He has unlimited power, and he is with us always (verses 18, 20). He will turn our trials into good, our tears into joy. We are thankful for that, and thankful to be called into the work of the King of kings. Like the Samaritan leper, we fall on our knees before Jesus and praise the Lord for what he has done for us! We have been cleansed, and like Isaiah, we say: "Here I am, O Lord. Send me!" (Isaiah 6:5-8).

Joseph Tkach

SPIRITUAL GIFTS ARE GIVEN FOR SERVICE

We understand from Scripture some basic points about the spiritual gifts God gives his people:

- Every member has at least one spiritual gift, usually two or three.
- Every member should be using his or her gifts to serve others in the church.
- No member has all the gifts, so we need each other.
- No gift is given to all members.
- God decides who receives which gift.

We have always had spiritual gifts — but only recently have we become aware of them to the point that we realized that every member ought to be involved in some ministry, some area of service ("ministry" refers to all types of service, not just pastoral work). Every Christian should be using his or her gifts to serve others "for the common good" (1 Cor. 12:7; 1 Pet. 4:10).

This awareness of spiritual gifts has been a great blessing for members and congregations. However, even good things can be misused, and a few problems have developed in connection with spiritual gifts. These problems are not unique to us, of course, and it is sometimes helpful to see how other Christian leaders have dealt with them.

Refusing to serve

For example, some people use the concept of spiritual gifts as an excuse to refuse to serve others. For example, they say that their gift is administration and they refuse to do anything except try to meddle in how the church is administered. Or they may claim to be a teacher and refuse to serve in any other way. I believe that this is the opposite of what Paul intended — he explained that God gifts people for service, not for refusal.

Sometimes work needs to be done whether anybody is especially gifted for it or not. Meeting halls need to be set up and cleaned up. Compassion needs to be given when tragedies strike, whether or not you happen to have the gift of compassion. All members need to be able to teach (Col. 3:16) whether or not they have the gift of teaching. All members need to be able to explain the gospel (1 Pet. 3:15) whether or not they have the gift of evangelism.

It is unrealistic to think that every member will do only those forms of service for which he or she is *specially* gifted. Not only do other forms of service need to be done, each member needs to experience other forms of service. Service often requires that we get out of our comfort zones, out of the area in which we feel gifted. After all, God may be wanting to develop in us a gift we did not know we had!

Most people have been given one to three major gifts, and it is best if the person's primary area of service uses one or more of those primary gifts. But each person should also be willing to serve in other ways, as the church has needs. One large church uses the principle that, "you choose your primary ministry based on your own gifts, and be willing to serve in a secondary ministry based on the needs of others." Such a policy helps members grow — and the secondary ministries are assigned only for limited periods of time. Those less-desirable service roles are then rotated to other members. Some experienced pastors estimate that members can expect only about 60 percent of their service to be within their primary spiritual gifts.

The most important thing is that each member serve in some way. Service is a responsibility, not a matter of "I will accept it only if I like it."

Finding your gifts

Now a few thoughts about how we determine what spiritual gifts we have. There are several approaches to this: 1) written tests, surveys and inventories, 2) self-analysis based on interests and experiences, and 3) confirmation from people who know you well. All three approaches can be helpful, and it is especially helpful if all three lead to the same answer. But none of the three is infallible.

Some of the written inventories are simply a method of analyzing yourself and others' opinions about you. The questions might go like this: What do you like to do? What have you done well? What do other people say that you do well? What kinds of needs do you see in the church? (This last question is based on the observation that people are usually most aware of the needs that they are able to help with. For example, a person with the gift of compassion will think that the church needs more compassion.)

Often, we do not know our gifts until we have put them to use and seen whether we do well in that type of activity. Not only do gifts grow through experience, they can also be discovered through experience. That is why it is helpful for members to occasionally try different areas of service. They may learn something about themselves, as well as helping others.

Joseph Tkach

QUESTIONS & ANSWERS
ABOUT SPEAKING IN TONGUES

Question: Many people in our fellowship have visited other churches. Some have spoken in tongues. Are members allowed to speak in tongues?

Answer: Yes. Speaking in tongues is a New Testament practice, described as a gift of the Holy Spirit. Members may worship as the Spirit leads them. However, they should keep in mind that the Spirit does not lead to confusion, nor to division. Speaking in tongues should not be done in a situation in which others will be offended, frightened or made uncomfortable, such as in a regular worship service.

Spiritual gifts, including tongues, must always be used as God intends — to lead a person to growth in godly living, to edify the body of Christ, or to otherwise build the kingdom. As soon as a person focuses on the gift instead of the intended result of the gift, they are misusing it. Gifts are not for goosebumps or "good feelings." They are given by God for a purpose — to edify the body and produce spiritual growth. They are not an end in themselves.

We are created to bring glory to God. Gifts are given to help us do that — never to bring glory or attention to ourselves. The more unusual gifts are not a sign that we are more spiritual than others. In some cases, they may even be given because we are dull of hearing, and God uses the gift as an extraordinary method of trying to get our attention. So, if a person has a particular gift, he or she should enjoy it, be thankful for it, and use it to edify — not to hurt or tear down or make others feel inferior.

Question: GCI does not allow tongues speaking in its worship services. Doesn't this contradict 1 Corinthians 14:39, which says that we should not forbid tongues speaking?

Answer: We do not forbid tongues speaking. We forbid it only during worship services. Members are welcome to speak in tongues as a private prayer language or in small groups composed of people who know that tongues-speaking is allowed in that particular small group.

We believe in the gifts of the Holy Spirit, including miraculous gifts such as healing. But we do not believe that every Christian should have the same gift. We do not believe that all Christians ought to seek the gift of tongues. We welcome tongues-speakers into our fellowship, as long as they do not use their gift in a contentious or offensive way. Paul's message in 1 Corinthians

14, summarized in verse 40, emphasizes order in the worship service, each activity at an appropriate time. In our tradition, we do not use the worship services for any of the miraculous gifts. There are other times when such gifts are more appropriate.

Comment: Some Pentecostal churches have slaying in the Spirit, holy laughter, crying, moaning and barking. Haven't these practices (with the possible exception of tongues) been denounced by many evangelicals as unbiblical?

Response: Most charismatic churches believe in and practice the gift of tongues. However, they are not all alike. The degree of pentecostalism varies from congregation to congregation. Some Pentecostal pastors do not accept practices such as being slain in the Spirit, holy laughter, etc. Although these "manifestations" happen in some Pentecostal churches, their denominational headquarters do not also encourage or emphasize them. Simply because a minority of members in a denomination are teaching or practicing something, it doesn't mean that every church in that denomination is in favor of it.

We do not condemn the gift of tongues, but we do not allow it in our worship services. If a member has that gift, we would see it primarily as a "prayer language." We do not foresee any place in our worship services for manifestations such as holy laughter, barking or being slain in the Spirit.

ABOUT THE AUTHORS

This book is a corporate product. Most chapters give the name of the author at the end. Others are corporate products, perhaps drafted by one person but extensively edited by others. Most of the authors were, at the time of writing, employed by Grace Communion International.

Terry Akers worked in the letter-answering department for Grace Communion International.

Gary Deddo worked for InterVarsity Press for many years. He now works for Grace Communion International and is president of Grace Communion Seminary.

Neil Earle was a pastor of a GCI church in Glendora, CA, and an instructor in church history at Grace Communion Seminary.

J. Michael Feazell was vice-president of Grace Communion International and the author of numerous articles.

Sheila Graham was a writer and editor for Grace Communion International. She is the author of one of our most popular articles, on the Proverbs 31 woman.

John Halford was the editor of *Christian Odyssey* magazine and the author of numerous articles. He died in 2014.

James Henderson was the GCI mission developer in Africa; he is now the national director in the United Kingdom.

Paul Kroll is a now-retired journalist and researcher for Grace Communion International.

John McKenna was adjunct faculty at Azusa Pacific Seminary and Grace Communion Seminary. He died in 2018.

Michael Morrison, PhD, is Dean of Faculty at Grace Communion Seminary. He is the author of several books, numerous e-books, and is the editor of this volume.

Ralph Orr was a pastor, research, and writer for Grace Communion International.

Joseph Tkach, D.Min., has retired as president of Grace Communion International; he is the author of numerous articles and e-books.

ABOUT THE PUBLISHER...

Grace Communion International is a Christian denomination with about 50,000 members, worshiping in about 750 congregations in almost 100 nations and territories. We began in 1934 and our main office is in North Carolina. In the United States, we are members of the National Association of Evangelicals and similar organizations in other nations. We welcome you to visit our website at www.gci.org.

If you want to know more about the gospel of Jesus Christ, we offer help. First, we offer weekly worship services in hundreds of congregations worldwide. Perhaps you'd like to visit us. A typical worship service includes songs of praise, a message based on the Bible, and opportunity to meet people who have found Jesus Christ to be the answer to their spiritual quest. We try to be friendly, but without putting you on the spot. We do not expect visitors to give offerings – there's no obligation. You are a guest.

To find a congregation, write to one of our offices, phone us or visit our website. If we do not have a congregation near you, we encourage you to find another Christian church that teaches the gospel of grace.

We also offer personal counsel. If you have questions about the Bible, salvation or Christian living, we are happy to talk. If you want to discuss faith, baptism or other matters, a pastor near you can discuss these on the phone or set up an appointment for a longer discussion. We are convinced that Jesus offers what people need most, and we are happy to share the good news of what he has done for all humanity. We like to help people find new life in Christ, and to grow in that life. Come and see why we believe it's the best news there could be!

Our work is funded by members of the church who donate part of their income to support the gospel. Jesus told his disciples to share the good news, and that is what we strive to do in our literature, in our worship services, and in our day-to-day lives.

If this book has helped you and you want to pay some expenses, all donations are gratefully welcomed, and in several nations, are tax-deductible. If you can't afford to give anything, don't worry about it. It is our gift to you. To donate online, go to www.gci.org/online-giving/

Thank you for letting us share what we value most – Jesus Christ. The good news is too good to keep it to ourselves.

See our website for hundreds of articles, locations of our churches, addresses in various nations, audio and video messages, and much more.

www.gci.org
Grace Communion International
3120 Whitehall Park Dr.
Charlotte, NC 28273
800-423-4444

You're Included...

Dr. J. Michael Feazell talks to leading Trinitarian theologians about the good news that God loves you, wants you, and includes you in Jesus Christ. Most programs are about 28 minutes long. Our guests have included:

Gordon Fee, Regent College

C. Baxter Kruger, Perichoresis

Cherith Fee Nordling, Northern Seminary

Alan Torrance, University of St. Andrews

Robert T. Walker, Edinburgh University

N.T. Wright, University of St. Andrews

William P. Young, author of *The Shack*

Programs are available free for viewing and downloading at www.youreincluded.org.

GRACE COMMUNION
SEMINARY

GRACE COMMUNION SEMINARY

Ministry based on the life and love of the Father, Son, and Spirit

Grace Communion Seminary serves the needs of people engaged in Christian service who want to grow deeper in relationship with our Triune God and to be able to more effectively serve in the church. We offer three degrees: Master of Pastoral Studies, Master of Theological Studies, and Master of Divinity.

Why study at Grace Communion Seminary?

- Worship: to love God with all your mind.
- Service: to help others apply truth to life.
- Practical: a balanced range of useful topics for ministry.
- Trinitarian theology: a survey of theology with the merits of a Trinitarian perspective. We begin with the question, "Who is God?" Then, "Who are we in relationship to God?" In this context, "How then do we serve?"
- Part-time study: designed to help people who are already serving in local congregations. There is no need to leave your current ministry. Full-time students are also welcome.
- Flexibility: your choice of master's level courses or pursuit of a degree.
- Affordable, accredited study: Everything can be done online.

For more information, go to www.gcs.edu.

Grace Communion Seminary is accredited by the Distance Education Accrediting Commission, www.deac.org. The Accrediting Commission is listed by the U.S. Department of Education as a nationally recognized accrediting agency.

Made in the USA
Columbia, SC
15 November 2020

24630106R00220